SEMITES, IRANIANS, GREEKS, AND ROMANS

Program in Judaic Studies
Brown University
BROWN JUDAIC STUDIES
Edited by
Jacob Neusner, Ernest S. Frerichs, William Scott Green,
Wendell S. Dietrich, Calvin Goldscheider, David Hirsch, Alan Zuckerman

Project Editors (Projects)

David Blumenthal, Emory University (Approaches to Medieval Judaism)
Ernest S. Frerichs, Brown University (Dissertations and Monographs)
Lenn Evan Goodman, University of Hawaii (Studies in Medieval Judaism)
William Scott Green, University of Rochester (Approaches to Ancient Judaism)
Norbert Samuelson, Temple University (Jewish Philosophy)
Jonathan Z. Smith, University of Chicago (Studia Philonica)

Number 217
SEMITES, IRANIANS, GREEKS, AND ROMANS
Studies in their Interactions

by
Jonathan A. Goldstein

SEMITES, IRANIANS, GREEKS, AND ROMANS
Studies in their Interactions

by

Jonathan A. Goldstein

Scholars Press
Atlanta, Georgia

SEMITES, IRANIANS, GREEKS, AND ROMANS

Copyright © 1990 by Brown University

Paperback edition published 2007 by Brown Judaic Studies

All rights reserved. No part of this work may be reproduced or transmitted in any form or by any means, electronic or mechanical, including photocopying and recording, or by means of any information storage or retrieval system, except as may be expressly permitted by the 1976 Copyright Act or in writing from Brown Judaic Studies, Brown University, Box 1826, Providence, RI 02912.

Library of Congress Cataloging-in-Publication Data

Goldstein, Jonathan A., 1929–
  Semites, Iranians, Greeks, and Romans : studies in their interactions / by Jonathan A. Goldstein.
  p. cm. — (Brown Judaic studies ; no. 217)
  Includes index.
  ISBN 1-55540-512-6 (alk. paper)
  1. Judaism—Relations—Greek. 2. Jews—Civilization—Greek influences. 3. Synagogues—Syria—Dura Europos (Ancient city). 4. Apocryphal books (Old Testament)—Criticism, interpretation, etc. I. Title. II. Series.
BM536.G7G58   1990
296'.09'015   90-41250
                                                CIP

ISBN 978-1-930675-43-8 (alk. paper : paperback)

Printed in the United States of America
on acid-free paper

To my wife,
Helen

Table of Contents

Preface ix

Part One
INTERCULTURAL BORROWING

1. Jewish Acceptance and Rejection of Hellenism 1
2. The Syriac Bill of Sale from Dura-Europos 33
3. Review of Goodenough..57
4. The Central Composition of the West Wall of the Synagogue of Dura-Europos 67
5. Tales of the Tobiads...115

Part Two
RELIGIOUS RESISTANCE TO FOREIGN RULE

6. Uruk Prophecy...155
7. The Date of the Book of Jubilees..161
8. The Testament of Moses: Its Content, Its Origin, and Its Attestation in Josephus 181
9. Apocryphal Book of Baruch..191
10. Review of Doran's *Temple Propaganda*...............................209
11. How the Authors in I and II Maccabees Treated the "Messianic" Promises...221

List of Abbreviations..251

Index 253

Preface

Did I really write all these articles? As a graduate student in 1956, I was sure I would perish before I published. My first scholarly discovery did not come until 1957, when I was 28. I hope in the present volume to convey to the reader something of the surprise and joy of my subsequent discoveries.

I have to be grateful for my scholarly pleasures: to my genetic endowment and its Creator, to my parents and teachers, and to the University of Iowa.

This volume was the idea of Professor Jacob Neusner. We have enjoyed relations of affection and esteem since our days as students at Harvard. The University of Iowa contributed money generously to support publication. I thank them both.

All the articles in this volume were first published elsewhere, as follows: "Jewish Acceptance and Rejection of Hellenism," in *Jewish and Christian Self-Definition*, Vol. II: *Aspects of Judaism in the Greco-Roman Period*, edited by E.P. Sanders with A.I. Baumgarten and Alan Mendelson (Philadelphia: Fortress, 1981); "The Syriac Bill of Sale from Dura-Europos," *Journal of Near Eastern Studies* 25 (1966), 1-16; Review of Goodenough, ibid., 28 (1969), 212-18; "The Central Composition of the West Wall of the Synagogue of Dura-Europos," *Journal of the Ancient Near Eastern Society* 16-17 (1984-85), 99-141; "The Tales of the Tobiads," in *Christianity, Judaism, and Other Greco-Roman Cults: Studies for Morton Smith at Sixty*, edited by Jacob Neusner (4 vols.; Leiden: Brill, 1975), Part III, pp. 85-123; "The Historical Setting of the Uruk Prophecy," *Journal of Near Eastern Studies* 47 (1988), 43-46; "The Date of the Book of Jubilees," *Proceedings of the American Academy for Jewish Research* 50 (1983), 63-86; "The Testament of Moses: Its Content, Its Origin, and Its Attestation in Josephus," in *Studies on the Testament of Moses*, edited by George W.E.

Nickelsburg, Jr. ("Septuagint and Cognate Studies," No. 4; Cambridge, Mass.: Society of Biblical Literature, 1973), pp. 44-52; "The Apocryphal Book of I Baruch," *Proceedings of the American Academy for Jewish Research* 46-47 (1979-80), 179-99; review of Doran's *Temple Propaganda*, *Jewish Quarterly Review* 75 (1984), 79-88; "How the Authors in 1 and 2 Maccabees Treated the Messianic Promises," in *Judaisms and their Messiahs*, edited by Jacob Neusner, William S. Green and Ernest Frerichs (Cambridge: University Press, 1988), pp. 69-96.

I have made some additions and corrections. The various editors who first published my articles differed from me and among themselves in their principles of spelling and style. I became aware of the resultant inconsistencies only as I read the proofs of this volume, and I decided it was not worthwhile to remove them. The articles of J.H. Charlesworth, George Nickelsburg, and John J. Collins in Chapter 11 which are cited only by author's name and article title or as being "in this volume" all are to be found, not in this volume but in the volume of the original publication, *Judaisms and their Messiahs*. Though *Aristeas to Philocrates* in fact is not a letter, there is little harm in calling it that, as one of my editors insisted on doing. The other inconsistencies will not mislead the reader. Chapters 2, 4, and 11 each have at the end a list of the abbreviations used, as they did when first published. The list of the abbreviations used in the other chapters is at the end of this volume, before the index.

I thank the holders of the rights to the articles and figures in this book for granting permission to republish. The University of Chicago granted permission for the articles in the *Journal of Near Eastern Studies*. I thank Joshua Bell for his services as editor.

Jonathan A. Goldstein
August 2, 1989

Part One

INTERCULTURAL BORROWING

1

Jewish Acceptance and Rejection of Hellenism

I. Introduction

"The Greek confronted the Hebrew. Judaism confronted Hellenism." Thus runs the conventional wisdom of our time. Surely that confrontation has been a major theme in the modern study of the cultural history of the period extending from the fourth century B.C.E. to the fifth century C.E. and even later. Still more fruitful in modern research has been the extended concept of a Hellenistic culture which confronted all other ancient Mediterranean and near eastern civilizations from the fourth century B.C.E. on. The concepts of Hellenistic culture and of confrontation themselves have a history, which began no later than the sixteenth century. The early investigators took as their point of departure the text of the Acts of the Apostles 6.1, which opposes Hebrews to Hellenists: "Now, in those days, when the disciples were increasing in number, the Hellenists murmured against the Hebrews because their widows were neglected in the daily distribution." Whatever the text may mean, clearly it opposes Hebrews to Hellenists, and it was Johann Gustav Droysen[1] in the nineteenth century who continued the misinterpretation of Acts 6.1 and produced the fruitful extended concept of Hellenism as the great confronting culture which arose in the fourth century B.C.E.[2]

Though the concepts of Hellenism and of the confrontation had their origin in the interpretation and misinterpretation of Acts 6.1,

---

[1] J.G. Droysen, *Geschichte des Hellenismus*, 1836-43,[2]1877-78.
[2] See Arnaldo Momigliano, "Hellenism," *EJ* VIII, 1972, col. 291, and *Essays in Ancient and Modern Historiography*, Middletown, Connecticut 1977, pp. 307-12.

they fit well the usage of Paul and the church fathers, who oppose "Jew" to "Greek."[3] Better yet, there would seem to be strong confirmation of the validity of the concept of Hellenism as opposed to Judaism, in the fact that II Maccabees tells of the war to defend *Ioudaismos*[4] and condemns *Hellēnismos*.[5]

Great works have been written on the broad phenomenon of Hellenism and on the narrower problem of how the Jews reacted to it. The latest important study is that of Martin Hengel,[6] who has assembled a mass of evidence in the attempt to show that the Judaism even of believers in the Torah, down to the reign of Antiochus IV, was heavily Hellenized, though there was some Jewish opposition to Hellenism as evidenced in the book of Ben Sira. Hengel goes on to argue that as a result of the persecution under Antiochus IV, those devoted to the Torah closed ranks against full assimilation of Hellenism. Though Hengel himself insists that even the later Palestinian Judaism of the Pharisees and the Essenes must be regarded as Hellenistic Judaism,[7] still he gives his Part III the title, "The Encounter and *Conflict* between Palestinian Judaism and the Spirit of the Hellenistic Age," and he labels his summary of Part III as "Palestinian Judaism between the Reception and the *Repudiation* of Hellenism." The feat of fully assimilating Hellenism into a monotheistic religion, Hengel implies, was left for Christianity.

If a historical concept was discovered through the misinterpretation of a text, one must test its validity very carefully. With all due respect to the industry and intelligence of my predecessors, including Hengel, I believe it is necessary to make a fresh beginning: one must define terms more carefully, and one must examine the sources on each period for what they themselves say. I believe that Hengel, too, stands in the tradition of the misinterpreters of Acts 6.1. In some respects he has far overstated the opposition between Judaism and Hellenism.

It goes without saying that the present paper cannot deal with the subject on the scale of Hengel's work, but nevertheless the proposed fresh beginning can be made. As a first limitation in scope, I intend to

---

[3] Walter Bauer, *Wörterbuch zum Neuen Testament*, [5]1958, col. 499; ET, *A Greek-English Lexicon of the New Testament*, [2]1979, pp. 251f.; G.W.H. Lampe, *A Patristic Greek Lexicon*, 1961-68, p. 451b; cf. H. Windisch, "*Hellēn*," TDNT II, pp. 507-16.
[4] II Macc. 2.21.
[5] II Macc. 4.13; much later, Tacitus (*Hist.* V.8.2) recorded the false tradition that Antiochus IV had tried to impose Greek ways upon the Jews; see Jonathan A. Goldstein, *I Maccabees*, 1976, pp. 131-59, 250f.
[6] M. Hengel, *Judaism and Hellenism*, ET, 2 vols., 1974.
[7] *Ibid.* I, p. 252.

look only at Jews who believed in the validity of the Torah: what was *their* reaction to Hellenistic culture? The restriction is not very great, since such Jews wrote most of our sources, and they, if anyone, felt the supposed confrontations with Hellenism. Pagan writers hardly mention Jews who rejected the authority of the Torah.[8]

"Culture" is a modern concept. There was no word for it in ancient Latin or Hebrew or Aramaic, and even the Greek *paideia* has different connotations.[9] Nevertheless, we can validly distinguish, even in the ancient world, resistance to foreign rulers from resistance to the foreign culture of those rulers. Hindus and Muslims of British India could adopt the culture of English gentlemen and still work for the independence of India and Pakistan. The pious Daniel of the biblical stores bore a Babylonian name, was adept in Babylonian wisdom, spoke and wrote Babylonian Aramaic, and still prayed for an end to foreign domination. Fighters in the army of Judas Maccabaeus bore Greek names,[10] and the martyr mother and her seven sons are presented as speaking Greek.[11] Thus, in looking for evidence of resistance to Hellenistic culture, we must be careful to exclude the abundant evidence which points only to hostility towards Greek-speaking rulers.[12]

We must take account of the religious impediments to Jewish adoption of Hellenistic culture, but we must not overestimate them. The members of the Muslim Aligarh movement in British-ruled India on no account would adopt Christianity, but otherwise the members of the movement aimed at becoming gentlemen in the English mould.[13] Just as Islam left the way open for many forms for Anglicizing, so the Torah left the way open for many forms for Hellenizing. Jews who accepted the authority of the Torah could not worship Greek gods[14] or practice or tolerate (as did many Greeks) male homosexual intercourse. Some Jews were rigorous in interpreting the sacred texts which put restrictions on Jewish contacts with Gentiles, and some were more

---

[8]See, e.g., Hecataeus of Abdera apud Josephus, *Ap.* I.190-93. On the authenticity of the passage, see below, n. 62.
[9]See Werner Jaeger, *Paideia*, ET, 3 vols., 1939-45.
[10]II Macc. 12.19, 24.
[11]II Macc. 7; the author finds it necessary to mention the fact that on occasion the martyrs speak, not Greek, but "the ancestral language" (vv. 8, 21, 27).
[12]The greater part of the protest literature of the conquered peoples was indeed directed against the Greek-speaking rulers. See the perceptive remarks of Samuel K. Eddy, *The King Is Dead*, 1961, pp. 333f.
[13]See David Lelyveld, *Aligarh's First Generation*, 1978.
[14]Greeks resented the fact that *Hellenized* Jews would not worship Greek gods; see, e.g., Josephus, *Ant.* XII.125.

lenient.[15] But for most Jews, some Greek practices and some polite intercourse with Greeks remained compatible with obedience to the Torah. In the *Letter of Aristeas to Philocrates*, The high priest Eleazar and the Jewish elders who translated the Torah into Greek will not violate Jewish law but manage otherwise to behave like perfect Greek *kaloi kai agathoi*. Condemnations of Gentile idolatry and immorality are commonplaces of Jewish biblical and post-biblical literature. Even if a Jewish source should specify that it is condemning *Greek* idols or *Greek* homosexuals, we should hesitate to take the passage as evidence that *Hellenism* rather than mere idolatry or homosexuality was an issue for pious ancient Jews. In each period we must try to ascertain which aspects of Hellenism were permitted and which were forbidden by the Torah as then interpreted. In every period we must expect to find pious Jews differing on how the Torah should be interpreted.

II. The Characteristics of Hellenism and Biblical Law

We cannot proceed further without defining Hellenism itself, a highly controversial task. I shall not attempt a complete definition. Rather, I shall list a number of traits or distinguishing characteristics on which all observers, ancient and modern, should agree:

1. "Hellenism," even in a non-Greek environment, implies that some Greeks are present, and that the non-Greeks have some contacts with them.
2. In a Hellenized culture, there must be some knowledge and use of the Greek language.
3. For intellectuals, the Hellenistic age was characterized by the development and spread of rational philosophies which often were skeptical of traditional religion.
4. In literature, Hellenistic culture typically produced highly emotional epic, dramatic, and lyric poetry.
5. Very important in Hellenistic culture were the athletic and educational pursuits of the Greek gymnasium.[16]
6. In architectural remains, these cultural traits of Hellenism left an enduring legacy, in the surviving traces of ancient gymnasiums, stadiums and theaters. Greek stone theaters are especially durable and conspicuous among archaeological remains.

---

[15]See below, pp. 15-28.
[16]See Martin P. Nilsson, *Die hellenistische Schule*, 1955; Henri I. Marrou, *A History of Education in Antiquity*, ET 1964, pp. 147-86 (to be corrected by Nilsson, pp. 34-42), 256-60; Jean Delorme, *Gymnasion*, 1960.

Our six traits are peculiarly Greek. Modern investigators such as M.I. Rostovtzeff have suggested that Hellenistic civilization was marked also by rational organization of human enterprises, by vigorous and often unscrupulous business methods, and by daring experiments in technology and social organization.[17] Jews may on occasion have disapproved of the business acumen shown by wealthy Israelites in the Hellenistic age. But acumen and rationality are *human* traits, conspicuous in but not limited to Hellenistic Greeks. Amos, long before the Hellenistic age, condemned Israelite business acumen (8.4-5; cf. Hosea 12.8-9). If an ancient Jewish moralist attacks Jews for exhibiting the traits which so interested Rostovtzeff, one cannot assume that moralist is attacking Hellenism unless he stigmatizes the traits as Greek.

What do the Torah and the rest of the Hebrew Bible have to say concerning our six traits? Not one is specifically forbidden. Some Jews could hold that all were permitted, while rigorists could infer from sacred texts that all were forbidden.

Thus, according to the Torah, the nations which inhabited the Promised Land before Joshua conquered it were to be driven out or killed. They were not to reside in it with the Jews, nor were Jews to make any covenant for peaceful relations with them.[18] Nothing in the Torah directly bars tolerating the residence of other Gentiles or making covenants with them. Indeed, covenants with "distant nations" are specifically permitted.[19] Surely Greeks came from a distant country!

Rigorists, however, could point out that the texts give a reason for removing the former inhabitants of the Promised Land: otherwise Israelites would copy their idolatry and their abominations. Greeks, too, worshipped idols and might practise abominations. Should they not, therefore, be excluded from Judaea?[20] On the other hand, some Jews who accepted the rigorist interpretation could believe that God would allow residence on Jewish soil by Greeks who abstained while there from acts forbidden by the Torah, and that God permitted association

---

[17]M.I. Rostovtzeff, *The Social and Economic History of the Hellenistic World*, 2 vols., ²1957.

[18]Ex. 23.31-33; 34.15f.; Deut. 20.15-19; cf. Ex. 23.23f. Ideally, the Promised Land should be defined by the borders given in Num. 32.33-42; 34.1-15; and Josh. 15-19, including the holdings of the Transjordanian tribes, who surely were bound by the laws against idolatry. If the Jews could not hold all of the promised territory, they were still bound to enforce the Torah in whatever part of it they controlled.

[19]Josh. 9.3-27; cf. Deut. 20.10-15.

[20]Ezra 9.1f.; Neh. 9.2.

even with idolatrous Greeks at times when those Greeks were not engaged in prohibited acts.

Nehemiah[21] found it dreadful that Jewish children spoke the language of Ashdod and did not speak or understand the Jewish tongue. Though the use of Aramaic had already invaded scripture itself, rigorists could have objected to Jewish use of Greek as Nehemiah objected to Ashdodite.[22]

The biblical texts forbidding Jews to practise Gentile customs also lend themselves to various interpretations. The passages in the Torah specify that the practices not to be imitated are those of Egypt and Canaan and involve idolatry, human sacrifice, and forbidden sexual acts.[23] Greeks were neither from Egypt nor from Canaan. Could not Jews imitate those Greek practices which involved neither idolatry nor human sacrifice nor forbidden sexual acts? On the other hand, almost all Greeks were idolaters, and some practised forbidden sexual acts. Rigorists could claim that the Torah forbade imitating the practices of any nation, the members of which were widely guilty of idolatry and forbidden sexual acts. Then should not Greek literature and Greek-style theaters be banned?[24] Those who would ban them would have to explain away the implications of Dan. 1-6, chapters accepted as true by many, if not most, Jews before the middle of the fourth century C.E. Babylonians certainly practised both idolatry and forbidden sexual acts, yet those chapters attest that the pious Daniel and his friends could adopt Babylonian names and study and use Babylonian wisdom.[25]

III. The Rejection of Hellenism by Conservative Romans

Rejection of Hellenistic culture by ancient peoples is not a figment of the imagination of modern scholars. Members of at least one ancient nation other than the Jews confronted Hellenistic culture in hostile fashion, and the writers and especially the moralists of that nation condemned the six traits listed above as well as those singled out by

---

[21]Neh. 13.24.
[22]Mek. Pisḥa 5 (Lauterbach, I, pp. 34, 36).
[23]Ex. 22.23-24; Lev. 18.3-30; cf. Deut. 20.19; II Kings 17.8-12.
[24]See below, n. 113.
[25]I shall discuss the origins and date of Dan. 1-6 in my commentary on Daniel. Though there are some later interpolations, the basic stuff of the chapters was written well before the time of Alexander the Great. For argument placing Jewish acceptance of Dan. 1-6 as early as the second half of the third century B.C.E., see Elias Bickerman, *Four Strange Books of the Bible*, 1967, pp. 92, 100.

Jewish Acceptance and Rejection of Hellenism

Rostovtzeff. The Romans so confronted Hellenism and labelled the traits they condemned as Greek.[26]

Latin vocabulary shows that Romans viewed many types of immorality as peculiarly Greek. Plautus and Titinius, Roman writers of comedy, were contemporaries of Ben Sira in the early second century B.C.E. In their plays, "to Greek it thoroughly" (*pergraecari, congraecare*) means to pursue pleasure or gluttony without any sense of shame.[27] Cicero and his contemporaries used the contemptuous Latin diminutive *Graeculus* ("Greekling") to express their low opinion of Greeks and to stigmatize any feature of Hellenistic civilization which they did not like.[28] If a Roman political figure exhibited any of the despised Hellenistic traits, his enemies were quick to twit him with being an imitator of Greeks.[29]

We may study the Roman reactions to Hellenism under the headings of our six traits:

1. Archaeological and literary evidence shows that Greeks were present in Campania, just to the south-east of Rome's own district of Latium, from the middle of the eighth century B.C.E., the traditional date of her foundation. The Greeks' settlements in Italy were numerous and deep-rooted.[30] Nevertheless, in the second century B.C.E. the outspoken conservative Marcus Porcius Cato, a contemporary of Jesus ben Sira, repeatedly called for the expulsion of the Greeks, not merely from Rome but from all of Italy.[31]

2. Romans could condemn the very use of the Greek language, even when employed to address Greeks.[32]

3. Conservative Romans tried to exclude all kinds of Greek philosophy, especially Epicureanism,[33] and even Cicero could echo Roman contempt for Greek philosophy in general.[34]

---

[26] For a general treatment of the confrontation in the second century B.C.E., see Gaston Colin, *Rome et la Grèce de 200 à 146 avant Jésus-Christ*, 1905, pp. 348-72.

[27] Plautus, *Bacchides* IV.4.101-2 (742-43); *Mostellaria* I.1.21 (22) and I.1.61 (64); Titinius apud Paulus Diaconus (ed. Müller), p. 215, line 5. Cf. Horace, *Satires* II.2.11.

[28] Cicero, *Pro Flacco* 11-12, 23; *Post reditum in Senatu* 6.14; *In Pisonem* 29.70; *De oratore* 1.47 and 102; *Epistulae ad Quintum fratrem* I.1.

[29] Polybius XXXIX.1; Plutarch, *Cato Major* 3.7.

[30] See Jacques Heurgon, *The Rise of Rome to 264 B.C.*, 1973, pp. 75-94, 239-44.

[31] Pliny, *Historia naturalis* VII.30.113.

[32] Valerius Maximus, *Factorum et dictorum memorabilium libri* II.2.2; Cicero, *In Verrem* II.4.66, §147,

[33] Cicero, *Academica priora* II.2.5; Plutarch, *Cato Major* 22.1-23.3; Gellius XV.11.1; Valerius Maximus, *Factorum* IV.3.6; Plutarch, *Pyrrhus* 20.3-4; Suetonius, *De rhetoribus* 1; Athenaeus XII.547a. Plautus, *Curculio* II.3.9-19 (288-

4. Cato disapproved of any Greek poetry on the lips of a Roman.[35] His general assessment of Greeks and Greek literature is worth quoting in full:

> Concerning those contemptible Greeks, Marcus my son, I shall speak to you in the proper place. I shall show you what I learned from my own experience at Athens: that it may be good to dip into their literature, but not to learn it thoroughly. I shall convince you that they are a most wicked and intractable nation. You may take my word as the word of a prophet: whenever that contemptible nation bestows its literature upon us, it will ruin everything....[36]

5. Cato and other Roman conservatives had the same contempt for the Greek gymnasium.[37] There were no public gymnasia at Rome under the republic, and even private gymnasia are not attested until the time of Cicero.[38]

6. The typical structures of Greek culture – the gymnasia, stadia and theaters – are strikingly absent from republican Rome before the first century B.C.E., and we hear that Roman conservatives brought about the demolition of such structures when they were erected.[39]

We may add that Romans could disapprove of Greek business methods and found strange the Greek insistence on doing business for cash and their refusal to grant credit.[40] Cicero believed Greeks were bent only on making money and would do anything for money.[41] Thus, conservative Romans and even Cicero felt themselves to be in hostile confrontation with Hellenistic culture.[42]

---

98) may be a blast against philosophers, but it could also be a mere attack on Greek parasites.

[34] *Post reditum in Senatu* 6.14.

[35] Cato, *Oratio* apud Gellius I.15.8, and *Carmen de moribus* apud Gellius XI.2; M. Catonis praeter librum de re rustica quae extant (ed. Henricus Jordan), Lipsiae 1860, pp. 58, 83. Cf. Cicero, *De re publica* IV.9.

[36] Cato, quoted by Pliny, *Historia naturalis* XXIX.7.14. Cf. Livy XXIX.19, where Scipio is condemned for reading Greek books, and Cicero, *Academica priora* II.2.5.

[37] Livy XXIX.19; Plutarch, *Cato Major* 3.7; cf. Cicero, *De re publica* IV.4.

[38] Cicero, *Epistulae ad Atticum* II.4.7; Delorme, *Gymnasion*, pp. 223-432.

[39] Livy, *Periocha* XLVIII; Velleius Paterculus I.15; Valerius Maximus II.4.2; Augustine, *De civitate Dei* I.31; Tertullian, *Apol.* 6; *De spectaculis* 10; Colin, *Rome et la Grèce*, p. 370. Cf. Cicero, *De re publica* IV.10.

[40] Plautus, *Asinaria* I.3.47-49 (199-201); Colin, *Rome et la Grèce*, p. 364; Fritz Pringsheim, *The Greek Law of Sale*, 1950, pp. 87-92.

[41] Cicero, *Epistulae ad Quintum fratrem* I.1.

[42] The confrontation continued, long beyond the fall of the Roman republic. See Juvenal III.60-125.

One would think that Jews devoted to the Torah felt a similar confrontation. But did they? Let us search the many and varied remains of Jewish literature, whether written originally in Hebrew, Aramaic or Greek.

IV. Jewish Attitudes Towards Hellenism

Scholars hitherto have not taken note of the stark contrast between ancient Jewish literature and the Roman texts we have just examined. Although ancient Jewish literature is full of ethnic, moral and religious polemics against non-Jews, Jewish texts, whatever their language, contain no verb comparable to the Latin *pergraecari* and no contemptuous noun or adjective comparable to the Latin *Graeculus*. Jews could have created a verb *hityavven* ("become, or act, Greek") on the model of *hityahed* ("become, or act Jewish"; Esth. 8.17), as has been done in modern Hebrew. Ancient Jews could so have used the Greek *Hellēnizein*, as the church Fathers did.[43] Jews could have used *yavan* ("Greece") and *yevani* ("Greek") as terms of reproach. Yet there is no trace that Jews so used such expressions. The word "Greek" is somewhat infrequent in the Jewish Apocrypha and Pseudepigrapha, in Qumran texts, and in rabbinic literature. Philo and Josephus employ it as a linguistic and ethnic term, usually without suggesting any opposition between "Jewish" and "Greek."[44]

One who nevertheless believes in the sharp confrontation between the Jews and Hellenism might insist that in the Jewish vocabulary of the Hellenistic age, the word "Gentile," so frequently opposed to "Jew," really means "Greek." Indeed, in Paul's epistles and in patristic literature, "Greek" often means simply "non-Jew" or "pagan."[45] Modern

---

[43]Lampe, *Lexicon*, p. 451b.
[44]Cf. Windisch, *"Hellēn," TDNT* II, pp. 507-8. One of the most frequent meanings of *yavan* in Jewish texts is "the Seleucid empire," and *yevani* then correspondingly means "of the Seleucid empire." See Goldstein, *I Maccabees*, p. 192. Mere Jewish opposition to rule by a foreign empire, even if that empire bears the name "Greece," is not to be viewed as Jewish opposition to Hellenism. On the references in Jewish literature to the real confrontation with the Seleucid Antiochus IV, see below, pp. 75-81.
[45]Windisch, *TDNT* II, pp. 509-16; Lampe, *Lexicon*, p. 451b. Pagan writers seem to have followed the same practice as Paul and the church Fathers, in opposing "Jew" to "Greek." See Menahem Stern, *Greek and Latin Authors on Jews and Judaism* I, 1974, pp. 96 (Hermippus of Smyrna apud Origen, *Contra Celsum* I.15 [GCS I, p. 67]), 145-7, 152-54 and 410-12 (Poseidonius, Apollonius Molon, and Apion apud Josephus, *Ap.* II.89-96), 218 (Nicolaus of Damascus, *Historiae*, apud Josephus, *Ant.* XII.125-26), and 252 and 254 (Nicolaus of Damascus, *De vita sua*, apud Constantinus Porphyrogenitus, *Excerpta de insidiis* [ed. de Boor], pp. 2f.); cf. Julian, *Adv. Gal.* 229c-230a and *Fragmenta breviora* 6, and the pagan

scholars have argued, however, that the word "Greek" in *Jewish* texts cannot be taken to mean "Gentile."[46] Thus, one may expect that the word "Gentile" in Jewish texts ought not automatically to be taken to mean "Greek." Nevertheless, we shall leave open the possibility that "Gentile" (*goy, ethnos*) in Jewish texts may on occasion mean "Greek."

For the purpose of this paper we shall divide the history of the Jews in the times when Hellenism was a factor into four periods. First, there is the time before the priest Jason usurped the high priesthood at the beginning of the reign of Antiochus IV (in late 175 or early 174 B.C.E.) Second, there is the period which began with Jason's high priesthood and extended down to the time when the Jews received from Antiochus V the letter restoring to them their laws and their temple (II Macc. 11.23-26; early 163 B.C.E.).[47] So important was this period that it deserves a special name; let us call the time from 175 to 163 B.C.E. the "critical period." Third, there are the years between the critical period and the death of the Hasmonaean prince Simon in 134 B.C.E. Fourth, there is the time between the death of Simon and the completion of the Babylonian Talmud in the fifth century C.E.

From all these periods we have evidence on our topic. In particular, we have Jewish literature either written in or reflecting each period. In this study we cannot possibly give a thorough survey of the literature of all four periods. I believe, however, that the essential truths can be demonstrated by a proper study of the first two.

V. Jewish Reactions to Hellenism: The Early Period

Let us proceed to consider the evidence for the earliest period, the one before Jason usurped the high priesthood. Hengel[48] tried to prove that it was a period of high Hellenization, obstructed or opposed only by a few Jewish conservatives such as Ben Sira. If we examine the evidence under the headings of our aspects of Hellenism, we shall find that Hengel, surprisingly, has overestimated the opposition to Hellenism and has read into the words of Ben Sira an opposition which does not exist there. For this period we have the testimony not only of

---

spokesman (Porphyry?) quoted apud Eusebius, *Praep. evang.* I.2.1-4. Hellenized Jews, it would appear, usually did not wish to give the impression that they were not Greeks, whereas pagan Greeks, especially those who were anti-Jewish, found the antithesis natural. Thus, Paul and the church Fathers may be reflecting pagan Greek, rather than Jewish usage.

[46]Windisch, *TDNT* II, pp. 507f.
[47]I treat the document at II Macc. 11.23-26 in my *II Maccabees*, pp. 414-17.
[48]*Judaism and Hellenism* I, pp. 6-266.

Jews but of pagans, especially of Hecataeus of Abdera. Since the Jews were under Graeco-Macedonian rule, they could not cut themselves off from all contact with Greeks. Contacts are attested both in the literary remains and in the papyri, to say nothing of the Greek pottery and artifacts found in the archaeological strata.[49] The period shows no opposition to the use of the Greek language. Indeed, the Torah itself was translated into Greek.[50] Far from sealing themselves off from Greek literature, pious Jews drew even upon its myths[51] and took to writing Greek poetry themselves.[52]

Greek tourists with philosophic training at first found the Jews so interesting that Jews for a while may have been as much pestered by visiting "philosophers"[53] as modern primitives are by anthropologists. There is no sign that Jews tried to exclude the teachings of the philosophers. Indeed, they soon claimed that the philosophers, when correct, had borrowed from the Torah.[54] Modern scholars have found traces of Greek philosophy in the thought of Qohelet and Ben Sira,[55] and even in the Greek translation of the Torah.[56] It is not beyond

---

[49] Clearchus apud Josephus, *Ap.* I.176-83; Hecataeus of Abdera apud Diodorus XI.3 and apud Josephus, *Ap.* I.183-204 (see below, n. 62); Victor A. Tcherikover and Alexander Fuks, *CPJ* I. A brief survey of the archaeological evidence can be found in the notes to Morton Smith, *Palestinian Parties and Politics that Shaped the Old Testament*, 1971, pp. 57-81.
[50] See Elias Bickerman, *Studies in Jewish and Christian History* I, 1976. pp. 167-200.
[51] See George W.E. Nickelsburg, "Apocalyptic and Myth in 1 Enoch 6-11," *JBL* 96, 1977, pp. 383-405; cf. *Sib. Or.* 3.105-57 (but there the author pretends to be a pagan Greek).
[52] Noteworthy are the following, though we lack clear evidence for dating them in the first of our four periods: (i) The Orphic Hymn apud Pseudo-Justin, *Cohortatio ad gentiles* 15 and Eusebius, *Praep. evang.* XIII.12. See Nikolaus Walter, *Der Thoraausleger Aristobulos*, 1964, pp. 184-86, 202-61; Yehoshua Gutman, *The Beginnings of Jewish-Hellenistic Literature* I, 1958, pp. 148-70 (in Hebrew). (ii) The epic *On Jerusalem* of Philo the poet apud Eusebius, op. cit. IX.20, 24, and 37. See Y. Gutman, "Philo the Epic Poet,"*SH* 1, 1954, pp. 36-63. (iii) The tragedy *Exagoge* by Ezekiel apud Eusebius, *op. cit.* IX.28.4; 29.16. See Gutman, *Beginnings* II, pp. 9-65 [in Hebrew]. (iv) *Sib. Or.*, especially Book 3. See John J. Collins, *The Sibylline Oracles of Egyptian Judaism*, 1974.
[53] Hecataeus of Abdera (see above, n. 49, and below, n. 62); Megasthenes apud Clement of Alexandria, *Stromateis* I.15.72.5 (GCS 2, p. 46); see Gutman, *Beginnings* I, pp. 39-107.
[54] Aristobulus apud Eusebius, *Praep. evang.* XIII.12.1.
[55] Hengel, *Judaism and Hellenism* I, pp. 115-52.
[56] Hengel (*ibid.* II, p. 105 n. 372) does not accept Morton Smith's confident assertion ("The Image of God," *BJRL* 40, 1958, p. 474), that *ho ōn* at Greek Ex. 3.14 reflects Platonic vocabulary. Plato, however, on a few occasions may have

question that those scholars are correct. For example, Qohelet did not need the help of Greek thinkers in order to question the general biblical belief in providence. The mere amoral facts of history could lead him to do so. Nevertheless, Greek influence on those writings is possible and even likely.

Strange, however, is Hengel's insistence that Ben Sira wrote in opposition to Hellenism.[57] Hengel himself may have been aware of the insecure basis of his theory here, for his argument is full of words like "probably" and "presumably." Nevertheless, his conclusions on Ben Sira have gained unjustifiably wide acceptance. Simple considerations suffice to refute them. The words "Greek" and "Greece" nowhere appear in Ben Sira's work. And should one suggest that he abstained from hostile mention of Greeks for fear of his Graeco-Macedonian overlords, Ben Sira certainly could have directed his hostility at unnamed "Gentiles," as does so much of Jewish literature. Yet in the entire book of Ben Sira there is no preaching against the Gentiles. Ben Sira does not tell his fellow Jews that they must not imitate foreigners, nor does he tell Jews to shun pagans. He may deplore the oppression of the poor by the rich or the questioning of divine providence, but nowhere does he say that the oppressors or the questioners imitate Greeks or Gentiles.[58] For Ben Sira, Hellenism was simply not an issue.

Surely Hellenistic culture must have challenged the Jews; even the mighty Romans felt the challenge. How are we to explain the strange fact that Ben Sira shows no trace of such a challenge? To answer this question, we must consider evidence ignored by most modern writers. In this earliest period, the Jews in fact could not be completely open to

---

used *to on* (not *ho ōn*) to mean "God"; see *Phaedo* 65c, *Republic* VI.501d, VII.518c and 537d, and IX.582c; hence, Smith may be right.

[57] Hengel, *Judaism and Hellenism* I, pp. 131-53.

[58] Ben Sira 36.9-17 is an exceedingly bold prayer asking God to overthrow the foreign rulers, even if the enemy is not named. We have taken care to exclude from our study expressions of mere opposition to foreign rule. Otherwise, in Ben Sira's book, the only attacks on non-Jews are in 50.25-26. Mentioned there are the inhabitants of Seir (i.e., the Idumaeans) and of Philistia, as well as that foolish nation that dwells in Shechem (i.e., the Samaritans). Of these, only the inhabitants of Philistia could at all be called Greeks, and even they were probably still regarded as non-Greek; see Goldstein, *I Maccabees*, p. 260, 420-21. The Greek manuscripts of Ben Sira, instead of "Seir" have "the mountain of Samaria." If correct, that reading might refer to the Greco-Macedonian military colony in the city of Samaria; see Goldstein, *I Maccabees*, pp. 245f. Even then, Ben Sira does not attack them as Greeks or even as pagans, but only as vexatious neighbors. He does not bother to praise Nehemiah or the high priest Simeon II for seeing to the separation of Jews from Gentiles.

Hellenism and were not. So great was the interest of philosophers in Jews that one might have expected Jews to have taken advantage of it to propagate their own religion among philosophers. One would then expect that the Greek translation of Genesis would have been full of the technical cosmological terminology of the Greek philosophers, yet that terminology is strikingly absent.[59] At least from the time when Aristophanes wrote his *Clouds*, ordinary Greeks knew enough of that terminology to make fun of it, even when they could not understand it. Thus, I believe the Jewish translators, too, knew something of the cosmological vocabulary of Greek philosophy.[60] They knew enough of it to avoid it completely in rendering Genesis.

This avoidance of philosophical vocabulary was not necessarily hostile. Very likely the purpose was to prevent Greeks from making the charge that Jews had plagiarized from the philosophers. Hence, this fact is but a feeble example of Jewish rejection of Hellenism.

More significant is the evidence of Hecataeus of Abdera,[61] that the Jewish way of life, even in his time, was "misanthropic" (ἀπάνθρωπον) and "hostile to strangers" (μισόξενον). How much contact did Jews of Judaea have with Greeks? Rigorist interpretations of the Torah in fact shaped much of life in Judaea. Hecataeus also lets us know that Jews did not tolerate the existence of pagan altars and shrines in Judaea: sometimes by paying fines for insubordination, sometimes by obtaining pardon from the provincial governors, the Jews of Judaea, by the late fourth century B.C.E., secured the privilege of not having to tolerate pagan worship on their own soil. It was a privilege they needed, for they believed their God would inflict ruinous punishment upon them if they tolerated idol-worship in the Holy Land, even if only pagans practised it.[62]

---

[59]See Gutman, *Beginnings* I, pp. 129-31.

[60]Cf. *Aristeas* 121.

[61]Hecataeus apud Diodorus XL.3.4; cf. Diodorus XXXIV-XXXV.1.2-3 (from Poseidonius?).

[62]Hecataeus apud Josephus, *Ap.* I.193. On the authenticity of the passage, see Hans Lewy, "Hekataios von Abdera," ZNW 31, 1932, pp. 117-32; Gutman, *Beginnings* I, pp. 66-71. Menahem Stern (*Greek and Latin Authors on Jews and Judaism* I, pp. 21-24) still has doubts about the passage of interest to us, because Josephus quotes Hecataeus as *admiring* the Jews for destroying pagan shrines and altars. Hecataeus, however, is known to have shared Plato's admiration for peoples who adhered tenaciously to their own laws. It is not inconceivable that Hecataeus and Plato could have admired even Jewish abhorrence of idolatry. No one has shown why Hecataeus could not have admired the Jews for adhering to their own laws. Even as a Jewish forgery, the passage would be important testimony for our purposes: it would attest that long before the time of Josephus it was believed that Jews in the days of

Scholars have not considered the implications of this privilege. Few if any non-Jews would reside on Jewish soil if they could not practise their own religion there. There were numerous Greek cities and villages in Palestine, but until Antiochus IV established the Akra, in Judaea proper there was not even a Greek village, much less a Greek city. In mentioning how Jews destroy pagan altars and shrines, Hecataeus does not speak of foreign settlers but of foreign "arrivals" or "visitors" (τῶν εἰς τὴν χώραν πρὸς αὐτοὺς ἀφικνουμένων). There must have been many Greek visitors, even pilgrims to the famous temple in Jerusalem, such as were said to have been contemplated already by King Solomon.[63] Even Graeco-Macedonian kings brought or sent sumptuous gifts.[64]

The Zenon papyri from our period attest estates held by Greek landlords in Palestine, but none in Judaea proper.[65] They also attest that Greeks did business at Jerusalem and Jericho, but not that they resided there. Finds of Greek pottery and other artifacts give more evidence of business contacts.[66] Even resident pagan *soldiers* were few. In Judaea proper, we hear only of a small garrison of pagan soldiers in the citadel of Jerusalem,[67] and they may have been selected for their willingness to conform to the Jews' laws barring pagan worship. The Gentiles whom Judas Maccabaeus drove out of Judaea may have been settled there only a few years before as part of the punishment of the Jews by Antiochus IV.[68]

A royal decree directly excluding Gentiles from settling in Judaea would have been so great a privilege for the Jews that our sources could not have passed over it in silence. Hence, the absence of Greeks from Judaea probably was a consequence of the ban on pagan worship there.

Hecataeus did not tolerate pagan worship on their own soil. In this case, the evidence of the lack of pagan settlement in Judaea proper, which we are about to consider, would confirm the veracity of the hypothetical forger's testimony.

Ruinous punishment for tolerating idolatry even of pagans on the holy soil: Ex. 34.13f; Deut. 7.25f.; I Kings 11.1-13; 18.18f. (many of the prophets of Baal probably came with Jezebel from Tyre). Cf. Philo, *Legat.* 200-2; Josephus, *Ant.* XVIII.120-22.

[63] I Kings, 8.41-43.
[64] II Macc. 2.12; 3.2; Josephus, *Ant.* XII.138-41.
[65] Victor Tcherikover, *Hellenistic Civilization and the Jews*, 1959, pp. 431f. n. 73.
[66] Tcherikover and Fuks, *CPJ* I, Nos. 2a and 2b. For the archaeological finds, see above, n. 49.
[67] II Macc. 4.28f. The garrison was so small it did not even attempt to restore order during the riot against Lysimachus (vv. 40-42).
[68] II Macc. 14.14; I Macc. 1.34; 3.36; Dan. 11.39.

This absence of resident Greeks goes far to explain the slow progress of the Greek language in Judaea,[69] whereas Jews in the Diaspora quickly adopted Greek as their sole vernacular. It also explains why in Ben Sira's Judaea Hellenism was still no issue. There were few if any Greeks in the country to imitate. Cato would well have envied Judaea's freedom from Greeks.

The exclusion of resident Greeks removed from Judaea one important ingredient of Hellenism, but the exclusion in itself was certainly not directed at others of our traits of Hellenism. Not only Greeks but all idolaters were excluded from residence, and pagan Syrians seeking to enter Judaea may have been far more numerous than Greeks.

Against this background one can also easily understand how demand for the institutions of the gymnasium might have been slow to develop, and why no traces from this period have been found in Judaea of the typical Hellenistic structures, gymnasia and stadia and theaters.[70] How much was their absence owing to lack of demand, and how much to interpretations of the Torah which blocked their introduction? Whatever the answer, there is only one of our ingredients of Hellenism against which we can be sure that the expounders of the Torah in the earliest Hellenistic age put strong restrictions: contacts with Greeks were reduced by the absence of permanent Greek settlers. Nothing forbade Jews in the Diaspora to live among pagans; indeed, though some Jews of the Diaspora tried to avoid contact with pagans,[71] they could hardly achieve complete success. We can thus account for most of the contrasts between the Jews of Judaea and those of the Diaspora.

Concerning the other ingredients of Hellenism, there probably was controversy, and many believers, both in Judaea and in the Diaspora, may have been inclined to view them as having been permitted by the Torah. The significance of the second, "critical" period is that within it the course of history seemed to demonstrate that God himself viewed

---

[69]See Joseph A. Fitzmyer, "The Languages of Palestine in the First Century A.D.," *CBQ* 32, 1970, p. 502f., 507-12.

[70]Contrast Babylon, where a theatre was built early in the Hellenistic age. Even if the theatre was built by Greek settlers, not by Hellenized Babylonians, the contrast with Judaea remains. The gymnasium at Babylon seems to have been founded later than the theatre. See Erich Schmidt, "Die Griechen in Babylon und das Weiterleben ihrer Kultur," *Archäologischer Anzeiger*, 1941, pp. 834-44; Delorme, *Gymnasion*, pp. 431f., 475, 483f.; A. Mallwitz, "Das Theater von Babylon," in F. Wetzel, E. Schmidt and A. Mallwitz, *Das Babylon der Spätzeit*, 1957, pp. 17-27.

[71]E.g., the Jews of Alexandria; see Josephus, *Bell.* II.488 and Salo W. Baron, *A Social and Religious History of the Jews*, ²1952, I, pp. 188, 380f. (n. 29).

some of our distinguishing characteristics of Hellenism as abominations.

VI. The Critical Period

Only a few years after Ben Sira wrote, fateful innovative movements brought on the critical period. Among some Jews of Judaea grew a desire for closer associations with Greeks and for the establishment of a gymnasium at Jerusalem. The leader of this group was Jason, brother of the incumbent high priest, Onias III.[72] The strange policies of the new Seleucid king, Antiochus IV, gave Jason his opportunity. I have argued that Antiochus IV sought to make his realm a fit match for the Roman empire by establishing republican institutions on the Roman model, an Antiochene republic with an Antiochene citizenship. I have presented evidence to show that among the civic institutions of the Antiochene republic were the gymnasium and the associated athletic and educational pursuits. Just as Roman citizens were able to mingle freely with one another, so should Antiochene citizens be. Near the beginning of his reign the king invited his subjects as communities or as individuals to accept Antiochene citizenship. Jason was quick to exploit the opportunity, in 175 or early in 174 B.C.E.[73] The king might have been sufficiently pleased by the acceptance of citizenship. When Jason added to the acceptance strong financial inducements, the extravagant king, perennially in need of money, not only issued decrees permitting the goals desired by Jason and his followers; he also deposed Jason's brother Onias and made Jason high priest in his place.[74]

The mere fact that Jason had to approach the king for permission shows that the hitherto prevailing interpretations of the Torah forbade important aspects of what he desired. We are told, indeed, that the king's decrees for Jason set aside the earlier "humane concessions" which the ambassador John had won for the Jews, surely from Antiochus III.[75]

Unfortunately, we do not know the exact manner in which the dominant rigorists interpreted the Torah before Jason's reform. Theirs were the interpretations ratified by Antiochus III. Nor do we know the

---

[72] I Macc. 1.11-14; II Macc. 4.7-9.
[73] On all this, see Goldstein, *I Maccabees*, pp. 162, 173 n.4.
[74] II Macc. 4.7-10; Goldstein, *I Maccabees*, pp. 104-21.
[75] II Macc. 4.11: Josephus, *Ant.* XII.138-46; see E. Bickerman, "La charte séleucide de Jérusalem," *REJ* 100, 1935, pp. 4-35; Élie Bikerman [sic], "Une proclamation séleucide relative au temple de Jérusalem," *Syria* 25, 1946-48, pp. 67-85.

exact content of the decrees of Antiochus IV which enabled Jason to proceed. We must try to make sense of the somewhat incoherent clues in the sources.

Our earliest explicit information on Antiochus' decrees in response to Jason's petitions is in I and II Maccabees. Both texts were written over half a century after the events, so that in interpreting them, we would do well to look at any evidence contemporary with the events. Jason of Cyrene, the author of the work of which II Maccabees is an abridgement, quoted verbatim near-contemporary evidence in the letter of Antiochus V to Lysias, which is datable in very late 164 or early 163 B.C.E.[76] That document refers to the decrees of Antiochus IV as "the changeover to Greek practices" (τῇ ἐπὶ τὰ Ἑλληνικὰ μεταθέσει) (II Macc. 11.24).[77]

A document of Antiochus IV himself, dated in 166 B.C.E., can be used to confirm that he viewed his grants to Jason as involving the introduction of Greek practices. In the document the king states that the Samaritans are not to be punished along with the Jews because they have proved that "they are not implicated in the charges against the Jews but rather live according to Greek ways."[78]

What was permitted to Jason and his followers that had not been permitted before? In the seemingly detailed account at II Macc. 4.7-9, Jason applies for the power to establish a gymnasium and an ephebic organization and to draw up the list of the Antiochenes in Jerusalem. Gymnasia and ephebic organizations were purely Greek, and to be an Antiochene citizen was to be a citizen of a Greek commonwealth. Nevertheless, the writer in II Maccabees does not let the word "Greek" appear either in his account of Jason's petition or in his report of the king's decrees. We can draw the inference that the Jewish Antiochenes must have associated at Jerusalem quite freely with Gentile Greek Antiochenes, but the writer in II Maccabees says nothing of the kind. He presents the facts as if only Jason, not Antiochus IV, perceived the Hellenizing implications of the petition. Only after Jason has received

---

[76]See n. 47.
[77]The document cannot refer to the decrees of Antiochus IV which imposed a "pagan" cult upon the Jews. As I have shown, the imposed cult was not Greek (Goldstein, *I Maccabees*, pp. 131-58). Thus, "the changeover to Greek practices" must be an expression referring to the decrees on behalf of Jason the high priest. The secretaries of the royal government must have had good reason so to refer to those decrees. Something must have been said in them about permitting Jews to follow Greek patterns of living.
[78]See Goldstein, *II Maccabees*, pp. 523-28, 538-39.

from the king the coveted powers does "Hellenism" come on the scene,[79] purely through Jason's perverse initiative.

The writer says that Jason "overthrew the civic institutions of the Torah" and "brought in new usages which were contrary to the law." What new usages? Jason founded the gymnasium "beneath the very citadel of Jerusalem," and he "made the education of the noblest adolescent boys consist of submission to the broad-brimmed Greek hat."[80] The very peak of "aping Greek manners" (*Hellēnismos*) lay in the fact that priests were interested more in the activities of the gymnasium than in their tasks as professional butchers in the offering of sacrifices![81] For anyone aware of how far Hellenism could go, with idolatry, sin, and truly complete abandonment of the Torah, the assertions of Jason of Cyrene have a touch of the ridiculous. Nothing explicit in the Torah forbade the existence of a gymnasium down the slope from the temple itself; much less did anything forbid a gymnasium beneath a secular citadel, manned at least in part by Gentile soldiers.[82] Had the Hellenizers dared to ape the Greeks completely by having the participants at the gymnasium of Jerusalem exercise naked, surely our indignant writer would have trumpeted the fact! All he can say is that the boys wore the broad-brimmed hats. Hence, at least they covered their loins (cf. Thucydides 1.6).

Some Jewish priests may have preferred the activities of the gymnasium to their duties in the temple, but the number of priests far exceeded the number required for temple functions.[83] We know that the offering of sacrifices at the temple remained uninterrupted until the fateful days in Kislev, 167 B.C.E., which saw the desecration of the temple and the full implementation of the punitive decrees of Antiochus IV.[84] So loyal to the Torah were the Hellenized Jewish participants in the pagan gymnastic games at Tyre, that they would not even go through the perfunctory form of paying their admission-fee

---

[79]II Macc. 4.13; in the wide sense of "Greek culture," "Greek behavior," the term appears here for the first time in the surviving Greek literature.

[80]II Macc. 4.12.

[81]II Macc. 4.13-15.

[82]II Macc. 4.27. The writer's indignation, far from being shared by many contemporaries of the events, could at that time have been only a sectarian view. The Essenes similarly were scandalized that Jerusalem's privies lay beneath the temple mount. See *Jerusalem Revealed* (ed. Yigael Yadin), 1976, pp. 90f.

[83]Emil Schürer, *Geschichte des jüdischen Volkes im Zeitalter Jesu Christi*, § 24.1, ⁴1901-11, vol. II, p. 286-90; ET, *The History of the Jewish People in the Age of Jesus Christ*, rev. ed., vol. II, 1979, pp. 245-50.

[84]Dan. 8.12f.; 11.31; 12.11; I Macc. 1.45, 54-59.

until they received the assurance that the money would be employed for building ships rather than for the usual purpose of paying for a sacrifice to Tyrian Herakles.[85]

Thus the account in II Maccabees is strange indeed. We can readily find the reason why the writer did not use the word "Greek" in summarizing the decrees of Antiochus IV and ascribed all the Hellenization to the wicked usurping high priest. At this stage of his narrative, the writer wished to portray Antiochus IV as an ordinary, reasonably benevolent Seleucid king. He believed that the sins of Jason and his followers brought God to turn Antiochus IV into the "rod of his anger."[86] But the evidence of II Macc. 11.24 shows that the royal government must have been aware of Hellenizing aspects in the decrees of Antiochus IV on behalf of Jason. Surely the word "Greek" must have appeared somewhere in the decrees. The account in II Macc. 4 must therefore be tendentious and distorted. Probably the writer of II Maccabees could write as he did because he took II Macc. 11.24 to refer to the persecution rather than to Jason's "reform."[87]

The author of I Maccabees does not deign to mention the names of the wicked,[88] nor does he specify that their goal was Hellenization. He views the events from the perspective of a rigorous interpreter of the commandments in the Torah, in which Gentiles, not Greeks, are mentioned. He does not pretend to quote either the exact words of the Hellenizers' petition or those of the king's decrees. Rather, he describes their content and effects in terms taken from the Torah. For the author of I Maccabees, the goal of the new deviant group among the Jews was closer association with the neighboring Gentiles. They presented a petition to the king, who granted them liberty to follow the practices of the Gentiles.[89] "Thereupon, they built a gymnasium in Jerusalem according to the customs of the Gentiles....They joined themselves to the Gentiles and became willing slaves to evil-doing."[90]

Our author, unlike the writer of II Maccabees, openly condemns civic association with Gentiles. On the other hand, just as the writer of

---

[85] II Macc. 4.18-20. Just as the mention of Antiochene citizenship for Jews implied increased association of Jews with Greek pagans, so did participation of Jews in the games at Tyre. Yet the writer does nothing to call attention to the fact. We may guess that Jason of Cyrene, a Jewish Greek, did not regard Jewish association with Greeks, even on the holy soil, as a sin in itself.

[86] II Macc. 4.16f.

[87] In II Macc. 6 the non-Greek traits of the imposed cult are not visible. The gods to be worshipped seem to be Greek Zeus and Dionysus.

[88] See Goldstein, *I Maccabees*, p. 67.

[89] I Macc. 1.11.

[90] I Macc. 1.14f.

II Maccabees identified the "new usages contrary to the law" only as the gymnasium and its activities, so the author of I Maccabees identifies the "practices of the Gentiles" at first only as the gymnasium. He does go on to assert that the deviants "underwent operations to disguise their circumcision, rebelling against the sacred covenant."[91] Isolated cases of such acts may have occurred then, as in many other periods, but there is good evidence in the sources contemporary with the events that our author's sweeping generalization here is false.[92]

Further removed from the time of the events, Josephus found the basically accurate account in I Maccabees vague and unsatisfactory. In paraphrasing it,[93] he added what he thought was precision: the Jewish deviants wished to *desert* the ancestral laws and to follow the Greek way of life. He infers that the Jews in the gymnasium exercised naked. The added precision probably reflects Josephus' preconceptions. Using another source, Josephus identified the deviants as Menelaus and the Tobiads. I show elsewhere that Josephus' other source contains untrustworthy material.[94] Hence, we need give no further consideration here to Josephus' account.

In the absence of good evidence, we can only guess at how the content of Antiochus' decrees made it possible for the royal government to refer to them as "the changeover to Greek practices." We may assume that the decrees provided that Greek law rather than the Torah was to be followed in at least some aspects, which surely included those touching the civic pursuits of the Jews who became Antiochenes.

The authors of both I and II Maccabees are indignant over the wicked acts of the deviants, but neither reports that pious Jews resisted the deviants in any way until much later. Indeed, both authors imply that the wickedness of the deviants and the acquiescence of the pious roused the wrath of God, who turned Antiochus IV into the rod of his anger.[95] Hecataeus of Abdera reported how in his times pious Jews took to violence and faced martyrdom rather than tolerate on their soil the things known to provoke the wrath of God.[96] We can explain the acquiescence of the pious to the programme of the high priest Jason only

---

[91] I Macc. 1.15.
[92] See Goldstein, *I Maccabees*, pp. 200f. At Jub. 15.1-14, the author condemns only the omission of circumcision, not the operation to disguise it.
[93] *Ant.* XII.241.
[94] J.A. Goldstein, "The Tales of the Tobiads," in *Christianity, Judaism, and Other Greco-Roman Cults* III (ed. Neusner), 1975, pp. 85-123, esp. pp. 121-23.
[95] II Macc. 1.11-15, 64; II Macc. 4.16f.; 5.17-20; 6.12-17; 7.18, 32f., 38.
[96] Hecataeus apud Josephus, *Ap.* I.191f. See above, n. 62.

if the vast majority of Jews at the time saw nothing contrary to the Torah in it. The assertions in I and II Maccabees, that Jason's programme constituted heinous sin, would then be conclusions after the fact. If God himself suddenly allowed the sacking of Jerusalem and of the temple and thereafter the desecration of the temple and the persecution of the Jews, he must have been suddenly and grievously provoked by sin. Only one set of great innovations came in the years which just preceded those disasters: the "reforms" of the high priest Jason. How could they not be the cause of God's wrath?

Fortunately, we have Jewish sources contemporary with the events to let us know that the authors of I and II Maccabees are indeed giving us judgments after the fact, and we also have sources after the time of the events which disagree with the judgments in I and II Maccabees.

For our purposes, the book of Jubilees is the most important of the contemporary sources. It was written between autumn, 169, and spring 167 B.C.E.,[97] almost in the immediate aftermath of Jason's reforms. The book shows that the author and his sect[98] regarded some aspects of Jason's policies as violations of the will of God. Running through the entire book is the theme that God requires Israel to shun *all* Gentiles, including Greeks.[99] I Macc. 1.11 thus could reflect misgivings of contemporaries of the events. On the other hand, nothing in Jubilees attacks the institution of a gymnasium at Jerusalem. Since the participants there did not exercise naked, at most Jub. 3.31 is a warning against the possibility that they might do so.

Already in his own time, the author of Jubilees had to explain how God, beginning in 169 B.C.E., could permit "the sinners, the Gentiles," to perpetrate cruel attacks upon the Jews and sack their city and their temple. In cataloguing the sins which brought God to do so,[100] the author says not a word about a gymnasium or about imitating the Gentiles or about idolatry. His chief concern seems to be with violations of Jewish laws peculiar to his own sect, especially those requiring a calendar with a 364-day year and a 49-year jubilee, as well as rules of ritual purity. The author's "prediction" to Moses reflects how the sect came violently to resist the wicked,[101] who, however, are described not as Hellenizers but as embezzlers, robbers, and violators of the laws of ritual purity. On recalling the detailed narrative of II Maccabees,[102]

---

[97]See below, "The Date of the Book of Jubilees."
[98]The sect was ancestral to the Essenes of Qumran.
[99]See especially Jub. 22.16-22.
[100]Jub. 23.16-24.
[101]Jub. 23.20.
[102]II Macc. 4.32-50; 13.8.

we recognize here the sins of the high priest Menelaus[103] rather than the Hellenizing reforms of Jason.

In Enoch 85-90, one passage (90:6-9 [first half], 11, 17-18) clearly belongs to the earliest stratum and was written at the end of the third century B.C.E. To that earliest stratum a supplementer in the 160's added 90.9 (second half) -10, 12-16, to reflect Judas Maccabaeus and his victories,[104] Also from the 160's are Dan. 7-12, written at various times between spring 167 and summer 163 B.C.E.[105] In Enoch 90.1-19 and Dan. 11.5-39 there are surveys of the important events or trends in the history of the Jews and their region under the rule of the Ptolemies and the Seleucids. If Jason's acts had been of pivotal importance, they would have been singled out for mention in both surveys. Far from ascribing the sack or the persecution to the effects of Jason's programme, Enoch and Daniel do not even allude to Jason's Hellenizing reform as an event. Jason's reform occurred at the beginning of the reign of Antiochus IV, in 175 or 174 B.C.E. Acts of violence against the Jews in the reign of Antiochus IV did not begin until after Menelaus became high priest in 172 B.C.E. At most, Jason and the Hellenizers are included among the "blind sheep" of Enoch 90.7f. (a passage which refers to the acts of violence against the Jews perpetrated in the reign of Antiochus IV) and among the "deserters of the Holy Covenant" of Dan. 11.30 (a verse which describes only events of 168 B.C.E.).[106]

The Testament of Moses was written in 166 or early in 165 C.E.,[107] and it places part of the blame of the disasters on the contemporary sins of Israel. But the sins are listed as sectarian division over interpretation of the Torah, perversion of justice, and ritual defilement of the temple, especially by unfit priests.[108] The words suggesting that

---

[103]Menelaus is never accused in II Maccabees of aping the Greeks.
[104]See for the present my *II Maccabees*, p. 86, n. 16, and my *I Maccabees*, pp. 40-42, n. 12.
[105]*Ibid.*, pp. 42-44.
[106]For the chronology and the interpretation of the texts, see Goldstein, *I Maccabees*, pp. 41f., 162-64, 212f. I Enoch 92-104 also may be early and antedate the persecution. See G.W.E. Nickelsburg, *Jewish Literature between the Bible and the Mishnah*, 1981, pp. 149-50. Nickelsburg informs me that the Ethiopic at I Enoch 99.2, 14 accurately reflects the Greek and was wrongly translated by Charles. Nothing is left in those chapters to suggest that the author refers to Jews who participated in the gymnasium. Though idol-worship is mentioned, nothing shows that the cults are Greek. The author is offended, not by their Greekness, but by the fact that they are pagan.
[107]Goldstein, *I Maccabees*, p. 40.
[108]Test. Mos. 5.1-6.

Jewish Acceptance and Rejection of Hellenism 25

idolatry was involved contradict our other sources and are probably an interpolation.[109]

Thus, of the contemporary sources, only Jubilees expresses concern over closer contacts with Gentiles. Not even one contemporary source speaks out against the gymnasium or against any of the reforms of Jason or regards them as the cause of God's subsequent wrath. We may conclude that the authors of I and II Maccabees were truthful in implying that there was no resistance to the introduction of Jason's programme: most pious Jews then believed that his Hellenizing innovations were not serious violations of the Torah.

VII. The Third and Fourth Periods

I Maccabees is propaganda for the Hasmonaean kings and may well reflect the opinions of early members of the dynasty.[110] Already Mattathias and Judas Maccabaeus may have held that the "covenant with the Gentiles" and the gymnasium were what roused the wrath of God. The writer of II Maccabees, who so often disagrees with I Maccabees, here agrees on the gymnasium as the cause which provoked God's wrath. We must take note of another striking feature in I and II Maccabees. In neither book is there a report of the closing or destruction of the gymnasium. One can only guess at the reason for such silence. Could it be that the Hellenizers themselves were appalled at the effects of the divine wrath and closed the gymnasium? Could Menelaus himself have been the one who put an end to the gymnasium? In any case, most pious Jews eventually came to agree that the gymnasium brought dire punishment upon Israel.

Nevertheless, from Hasmonaean-ruled Jerusalem two strange documents survive. We have them preserved, one quoted within the other, at II Macc. 1.1-10.[111] In a letter of 143 C.E., the Jews of Judaea and Jerusalem called upon the Jews of Egypt to observe the "Days of Tabernacles in the month of Kislev," i.e., the festival of Hanukkah. The writers describe the persecution as punishment for sins of the high priest Jason but say *nothing* of his Hellenizing policies. One might

---

[109]Test. Mos. 5.3 speaks in general terms of "whoring after strange gods." The words, however, are strangely joined to their context by *et quia: "deuitabunt iustitiam et accedent ad iniquitatem et contaminabunt inquinationibus domum seruitutis suae et quia fornicabunt post deos alienos."* The strange syntax suggests that the words are an interpolation by a later writer who was convinced that the Hellenizers were idolaters. Moreover, the author goes on in 5.4-6 to give a long series of explanatory details (expressed in Latin by clauses beginning with *enim*), and not once there does he speak of idol worship.
[110]Goldstein, *I Maccabees*, pp. 4-26, 62-89.
[111]See Goldstein, *II Maccabees*, pp. 138-53.

explain this peculiar silence by suggesting that the writers were being tactful with their audience, the Greek-speaking Jews of Egypt. It is likely, however, that the senders, like the authors of Jubilees, Enoch, Daniel, and the Testament of Moses, still did not regard Jason's Hellenizing policies as heinous sin. Late in 124 C.E., a second letter from the Jews of Judaea and Jerusalem went out to the Jews of Egypt, to the same effect.

Despite this surprising evidence, we can infer from the points of agreement between I and II Maccabees that after the critical period most Jews believed God's wrath would be roused if they tolerated either permanent Gentile residents or a gymnasium in any part of the Holy Land held by Jews.[112] Pious Jews seem to have inferred from God's disapproval of a gymnasium in Judaea that he would also be displeased there by the other large structures characteristic of Greek culture: theaters, stadia and hippodromes.[113]

Before the critical period theaters and the other structures may have been absent from Judaea proper only because there was no demand for them. Archaeology and the explicit testimony of Josephus show that Herod was the first to dare to erect theaters and amphitheaters in Judaea proper.[114] Through Herod built gymnasia for pagan cities

---

[112] The Hasmonaeans either expelled non-Jews from the reconquered Promised Land or required them to become Jews (I Macc. 13.11; 14.46, 50; II Macc. 14.14; Josephus, *Ant.* XIII. 257f., 318, 397; *Megillat Ta'anit* 15 Sivan; see also Michael Avi-Yonah, *The Holy Land*, 1966, pp. 74-6, and cf. Josephus, *Vita* 112f).

Hengel (*Judaism and Hellenism*, I, pp. 304-9) misreads the minds of ancient pious Jews in thinking their fear that *Hellenizers* might again bring apostasy upon them made them "repudiate" Hellenism. Not Hellenizers, but the wrath of God was what they feared, and they knew from experience that the wrath of God had been directed only against a few aspects of Hellenism.

[113] Gymnasia were so obviously abominable to God that the rabbis did not need to mention them. Concerning the other structures, we have the tradition preserved in Sifra Ahare Mot pereq 13 (to Lev. 18.3; ed. Weiss, p. 86a). I translate from *Sifra or Torat Kohanim according to Codex Assemani LXV* (ed. Louis Finkelstein), 1956, p. 372: "What is the meaning of the text (Lev. 18:3), 'Nor shall you follow their customs?' That you should not adopt their established usages, such as theatres, circuses, and stadia." On the origins of the passage, see J.N. Epstein, *Mebo'ot le-sifrut ha-tannaim*, 1957, p. 640. For *haquqin* as "established," cf. *Sifra*, p. 85d top (ed. Weiss), and p. 370, lines 4f. (ed. Finkelstein).

[114] Josephus, *Ant.* XV. 268, XVII. 161, 175, 194, 255; *Bell.* I. 659, 666; II. 44; Schürer, *Geschichte*, §22.II.2, vol. II, p. 61; ET, *History*, vol. II, p. 55. Cf. Josephus, *Ant.* XV. 328-33, 341.

outside Judaea,[115] apparently even he did not dare to build one in Judaea proper.[116]

Jews thus inferred from the harsh facts of history that God hated the residence of pagans in the Holy Land and the presence there of the characteristic Greek structures. Most Jews seem to have refrained from further generalizing to conclude that God hated the introduction there of the other distinguishing characteristics of Hellenism. Nevertheless, we have seen how biblical texts could be interpreted as excluding all the characteristics which we listed above, and it is conceivable that in the third of our periods (the time between the end of the critical period and the death of the Hasmonaean prince Simon) some Jews drew the broad inference that all our traits of Hellenism were forbidden. We have one important piece of evidence on this topic: the *Letter of Aristeas to Philocrates* which was written c. 138 C.E.[117] In my view *Aristeas* is a reply to claims that now Jews must not live in the Diaspora, must not submit to pagan rulers, must not use Greek, must not associate with Greeks, must not read Greek literature, and must not dabble in Greek philosophy.[118] The work demonstrates that pious Jews did all those things and prospered and produced an authoritative Greek translation of the Torah. Even the author of *Aristeas* does not venture to suggest that Jews can participate in gymnasia, and though he gives a favorable opinion of watching serious plays in the theater, he recommends them only to the pagan king, not to Jews.[119] Association with Gentiles can be compatible with the Torah, he suggests, but only if the laws of diet, ritual purity, and abstinence from idolatry are strictly observed.[120]

The probable opponents against whom *Aristeas* was written may have been the last considerable group of Jews to take the extreme position, the one regarding all our traits of Hellenism as forbidden. At least, I have found no further traces of such a group. The author of *Aristeas* is more cautious about association with Greeks and approval of the theater than were later writers from the Jewish Diaspora.

Indeed, God had manifested his wrath against association with Gentiles and against the building of a gymnasium only in the case of the

---

[115] Josephus, *Bell.* I. 422.
[116] Cf. Josephus, *Ant.* XV. 328-30. On the supposed Herodian gymnasium at Jericho, see Ehud Netzer, "Jericho from the Persian to the Byzantine Periods," *Encyclopedia of Archaeological Excavations in the Holy Land* II, 1976, pp. 568-70.
[117] See for the present Bickerman, *Studies* I, pp. 109-36.
[118] I shall argue these points in a future study of *Aristeas*.
[119] *Aristeas* 284.
[120] *Aristeas* 128-42, 180-84. Cf. bAZ 8a (bottom).

Holy Land, never in the case of the Diaspora. From the last of our four periods of ancient Jewish history we have good evidence that Jews believed all our traits of Hellenism to be permitted by God to Israelites living on Gentile soil.[121]

The synagogue of Delos, first built in the second or early first century C.E., was situated near the gymnasium and the stadium, and after the gymnasium was abandoned, stones from it were used to build a partition-wall inside the synagogue.[122] Unfortunately, nothing informs us whether the Jews at Delos who used the synagogue also participated in the gymnasium. However, the great synagogue of Sardis, begun in the second half of the second century C.E., was an integral part of the gymnasium complex.[123] Jews of Antioch who were too pious to use the oil of pagans nevertheless seem to have participated in the gymnasium there.[124]

Philo admits he has seen plays in the theater[125] and has watched the fights of pancratiasts in the stadium.[126] He takes it for granted that cities contain gymnasia[127] and that parents see to it that their children receive training in one.[128] He freely uses metaphors taken from the gymnasium.[129] From the Emperor Claudius we learn that Jews infuriated the pagans of Alexandria by intruding themselves into the games presided over by the gymnasiarchs and ephebic officials of the city.[130] Rabbinic authorities disapproved of the close and friendly social contacts between Jews of the Diaspora and their pagan neighbors, but even the rabbis felt compelled to be lenient.[131] On the other hand, there is no sign that the pious in Judaea ever believed that God might accept a Jewish gymnasium or theater in the Holy Land.

---

[121] Cf. Hengel *Judaism and Hellenism* I, pp. 67-9.
[122] See *Greece* ("Hachette World Guides"), 1955, p. 532, and Philippe Bruneau, *Recherches sur les cultes de Délos à l'époque hellénistique et à l'époque impériale*, 1970, pp. 480-93.
[123] See D.G. Mitten, "A New Look at Ancient Sardis," *BA* 29, 1966, p. 61-5.
[124] Josephus, *Ant.* XII. 120.
[125] Philo, *Quod omnis probus* 141; *Ebriet.* 177; see also Baron, *Social and Religious History* II, p. 9.
[126] Philo, *Quod omnis probus* 26.
[127] Philo, *Opif. mund.* 17.
[128] Philo, *Spec. leg.* II. 230.
[129] E.g. Philo, *Mut. nom.* 172; *Somn.* I. 69.
[130] Tcherikover and Fuks, *CPJ* II, no. 153, lines 92-93; cf. Josephus, *Ant.* XII. 120.
[131] BAZ 8a (bottom).

VIII. Conclusion

We have now considered throughout our four periods of Jewish history those of our aspects of Hellenism which Jews came to reject most, as a result of the experiences of the critical period. I do not propose to examine in detail the voluminous literary sources reflecting the Jews' acceptance and rejection of our traits of Hellenism from the death of the Hasmonaean prince Simon down to the completion of the Babylonian Talmud. The general picture is that the Jews regarded each one – with the exception of participation in the gymnasium and unlimited association with Greeks – as permissible and sometimes even desirable.

In Judaea itself, pious Jews and Hasmonaean princes bore Greek names and spoke Greek. King Aristobulus I was called *Philhellēn*.[132] Hasmonaean rulers put Greek legends on their coins. Although the Hasmonaeans were bitterly opposed by some of the pious Jewish sects, in no ancient source do we find them condemned for Hellenizing. The Qumran texts never mention the sin of imitating the Greeks. Josephus, writing for a Greek audience, could well abstain from adverse judgments upon Herod as a Hellenizer in summarizing the king's character.[133] But *no* ancient Jewish or Christian writer attacks Herod for being a Hellenizer.[134]

A pious Jew not only translated the Hebrew book of Esther into Greek; he also altered it to fit the patterns of Greek romances.[135] Rabbis in Jewish Palestine used Greek widely and praised the Greek language.[136] Only in a period of grave stress did they decree that Greek not be taught to Jewish children.[137]

---

[132]Josephus, *Ant.* XIII. 318.
[133]Josephus, *Ant.* XVI. 150-59, 400-3; XVII. 191, 304-14.
[134]See the interpolation at Test. Mos. 7.2-6; bBB 3b; Abraham Schalit, *König Herodes*, 1969, pp. 646-49. Josephus (*Ant.* XV. 328-30) tells how Herod excused himself to Jews for having erected Hellenizing and even idolatrous structures and sculptures *outside Judaea proper*, but Josephus himself does not there censure Herod. For demonstration that Test. Mos. 6-7 contains interpolations, see *Studies on the Testament of Moses*, ed. G.W.E. Nickelsburg, Jr., 1973, pp. 5-58.
[135]See Bickerman, *Studies*, I, pp. 225-74.
[136]See Saul Lieberman, *Greek in Jewish Palestine*, 1942, esp. pp. 15-28.
[137]See Saul Lieberman, *Hellenism in Jewish Palestine*, 1950, pp. 100-4. In an article, as yet unpublished, "Rabbinic Bans on Aspects of Hellenistic Culture," I deal with the prohibition on teaching Greek recorded at mSot 9.14 and related matters.

Aristobulus' comments on the Torah,[138] the books of Wisdom and of IV Maccabees, and Philo's writings give eloquent testimony to how pious Jews in the Diaspora could adopt and study Greek philosophy. Jason of Cyrene himself took pains to have the martyred sage Eleazar resemble Socrates in character.[139] The rabbis believed in devoting almost all their waking hours to Torah. Nevertheless, they did not forbid the *study* of philosophy. Whatever the supposed rabbinic ban on teaching *ḥokmat yevanit* ("Greek wisdom"?) was, it is unlikely to have been a ban on philosophy, and we hear how the patriarch Gamaliel II himself kept five hundred Jewish youths studying *ḥokmat yevanit!*[140]

Plato banned the reading of Homer from his projected ideal state.[141] In the Diaspora, the Jewish sibyl calls Homer a liar and a plagiarizer, but praises his art and certainly does not suggest that his poems must not be read.[142] The rabbis specifically forbid Jews to read the book of Ben Sira and permit them to read the books of Homer and later Greek authors.[143] Only once in the whole Babylonian Talmud is there any suggestion that Greek literature can lead to ruin. The question is asked concerning the heretical Rabbi Elisha b. Abuyah: why did not his knowledge of Torah protect him from error? The answer is given: because he was continually singing Greek songs.[144] The isolation of this instance speaks for itself.

Jewish rejection of the gymnasium in the Holy Land continued. In principle, Jews also continued to believe that God wanted to exclude

---

[138]Fragments in Eusebius, *Hist. eccl.* VII.32.16-18; *Praep. evang.* VIII.9.38-10.17; XIII.12.1-16. See the work of Walter cited above, n. 52.

[139]See my *II Maccabees*, on II Macc. 6.18-31.

[140]BBK 83a, Sot 49b; Lieberman, *Greek*, pp. 1 and 20, and *Hellenism*, pp. 104f. I treat the rabbinic texts on *ḥokmat yevanit* in the article mentioned in n. 137. The Rabbinic term *epikuros* (mSanh 10.1 and Ab 2.4) is derived from colloquial anti-Epicurean Greek usage ("an undisciplined person"). Cf. Joseph Geiger, "To the History of the Term *Apikoros*," *Tarbiz* 42, 1972-73, pp. 499-500 (in Hebrew, with English summary on p. xiv). The rabbis mostly use the word to refer to Jews and never to refer to a member of a philosophical sect or even to an imitator of Greeks; see bSanh 99b-100a, pSanh 10.1 (27d-28a). The word is used of a Gentile at bSanh 38b.

There is no evidence that rabbinic authorities after the time of Gamaliel II so actively fostered the study of *ḥokmat yevanit*. The abstention of the rabbis from forbidding the study of philosophy does not mean that they themselves studied it or valued it highly. See Saul Lieberman, "How Much Greek in Jewish Palestine?" *Biblical and Other Studies* (ed. Altmann), 1963, pp. 123-32.

[141]Plato, *Republic* X. 595-607.

[142]*Sib. Or.* 3. 419-31.

[143]BSanh 100b; pSanh 10.1 (28a); Lieberman, *Hellenism*, p. 105-14.

[144]BHag 15b.

Jewish rejection of the gymnasium in the Holy Land continued. In principle, Jews also continued to believe that God wanted to exclude Gentile residents and idolatry from Judaea, but they had to yield to the pressure of events. When the Romans put an end to the independence of Hasmonaean Judaea, they restored the Greek cities of Palestine,[145] and Jews could hardly prevent the residence of pagans and the practice of pagan religion on what they still regarded as their own soil.[146] The situation became much worse with the influx of Gentiles and the removal of Jews after the failure of the revolts against Rome. Jews had to acquiesce. Even so, Jews did what they could to exclude idolatry and keep to a minimum the number of Gentiles residing in the Holy Land.[147]

How, then, can we explain the contrast between the Jews and the conservative Romans? The factor of the long absence of Greeks from Judaea proper goes far to explain the phenomena in Judaea, but the Jews of the Diaspora lived surrounded by Greeks. Perhaps we can suggest an answer along the lines of the McMaster project: Romans, long before the moral crisis of the time of Cato, had been exposed to Greek influences. Roman religion had come in large measure to be identified with Greek religion. Greek Bacchus was worshipped at Rome on the Aventine Hill. Roman Jupiter was held to be Zeus, etc. Conservative Romans felt it urgent to distinguish themselves from immoral Greeks. It was a problem of self-definition. The Jews, in contrast, found their self-definition in the Torah, which sufficed to distinguish them from any pagan, Greek or non-Greek. The "immoral" traits which so shocked Cato drew the opposition of Greek moralists as well. Jews knew that some Greeks lived upright lives. As for the other Greeks, Jews saw them as no more wicked than the rest of the pagans and viewed them on a par with Syrians, Phoenicians and Babylonians.

To summarize: initially the Jews were open to all our traits of Hellenism, except that Greeks were excluded from residence in Judaea proper. This exclusion slowed the growth of a demand for the introduction of non-idolatrous Hellenistic patterns into Judaea. When that demand finally developed, in the 170s B.C.E., Hellenistic patterns, of the gymnasium and of civic organization, came to Jerusalem, and there was no resistance by pious Jews. A complex and

---

[145] Josephus, *Bell.* I. 155-56; *Ant.* XIV. 74-76.
[146] See, e.g., Philo, *Legat. ad Gaium* 200-2.
[147] mAZ 1.8; Maimonides, *Mishneh torah, Madda', Hilkot 'abodah zarah* 7:1; *Abot de Rabbi Nathan* 31 (ed. Schechter, p. 33b), translated in Anthony J. Saldarini, *The Fathers According to Rabbi Nathan (Abot de Rabbi Nathan)*, Version B, 1975, pp. 181f.; pAZ 4.4 (43d end). On the passage in *Abot de-Rabbi Nathan*, see also Jacob Neusner, *A Life of Rabban Yohanan ben Zakkai*, 1962, p. 106 n.1.

unforeseeable series of events brought it about that Antiochus IV punished the Jews severely and imposed upon them a cult which they viewed as pagan. In accordance with hints in scripture, pious Jews inferred that God in wrath had used Antiochus as the rod of his anger, but that Antiochus had arrogantly exceeded his mandate.[148] The inference allowed the Jews to resist Antiochus. Surprisingly, they won. They still had to ponder the question: what was the cause of God's wrath? Though not all Jews agreed, the ruling Hasmonaeans and many of their opponents came to believe that it was the existence, on the holy soil, of the gymnasium and of close associations with Gentiles. Thereafter, the Jews of Judaea never again built a gymnasium. Many Jews also held that God forbade the other characteristic Greek structures: theaters, stadia, and hippodromes. As long as Jews had the power, they barred Gentiles from permanent residence in Judaea proper. In the Diaspora, God had never demonstrated his opposition to Jewish participation even in these aspects of Hellenism. As for Jewish participation in the other aspects, God had shown no opposition either in Judaea or in the Diaspora, and we find Jews throughout regarding them as permitted.

---

[148]Cf. Isa. 10.5-19.

2

The Syriac Bill of Sale from Dura-Europos

P. Dura 28, a Syriac deed of sale written in 243 of the Christian era, is an extraordinary document.[1]

Almost perfectly preserved, it is the oldest extant piece of Syriac written on perishable material and one of the oldest Syriac texts.[2] It was the first document of an ancient slave sale in Hebrew or Aramaic to be published.[3] Written in their own native language for members of a Semitic population touched by Hellenism, who are Roman citizens, *P. Dura* 28 contains many evidences of cultural interaction. Finally, *P. Dura* 28 is an important link for tracing the evolution of Semitic documentary forms, for its date and the wording of its clauses show it to lie midway between earlier texts and those in the Talmudic literature and in the medieval Jewish formularies.[4]

---

[1] Photographs: *YCS*, V (1935), Plates I-III; W.F.G., Plates LXIX, LXXI. To the literature cited at W.F.G., pp. 145-46, add Goldstein and that given below, n. 9. For abbreviations used in this article see List of Abbreviations on p. 54-55.

[2] See Welles, *YCS*, V, 122-23; earlier epigraphic texts: below, n. 11.

[3] Frank Moore Cross published the second ("Samaria Papyrus 1: an Aramaic Slave Conveyance of 335 B.C.E. Found in the Wâdī ed-Dâliyeh," *Eretz-Israel*, XVIII [1985], 7-17) and says (ibid., p. 7) there are 11 more among the Samaria Papyri.

[4] Medieval formularies: Hay (died 1038), Bargeloni (*ca.* 1100) and *Maḥzor Vitry;* Simhah b. Samuel of Vitry died in 1105, but the formulary, like much else in Hurwitz's edition, may be somewhat later. In any case, though briefer, its bills of sale closely resemble those of Bargeloni.

To trace in detail the origins of the clauses of *P. Dura* 28 beyond the time of the Elephantine papyri is beyond the scope of this article. Cuneiform bills of sale and conveyance including those most recently discovered are collected and discussed (with refrence to their "satisfaction clause") by Muffs. In his judgment (p. 291), the Aramaic formulary was probably derived from neo-

The document was first read by C.C. Torrey,[5] who succeeded in grasping the general content. Although his transcription and translation, with a few improvements by H. Ingholt and C.B. Welles, were incorporated in the final edition of the Dura parchments and papyri, they now leave much to be desired.

To all appearances, *P. Dura* 28 is a tied double document of the type common in the third century and earlier.[6] Accordingly, the two uppermost lines of the document should be an abstract of the text below, giving "the place and date of the document; the nature of the transaction and certain of its details; the names of the principals."[7] Torrey's attempt to render the two lines lacked all plausibility. His reading of lines 12-16 of the lower text provoked immediate comment from Carl Brockelmann,[8] and Brockelmann's substantially correct suggestions were supported by other scholars.[9] In a review of the Dura *Parchments and Papyri*, I suggested further corrections and reported that I had read the upper text.[10] Although some passages of *P. Dura* 28 still elude me, I submit here a new text with notes justifying my readings, a translation, and a commentary relating the document to other ancient documents and systems of law.

I. Transliteration

Upper Text
   i. (Hand A) *b'yr d31 zbn m(rqy') '(wrly') mtr't' brt šmny zbn ltyrw br br b'š'*
   ii. *'mt' mtsyn b(dynr') 700 brt šnyn 28*

Lower Text
   1. (Hand B) *bšnt št d'wṭqrṭwr qsr mrqws 'nṭwnyws grdynws 'wsbws 'wṭwks*

Assyrian models, and those models in turn in many ways represent the culmination of the "fringe tradition" of cuneiform law represented in the provincial formularies of Susa, Kültepe, the Diyala region, Alalakh, and Ras-Shamra.

[5] *ZfS*, X (1935), 33-45.
[6] Tied double documents at Dura: W.F.G., p. 14. Cf. Y. Yadin, "Expedition D—The Cave of the Letters," *IEJ*, XII (1962), 236-38; and B.M.V., pp. 244-47 (exhaustive bibliography).
[7] W.F.G., p. 145.
[8] *ZfS*, X. 163.
[9] Arangio-Ruiz and Furlani, *Neg.*, p. 433, n. 1; E.Y. Kutscher, *Tarbiẓ*, XIX (1947-1948), 54, n. 8; C. Rabin in Pringsheim, p. 462, n. 4. Nevertheless, Brockelmann's reading was not adopted in W.F.G.
[10] Goldstein, pp. 431-32.

The Syriac Bill of Sale from Dura-Europos   35

2. sbstws bhpṭy' d'nyws 'rnyws wdṭrybwnyws ppws byrḥ 'yr šnt
3. ḥm šm" wḥm šyn w'rb' bmnyn' qdmy' wb šnt tltyn wḥd' d ḥrwryh
4. d'n ṭwnyn' 'ds' n ṣyḫt' qlwny' mtrpwls 'wrly' 'lksndry' bkmrwt'
5. dmrqws 'wrlyws 'nṭywks hpws rhmws br blšw wb'sṭrṭgwt' dmrqws
6. 'wrlyws 'bgr hpws rhmws br m'nw br 'g' wd'bgr br ḥpsy br br ?q?
7. dtrtyn zbnyn bywm tš't' mwdyn' mrqy' 'wrly' mtr't' brt
8. šm n brz br 'bgr d yrt' 'dysyt' llwqs 'wrls tyrw br br b'šm n
9. ḥrny' dqblt mnh dynr' šbm" wzbnt lh 'mtsyn 'mt' dyly
10. zbyn' thw' brt šnyn 'šryn wtmn' ytyr 'w ḥsyr mn šby' hkn
11. dmn ywmn' wl 'lm' thw' 'nt tyrw zbwn' wyrtyk šlyt b'mt' hd'
12. dzbnt lk lmqn' wlmzbnw wlm'bd bh kl dtṣb' w'n 'nš ndwn 'w
13. nthg' 'm tyrw zbwn' 'w 'm yrtwhy 'l ḥšbn 'mt' hd' dzbnt lh
14. 'qwm 'n' mtr't' mzbnnyt' wyrtr w'dwn w'mrq w'dk' w'qymyh
15. bgdh dtyrw zbwn' wl' 'štlṭ lmhpk bmly str' hn' wzbnth
16. lk 'mt' hd' ?? 'm?? ?? ?nmws dmk' w'dm' lyr ḥ' št' šlmyn
17. whkn' hwt tnwy bynthwn d'n t'rq lh 'mt' hd' mn ywmn'
18. wlhl mn gdh dtyrw zbwn' w'tktbw lzbynt' hd' šṭr' tryn
19. ḥd pḥmh 'ḥyd ld k'rwḥ n'l b'rkywn d'n ṭwnyn' 'ds' nsy ḫt'
20. w'ḥrn' pḥmh nhw' lwth dtyrw zbwn' (Hand C) mwdn' 'wrls ḥpsy
21. br šm šyhb 'dysy' mn pylys dtrt'šr' dktbt ḥlp 'wrly'
22. mtr't' 'ntty bršm' dspr' l' ḥkm' dzbnt 'mt' hd' dylh
23. wqblt dmyh 'yk dktyb mn l'l
24. (Hand D) mrqws 'wrls br kib šhd
25. (Hand E) mrqs 'wrls br p?? šhd
26. (Hand F) bršm' dmb ḥr' lštryn
27. (Hand G)   Αὐρ(ήλιος) Μάννος ὁ ἐπὶ τοῦ ἱεροῦ καὶ
28.   τοῦ πολειτικοῦ μ(α)ρ(τυρῶ)
29. (Hand B)   mrqs 'wrlyws blšw br
30.   mqymw spr' ktbt šṭr' hn'
31. (Seal bearing image of Gordian III)

Verso
1. (Hand H [= Hand B?]) 'wrly' mtr't' brt šmny mzbnnyt' 'l npš hšd'
2. (Hand C) 'wrls ḥpsy br šm šyhb ḥtmt 'l sṭr' hn'
3. (Hand I) 'wrls 'bgr sṭrṭg' šhd "Αβγαρος
4. (Hand J) 'bgr br brsmy' šhd
5. (Hand H) 'wrly' mtr't' brt šmny mzbnnyt' 'l npšh šhd'

II. Notes to the Transcription of the Text

i–ii. The numerals are of the type common in ancient Hebrew and Aramaic documents and inscriptions; they tally with the numbers written out in the lower text. "31" is written as "20 + 10 + 1." Probably as an adaptation to a cursive script, the figure "20," known from Elephantine, Palmyra, Nabataea, and Wadi Murabba'at, is here turned on its side; cf. B.M.V., p. 98, fig. 27. All the other figure forms in the upper text appear in the earliest dated Syriac inscriptions.[11]

In the first occurrence of *zbn* the cursive hand leaves the *b* almost unrecognizable. The letters which follow *zbn* are clear and can hardly be anything but the abbreviated Roman praenomen and nomen of the seller.

mtr't', the Aramaic cognomen of the seller, appears six times in the document (here, and at lines 7, 14, and 22 of the lower text, and then twice in the very clear signatures on the verso). Torrey read it as *mtb't'*, and treated it as a common noun, "the defendant," but such a common noun would follow the patronymic *brt šmny*. The third letter never appears joined to the letter which follows it and cannot be a *b*. The name is Mat-Tar'atha = Amath-Tar'atha = "handmaid of Atargatis." This type of name is well-attested in Syria, and so are the omission of the initial ' (cf. the slave's name in line ii) and the assimilation of the final *t* of *Amath*.[12]

br b'š'. In both upper and lower texts, the fourth letter of Tiro's father's name is ' rather than *l*. The name occurs in inscriptions[13] and, transliterated (Barbaessamen, Barbaesomen), in documents from Dura.[14]

mt syn. On the omission of the initial ', see above on *mtr't'*.

On the symbol *r* for "denarius," see B.M.V., pp. 90-91.

---

[11]André Maricq, "La plus ancienne inscription syriaque: celle de Birecik," *Syria*, XXXIX (1962), 88-100; H. Pognon, *Inscriptions sémitiques de la Syrie, de la Mésopotamie, et de la région de Mossoul* (Paris, 1907), No. 2 and Plate XIV; J.B. Segal, "Some Syriac Inscriptions of the 2nd-3rd Century A.D.," *Bulletin of the School of Oriental and African Studies*, XVI (1954), 13-36. See also M. Lidzbarski, *Handbuch der Nordsemitischen Epigraphik*, I, 198-202, and Tafel XLVI.

[12]Cumont, "Atargatis," *RE*, II (1896), 1896. Names formed with "Amath-": A. Caquot, "Sur l'onomastique religieuse de Palmyre," *Syria*, XXXIX (1962), 239. Loss of initial ': Nöldeke, sec. 32; cf. *Inscriptions grecques et latines de la Syrie* 1409, 1411 (Amath-Babea), 680. 4-5 (Math-Babea). Assimilation of final letter of "Amath-": Ed. Sachau, "Edessenische Inschriften," *ZDMG*, XXXVI (1882), 145-47 (*'mšmš* along with Greek transcrition 'Αμασσαμσης).

[13]Caquot, "Nouvelles inscriptions araméennes de Hatra," *Syria*, XXIX (1952), 117, n. 1, and pp. 89-105, Nos. 23-25; XXX (1953), 235, No. 29; Enno Littmann, *Semitic Inscriptions* (New York, 1904), p. 86, Nabataean inscription No. 1. Segal, "New Syriac Inscriptions from Edessa," *Bulletin of the School of Oriental and African Studies*, XXXI(1958), 38-39.

[14]W.F.G., index, p. 430.

3. *dḥrwryḥ: dḥrrwr'* W.F.G. At the end of this word the writing runs into a notch in the edge of the parchment. What is there bears no resemblance to an ' but is easily read as *y* and the right-hand stroke of *ḥ*.

4. *bkmrwt': b'mrwt'* W.F.G. In later Syriac the words for "priest" and "priesthood" are always written *plene*, but the defective spelling *kmr'* occurs in inscriptions from Hatra.[15] Difficulties of the earlier reading: Welles, *YCS*, V, 128-30, and W.F.G., p. 147, n. 15.

6. *?q?: kmr* W.F.G. The word is probably the divine element of the name of Abgar bar Ḥafsai's grandfather, Bar-?, son of the god X. In the scribe's hand the middle letter is surely *q*, not *m*. The first letter may be *b, y, l,* or *n;* the last, *d, w, z, y, l, ',* or *r*. The non-divine name *bqr* appears in Safaitic and Thamudic, Ryckmans, II, 55.

7. *mwdyn': mbdq'* W.F.G. The second letter is not joined to the one following and cannot be a *b,* and the *q* would be unlike any in this scribe's hand; finally, there is no support for Torrey's rendition of the reading as "of the aforesaid month."

'wrly': 'wdly' W.F.G. (misprint).

8. *šmnbrz*. I am not sure of the fourth and fifth letters since I do not know a suitable etymology for the name.

dyrt' 'dysyt': mzbnnyt' mskl' W.F.G. The first word is badly written. Torrey's reading is a guess from the context and from the signatures on the verso; it ignores the clear ' at the beginning of the second word, and the *m* of *mskl'* would be unique in the document. Moreover, in Hebrew and Aramaic documentary style the verb of saying precedes the declarer's name and is always *'mr*. Analogy with other documents and with the name of the buyer here requires that the seller's place of origin (or citizenship) and place of residence be given here. Cf. *P. Dura* 29, *Mur.* 19, etc.

br b'šmn: brblšmn W.F.G. See on line i, *br b'š'*.

10. *hkn: hkyn* W.F.G. The form *hkyn* is unknown in Syriac. The *y* was misread from the extended stroke leading to the *n* (cf. the *n* at the end of line 8).

12. *lmzbnw: lmdbrw* W.F.G. The next to last letter is joined to the *w* and cannot be *r*. The reading becomes certain when the passage is compared with other Aramaic *kyrieia* clauses; see commentary.

13. *ḥšbn: ḥšyn* W.F.G. Parallels make Brockelmann's reading certain. See commentary. Ingholt and Torrey may have rejected it because of the defective spelling, but see on line 4; the defective spelling is found in Enno Littmann, *Semitic Inscriptions*, p. 15, No. 6, line 4.

---

[15]Caquot, *Syria*, XXIX, 89-105, Nos. 5, 25, 27; XXXII, 55, No. 51.

14. *'qwm: 'qdm* W.F.G. Again the correct reading is proved by the parallels.

w'qymyh: w'qymh W.F.G.: *w'qymnh* Goldstein. Only the first reading fits both the letters on the parchment and Syriac grammar.

15. *bmly: bmny* W.F.G. The idiom, translated by Torrey "in any way whatsoever," would be strange in Syriac, whereas the reading adopted yields the well-attested *hpk bmlt'*, "break one's word," "retract."

wzbnth: zbnth W.F.G. The careless stroke joined to the *z* is probably a *w*.

16. *?? 'm?? ?? ?nmws: kd 'kyn ḥd nmws* W.F.G. The letters on the parchment are ambiguous or blurred, and I have not been able to find a satisfactory reading. Torrey translated, "while I establish a certain law," but this is very implausible language for a legal document. How would a private citizen "establish" a law? Brockelmann's suggestion, "indem ich den einen gesetzlichen Termin von jetzt bis zu sechs vollen Monaten festsetzte," makes sense but cannot be derived from the reading; see commentary.

The first two letters are blurred beyond recognition in the photographs. The ' seems certain; the *m* could also be a badly written *b* or *k* – cf. *wzbnth* in line 15; the next letter is not joined to what follows it and can be *d, z, r*, or final *y* or *n*. Next comes a faint long stroke sloping downward from left to right; if it is not a stray mark, it is a final *n*. After a space come the strokes read by Torrey as *ḥ*; however, the writing does not appear to be joined to what follows and can be read as two letters, the first being *b, y, k, l, n*, or ', and the second, *w* or perhaps *d* or *r*. Then comes a clear *d* or *r*, and then the word which Torrey probably was correct in reading as *nmws*. Passages in the Syriac-Roman laws lend support to this reading. Nevertheless, the *n* is badly formed and does not quite join the following letter; the *m* bears on its upper right a mark which disguises it; and the *w* is run into the *s* (cf. the *ws* of the scribe's signature, line 29).

17. *d'n: w'n* W.F.G. See commentary.

19. *pḥmh: pḥm* W.F.G. The word is faint and badly written both here and in line 20.

ldkṙwṅ. The writing here is faint and ambiguous. Torrey's reading can be made out from the photographs but is suspect. It ignores the mark sloping down from left to right after *'ḥyd*, thus leaving an abnormally large space between words. Furthermore, the noun "record" known from Syriac and Babylonian Aramaic is rather *d(w)krn' (dukhrānā)*, though the form read by Torrey is known in Biblical Aramaic (Ezra 6.2), the Christian Aramaic of Palestine, and modern Syriac; see H.L. Ginsberg, *Koheleth* (Tel Aviv-Jerusalem: M. Newman, 1961), p. 28 (in Hebrew).

The Syriac Bill of Sale from Dura-Europos

The traces on the parchment can also be read *lśhdw*, "as testimony," but then the faint stroke sloping down from left to right after the *w* must be ignored, and again an abnormally large space is left between words.

20. *pḥ mh*: *prwmywn* (?) W.F.G. See on line 19 and W.F.G., pp. 144, 148.

21. *'dysy'*: *'dsy'* W.F.G. (misprint).

22. *ḥkm'*: *ḥpm'* W.F.G. (misprint).

24. *klb śhd*: *blbśrbl* W.F.G. The reading *śhd* is certain. In Aramaic documents either the singular *śhd* stands by the signature of each witness or the plural *śhdy'* introduces them all (note, however, the Nabataean practice described by Yadin, *IEJ*, XII, 238, and the practice of some Jews of Jerusalem, *M. Giṭṭin* 9.8). The letters of *klb* are all ambiguous, and one would expect the *status emphaticus*; indeed, the name *br klb'* (Barchalbas) is well attested at Edessa and Dura (Welles, YCS, V, 126, n. 21; W.F.G., index, p. 430). Arabic names are common at Edessa and do lack the ' of the *status emphaticus* but usually have a final *w*. See Caquot, *Tessères*, p. 156; Ryckmans, I, 114. Several examples of a jar-stamp in Greek lettering have been found at Dura, *Abemmês Barchalb*, father's name apparently in the *status absolutus*, but the editors take the second word as an abbreviation for *Barchalba* (*The Excavations at Dura Europos...: Preliminary Report of the Ninth Season of Work (1935-1936)*, ed. by M.I. Rostovtzeff et al. [New Haven, 1952], Part III, p. 124, n. 986).

25. *p?? śhd*: *pnwdgl* W.F.G. See on line 24. With a list of names used in Osrhoene, one may well find a convincing reading. For the two doubtful letters, I would guess *t* (note the form in the upper text) and *r*. The extremely cursive *h* of *śhd* either has its right stroke reduced and crowded up against the *ś* or its left loop crowded up against the *d*.

Verso, 3. Αβγαρος: Ἄβγαρ ὁ στρ. W.F.G. Neither photograph shows the final tau and rho. The name is probably the witness' Greek signature, which he wrote after signing in Syriac. His pen was running dry as he wrote *śhd*, but he went on in Greek without dipping it again.

Verso, 5. *'l npśh*: *lnpśh*. There is a faint stroke to the right of the *l* which is surely an ink-mark. If it is read as ', verso, line 5, agrees with verso, line 1, and conforms to the common formula of the conceding party's signature in Aramaic documents.[16]

---

[16] Milik II and III; *Mur.* 18, 19, 21, 24, 28-30; Yadin, *IEJ*, XII, 237.

III. Translation

Upper Text

[1]In Iyyar of 31, a sale. Marcia Aurelia Mat-Tar'atha, daughter of Shamnai, has sold to Tiro, son of Bar-Ba'esha, [ii]a female slave, Math-Sin, for 700 denarii, 28 years old.

Lower Text

[1]In the sixth year of Imperator Caesar Marcus Antonius Gordianus Pius Felix [2]Augustus; in the consulship of Annius Arrianus and Cervonius Papus; in the month Iyyar of the year [3]554 of the former reckoning; and in the year 31 of the freedom of [4]Antoniniana Edessa, the glorious, Colonia Metropolis Aurelia Alexandria; in the priesthood of [5]Marcus Aurelius Antiochus, eques Romanus, son of Belshu; and in the term as strategoi of Marcus [6]Aurelius Abgar, eques Romanus, son of Ma'nu, grandson of Agga, and of Abgar, son of Hafsai, grandson of Bar-?q?, [7]for the second time, on the ninth day (of the month).

I, Marcia Aurelia Mat-Tar'atha, daughter of [8]Shamenbaraz, granddaughter of Abgar, resident (?), Edessene, declare to Lucas Aurelis Tiro, son of Bar-Ba'eshamen, [9]of Carrhae, that I have received from him 700 denarii and have sold to him Amath-Sin, my female slave, [10]whose age is 28 years, more or less, purchased from her captors, under the following terms:

[11]That from this day forth and forever, you, Tiro, the buyer, and your heirs shall have power over this slave [12]that I have sold you, to take possession, to sell, and to do with her whatever you wish; and if anyone shall bring suit or [13]raise a claim against Tiro, the buyer, or against his heirs concerning this slave that I have sold him, [14]I, Mat-Tar'atha, the seller, and my heirs shall rise and defend and clean and clear (her with respect to her title) and place her [15]in Tiro the buyer's possession. And I shall have no power to revoke the terms of this document. And I have sold [16]you this slave...law of from now until six full months have passed. [17]And an agreement was made between them as follows: if this slave shall run away from today [18]onward, it shall be at the risk of Tiro, the buyer.

Two documents of this sale have been written; [19]one copy of it, retained as a record, is to be entered in the archives of Antoniniana Edessa, the glorious, [20]and the other copy of it is to be for Tiro, the buyer.

I, Aurelis Ḥafsai, [21]son of Shamashyabh, Edessene of the Twelfth tribe, declare that I have written on behalf of Aurelia [22]Mat-

Tar'atha, my wife, in the subscription, because she is illiterate, that she has sold this slave of hers ²³and received the price thereof as written above.

²⁴Marcus Aurelis Bar-Klebh (?), witness.

²⁵Marcus Aurelis Bar-*p??*, witness.

²⁶With the signature of the inspector of documents:

²⁷I, Aurelius Mannus, superintendent of the sacred and ²⁸civic archives, bear witness.

²⁹I, Marcus Aurelius Belshu, son of ³⁰Moqimu, the scribe, have written this document.

³¹(Seal of Gordian III)

Verso

¹Aurelia Mat-Tar'atha, daughter of Shamnai, the seller, testifies for herself.

²I, Aurelis Ḥafsai, son of Shamashyabh, have signed this document.

³Aurelis Abgar, the strategos, witness; Abgar.

⁴Abgar, son of Bar-Samya, witness.

⁵Aurelia Mat-Tar'atha, daughter of Shamnai, the seller, testifies for herself.

IV. Synopsis of Grammar and Orthography

The one grammatical error in the upper text is probably the slip of a hasty pen. With the exception of line 10, where the scribe may have misplaced a word, the grammar of all the readable portions of the lower text is good. The names of both consuls have been misspelled, and one "ni" has fallen out of "Antoniniana" – the name, however, may have been so pronounced in Edessa. Otherwise, the scribe apparently took care to spell names in the manner preferred by their bearers: the Roman consuls, the eponymous local officials, and the scribe's own signature have the purist "-ius," whereas the husband's signature and subscription, the witnesses' signatures, and the buyer have the vulgar "-(i)s." The spelling of "witness" *(šhd)* is a stereotype, but the use of š in the word "twelfth" in line 21 is remarkable, and so is the consistently defective spelling of short "u" in native Syriac words.

V. Commentary

Upper Text

Lines i-ii. The decipherment of these two lines shows *P. Dura* 28 to be, as expected, a double document with an inner text reduced to a brief abstract. Double documents with such inner texts are known from Ptolemaic Egypt,[17] from third-century Dura,[18] and from the documents of the second century discovered in the "Cave of the Letters" in the Judean desert of Israel.[19]

In these documents, upper texts tend to be written in a more cursive script than the lower texts, and often by a different hand.[20] The upper text of *P. Dura* 28 with its neat but rapid cursive (note especially the forms for ' and *t*) is so different from the lower text as to suggest another hand, possibly that of Aurelius Mannus, superintendent of the sacred and civic archives (lines 27-28), for in Ptolemaic Egypt such texts were added to double documents by registry officials.[21] Unlike the lower text, the upper text is expressed in the third person, as would befit an official's summary of the contents. In summarizing, the writer of the upper text seems generally to have followed the order of the lower. In the date he retained only the Babylonian month and the year of the local era, by his omissions incidentally leaving the date in the normal Semitic order, with the month named before the year (see commentary to lines 1-7). The figure "20" in the age of the slave is very different from that used to form the "20 + 10 + 1" of the date, and the ' of Iyyar occurs only there in the upper text and is used several times in the lower. I prefer to view these as the normal inconsistencies of a cursive hand, rather than as evidence that two hands wrote the upper text.

In abbreviating, the writer of the upper text omitted the words *yrḥ* (month) and *šnt* (year). *yrḥ* is frequently omitted in documents (e.g., Cowley, Nos. 5-10 and the contracts from Wadi Murabbaʿat). I know no parallel, however, for the omission of *šnt*. The use of figures in the upper text and words in the lower to express numbers is common in double documents; the practice probably served the same function as it does in modern checks.[22]

---

[17]F. Bilabel, "Zur Doppelausfertigung ägyptischer Urkunden," *Aegyptus*, V (1924), 168-72; VI (1925), 94-96, 100-104.

[18]*P. Dura* 26, 29, 30, 32.

[19]See above, n. 6. Upper texts reduced to abstracts may be alluded to at *T. Baba Batra* 11:1, p. 413, lines 4-5 Zuckermandel (names of the principals, description of the purchase, the amount paid, the date) and by R. Idi quoting R. Jeremiah at *TP, Baba Batra*, p. 17c (names of the principals, names of the witnesses, date). On the inclusion of the witnesses' names, see Gulak, pp. 15-24. In neither case, however, is it clear that the upper text is briefer than the lower.

[20]*P. Dura* 29-32 (cf. 24 and 25); Bilabel, *Aegyptus*, V, 170-72; cf. Yadin, *IEJ*, XII, 236.

[21]Bilabel, *loc. cit.*

[22]*P. Dura* 26; *Mur.* 21, 22, 29, 30; Bilabel, *Aegyptus*, VI, 104; cf. V, 171, and VI, 94-96.

The Syriac Bill of Sale from Dura-Europos   43

zbn. The designation of the transaction (sale), according to Payne Smith, col. 1076, properly means *emptio*, not *venditio*, but cf. Pringsheim's remarks on *ônê* and *prasis*, pp. 111-26.

On the praenomen and nomen of the seller, see Welles, *YCS*, V, 140, n. 80; on her Aramaic cognomen, above, notes to transcription. On the worship of Tar'atha-Atargatis at Edessa, Duval, *Journal Asiatique*, 1891, pp. 230-32; at Carrhae, Martin, "Discours de Jacques de Saroug sur la chute des idoles," *ZDMG*, XXIX (1876), 110, 131-32.

The second occurrence of *zbn* is ungrammatical. As the verb, "sold," it should be feminine *(zbnt)*. The error may have arisen from the first occurrence, the noun *zbn*.

The upper text reduces the patronymics of seller and buyer to hypocoristics;[23] so do the seller's signatures, Verso, lines 1 and 5. For some reason, the writer of the upper text found it necessary to give the Roman names of only the conceding party; on the buyer's names, see below on line 8. On the slave's name, see W.F.G., p. 143; on the omission of the ', above, notes to transcription.

Lower Text

i. The Dating Formula

Lines 1-7. The elaborate formula begins with the year of the emperor's *imperium*. Under Roman rule, down to the time of Diocletian, the peoples of Egypt, Palestine, Syria, and Arabia continued their practice of dating by the regnal years of the monarch ruling over them, a practice followed by only some of the other subject peoples of the Empire.[24] Of the texts dating by both the regnal year and the consuls, *Mur.* 115 and probably other documents from Jewish Palestine[25] agree with *P. Dura* 28 in placing the regnal year first. In the rest of the surviving documents, the consuls appear first. The otherwise careful scribe of *P. Dura* 28 has misspelled the names of both consuls.

Other features of the dating formula are entirely unsemitic. The order in dates of Hebrew and Aramaic documents and in the medieval

---

[23]On such hypococoristics, see Caquot, *Tessères*, p. 154-57.
[24]Egypt: Mitteis, p. 88; Palestine: *Mur. 18* and *118*; Nabataea: Document 6, Yadin, *IEJ*, XII, 241; Syria: *P. Dura* 25, 31; and cf. Luke 3.1 and the dating prescripts of the *Doctrine of Addaeus the Apostle* and the *Acts of Sharbil*. The indices to *Inscriptiones Graecae ad res Romanas pertinentes*, Vols. I and III, show dating by years of the emperors only in Bithynia and Pontus, Cyprus, Egypt, Palestine, Syria, and Arabia. The Mishnah requires bills of divorcement to be dated by the year of the emperor (*Giṭṭin* 8.5; see the commentary of Albeck [Jerusalem, 1954], pp. 297, 405); cf. *Mur. 18* and *TP, Giṭṭin* 8.5, p. 49c.
[25]Such is the implication of *M. Giṭṭin* 8.5.

Hebrew formularies is day, month, year.[26] In the Greek date, the prevailing order is year, month, day,[27] which is the order here, except that the local designations of the year have been inserted between the month and the day.

The era of the colony of Edessa is described as that of its "freedom," probably its freedom from its own local dynasty. Cf. Bellinger, YCS, V, 152; E. Bickerman, *Chronologie* (Leipzig, 1963), p. 46. To Bellinger's chronological studies of the era of the colony in YCS, V, add André Maricq, "Hatra de Sanatrouq," *Syria*, XXXII (1955), 278, n. 3. On the titles of Edessa, see Bellinger, *op. cit.*, 143, n. 4.

4-5. Dating by eponymous priests was a common practice in the ancient world; at Dura there were four.[28] *P. Dura* 28 shows that there was only one at Edessa, though the Christian Syriac *Acts of Sharbil* date the fifteenth year of Trajan by two eponymous priests[29] and the Syriac *Doctrine of Addaeus the Apostle* speaks of two high priests of Edessa.[30] The Christian writers simply refused to leave the eponymous priesthood to a pagan alone and included the Christian bishop. In the *Acts of Sharbil* Barsamya is the name of the second eponymous priest and of the Christian bishop,[31] and Sharbil alone is called the chief priest.[32] Later Syriac martyrdoms replace the eponymous priest by only one name, that of the bishop.[33] Only one of the two chief priests mentioned in the *Doctrine of Addaeus* need have been eponymous.

5-7. The strategoi evidently became the annual chief magistrates of the city after the Romans ended the dynasty of Edessa.[34] In accordance with the parallels in Greek and Roman inscriptions, "for the second time" refers only to Abgar, son of Ḥafsai. The names Abgar and Ma'nu (Μάννος) were favorites of the dynasty of Edessa, and Ḥafsai occurs in aristocratic families there. The name Belshu, which is also the native cognomen of the scribe (line 29), is Akkadian, shortened from Ša-Bel-šu,

---

[26]R. Yaron, "The Schema of the Aramaic Legal Documents" *JSS*, II (1957), 33-34, 61; so, too, in the documents from the Judean desert and in the formula at *T. Baba Batra* 11.2, p. 413, lines 5-8.
[27]See, e.g., W. Larfeld, *Griechische Epigraphik*, 3rd ed. (München, 1913), pp. 334-38.
[28]*P. Dura* 25 and 37.
[29]Syriac p. 41, line 18.
[30]Syriac p. 14, lines 5-6 Cureton.
[31]Syriac p. 42, line 17.
[32]Syriac p. 42, lines 7-8.
[33]See Welles, *YCS*, V, 131, n. 44.
[34]Welles, *YCS*, V, 131-32.

"He is Bel's"; the cult of Bel at Edessa is well attested.[35] As one would expect, the native aristocracy and perhaps even the royal family remained prominent in the Roman colony of Edessa.

ii. The Seller's Declarations of Receipt of the Price and Sale of the Slave

Lines 7-10. The seller's declaration begins abruptly with the word "I declare," ὁμολογῶ, without any verb of saying in the third person. In the terms used by papyrologists, this document is a "subjective homology." To my knowledge there is no parallel to this aspect of *P. Dura* 28 among surviving ancient witnessed documents. The formulary of Hay, however, presents something of a parallel. In Jewish practice documents were formulated as the statement of the witnesses testifying to what they have seen and heard,[36] and hence the verb of saying in the third person must appear, but thereafter the document continues *q' mwdyn'*, "I declare...."

P. Dura 28 is the earliest extant Semitic bill of sale in the form of a homology; however, the Mishnah takes the existence of such bills for granted,[37] and the bills of conveyance in the formulary of Hay are all homologies. In Greek bills of sale from Egypt, this form first appears in the first century B.C.[38] and under Roman rule becomes the sole form for bills of sale.[39]

On the buyer's names and patronymic, see above, notes to transcription and synopsis of grammar and orthography, and Welles, *YCS*, V, 140, n. 80.

Another peculiarity sets *P. Dura* 28, along with the medieval Jewish formularies and the Greek Parchment 2 from Avroman,[40] apart from almost[41] all other known ancient bills of sale in Greek, Hebrew,

---

[35] Names of aristocrats: Jules Leroy, "Nouvelles découvertes archéologiques relatives à Edesse," *Syria*, XXXVIII (1961), 160-62; Belshu: K.L. Tallqvist, *Assyrian Personal Names* (Helsingfors, 1914), p. 62; Bel at Edessa: Duval, *Journal Asiatique*, 1891, pp. 228-29.

[36] See Gulak, pp. 15-24, and cf. the formula of the cuneiform *lišanšu* documents, Koschaker, pp. 21-23. Early cuneiform documents in subjective style: Muffs, pp. 35, 274-77.

[37] Gulak, pp. 2-6. Avroman 1 and 2 are homologies.

[38] Pringsheim, p. 124, n. 2.

[39] Pringsheim, pp. 109-11, 124.

[40] Not, however, Avroman 3; Avroman 1 has no verb of sale or conveyance in the declaration – rather, the sum of money received is called the price of the vineyard.

[41] A parallel exists in the Alexandrian *synchoresis* documents (Mitteis, pp. 182-83). However, they represent an entirely different procedure and documentary

Aramaic, cuneiform, and demotic: the declaration of receipt of the price precedes the declaration of sale.[42] Since the medieval Jewish formularies follow the practice of the Jewish academies in Babylonia, perhaps here is a significant difference between legal practice in the Roman world and among the Greek and Semitic subjects of the Parthian and Sassanian Empires. The problem deserves further study.

10. There are difficulties in the syntax of this line. Torrey translated the first word as "a purchase," meaning that the slave was bought, not home-born. The word then is a feminine noun in the *status absolutus*, a possible construction, particularly in an early text.[43] However, neither in the few extant ancient slave sales nor in the medieval formularies is there any parallel for so describing the slave; on the contrary, one would expect note to be taken only if the slave was home-born.[44]

There may be a helpful parallel in the declarations of sale in the medieval Jewish formularies. In them, at the corresponding point of the clause, appears the word *zbyny* (sale), as a cognate accusative, but there the word is needed as a noun for the adjectives describing the sale as final and irrevocable. Here a cognate accusative would seem to serve no purpose.

Difficult, too, is the presence of the word *thw'*. It can hardly be construed with *zbyn'* as an expression of the buyer's taking possession, "Bought let her be!" The grammar and word order would be odd,[45] the formula unparalleled[46] and out of place in a statement of the name and specifications of the slave. Hence, the word presumably is to be construed with what follows. But in normal Syriac, the imperfect of "to be" is not a simple copula but has a modal force, such as "let her be..."; that would be a strange way to state the slave's age, especially that of a handmaid past the bloom of youth. *Neg. 135*, a slave-sale from Ascalon showing considerable Semitism in its language and formulation, alone among Greek documents introduces the age of the slave with the participle *onta*. But the participle of *Neg. 135* is good Greek; the imperfect here is odd Syriac, though the scribe otherwise seems well-trained.

---

style; e.g., the amount of the price is not mentioned in the declaration of receipt.
[42]Cf. Welles, *YCS*, V, 101, n. 39.
[43]Nöldeke, sec. 202.
[44]Welles, *YCS*, V, 103, n. 48.
[45]See Nöldeke, sec. 300.
[46]But cf. the Middle Assyrian sale formula, Koschaker, pp. 28-30.

One must always hesitate to emend a legal document, especially one written by an evidently experienced scribe. Nevertheless, parchment was expensive, and an erasure might have invalidated the document. Hesitantly, therefore, as the basis for my translation, I suggest that the scribe wrote *zbyn'* too soon; in order to set off the declaration of the slave's age as a sort of parenthesis, he inserted the verb *thw'*. If so, *zbyn'* is to be construed with *mn šby'* and as a predicate adjective in the *status absolutus*. Literally translated, line 10 becomes, "She was purchased (she is 28 years old, more or less) from her captors." It is, indeed, usual for a bill of sale to mention how the seller acquired the property, and on the basis of parallels in other documents,[47] one would expect this to be expressed by something more than a prepositional phrase.[48]

The phrase "more or less" occurs in demotic and Semitic documents as early as Old Babylonian deeds and is found also in Greek papyri. By it, the sale is agreed to be final regardless of whether estimated measurements are too large or too small.[49]

šby' can be vocalized in two ways, as the abstract and collective *šebhyā* (captivity) or as the plural *šabbāyē* (captors). The latter is suggested by the parallels in other documents of sale, which name the previous owner, not the previous status of the slave or other property, and also by the language of a hymn to the Virgin Mary to Jacob of Sarug.[50] Here and in the hymn and at Joel 4.8 the word probably means "slave-dealers," a usage which hitherto has been unrecognized. See *TB Gittin* 58a; Joel 4.8 (reading *šabbā'im* for *šᵉbā'im*; cf. Greek Joel 4.8 and Jerome's comment, quoted at F. Field, *Origenis Hexapla*, I, 966). Like Greek *andrapodistês*, the word can also mean "marauder" (see *TP Terumot* 8.3, p. 46a).

To my knowledge, no other Aramaic document introduces the clauses following the declaration of sale and receipt with a formula like "under the following terms." The wording here probably is translated from a Greek model.[51]

---

[47] *P. Dura* 25, lines 24-25; 26, line 9; K. 12, lines 4, 12; Avroman 1, A, lines 11-12, and B, lines 12-13.
[48] But note the prepositional phrase in line 18.
[49] San Nicolò, pp. 208-209; M. *Baba Batra* 7.2 – see Gulak, p. 99. The words are found in Milik II, as corrected by B.M.V., p. 147, note to line 14; *Mur.* 22 and 30.
[50] J.B. Abbeloos, *De Vita et scriptis S. Jacobi Batnarum Sarugi in Mesopotamia Episcopi* (diss. Louvain, 1967), p. 256, line 13: *btym' rbtn zbnn ḥwbk mn šby'*, where the final word bears the dots of the plural.
[51] Cf. Avroman 1, line 15 (ἐφ' ᾧ).

III. The Kyrieia Clause

This formula occurs in documents from the Judean desert[52] and in the medieval formularies and, as a unit, can be traced back as far as the Aramaic papyri from Elephantine;[53] elements of it can be found in Mesopotamian, Ugaritic, and Egyptian documents of the second millennium B.C.[54] In Greek documents the earliest instance known to m e is Avroman 1 (88 B.C.); in Greek bills of sale from Egypt the clause first appears in the second Christian century.[55] Like the defension clause (lines 12-15), the *kyrieia* clause over the centuries increases in verbosity down to the prolix heaps of synonyms in the formulary of Hay. The verbosity comes as subtle traders find the word *šlyṭ* by itself too vague to express the nuances of ownership,[56] and later as the words used to supplement it change their meanings – for the conservatism of documentary style retains all the obsolete expressions while adding the new ones.[57] Hence, if the low number of verbs defining ownership is a criterion, K. 3, K. 12, Milik II, *Mur. 30*, *P. Dura* 28, and Avroman 1 are more primitive in formulation than the other Greek papyri.[58]

IV. The Guarantees

Lines 12-18. The seller (a) guarantees to defend title to the slave against challenge by a third party, (b) renounces all means of revoking the sale, and (c) grants the buyer a period of six months within which he may receive satisfaction should the slave be somehow unsatisfactory – the exact nature of the circumstances and the satisfaction is obscure because of the illegibility of the document. This combination in contiguous clauses following the *kyrieia* clause, of guarantee to defend, renunciation, and assurance of satisfaction for defects, recurs in the formularies of *Maḥzor Vitry* and Bargeloni[59] but

---

[52] Milik II; Nabataean Document 2, Yadin, *IEJ*, XII, 241; cf. *Mur. 30*, lines 22-23.
[53] Rabinowitz, pp. 124-41; Yaron, "Aramaic Deeds of Conveyance," *Biblica*, XLI (1960), 248-50, 256-61.
[54] Kutscher, *JAOS*, LXXIV, 239; Yaron, *Biblica*, XLI, 386-87; "Aramaic Marriage Contracts from Elephantine," *JSS*, III (1958), 31-32.
[55] Mitteis, pp. 182-83.
[56] Cf. Yaron, *Biblica*, XLI, 257.
[57] Cf. Kutscher, *Tarbiẓ*, XIX, 127-28; Yaron, *Bib. Or.*, XV (1958), 15-22.
[58] Note, however, the elaborate *kyrieia* and defension clauses in Nabataean documents mentioned by Yadin, *IEJ*, XII, 241, 249.
[59] In the order *kyrieia*, defects, renunciation, defension. In *Maḥzor Vitry* and Bargeloni the renunciation clause begins with the statement that the seller has retained no share in the slave. In Hay, first comes a statement that the seller has retained no share and that the buyer has received full possession, and then the *kyrieia*, defects, and defension clauses.

The Syriac Bill of Sale from Dura-Europos 49

in no other ancient document known to me.[60] The guarantees of *P. Dura* 28 stand with those of the medieval Jewish formularies also in lacking a penalty clause for nonfulfillment.

The juxtaposition of defension and renunciation clauses is logical and has parallels in bills of sale from many areas of the ancient world.[61] Also logical is the juxtaposition of the seller's renunciation of the means of revocation and a clause allowing the buyer a period of grace: the seller is denied the right to revoke the sale, the buyer is conditionally granted it.

a. The Defension Clause

Lines 12-15. For the history and the philological analysis of this clause, see Kutscher, *Tarbiz*, XIX, 53-59, 125-28; Yaron, *Bib. Or.*, XV, 15-22; Rabinowitz, pp. 142-52; Goldstein, pp. 431-32; Muffs, p. 171.

13. *'w nthg'*. The translation in W.F.G. follows Torrey, "or talk against." The Syriac word, however, does not mean simply "talk" but at least "raise a claim." The Syriac verb can also mean "plot," so that perhaps it means here "raise a false claim," but parallels suggest that the added word is another instance of the piling up of synonyms in documentary formulas. Compare the inflated defension clause of Bargeloni's formulary, "*dykwm wyt'wn wyhgh wyšt'y wy'r'r šwm dyn wdbrym b'wlm 'l plwny zh....*"

15. *bgdh*. Though the reading is beyond doubt, the idiom, literally, "in [or subject to] the fortune of," is strange, whereas the medieval Jewish formularies have the common idiom "in the hand of," suggesting the easy emendation *b'ydh*. Nevertheless, again it is well to beware of emending a document written by a good scribe. The strange idiom may be attested in a story in the Palestinian Talmud.[62] A fire broke out (on the Sabbath) on the property of R. Jonah (fourth century); he refused to let his Nabataean[63] neighbor put it out, whereupon the Nabataean held him responsible for damages should the fire spread, using the formula

---

[60]Old Babylonian and Assyrian slave-sales have no *kyrieia* clause, but do have a renunciation clause followed by a statement that the seller stands surety for designated periods against epilepsy and against contest of title (Koschaker, p. 31; San Nicolò, chap. 2 and pp. 209-23). The clause of standing surety is not found in late cuneiform slave sales, which lack all reference to hidden defects (Petschow, p. 63). In Greek papyri from Egypt, the guarantee against leprosy and epilepsy is included in the declaration of sale, not in a separate clause. *Neg. 135* contains no renunciation clause.

[61]Assyrian and Old Babylonian slave-sales: see n. 60; other examples: Petschow, p. 44; K.1 and K.3. See Yaron, *Biblica*, XLI, 261-68, 387-89.

[62]*Shabbat* 16.7, p. 15d, *Yoma* 8.5, p. 45b; *Nedarim* 4.9, p. 38d. I owe this reference to Professor Saul Lieberman.

[63]At *Nedarim*, loc. cit., a Samaritan neighbor.

bgdk mdly, "My property is subject to your fortune." The formula "in the fortune of so-and-so" may have had the connotation both of "in his charge" and "in his possession"; cf. *mn gdh* in line 18, and the use of *bršwt* in rabbinic Hebrew.

b. The Renunciation Clause

Line 15. This clause is not impersonally phrased but is a declaration of the seller that he has no power to revoke the conditions of the document.[64] Since it does not close the provisions of the sale, the formula here is not analogous to the Greek closing formula, *kyria hê syngraphê*.[65]

c. The Defects Clauses

Lines 15-18. Partly unread, the first of these clauses is recognizable because of its close affinities to the vocabulary of the Syriac-Roman lawbooks.[66] Syriac legal terminology as reflected here seems to have taken note of the logical connection of the renunciation clause with the defects clause. In the Syriac-Roman laws, the agreement (*tnwy*) between the buyer and the seller in a slave-sale may be either "good" or "bad" (for the buyer),[67] and the "bad" agreement is defined as one in which one party may not retract against the other (*dl' 'nš nhpwk 'l hbrh*),[68] with the use of the same root *hpk* (revoke, retract).

The parallel passages in the Syriac-Roman laws declare the seller of a slave liable for hidden defects for a period of six months, though in a "bad" agreement only for insanity. The first clause here probably indicates the extent of the seller's liability during the six months.[69] I would guess that here all conditions of a "good" agreement apply,

---

[64]Cf. Brockelmann, *ZfS*, X, 163. In *Maḥzor Vitry* and Bargeloni, the renunciation clause speaks of the irrevocability of the *sale*, not of the document.

[65]Cf. Welles, *YCS*, V, 110. One Aramaic equivalent for the Greek formula occurs in K. 9 (line 22–read myṣb) and K. 10; another was known to both Talmuds; see Rabinowitz, pp. 112-24, and Gulak, pp. 24-30. The latter occurs in *Maḥzor Vitry* and Bargeloni.

[66]L 39, 113; P 19, 20, 35; R I 19, 20, 28; R II 27, 28, 40, 41; R III 39, 114.

[67]Equivalent to the Greek καλή or κακή αἵρεσις and the Latin *venditio bonis condicionibus* or *venditio simplaria*; see Pringsheim, pp. 481-92. These distinctions and the Greek terminology are attested in a Semitic text of about the same time as *P. Dura* 28, *Exodus rabbah*, 43.8, ascribed to R. Levi b. Parṭa (third century). Read with Oxford ms. No. 147 *q'lwrysyn* and *q'q'rysyn* (this confirmation of Perles' and Krauss' emendation of the printed text I owe to Professor Sal Lieberman): "...A man...came to buy a slave. He said to the owner, 'Is this slave you are selling me a good acquisition [q'lwrysyn, καλή αἵρεσις] or a bad acquisition *q'q'rysyn*, κακή αἵρεσις....'"

[68]L 39; R II 28.

[69]Cf. *Neg.* 135. See also Welles, *YCS*, V, 105-107.

except for liability for flight — the exception being made by common agreement (lines 17-18). With Torrey's reading in line 17, *w'n*, the resultant clause, "And such was the agreement between them," serves no visible purpose.[70] Hence, read *d'n*. Pringsheim[71] viewed the clause placing the risk of the slave's flight upon the buyer as a "risk clause," a category he sharply distinguished from defects clauses. The distinction is logical,[72] but the Syriac-Roman laws do treat the tendency to flee as a hidden defect, though as one for which the seller is obligated to refund the price only under certain circumstances.[73]

18. *mn gdh dtyrw zbwn'*. This predicate phrase without a copula is grammatical but somewhat awkward. Perhaps the scribe omitted *hw* because of the *w* of *w'tktbw*.

V. The Statement of Number of Copies and Registry

Lines 18-20. See Welles, *YCS*, V, 111-12.

19. *n'l b'rkywn*. In Mishnaic Hebrew, a similar phrase, *'lh b'rk'wt*, is used of the registration of documents in official archives.[74] The use of the Hebrew root *'lh* surely reflects the Aramaic. On the archives of Edessa, see Welles, *YCS*, V, 126-27, 135-37.[75]

VI. The Subscription

Lines 20-23. On the subscription (*hypographê*) in Greek papyri from Egypt, see Mitteis, p. 56. In *P. Dura* 28, as in *P. Dura* 26, 27, and 29, and in a notarial practice described in the Palestinian Talmud,[76] the subscription serves as a closing formula to prevent anything from being added to the clauses of the document. Hence, no space is left between it and the operative part of the text.[77] On the name Shamashyabh, see Caquot, *Syria*, XXXIX, 245.

---

[70]It cannot be analogous to the *kyria* clause of Greek papyri because another operative clause follows (see above, n. 65), nor does it record the procedures of a Roman *stipulatio* (W.F.G., p. 16; cf. Welles, *YCS*, V, 110-11).
[71]Pp. 456-65; cf. San Nicolò, pp. 223-27.
[72]The formula does have a separate history; most ancient systems of law, including Jewish law, place the risk of the slave's flight solely on the buyer; see also Welles, *YCS*, V, 108-109.
[73]E.g., R I 19.
[74]*M. Giṭṭin* 1.5; *T. ibid.* 1.4; *T. Mo'ed qatan* 2.1; *T. Baba batra* 8.2-3; *T. 'Abodah zarah* 1.8; *TB Giṭṭin*, pp. 9ab, 10b-11a, 44a; *TP, ibid.*, 1.5, p. 43d.
[75]Remove the reference to a "*Strategos-Baḥora*" on p. 137.
[76]*TP Giṭṭin* 10.1, p. 49d; see Gulak, pp. 29-30. The procedure of *P. Dura* 26-29 sets aside Gulak's hesitations on p. 30.
[77]See W.F.G., Plate XX, and delete "*vacat*" in the transcription of *P. Dura* 26, lines 28-29.

VII. The Signatures

Lines 24-30 and Verso. The normal procedure, described by the Mishnah and found in the documents of the Judean desert and in *P. Dura* 26, 30, and 32, was for single documents to be signed on the recto only and double documents on the verso only, but the existence of "conflated"[78] procedures such as the one followed here is recognized by the Mishnah and described in the Palestinian Talmud.[79]

In both line 24 and line 25, the Semitic name which follows "Marcus Aurelius" is surely the native cognomen, not the patronymic; here and elsewhere in the Dura documents, names of Roman citizens may appear without the patronymic but never without the cognomen.[80] The first two signers identify themselves simply as witnesses. Hence, one cannot place them in the same category as the archivist Aurelius Mannus and explain the attesting signatures on the recto of *P. Dura* 28 as being all those of archivists (cf. *P. Dura* 17 and 25).

The scribe's identifying signature is a feature common in neo-Babylonian, demotic, and Aramaic documents. On its position here after the attesting signatures on the recto, see Yaron, *JSS*, II, 38-39, and Petschow, pp. 7-8, 44, 70. The vocalization of the scribe's patronymic is assured by the numerous Greek and Latin transcriptions of the name in the Dura documents. On the name itself, see Caquot, *Tessères*, p. 175; its occurrence at Edessa, Leroy, *Syria*, XXXIV, 322.

On the verso of a double document the common practice of the Semitic East placed the signature of the conceding party or his literate substitute first and then the signatures of the several witnesses, each signature adjacent to a knot of the tying string,[81] but *P. Dura* 28 exhibits some strange aspects. The "signature" of the illiterate Mat-Tar'atha appears before that of her husband, her literate substitute, and again as the last of the signatures on the verso. Practices mentioned in rabbinic literature give a key to understanding these phenomena.

At Edessa, four or five attesting signatures may have been sufficient, but in the "conflated" procedure of *P. Dura* 28, only two witnesses signed on the verso, along with Mat-Tar'atha and her husband. The documentary sheet, however, had five holes for the five knots of the tying string. From the Mishnah and the Tosefta we learn that a double document which did not bear a signature by every one of

---

[78]W.F.G., p. 145.
[79]*M. Baba batra* 10.1; *TP Giṭṭin* 8.10, p. 49d.
[80]*P. Dura* 26, 29-32.
[81]Milik II; *Mur.* 18-20, 28-30, 36, 38; Yadin, *IEJ*, XII, 237.

its knots was called a "bald" document and was invalid.[82] One did not, however, have to procure the signatures of legally eligible witnesses to fill the blank spaces. According to some authorities, even the signature of a slave would do.[83] This is the function of Mat-Tar'atha's second signature.

As for her illiteracy, it is possible that, though illiterate, she could sign her name. If so, it is odd that the letter forms are inconsistent in her two signatures (note especially the ' of *mtr't*'); one would expect an illiterate to know only one way of signing her name. But the letter forms in the two signatures are all found in the script of the scribe Marcus Aurelius Belshu, with one significant difference: very few of the letters are joined. Children and illiterates find it easier to copy manuscript "printing" than cursive "writing." Rabbinic sources mention several procedures by which an illiterate can write a signature: a stencil can be cut in another piece of paper and the illiterate can ink the document through it; the illiterate can trace over scratches or markings in lead, gall-nut juice, or spittle on the document itself.[84] In the case of *P. Dura* 28, none of these methods seems to have been used. With a stencil, both signatures would have been very much alike; in tracing, Mat-Tar'atha probably would not have become confused twice by the sequence *'l np*, whereas in line 1 she has omitted the *n*, which has been squeezed in, and in line 5 she seems to have been diffident writing the '. My guess is that the scribe wrote out an example for each line, and Mat-Tar'atha copied them.

The first witness to sign on the verso is one of the two chief magistrates of Edessa. In documents from Dura, too, the first attesting signature is that of a chief magistrate.[85] His signature may have been required for full validity of the document. As in the documents from Dura, the name of an official appears with his title and without his patronymic.

The name Bar-Samya occurs among the aristocracy of Edessa in the *Doctrine of Addaeus the Apostle* and is the name of the Christian bishop in the *Acts* of Sharbil and of Barsamya. On other instances of the name and on the vexed question of the vocalization and etymology, see H. Ingholt, *Parthian Sculptures from Hatra* ("Memoirs of the Connecticut Academy of Arts and Sciences," Vol. XII [New Haven, 1954]), pp. 17 ff., esp. p. 21; and Caquot, "Note sur le *semeion* et les inscriptions araméennes de Hatra," *Syria*, XXXII (1955), 59-69.

---

[82]*T. Giṭṭin* 8(6).9; *M. Giṭṭin* 8.9.
[83]*M. Giṭṭin* 8.10; *TB*, ibid., p. 21b-82a.
[84]*T B. Giṭṭin*, pp. 19a-b.
[85]*P. Dura* 17, 25.

VI. List of Abbreviations

The abbreviated titles used in this article are the following. *Acts of Sharbil and Barsamya*: see Cureton. Avroman: E.H. Minns, "Parchments of the Parthian Period from Avroman." *JHS*, XXXV (1915), 28-30. Bargeloni: *Sepher Haschetaroth: Dokumentenbuch von R. Jehuda ben Barsilai aus Barcelona*, ed. S.J. Halberstam (Berlin, 1898; bill of slave-sale: p. 69). *Bib. Or.*: *Bibliotheca Orientalis*. B.M.V.: P. Benoit, J.T. Milik, and R. de Vaux, *Discoveries in the Judean Desert, II: Les grottes de Muraba'ât* (Oxford, 1961). Cowley: A.E. Cowley, *Aramaic Papyri of the Fifth Century B.C.* (Oxford, 1923). Cureton: *Ancient Syriac Documents*, ed. W. Cureton (London, 1864). Demotic Documents: K. Sethe and J. Partsch (eds.), *Demotische Urkunden* ("Abhandlungen der philologisch-historischen Klasse der Sächsischen Akademie der Wissenschaften," Vol. XXXII [1920]). *Doctrine of Addaeus the Apostle:* in Cureton (incomplete) and *The Doctrine of Addai the Apostle*, ed. G. Phillips (London, 1876). Goldstein: J.A. Goldstein, Review of W.F.G., *JAOS*, LXXXI (1961), 429-32. Gulak: A. Gulak, *Das Urkundenwesen im Talmud* (Jerusalem, 1935). Hay: *Sefer ha-shetarot le-Rab Hay bar Sherira Gaon*, ed. S. Asaf, *Tarbiz*, Suppl. I (5690). *IEJ*: *Israel Exploration Journal*. *JAOS*: *Journal of the American Oriental Society*. *JSS*: *Journal of Semitic Studies*. K.: documents in E.G. Kraeling, *The Brooklyn Museum Aramaic Papyri* (New Haven, 1953). Koschaker: P. Koschaker, *Neue keilschriftliche Rechtsurkunden aus der el-Amarna Zeit* ("Abhandlungen der philologisch-historischen Klasse der Sächsischen Akademie der Wissenschaften," Vol. XXXIX [1928]). M.: *Mishnah*, ed. H. Albeck (Jerusalem and Tel-Aviv, 1952-1959). *Mahzor Vitry: Machsor Vitry*, ed. S. Hurwitz (Berlin, 1893; bill of slave-sale: pp. 792-93). Milik: J.T. Milik, "Deux documents inédits du désert de Juda," *Biblica*, XXXVIII (1957). Mitteis: L. Mitteis and U. Wilcken, *Grundzüge und Chrestomathie der Papyruskunde* (Leipzig-Berlin, 1912), Vol. II, Part I. Muffs: J.Y. Muffs, *Studies in the Aramaic Legal Papyri from Elephantine* ("Studia et documenta ad iura Orientis antiqui pertinentia," Vol. VIII; Leiden: Brill, 1969). Mur.: documents in B.M.V. Neg.: documents in V. Arangio-Ruiz, *Negotia*, Part III of *Fontes iuris romani antejustiniani*, ed. S. Riccobono et al. (Florence, 1943). Nöldeke: T. Nöldeke, *Compendious Syriac Grammar* (London, 1904). Payne Smith: R. Payne Smith, *Thesaurus Syriacus*. Petschow: H. Petschow, *Die neubabylonischen Kaufformulare* ("Leipsiger rechtswissenschaftliche Studien," Vol. CXVIII [1939]). Pringsheim: F. Pringsheim, *The Greek Law of Sale* (Weimar, 1950). Rabinowitz: J.J. Rabinowitz, *Jewish Law* (New York, 1956). San Nicolò, *Die*

Schlussklauseln der altbabylonischen Kauf- und Tauschverträge ("Münchener Beiträge zur Papyrusforschung und antike Rechtsgeschichte," Vol. IV [1922]). Syriac-Roman Lawbooks: *Syrisch-Römisches Rechtsbuch*, ed. K.G. Bruns and E. Sachau (Leipzig, 1880), and *Syrische Rechtsbücher*, ed. E. Sachau (Berlin, 1907). T.: *Tosefta*, ed. M.S. Zuckermandel (2d ed; Jerusalem, 1937). TB: *Babylonian Talmud*. TP: *Palestinian Talmud*. Tessères: H. Ingholt, H. Seyrig, J. Starcky, and A. Caquot, *Recueil des tessères de Palmyre* (Paris, 1955). W.F.G.: C.B. Welles, R.O. Fink, and J.F. Gilliam, *The Excavations at Dura-Europos: Final Report V, Part I, The Parchments and Papyri* (New Haven, 1959). YCS: *Yale Classical Studies*. ZDMG: *Zeitschrift der Deutschen Morgenländischen Gesellschaft*. ZfS: *Zeitschrift für Semitistik und verwandte Gebiete*.

3

Review of Goodenough

Jewish Symbols in the Greco-Roman Period. Vols. IX-XI: *Symbolism in the Dura Synagogue.* By Erwin R. Goodenough. New York: Pantheon Books ("Bollingen Series," Vol. XXXVII), 1964. Pp. xviii + 237 + xi + 251 + xv + 21 pls. + 354 figs. $25.00.

Jewish Symbols in the Greco-Roman Period. Vol. XII; *Summary and Conclusions.* By Erwin R. Goodenough. New York: Pantheon Books ("Bollingen Series," Vol. XXXVII), 1965. Pp. xii + 217. $6.00

One must approach the concluding volumes of the late Professor Goodenough's great work with reverence and gratitude for the treasures he has set before us. (A last volume containing maps and a general index is promised.) To Goodenough, the study of the Dura synagogue was the culmination of his efforts. In the volumes on it and in the summary and conclusions one perceives how this was a work of passionate devotion, not least in the way that its pages are occasionally scarred by the author's understandable acrimony toward obstinate and sometimes obtuse critics. Yet his humanity and humility shine through, and if in summarizing his achievement I suggest where he may have been mistaken, I hope it will be taken as a tribute to a work from which I have learned much.

Goodenough's solid achievement can be summarized as follows:

1. In Volumes I and III he has been the first comprehensive collector and, in large measure, the discoverer of a vast body of figured remains from the Greco-Roman world of the second to sixth centuries of the Christian era, remains which can be ascribed only to Jews, much as the ascription clashes with the assumed aniconic character of Judaism.

2. In Volumes IV to XI he has shown that the figures used consist of a very limited "vocabulary" of motifs, some drawn from Jewish sources (e.g., the menorah), others clearly pagan in origin and drawn from a symbolic "lingua franca" common to many religions in the Greco-

Roman world (e.g., birds eating grapes from a vine). Though many of the figured motifs are expressly forbidden for use by Jews in the authoritative texts of Jewish law, Goodenough has shown that the figures are not "mere decoration" but symbols which had deep religious significance for the Jews who used them, especially the meaning of life beyond the grave. He has shown how the symbolic remains and the paintings of the Dura synagogue can be understood as products of a type of Judaism in which mysticism was important. In my opinion he has come closest to a correct interpretation of the Dura paintings, certainly closer than C.H. Kraeling.

Having accomplished all this in eleven painstakingly erudite volumes, in Volume XII Goodenough does his reader the service of presenting a bird's-eye view of the whole along with a few additions and corrections. In a work of such vast scope he has committed numerous small errors which it would be carping to mention here. One must deal with his fundamental theses.

From the beginning of his work Goodenough has gone much farther in his assertions than what I have described as his solid achievement. In the preface to Volume XII he emphasizes to his reader that in his thirty years of labor, from his book *By Light, Light* in 1935 to the end of *Jewish Symbols*, he was "trying to make a point." He wished to trace to a "Mystic Gospel of Hellenized Judaism" the origins of Christianity as a religion "of salvation from the world and the flesh, of a Savior who in his person brought divinity to lost humanity, a religion of sacraments, organized priesthood, and theological formulation – that is a Greco-Roman religion even though it called itself the Verus Israel." Through the study of Philo he claimed to have discovered such a "Mystic Gospel." In Goodenough's interpretation of Philo, Moses taught a mystery religion which would "lead man out from bodily enslavement to the passions into the world of immaterial reality." Goodenough saw two levels in this mystery religion. The lower, the "mystery of Aaron," sought union with God and liberation through the observance of the actual written laws of the Torah and in the contemplation of the material cosmos. This lower mystery was symbolized in the high priest's vestments and in the structure and furniture of the Tabernacle except for the ark and was characterized by the number 5, the number of the senses. The higher mystery, the "mystery of Moses," sought its goals by leaving the material cosmos to go into the "darkness" of ultimate immaterial reality. This higher mystery was symbolized by the ark and was characterized by the perfect number ten or one.

Goodenough's study of the symbols and the Dura paintings is throughout an effort to prove that such a mystic gospel was a widespread phenomenon in ancient Judaism, not an isolated aberration in Alexandria. His effort to make his point inevitably determines his findings, however much he tries to let the ancient remains "speak for themselves." Material remains are mute. To discover what was in the mind of those who left them, in the absence of surviving written information, one can use only the methods of psychology. Goodenough, as he must, makes psychological assumptions. To him a religious symbol is "a form that reflects deeper meaning from the world of religion than what it actually depicts." To be a "live" symbol this form must have "emotional impact." This emotional impact he calls the "value" of the symbol, which he sharply distinguishes from the verbal "explanations" given by believers. Goodenough's pivotal assumption, his "working hypothesis" is the "principle of constant value": a live symbol when borrowed by another religion will presumably get new explanations but will be borrowed for its value. If the Jews of Dura had an Orpheus-figure painted on the walls of their synagogue, Goodenough supposes that they borrowed the figure for its Orphic values and that their Judaism included Orphic values. To interpret the varieties of religious experience, Goodenough distinguishes two fundamental types of the religious quest for security and salvation, the quest through "obedience to the father," best exemplified in halakhic Judaism, and the quest through union with the mother, which he sees in the mysticism of Philo and the material remains and Dura.

Goodenough finds the Dura paintings very close to the mysticism described in *By Light, Light*. He finds in the designer a "philosopher"[1] akin to Philo, who freely altered and allegorized biblical material, sometimes passing completely outside the Bible to Iranian and Greek speculations. While admitting that there is much that he does not understand, Goodenough sees in the parallelism and contrast of the left and right sides of the west wall of the synagogue the parallelism and contrast of the "mysteries of Aaron and Moses." For example, on the left side appears a painting with Aaron standing in a schematized temple complex drawn from the traditions of Greco-Roman mystic art, depicted as firmly grounded on earth. Around Aaron stand the appurtenances of the Jewish temple cult and priests busily carry out their duties. Five, the number of the senses, appears repeatedly, notably in the columns of the temple, and the material cosmos of the seven planets is emphasized by the prominent appearance of the seven-branched

---

[1] Goodenough's use of the term "philosopher" for the designer of the synagogue paintings is based on a misunderstanding of a passage in the *Passio Quattuor Coronatorum*. See E.J. Bickerman's review of Vols. IX-XI, *Harvard Theological Review*, LVIII (1965), 142, n. 57.

menorah. Correspondingly, on the right appears a closed temple of the higher mystery, with no relation to earth, surrounded by seven walls drawn from Iranian mystic doctrine, and with no cult depicted. Ten, the perfect number of the higher mystery appears in the columns of the closed temple. Under cosmic-material Judaism Goodenough classifies the "mundane" doctrines of the messianic triumph of the Jews over their enemies. Hence, he notes with satisfaction the contrast in the lowest tier of the biblical paintings of the west wall. On the left Elijah may be posing with the resurrected child, the Messiah son of Joseph (see XI, 167-68), and Mordecai, portrayed as the pagan cavalier god, rides in triumph over Israel's enemies. On the right, the true, higher victories are portrayed: the pagan goddesses, Anahita and the Nymphs (borrowed for their "value") pose with the resurrected child, the mystic hierophant Moses, and King David is initiated by Samuel into the mystic Seven Powers of God.

Even the skeleton I have presented here would be a great scholarly construct, and Goodenough has done far more. But apart from the points I have described as solidly established, it is honeycombed with dubious or false assumptions. Philo nowhere speaks of a "mystery of Aaron"; much of the "Mystic Gospel" may be only the creation of Goodenough. Goodenough's careful study has established the "principle of constant value" for what he calls the "lingua franca" of Greco-Roman symbols of immortality. But he knew well that Anahita and Orpheus did not belong to that lingua franca. To deal adequately with all the problems would require a long book. Morton Smith's review in the *Journal of Biblical Literature*, LXXXVI (1967), 53-68, treats well the weaknesses of the principle of constant value, of the psychological scheme, of Goodenough's falsely monolithic conception of "normative rabbinic Judaism" (a heritage from his teacher, George Foot Moore), and of Goodenough's undervaluing of the Hebrew and Aramaic sources which he could not read. Hence, I shall deal with other fundamental weaknesses, especially in the treatment of the Dura paintings, and suggest a different approach which seems to me correct, while acknowledging that Goodenough was often aware of his shortcomings and foresaw some of what I have to suggest.

Goodenough has established that there *was* mysticism in Philo and has found mysticism in the Jewish material remains and in the paintings at Dura. Jewish mysticism, however, was not peculiar to Philo. G. Scholem[2] and others have shown how pervasive a phenomenon mysticism was throughout Jewish history. If mysticism underlies the material treated by Goodenough, is it akin to the

---

[2] See his *Major Trends in Jewish Mysticism* (3d ed.; New York, 1954).

"Philonic" mysticism of *By Light, Light*? The distinctive feature of Philonic mysticism, well appreciated by Goodenough, is its condemnation of the passions and its contempt for the material, its total rejection of the conception that God is material. This feature is derived from Plato; Philo shares it with the medieval Jewish philosophers. There is a long history in Judaism of the antagonism between the Platonic-Philonic mysticism of the philosophers and the "material" mysticism of the Kabbalists.[3] The "material" mysticism has a much longer history than the Platonic-Philonic. Isaiah 6 and Ezekiel 1, if not the Book of Enoch, antedate any conceivable forerunners of Philo. Granted the difficulty of artistic representation of "immaterial reality," one is still entitled to be skeptical of an interpretation of the remains in terms of Platonic-Philonic mysticism.

Besides the issue of the relation of God to matter, there is the question of Goodenough's attitude toward eschatology. Goodenough was aware that he had not treated the possible eschatological implications of his material (see XII, 49). Indeed, it is quite clear that eschatology, in contrast to mysticism, bored him. Barely two pages of *By Light, Light*[4] deal with it. Philo was not so uninterested, much less the Jews and Christians known to us from the period. Moreover, the vast bulk of the material studied by Goodenough comes from after the destruction of the Temple in 70. For Philo, who lived before, eschatology might not be a burning question, but in other writers both before and after the destruction we find a burning interest in eschatology, even in the medieval philosophers who followed in the path of Philo. Certainly for the main-stream of Jewish mysticism the mystic approach to the divine and the hope of the victory "in the end of days" are equally important. Yet, as seen by Goodenough, the Dura artist portrayed the victory of the messianic king only by representing Mordecai as the "cavalier god."[5]

---

[3] See Scholem, *Major Trends*, pp. 22-37, 63-67; *Jewish Gnosticism, Merkabah Mysticism, and Talmudic Tradition* (New York, 1960), pp. 36-42; Maimonides, *Mishneh Torah, Mada', Hilkot Teshubah* 3.7 and the comment of R. Abraham b. David of Posquières *ad loc.*; I. Twersky, *Rabad of Posquières* (Cambridge, Mass., 1962), pp. 282-86. Note however, H.A. Wolfson's view, *Jewish Quarterly Review, Seventy-fifth Anniversary Volume* (1967), pp. 570-73.
[4] Pp. 81-82.
[5] In fact, Mordecai is not portrayed as the "cavalier god" but as a Persian king, as one would expect from Esther 6.8-11; cf. J. Neusner, *A History of the Jews in Babylonia*, II (Leiden, 1966), p. 58. The interpretations of Rachel Wischnitzer, *The Messianic Theme in the Paintings of the Dura Synagogue* (Chicago, 1948) are almost all wrong, but her intuition of a messianic theme is surely correct.

In a review I can give only a sketch of what I think is a correct approach, which I hope to develop in future studies. I believe it can be demonstrated that the Dura paintings represent the eschatological-material mysticism known from the texts of Merkabah mysticism and the Kabbalah and from the Palestinian and Babylonian Talmudic and Midrashic literature, not the Platonic mysticism of immaterial reality known from Philo. I believe that Goodenough was correct in seeing parallelism and contrast in the two sides of the west wall. However, the contrast is not between material and immaterial but between temporary and past foreshadowings on the left side and the permanent and eschatological on the right. I believe that the problem of the conflict of the pictorial representations with the prohibition of images in halakhic texts can be resolved by a proper approach to the history of the halakhah. Even now it is well known that some important rabbis allowed two-dimensional representations and even some sculpture.[6] One who undertakes to confirm these hunches may well fail; following up the clues discovered by Goodenough has convinced me, however, that the effort will be worthwhile. As a first step, I shall consider in the remainder of this review the only surviving Jewish liturgical text from Dura and then turn to some of the paintings which Goodenough saw as most reflecting a "Judaism of immaterial reality."

The parchment fragment found near the Dura synagogue, *P. Dura* 11, has been identified as a fragment of a Jewish grace after meals.[7] Because the text is so fragmentary, it is impossible to determine its precise nature.[8] In its opening words the passage does closely resemble the texts of the grace which stem from Babylonia, especially the Persian version.[9] Indeed, the opening words may reflect one of the formulas out of which the later Jewish texts of the grace were

---

[6]See E.J. Bickerman, "Sur la théologie de l'art figuratif à propos de l'ouvrage de E.R. Goodenough," *Syria*, XLIV (1967), 134-39.

[7]See my review, *JAOS*, LXXXI (1961), 431.

[8]Little doubt would be left about the opening formula if the last complete word in line 3 of frag. *a* could be read *bḥsd*, "with grace," instead of *bhmh*, "cattle." Crucial is the final letter of the word, which stands in a smeared context. Is it *he* or has a black stain disguised a *daleth*? Professor C.B. Welles has examined the document for me and agrees that the form of the *he* is suspicious, but he says that the black mark in question is ink, presumably the scribe's, and not an accidental stain.

[9]See L. Finkelstein, "The Birkat Ha-Mazon," *JQR*, XIX (1928-29), 235, n. 47 (Karaite version); p. 243 (non-Palestinian [Babylonian?] version from the Genizah); p. 244 (version of Seder R. Amram); p. 246 (Persian version and Sephardic version B). See also S. Lieberman, *Yemenite Midrashim* (Jerusalem, 1940), pp. 40-41 (in Hebrew), for Palestinian parallels to *P. Dura* 11, for its poetic character, and for the abbreviated divine name.

conflated. Nevertheless, short as it is, the fragment is not a primitive text; its style is elaborated by the parallelism of biblical poetry: "Who hath distributed food/who hath prepared sustenance...." It is peculiar in another respect: the normal biblical and rabbinic expression is *kl bśr*, "all flesh." I know only one Hebrew text which shares with *P. Dura* 11 the expression *kl bny bśr*, "all the children of flesh," the *'Alenu* prayer of the Rosh Ha-shanah liturgy. *'Alenu* exhibits the same use of biblical poetic style. It contains prominent references to the mysteries of creation and the Heavenly Throne and teems with allusions to eschatological prophesies. *'Alenu* appears prominently in the texts of Merkabah mysticism.[10] Possibly composed while the Temple still stood, the portion of the Rosh Ha-shanah liturgy of which *'Alenu* is a part is known to have been recited in the Babylonian school of Rab, a fact most important for the student of the Dura paintings. Rab was a contemporary of the Dura synagogue; he was concerned with fixing the formulas of the grace; he and his contemporaries "glorified Moses in the manner of the Dura synagogue." He was also a mystic, devoted to the thought patterns known to us through the Merkabah texts and the *Sefer Yeṣirah*. He and his contemporaries in Jewish Babylonia, suffering under Sassanian persecution, sought solace in the study of two biblical episodes on the west wall at Dura, the book of Esther and the Exodus. As in *'Alenu*, their thoughts turned to the eschatological prophesies.[11]

The hints afforded by this tiny fragment cannot be taken as proof that the biblical paintings at Dura stem from the thought-world of Rab and contemporary rabbinic thinkers in Babylonia. However, the hypothesis is worth testing. With these possibilities in mind, let us approach first the central composition of the west wall at Dura in its final form, the composition which Goodenough calls the reredos. Let us begin with the undisputed, the parting blessings of Jacob to his descendants portrayed in the lowest tier. "In the end of days" (Gen. 49.1), for any Jewish reader in the time of the Dura synagogue, identified Jacob's blessings as eschatological prophesy. Far be it from me to say that any one interpretation exhausts the meaning of the great "tree-vine" which grows up from the blessing scene, and fills the center of the reredos. Nevertheless, in the blessing of Jacob it appears in the words to Judah (Gen. 49.8-12), taken by Jews and Christians as a messianic prophesy. If a tree-vine grows up from Jacob's eschatological

---

[10]See Scholem, *Jewish Gnosticism*, pp. 20-30. For "all the children of flesh," cf. Romans 9.8. There, however, "children of the flesh" occurs as part of an antithesis, and "flesh" has the definite article.

[11]See Neusner, *op. cit.*, I (1965), 158-63; II, 151-59, 163-66, 180-87.

prophesy to Judah, what can the Orpheus figure portrayed on the next level of the reredos as a shoot from the trunk be but the messiah of Isaiah 11, whose coming tames the wild beasts? If I am right in assuming that two-dimensional representations were halakhically permitted, Jews under rabbinic influence would use the ready-made Orpheus figure for that messiah just as Joseph would have been portrayed by ready-made Sarapis and Eve by Isis.[12]

According to Isa. 11.10-13, the taming of the beasts is followed by the regathering of the tribes around the messianic king (cf. Deut. 33.5), precisely what is shown by the top level of the reredos. Who, then, are the two figures in the Greek robe standing before the messianic king?[13] Surely Moses and Elijah, as both Jewish and Christian sources testify.[14] Goodenough was aware of these possibilities, but his bias against eschatology and his insistence on "making the point" of *By Light, Light* blinded him to so straight-forward an interpretation, though it could be reconstructed from Philo, too.[15] Instead he saw a mystic ascent under the leadership of great hierophants to the goal of being slaves in the presence of a Philonic, pre-Christian trinity.

Goodenough denies that the "closed temple" represents any biblical scene. He connects it with Philo's immaterial mystery of the ark. Unfortunately, this is the one of two surviving paintings in the middle tier at Dura in which the ark does *not* appear, and in the context of the Dura paintings one must have *some* biblical connection. In fact, the closed temple is the Heavenly Temple,[16] a concept which originated with Isaiah 6. The Heavenly Temple has both mystical and eschatological significance. In the end of days it will descend to earth. Until then its doors are shut.[17] Most of the relevant Jewish texts have the Heavenly Temple in the fourth heaven (*Zebul*), as does the Dura

---

[12]See *TB Abodah zarah* 43a; H. Blaufuss, *Aboda zara: Mischna und Tosefta* (Nürnberg, 1916), p. 25 and n. 221; Saul Lieberman, *Hellenism in Jewish Palestine* (New York, 1950), pp. 136-38.

[13]Goodenough assumes (IX, 84-85) that the preference for portraying kings with two companions is Jewish and Christian, not pagan. As Morton Smith informs me, this assumption is disproved by Trajan's column. See the plates of K. Lehmann-Hartleben, *Die Trajanssäule* (Berlin und Leipzig, 1926), Scenes IX, X, XVIII, etc.

[14]L. Ginzberg, *Legends of the Jews*, VI, 167, n. 966; Luke 9.28-36; Mark 9.2-8; Matt. 17.2-8; Rev. 11.3-19. Cf. Goodenough, IX, 85. The transfiguration story and early artistic representations of it draw on Jewish prototypes. See below, "The Central Composition," section B.

[15]See H.A. Wolfson, *Philo* (Cambridge, Mass., 1948), II, 407-15.

[16]See the thorough study of A. Aptowitzer, "Bet-hamiqdash shel ma'alah 'al pi ha-agadah," *Tarbiz*, II (5691 = 1930-31), 137-53, 257-77.

[17]See Rev. 11.15-19, 15.5; cf. Ezek. 44.1-3.

painting. I hope to deal with other details of the Heavenly Temple and its counterpart on the left side of the west wall in a later study.

The scene to the right of the closed temple contains the ark desiderated by Goodenough for his Judaism of immaterial reality, but the scene proves again, I think, to belong to the Judaism of eschatological-material reality and is drawn again from Isaiah. All students of the Dura synagogue have been perplexed by the discrepancies between the painting and the story of the ark in I Samuel 6 and perhaps II Samuel 6 with which it has been identified. The midrashic mind was fond of repetitions in history. The scene is influenced by the story of the ark in Samuel but represents a midrash on Isa. 46.1-2, 52.11-12, and perhaps 48.20.[18] The Targum and the Septuagint of Isa. 46.1-2 say that the idols of Bel and Nebo have been smashed and have been transformed into cattle struggling under a heavy load.[19] The "bullwhackers," dressed like the priests of the earthly temple on the left side of the west wall, are probably the "bearers of the vessels of the Lord" of Isa. 52.11, though they conduct and do not bear. Following them is the ark, which one would expect to be the burden except that nothing connects it with the beasts or even with the axle under it. The ark, according to old Jewish traditions, disappeared after being taken into exile in Babylon by Nebuchadnezzar, but it is destined to return to the end of days. No one, to my knowledge, has noticed that the ark here is portrayed as an ancient near-eastern throne, even to having cushions; cf. Stanley A. Cook, *The Religion of Ancient Palestine in the Light of Archaeology* (London, 1930), p.22. When one considers this throne with the other thrones portrayed in the Dura paintings and with the relevant midrashic texts, one immediately recognizes the Throne of the Merkabah, suspended above the wheels, as in Ezekiel 1, not an ark on a clumsily drawn cart with a misdrawn axle. The Divine Throne has no need of transformed pagan idols to pull it; according to the Targum the

---

[18] I Samuel 6 in Merkabah mysticism: Scholem, *Jewish Gnosticism*, pp. 20-30. Evidently, the connection of Isa. 46.1-2 with I Samuel 6 was known to Hellenistic Jews, for the *Sinaiticus* and *Alexandrinus* at Isa. 46.1 read "Dagon" instead of "Nabo."

[19] Cf. TB *Megillah* 25b, *Sanhedrin* 63b; *Shir hashirim rabbah* 7.9. Bel as bull: L. Malten, "Der Stier in Kult und mythischem Bild," *Jahrbuch des Deutschen archäologischen Instituts*, XLIII (1928), 106. Goodenough (X, 78-79; XII, 174) was correct in seeing "short-range polemic" here but wrongly assumed Iranian deities to be the targets. Bel and Nabu were widely worshipped in Syria and Mesopotamia; see Cumont, *Fouilles de Doura-Europos*, pp. 199-201. Bel was worshipped in several temples at Dura. If Nabu had no temple there, veneration for him is abundantly attested in the names of the inhabitants.

burden of the ridiculous beasts is their own excrement. Goodenough labored mightily but confessed his failure to make the pattern of the rosettes and jewels on the ark conform to the scheme of the immaterial powers of God as taught by Philo. But the pattern on the ark exactly fits the pattern of the ten *Sefirot* known from Kabbalistic texts, as Goodenough probably knew.[20] The doctrine of the ten *Sefirot* is known from the *Sefer Yeṣirah* and may well have been known in the same patterned form to Rab.[21] The Dura painting would be the earliest attestation of the patterned arrangement. If this identification is correct, it is an important addition to Scholem's demonstration of the antiquity of the Kabbalah.

Goodenough's study of the symbolism of dress (IX, 124-74; XII, 164-65) is open to criticism, but he is surely correct that the three men in the Greek robe following the ark are divine beings, though in no way a parallel to the Christian trinity, as he is so eager to assume wherever a three appears. They are three archangels who attend the Merkabah.[22] Merkabah mysticism would indeed interpret "the Lord...the God of Israel" at Isa. 52.12 to mean angels.[23]

From the examples I have presented, the suggestion is clear that the Dura paintings are much closer to well-known patterns of Jewish mysticism and eschatology than they are to Philo's thought or to Goodenough's hypotheses. However, there is much in the paintings that is not preserved in extant rabbinic sources, so that the paintings constitute an invaluable source for Jewish attitudes in the Euphrates valley at the time of Rab. Whether Rab's direct influence is to be seen at Dura remains to be established. If Goodenough's shade survives to know the fate of his work, let it not be small in his eyes that in failing to make the point of *By Light, Light* he has cast a flood of light on the symbolic world of ancient Jews and that he may have opened the way to new light on the mystical and eschatological beliefs of the Babylonian rabbis and the ordinary Jews around them.

---

[20]See *By Light, Light*, p. 363; Scholem, *Major Trends*, p. 214, and *Ursprung und Anfänge der Kabbala* (Berlin, 1962), pp. 109-43.

[21]Similarly, the eleven jeweled ornaments on the ark (see I Chron. 28.18), in the scene on the north wall of "the ark in battle" may be Rab's eleven attributes of God's mercy (*Midrash Tehillim*, 93.8).

[22]Although in most accounts four archangels surround the Throne, there were traditions which counted only three archangels (Ginzberg, *Legends*, V. 70-71, n. 13). Alternatively, since not the heavenly but the earthly Merkabah, the ark (see the Hebrew text of I Chron. 28:18), is shown, the artist may have had reason to portray three angels instead of four. Uriel may be absent in the absence of the Temple cult (*Zohar*, III, 32b).

[23]Scholem, *Major Trends*, p. 363, n. 57; *Jewish Gnosticism*, pp. 43-55.

4

The Central Composition of the West Wall of the Synagogue of Dura-Europos

We grieve over the death of our teacher, Elias Bickerman, but he lives on not only in his scholarly works but also in us, his students, and in our works. I have repeatedly acknowledged my debt to him because so much of my research is built directly upon his. Our teacher's brilliance extended to interpreting enigmatic aspects of paintings on religious topics so as to cast light on what human beings did and believed in antiquity.[1] He made a significant contribution to the study of the paintings of the synagogue of Dura-Europos.[2] I am pleased to offer this article as one more tribute to him. In it I return to the paintings of the synagogue of Dura-Europos, a topic on which I began to publish long ago and promised to publish more.[3] Even now I shall treat only some of the paintings.

Archaeological and historical evidence shows that the town of Dura (or Europos as it was called by Macedonians and other speakers of Greek) in the third century C.E. was a heavily fortified Roman army

---

[1] E.g., His "Héliodore au temple de Jérusalem," in his *Studies in Jewish and Christian History*, Part II (Leiden: Brill, 1980), pp. 159-91; "Sur la théologie de l'art figuratif: à propos de l'ouvrage de E.R. Goodenough," *Syria* 44 (1967), 131-61.
[2] See his "Symbolism in the Dura Synagogue," *Harvard Theological Review* 58 (1965), 127-51. There is also his treatment of the synagogue in his review of *The Excavations at Dura-Europos: Preliminary report of Sixth Season of Work, October 1932 – March 1933*, ed. by M.I. Rostovtzeff, A.R. Bellinger, C. Hopkins, and C.B. Welles, *Syria* 18 (1937), 220-21.
[3] Began: in my review of *Jewish Symbols in the Greco-Roman Period*, Vols. IX-XI: *Symbolism in the Dura Synagogue*, by Erwin R. Goodenough, *JNES* 28 (1969), 212-18, reprinted above, No. 3. Promised: in the same review, above, p. 62.

post. Shapur I, king of Persia, the second ruler of the Sassanian dynasty, marched westward and upstream along the Euphrates River, seeking to reconquer the empire which had been held by the Old Persian Achaemenian dynasty until it fell to Alexander the Great in the 330s B.C.E.[4] The Roman force at Dura prepared well to resist. To enable the already strong western wall to resist enemy efforts to undermine it, the defenders filled the street adjacent to the wall with an earth embankment. At first they took care to protect the walls of the buildings along the street from the pressure of the embankment by buttressing them on the inside with packed earth, but finally they took off the roofs and filled the roofless walls with debris, further to thicken the defense-works. Even so, the city fell, possibly in 256 but more likely in 257, never to rise again. However, the burial of the buildings along the city wall preserved them and their paintings, including the synagogue.[5]

The synagogue with the paintings was an enlargement of an earlier structure. Inscribed ceiling tiles date the completion of the enlarged building to the second year of the Emperor Philip and the year 556 of the Seleucid Era (245/6 C.E.).[6] The paintings of the synagogue were executed between the completion of the enlarged building in 245/6 and some time when visitors who wrote in Middle Persian painted and dated their approving comments on the walls, perhaps in 253/4.[7]

The west wall of the synagogue was the one facing Jerusalem. In the center of that wall, just above the floor was the niche in which the Torah-scroll was kept. Like Daniel in Babylon-by-the-Euphrates (Dan. 6.11), the Jews in Dura-by-the-Euphrates prayed facing in the direction of Jerusalem. In so doing, they would see the paintings of the west wall and especially those in its center, above the Torah niche. Indeed, a symmetry in design and in concepts can be shown to exist in the paintings of the west wall, further directing the eye of the worshiper to the central composition above the niche.[8] By "central composition" I mean the four conspicuous portraits, each of a single standing man, and

---

[4]Clark Hopkins, *The Discovery of Dura-Europos* (New Haven and London, 1979), pp. 251, 261-64.
[5]*Ibid.*, pp. 239-49; Carl H. Kraeling, *The Synagogue* ("The Excavations at Dura-Europos," Final Report VIII, Part I; New Haven, 1956), pp. 4-5; David MacDonald, "Dating the Fall of Dura-Europos," *Historia* 35 (1986), 63-64.
[6]Kraeling, *Synagogue*, pp. 5-6, 263.
[7]Kraeling, *Synagogue*, pp. 291-92, 297-307; on the uncertainty of the dates of the painted comments in Middle Persian, see MacDonald, "Dating," *Historia* 35 (1986), 61-63.
[8]See for the present my review, above, pp. 59-62.

everything between them.[9] Erwin R. Goodenough called the area between the four portraits the "reredos"[10] (a name useful for its brevity). In the synagogue of Dura the central composition occupied a place similar to the mural decoration of the apse in the Christian churches of the fourth century and later.

Unfortunately, the reredos is not among the best-preserved portions of the paintings on the west wall. Upper parts of it were destroyed long before it was excavated. The ancient artist or artists[11] revised the reredos more than once, not by removing paint but by adding more, so that the composition had several layers of paint.[12] The excavators reported that the figures were at first clear, but exposure to sun, heat, and air almost immediately began to bring about cracking and fading. One result was that part of the lower layers became visible. The pictures are not frescoes painted on absorbent, still-wet plaster. Rather, the paint is powdery tempera which was brushed onto dry plaster, so that the layers of pigment even at the moment of application could readily mix with one another and may have mixed even more when Henry Pearson put a preservative varnish over the paintings. Pearson also partly restored them before setting them up permanently in the Damascus museum.[13] The work of a restorer may save what was originally there, but it may also represent merely what was in his imagination. No record remains to tell us precisely what Pearson did. Hence, the best evidence for the content of the reredos and, indeed, for all the paintings of the synagogue, is usually in the early photographs and drawings, especially the drawings of Herbert Gute.[14]

---

[9]See fig. 1, reproduced with the permission of the Princeton University Press from Goodenough, *Jewish Symbols in the Greco-Roman Period* (13 vols.; "Bollingen Series," XXXVII; New York, 1953-68), Vol. XI (1964), Pl. I (photograph by Fred Anderegg). On the central composition, see also Kraeling, *Synagogue*, pp. 62-64, 67, 214-29, with bibliography on pp. 215, 227; Goodenough, *Jewish Symbols*, IX, 78-123. Goodenough's visual observations of what is in the paintings are always valuable; as for interpreting their meaning, he is mostly correct on the four portraits and mostly wrong on the scenes of the reredos.
[10]*Ibid.*, IX, 78.
[11]From now on, I shall use the singular, leaving open the possibility that there was more than one painter.
[12]For the efforts of scholars to reconstruct the stages of the painting, see below, pp. 70-75.
[13]See Clark Hopkins, "The Excavation of the Dura Synagogue Paintings," in Joseph Gutmann (ed.), *The Dura-Europos Synagogue: a re-evaluation (1932-1972)* ("Religion and the Arts," I; Chambersburg, PA: American Academy of Religion and Society of Biblical Literature, 1973), pp. 15, 17.
[14]See Goodenough, IX, 78-79; Kraeling, *Synagogue*, p. 217.

All observers agree that first to be painted was the great "tree-vine," a tree with branches and leaves like a grapevine, but without grapes, which spread to the top of the reredos area.[15] At an early stage and perhaps from the beginning, at either side of the foot of the tree-vine was a set of objects, very faint now because both were later painted out. To the left was an ornate table with an elliptic object on top and a round object underneath it; to the right seemed to be a rampant pair of lions with perhaps a small crater behind them[16] or perhaps a table surface above them and a complicated structure between them.[17]

The two sets of objects at the foot of the tree-vine were painted out. Drawn right across the space occupied by them are two scenes: to the left, the dying Jacob blesses his twelve sons; to the right, he blesses his grandchildren, Ephraim and Manasseh, in the presence of their father, Joseph.[18] Just above those scenes, apparently painted across or amid the spreading branches of the tree-vine is a figure wearing the Phrygian cap and playing the lyre to a set of peacefully-listening wild beasts, clearly after the pattern of Greco-Roman portrayals of Orpheus. The lyre-player is at the left, with an eagle to the left of his head and the rest of the beasts standing to the right of him. Observers disagree on their number and identity, but not about the conspicuous lion in the center of the field.[19] Kraeling insists that the lyre-player sits upon a

---

[15]Fig. 6 is Gute's meticulous painting of the reredos as he saw it in 1933-34; on Gute's skill, see Hopkins, *Discovery*, pp. 180, 208, and Goodenough, IX, 79. Gute held that originally the tree may have grown out of a vase as in the later drawing (fig. 3) which he made on the basis of fig. 6 at Goodenough's request; Gute believed that he saw the handle of such a vase painted "on" (I think he meant "showing through") the left "rampant lion." If so, the vase necessarily was painted out when the "rampant lions" were put in. Goodenough quotes this view of Gute with approval (IX, 79). Nothing, however, compels us to take the trace observed by Gute as a vase-handle. The ancient Near Eastern parallels I shall bring below go far to refute Gute's conjecture. Fig. 5 shows the lower and middle sections of the reredos as sketched by Robert Du Mesnil du Buisson in 1932-33 (on his activity, see Hopkins, *Discovery*, pp. 119, 129-36, 211); probably Du Mesnil was much less accurate than Gute, but he drew during the year when the paintings were discovered, "when much may have been visible that later disappeared" (Goodenough, IX, 79). Figs. 2 and 4 were drawn by H. Pearson in 1934-35 to give his conception of the earliest design in the reredos. Figs. 2-6 are taken from Goodenough, XI, figs. 73-77, 323, with the permission of the Yale University Art Gallery, Dura-Europos Collection.
[16]Fig. 3 (Gute).
[17]Figs. 2 and 4 (Pearson).
[18]Fig. 6.
[19]See Robert Comte Du Mesnil du Buisson, *Les Peintures de la synagogue de Doura-Europos* ("Scripta Pontificii instituti biblici," 86; Roma, 1939), pp. 48-51; André Grabar, "Le Thème religieux des fresques de la Synagogue de Doura,"

Figure 1

Figure 2

Figure 3

Figure 4

Figure 5

throne and wears the costume of a Persian king, including the long-sleeved tunic ornamented down the front and at the hem with yellow bands, trousers similarly ornamented, soft white boots, and even the Phrygian cap, the same garb as is worn by King Ahasuerus and by Mordecai in the scene just to the left of the Torah-niche.[20]

Still higher, painted amid or across the branches and leaves of the tree-vine is an enthroned figure, clothed and posed as a Persian king, with two men in himation and striped chiton standing close by in front of him on either side. Grouped around the king and his two attendants are twelve or thirteen figures wearing Persian-style tunics and trousers. As seen by Gute, seven stand in a front row, in line with the two attendants, four to the left and three to the right; and in the back row, in a line on a level behind the king, three stand to the left and three to the right.

A schematic spiraling vine stem with grapes but without leaves frames all the paintings of the synagogue (except those of the bottom dado). The part of this border-pattern which separates the top two registers of paintings continues straight across the branches and leaves of the tree-vine on a line just above the centered lion and just below the

---

RHR 123 (1941), 170-72; Henri Stern, "The Orpheus in the Synagogue of Dura-Europos, *JWCI* 21 (1958), 1-6; Goodenough, IX, 89-93; Kraeling (*Synagogue*, pp. 223-25) agrees in part on the influence of the classical Orpheus figure on the designer of the reredos, but Kraeling has doubts based upon his conception of the stages by which the painting arose. Goodenough (IX, 92-93) and Stern ("Un Nouvel Orphée-David," *CRAI*, 1970, pp. 63-76) argued against Kraeling's skepticism, but Sister Charles Murray ("The Christian Orpheus," *CA* 26 [1977], 19-27) vigorously restated Kraeling's case against theirs. There can, however, be no doubt that the final composition of the reredos has too much in common with the classical Orpheus scene for the resemblance to be coincidental, and even Kraeling admitted that it influenced the designer. I hope my present article will settle the matter.

[20] *Synagogue*, pp. 223-24 (including n. 889); other observers fail to notice the throne or the ornamenting of the tunic. Du Mesnil (*Peintures*, p. 50) seems to agree that the lyre-player's apparel is royal but inaccurately asserts that the usual garb of Orpheus happens to be identical with the Persian royal costume. Stern is unsure that the throne is there (*JWCI* 21 [1958], 2); Moshe Barasch denies that the lyre-player is sitting upon it ("The David Mosaic at Gaza," *EI* 10 [1971], 97 [in Hebrew]). One should also note that as seen by Kraeling and Du Mesnil and perhaps by Gute, the lyre-player has the same posture with spread knees as do the kings in the other paintings of the synagogue. But the posture with spread knees is also typical of the classical Orpheus scene. See the examples presented or cited in Henri Stern, "La Mosaïque d'Orphée de Blanzy-lès-Fismes (Aisne)," *Gallia* 13 (1955), 41-77 (of the printed illustrations, only figs. 17 and 19 do not have Orpheus' knees spread), and R.M. Harrison, "An Orpheus Mosaic at Ptolemais in Cyrenaica," *JRS* 52 (1962), 13-18.

king's two attendants. It thus divides the reredos into an upper and a lower zone.[21] To the left and right of each zone of the reredos are two framed "wing-panels," each containing a picture of a standing man who wears a striped chiton and a fringed himation. The designer appreciated symmetry: though the arms of the men pictured vary in position, the legs are symmetrically posed in the two horizontal pairs, as are the removed boots of the two upper figures. An Aramaic label identifies the man in the upper right panel as "Moses son of Levi," and it is easy to recognize him as a portrayal of Moses at the burning bush (Exod. 3.1-5).[22]

In view of the nature of the powdery paint, it is not surprising that observers have disagreed on the order of painting, though all agree that a tree-vine was painted first and that the table and "rampant lions" and the things accessory to them stood early in the painting and were later painted out. Du Mesnil was at Dura when the paintings were discovered in 1932 and sketched them while they were fresh. He believed that the king and his two attendants and the surrounding figures in trousers were painted after the tree-vine and later still were covered over with vine-leaves in an effort to conceal them, supposedly in response to objections to the portrayal of human figures in a synagogue or to the apparent deification of the presumably-human king (in the pagan temples of Dura, a portrait of the deity to be worshiped occupies a comparable position).[23]

Carl H. Kraeling visited Dura briefly in 1934, but his two detailed accounts of the reredos were based upon his observation of the restored original as set up in Damascus, upon the early sketches and photographs, and upon his own consultations with Pearson.[24] In his first account, in *Report VI*, Kraeling expressed his belief that the original tree-vine had its branches spread in circular fashion to produce on high a vertical medallion, the upper part of which contained the enthroned king and his two attendants, whereas the lower part contained the lion and other animals. To the left and right of the trunk stood the table and the "rampant lions." Then, everything except the central medallion was painted out, covered with a red wash. The

---

[21]See fig. 6.
[22]See fig. 1, in which, however, the Aramaic label is not visible; on it, see Kraeling, *Synagogue*, pp. 229, 271.
[23]Du Mesnil at Dura: see n. 15; his observations: *Peintures*, pp. 27-28, 43-45, 48-52.
[24]Visit: Hopkins, *Discovery*, p. 215, and cf. Goodenough, IX, 79; detailed accounts: *Report VI*, pp. 367-71, and *Synagogue*, pp. 62-64, 67, 214-19. Bases: *Report VI*, p. 367, and *Synagogue*, p. 62 (n. 148), 214-19 *passim*, and Goodenough, IX, 79.

Figure 6

Figure 7

Figure 8

Figure 9

Figure 10

border pattern separating registers and scenes was drawn across the field. Above it, said Kraeling, nothing was left of the tree-vine. Thereafter, the figures in trousers were added around the king and his attendants, the "Orpheus" was drawn to the left of the animals, the blessing-scenes were put in to the right and left of the tree-vine, and the tree-vine itself seems to have been reinforced in a darker shade of green. The four flanking portraits, he implied, belong to this later stage, for he wrote that the underpainting ran at one point into the neighboring portrait panel.[25] Nevertheless, he admitted[26] that "the overpainting preserved most of the elements of the underpainting in some form or other." At this point Kraeling said nothing of what Du Mesnil observed as the effort to cover over the king and his attendants with vine-leaves.

Kraeling changed his mind on some topics in his later account. For one thing, he tried to explain the numerous holes which scar the surface of the reredos, mostly in the vicinity of the trunk of the tree-vine and its spreading branches.[27] He held that most of the holes received the wooden pegs supporting applied plaster rosettes, which supposedly represented blossoms on the tree-vine. Fragments of plaster rosettes were indeed found on the floor of the chamber. A few of the holes, he said, received the nails that anchored a canopy over the Torah shrine. According to him, the rosettes were removed when the tree-vine was entirely painted out by the red wash or "cover coat." If so, the craftsmen proceeded inconsistently: only three of the holes were filled in with plaster and painted over. The rest were left open and daubed heavily with the red wash.[28]

Nothing proves (or disproves) that there was a canopy over the Torah-niche. If the worshipers wanted one, it could have been attached even after the paintings were complete, at the price of covering up or defacing a small part of the lower reredos. Goodenough demolished Kraeling's theory on the holes and rosettes: "It is inconceivable that the rosettes taken from the tree painting would have been kept for several years lying on the synagogue floor." Nothing connects the rosettes with the tree-vine. They cannot have represented blossoms, for "[many of] the holes were made in the trunk or below the

---

[25]P. 367.
[26]P. 370.
[27]*Synagogue*, p. 63 and n. 152 there; p. 218, n. 862, and Pl. XXXIV with overleaf. Not all the holes can be connected with the tree. One cluster of them is far off to the lower right, near the upper paw of the right "rampant feline," and two single holes are off to the lower left, one by the right end of the couch supporting Jacob, another on the elliptic object resting on the table.
[28]*Ibid.*, p. 218, n. 862.

branches in spaces beside the trunk."[29] There is no evidence to tell us why and how the holes came to be there. Clearly the painter was usually not disturbed by their presence, for he applied his paint right over the open holes.

Kraeling's untenable theory on the holes and rosettes plus (unspecified) features of the distribution of the foliage drove him to abandon his earlier position, that the top of the original reredos showed within the spreading branches of the tree-vine a "medallion" containing the king and his two attendants and below them the lion and other animals. Rather, king, attendants, and lion were added in a second stage.[30] Indeed, the area around the king's left leg is painted over the three filled holes.

Kraeling now believed that the reredos in this second stage was not yet divided into two parts by the border pattern but it already was framed by the four flanking portraits in the "wing panels"; presumably the border pattern, too, framed both the reredos and each of the wing panels. Thereafter, Kraeling held, the canopy and rosettes were removed, the border pattern was drawn across the reredos, dividing it into 2 registers, and the table and the "rampant lions" at the lower left and the lower right were covered over with the red wash. Across the bottom of the reredos were drawn the two blessing scenes. At the top of the lower register, over the red wash, the lyre-player was painted to the left of the lion and, over his shoulder a large yellow bird, and perhaps other animals around the lion. Above the dividing border pattern, the figures in trousers were painted around the king.[31]

Kraeling was now aware of the confusing state of the reredos, which led Du Mesnil to suppose that vine-leaves were painted in a last stage to obscure objectionable human figures. According to Kraeling, the powdery paint tended to flake off the hard plaster and thus brought to light again the original tree and the symbols at its foot, and "It is possible that before the Synagogue was buried in the embankment, its elders, bowing to necessity, sanctioned a reintroduction of the tree design in the central area."[32]

Goodenough's superb powers of visual observation and painstaking efforts to seek out the best witnesses require that we present his views here. Rightly, he put greatest reliance on the careful copies which Gute, a good artist, made of the paintings in 1933-34, when they were

---

[29]IX, 83, n. 23.
[30]*Synagogue*, p. 218, n. 862.
[31]*Ibid.*, pp. 221-25.
[32]*Ibid.*, p. 227, n. 898.

still relatively fresh.[33] Goodenough believed that originally there was only the tree-vine, which perhaps grew out of a vase.[34] If the vase was ever there, it was then painted out, and the table and the rampant felines and their associated objects were put in.[35] Perhaps even then, perhaps a bit later, the king and his two attendants were painted directly across the upper branches of the tree-vine.[36] At about the same time, the lyre-player and the listening animals were drawn across the middle branches of the tree-vine as a single composition. If the lyre-player, unlike the lion, is painted over the red cover coat, Goodenough argues that the lion indeed was painted before that coat was put on, but the coat was applied almost immediately after the lion was painted, and for the purpose of accommodating the lyre-player.[37]

Disagreeing with Kraeling, Goodenough held that the tree-vine was never completely covered over: the red wash obliterated only the upper part of the tree-vine at either side of the king and his attendants and also the two original sets of figures at the foot of the trunk.[38] From that point on, Goodenough's descriptions of the insertion of the dividing border-pattern, the blessing scenes, and the standing figures in trousers substantially agree with Kraeling's.

We thus have important disagreements among competent observers. Did the designer of the reredos ever intend to have the tree-vine obliterated? Did he intend from the first to have the lyre-player be a part of the composition which included the lion? Were the worshipers ever so embarrassed by the figures of the king and the "Orpheus" that they wanted to obscure them by vine-leaves? The last question is easy to answer: the "repainted leaves" hide little if anything; the red wash shows how the painters could obliterate scenes if so ordered. If the reredos was objectionable, why were the four wing-panel portraits or the other paintings of the synagogue so acceptable that no vine-leaves were painted across them?

We should also ask, was the tree-vine ever intended to stand either alone or merely accompanied by the original figures at its base? The Torah contains an emphatic prohibition of planting "an asherah, any tree" by the altar of the LORD (Deut. 16.21). An asherah was a tree or

---

[33]See nn. 9, 15.
[34]See n. 15.
[35]Goodenough, IX, 79-81.
[36]*Ibid.*, pp. 83, 92 (par. 3).
[37]IX, 89-92. On the view of Sister Charles Murray, see n. 19.
[38]IX, 104.

stump representing a deity.[39] In a pagan shrine, an image of the god to be worshiped would occupy the reredos. A tree, an asherah, would seem to be inacceptable in a position where it could be taken as a representation of the LORD! One might reply that the synagogue of Dura is unique. Without it we never would have assumed that Jews could construe so loosely the prohibition on images in the Ten Commandments. Therefore, for the present we cannot exclude that originally the designer intended the reredos to contain little if anything more than the tree-vine.

Controversy reigns also in the discussions of the meaning of the compositions within the reredos and the wing-panels, though observers agree that Jacob's deathbed blessings stand at the foot of the reredos and the upper right wing-panel depicts Moses at the burning bush (an Aramaic label identifies him as "Moses son of Levi"). But who are the figures in the other three wing-panels? What is the meaning of the tree-vine, the painted-out figures at its base, the lyre-player and the animals, the king and his two attendants, and the standing figures in trousers?

I believe that despite the gaps in our information on the Jews in the third century C.E. we possess sufficient clues to solve these problems. Not all the paintings at Dura are enigmatic. Easily understood scenes, some identified by written captions,[40] strongly suggest that there is a scriptural basis for every one of the paintings. We know something of the aspirations of Jews of the time. We know something of how they read scripture as promising fulfilment of those aspirations. On the basis of that knowledge, I shall first (in Part II) suggest a straightforward interpretation of all the details of the reredos which ties them into a coherent whole. Then (in Parts III and IV), I shall confirm that interpretation and seek answers to the remaining problems of the reredos and wing-panels through a detailed study of the position of the paintings in the history of ancient Near Eastern and early Christian and Jewish art. In this manner I shall be able to identify and explain the enigmatic scenes of the central composition and shall demonstrate that the final plan of the reredos was from the first in the mind which directed the hands of the painter and that other factors than changes

---

[39] Asherah: Du Mesnil du Buisson, *Etudes sur les dieux phéniciens hérités par l'Empire romain* (Leiden, 1970), pp. 32, 58-59. See, however, Morton Smith, "The Image of God," *Bulletin of the John Rylands Library* 40 (1957-58), 497-512. Smith presents evidence to show that the seven-branched menorah and a similarly shaped tree were used as symbolic images of the God of the Jews. Even if he is right, the tree-vine of the Dura synagogue and its setting bear no resemblance to the examples presented by Smith.

[40] E.g., the Exodus scene at the top right of the west wall.

in the designer's intentions are responsible for the strange stages in the artist's execution of those intentions.

II. What Jewish Aspirations and Scriptural Interpretations Are Expressed in the Reredos?

From the first century B.C.E. on, Jewish beliefs in a Messiah descended from David who would rule over a liberated Israel become more and more evident.[41] Josephus passed in almost complete silence over such beliefs and their role in the Jewish revolt of 66-70 C.E., surely because they would have evoked the contempt and hostility of his Graeco-Roman audience. He took care, however, to assert that the crucial verse, Num. 24.17, was fulfilled, not by a Jewish monarch, but by Vespasian.[42] Furthermore, he published a version of his *Jewish War* in Aramaic and implied he did so with a view to the Jews living in Babylonia.[43] We may infer that he intended to counter their messianic hopes.[44]

The disastrous defeat of 70 C.E. did not put an end to the messianic hopes among the Jews, based as they were on irrevocable scriptural promises, as we can see from the books of II Baruch and IV Esdras and from statements ascribed to Tannaim. Perhaps messianic notions were involved in the rising of the Jews of Mesopotamia against Trajan.[45] Around 132 C.E. Rabbi 'Aqiba quoted the same Num. 24.17 as referring to Bar Kokheba and his revolt against the Romans.[46] The near silence of the Mishnah on messianic hopes suggests that its compiler, Rabbi Judah the Patriarch, working early in the third century C.E., wished to avoid the danger that faith in those hopes might lead to yet another disastrous war against hopeless odds. Surely the Patriarch continued to believe the irrevocable scriptural promises, but his Mishnah did not have to serve as a reminder of them. Otherwise, it is clear that the

---

[41]Beginning with Psalms of Solomon 17:21-43, 18:6-7. See n. 2 of my article, "How the Authors in I and II Maccabees Treated the 'Messianic' Promises," reprinted as Chap. 11 in this volume. See also the contributions of de Jonge, van der Woude, and Grundman to the article *"chriô ktl."* *Theological Dictionary of the New Testament,* ed. by Gerhard Kittel and Gerhard Friedrich (Grand Rapids, MI, 1964-76), IX (1974), 513-13, 515-16, 517-34, 537-50, 566-69, 572-73; Joseph Klausner's survey of the early rabbinic sources is convenient but antiquated (*The Messianic Idea in Israel* [New York, 1955], pp. 391-517).
[42]*BJ* vi 5.4.312-13.
[43]*BJ* i 1.1-4.3-12.
[44]Cf. however, Jacob Neusner, *A History of the Jews in Babylonia,* Vol. I (2nd printing, revised; Leiden, 1969), pp. 69-70.
[45]See *ibid.,* p. 78.
[46]*JT Ta'anit* 4:5, p. 68d, *Lam. Rabbah* on 2:2.

disastrous end of Bar Kokheba's revolt did not quench the fire of the messianic hopes among Jews in the Holy Land or in Mesopotamia.[47]

Several prophets predicted a last great war pitting the gentile powers against each other and/or the Chosen People.[48] By the first century C.E., this war, which would immediately precede the Messianic era, came to be called the "War of Gog and Magog," a name derived from a popular misreading of Ezek. 38.2, as if Gog and Magog were rival powers.[49] The superpowers of the period of the Dura synagogue were Rome and the Iranian empires, first that of the Parthians and then, after 224, that of the Sassanian Persian dynasty. The repeated clashes of the rival superpowers gave rise in the minds of Jews to the belief that the War of Gog and Magog would be a war between Rome and Parthia or Sassanian Persia.[50] All Mesopotamian Jewry lived near the theater of those wars, and Dura was a strategic Roman border post facing the rival power throughout the time that the Jews there could look at the paintings on the walls of their synagogue.

It is, then, a legitimate working hypothesis to assume that there is a messianic theme to the reredos. We shall find ample confirmation for that hypothesis in the rest of this article. Now let us examine the contents of the reredos.

The tree-vine is peculiar: though its branches and leaves are those of a grapevine, it has no fruit. The hands that painted the synagogue were obviously familiar with fruitbearing vines, for the border pattern consists of a spiral vine-stem with grapes. Du Mesnil and Goodenough insist that part of the tree-vine survived or was repainted into the

---

[47]See Neusner, I, pp. 85, 151 (n. 3), and Vol. II (Leiden, 1966), pp. 52-57, 71, 159-60, 167-68, 197, 205-6, 214 (n. 3), 238-40, 286. In this article I use "Mesopotamia" in the broad sense, to mean the entire Tigris-Euphrates valley, including both Dura and the area of dense Jewish settlement in Babylonia farther downstream.

[48]Ezek. 38, Joel 3:9-14, Hag. 2:22, Zech. 12:1-9, 14:2, 13.

[49]See Rev. 20:8, *Sibylline Oracles* iii 319-22; Klausner, pp. 375-76, 398, 401, 422, 450, 464, 496-501; and the statement of R. El'azar bar Abina at *Gen. Rabbah* 42:4. The scene of the "Ark in Battle" in the register above the Ezekiel sequence on the north wall of the Dura synagogue depicts the War of Gog and Magog, as I hope to demonstrate elsewhere. The painting shows a *drawn battle*, in which the powers dominating Israel are destroying each other while the people of the Torah stand by in quiet confidence and faith. For the present, in confirmation of my theory it is enough to contrast that scene with the cameo depicting the *victory* only a few years later of the Sassanian Shapur I over the Roman emperor Valerian (Roman Ghirshman, *Persian Art: the Parthian and Sassanian Dynasties* [New York, 1962], Pl. 195).

[50]Neusner, I, pp. 31 (n. 1), 84-85; cf. III (Leiden, 1968), 182, and IV (1969), 35, 53-54, 68, 319, 375.

final composition, and even Kraeling admitted that possibility. Yet the king and his attendants and the Orpheus were painted right across the tree-vine. Can we not infer that the designer intended those figures to be viewed as the fruit?

The vine grows up as if from the blessing scenes. We have our working hypothesis (that the paintings have a messianic theme); we know how the messianic texts of scripture were being read at the time of the Dura synagogue; we have access to how the Orpheus myth was interpreted then. On this basis we are led directly to the following provisional interpretation of the reredos.

The tree-vine symbolizes Israel and her destiny.[51] The tree-vine seems to sprout from the Torah-niche. At the end of the first book of the Torah, in Jacob's deathbed benedictions, the vine appears in a part of his blessing to Judah (Gen. 49.10-11) that was taken as a messianic prophecy, very likely already by the writer of Zech. 9.9.[52]

The first "fruit" to be displayed on the rising vine of Israel's destiny is the Orpheus scene, known to have been taken in the Graeco-Roman world as a symbol of the taming of the violent and savage forces in the world which peace-loving human beings long for.[53] The royal Orpheus image in the tree-vine rising from Jacob's blessing to Judah fits well the messianic prediction at Isa 11.1-9 of a royal "shoot from the trunk of Jesse" (father of David and descendant of Judah). With the coming of that "shoot" even carnivorous beasts will be tamed and will turn into harmless herbivores. Nothing is said in Isa 11 to indicate that the king's musical ability will be the force that tames the beasts. On the other hand, nothing in the Orpheus myth hints that Orpheus was a king, yet the lyre-player of the reredos probably sits on a throne and wears the same garb as Persian King Ahasuerus in the center left painting of the bottom register of the west wall.[54] Surely, then, the lyre-player is the king predicted by Isa. 11.1-9, with the image of

---

[51]See Jer. 2:21, Hos. 10:1, Ezek. 19:10-14, Psa. 80:9-20, and cf. Isa. 5:1-7. Babylonian Jews are reported to have recited the following prayer formula (based upon Psa. 80:9-11) which received the disapproval of rabbinic authorities: "A vine from Egypt our God brought out, and he drove out nations and planted it; he watered it with water from Sinai and with streams from Horeb. Blessed art Thou, O LORD, who lovest Israel" (B.M. Lewin, *Otzar ha-Gaonim* [Haifa, 5688=1928], Vol. I, Part I, p. 71, and Part II, p. 73). See also Kraeling, *Synagogue*, p. 63, n. 150.

[52]See *Gen. Rabbah* 98:8-9, 99:8, BT *Berakot* 57a, *Targum Onqelos* Gen. 49:10, LXX Gen. 49:10 (perhaps); Adolf Posnanski, *Schilo: Ein Beitrag zur Messiaslehre* (Leipzig, 1904-); Louis Ginzberg, *The Legends of the Jews* (7 vols.; Philadelphia, 1909-38), V, 367-68 (n. 388).

[53]Goodenough, IX, 93; Stern, *JWCI* 21 (1958), 4, and *CRAI*, 1970, pp. 78-79.

[54]See n. 20.

Orpheus' musicianship borrowed to symbolize the power by which that wonderful king's presence will tame the beasts.[55] Because one or more trees usually appeared in the pagan Orpheus scene,[56] the messianic figure symbolized by that scene and based upon Isa. 11.1-9 was all the more easily integrated into a composition tied together by a tree-vine.

To explain why there are two blessing scenes at the base of the tree-vine and why the king above is surrounded by 13 standing figures in the garb of Persian commoners, we need only bear in mind the stories of the strife between Joseph and his brothers in Genesis and the history of the rivalry between Israel and Judah in the books of Samuel and Kings and combine those two factors with Isa. 11.11-13. In many periods Jacob's descendants have been troubled by the propensity of their nation to to be split into quarreling factions.

The biblical narrative presents Jacob as foreseeing that the descendants of each of his sons will maintain a separate tribal identity (Gen. 49.3-26), though within the structure of a single nation (Gen. 49.2, 28). In the separate scene of his blessings to Joseph's sons, he foresaw a distinct glorious destiny for the Joseph tribes, especially Ephraim (Gen. 48.3-4, 9-22), even though he was to include them within the structure of the single nation (Gen. 49.22-26 in Gen. 49.1-28). Isa. 11.11-13 predicts that in the time of the wonderful king God himself will gather together the scattered tribes of Jacob's descendants; though Ephraim and Judah will continue to maintain their separate identities (and so, we may infer, will the tribes which follow the leadership of those two), the twelve or thirteen tribes will henceforth live together in harmony, an idea well symbolized by the twelve or thirteen subjects standing in obedient order around their king.

Nothing in scripture suggested that the prophetic promises[57] of the return of the "Lost Ten Tribes," the ones led by Ephraim, had been revoked. The Jews of Dura lived not far from the valley of the Habur river, to which the Lost Tribes had been exiled (2 Kgs. 17.6), and because of that fact were probably all the more conscious of the destiny promised by the prophets and by dying Jacob to Ephraim and to the tribes subordinated to his. Thus we can account for the appearance of

---

[55] When I announced this interpretation in my review, above, pp. 63-64, I was not aware that Henri Stern had elaborated it before me, in *JWCI* 21 (1958), 4-6. Stern, however, in his articles has not noted that the top scene of the reredos, the king and his subjects, also is derived from Isa. 11 (vss. 11-13).

[56] See the examples presented or cited in Stern, *Gallia* 13 (1955), 41-77, and Harrison, *JRS* 52 (1962), 13-18. Trees are also found in Christian Orpheus scenes; see Stern, "Orphée dans l'art paléochrétien," *CA* 23 (1974), 2, 4, 6, 8.

[57] E.g., Isa. 11:11-16, 27:12-13, Jer. 31, etc.

both sets of blessings at the base of the tree-vine and for the presence of all twelve or thirteen tribes around the messianic king at the top.[58]

We have now identified and explained all figures in the reredos except for the king's two attendants who are dressed in chiton and himation. A group of texts gave rise to the vine figure as a symbol for Israel and her destiny. Otherwise, however, the reredos is an illustration of only Gen. 49 and Isa. 11. We have yet to ascertain the meaning of the three wing panels other than the one at the upper right.

III. What Can the Jewish and Christian Art and Literature of the First Six Centuries Tell Us About the Enigmatic Aspects of the Reredos?

A. The Orpheus Composition

Dura was a provincial outpost with a relatively small Jewish community which can hardly have been distinguished for artistry and intellectuality. If its synagogue exhibits elaborate artistic and theological schemes, they must be derived from traditions formulated in centers culturally more favored, traditions which can be expected to have had their origins in times well before the mid-third century C.E. and to have persisted into times long after.[59]

Pieces of Jewish and Christian art have been discovered which strikingly confirm my interpretation of the Orpheus scene of the reredos and also cast light on the traditions which gave rise to it. Good articles by Henri Stern and Moshe Barasch have treated important aspects of this evidence.[60] However, there are still problems to be solved.

Outstanding among the discoveries is the mosaic of a royal Orpheus in the floor of the central nave, near the entrance, of the ancient

---

[58]Nothing in the reredos can be taken to symbolize the Messiah descended from Joseph who is found in rabbinic traditions (see Klausner, pp. 400-1, 483-501), so that those traditions can hardly explain the inclusion of Jacob's blessing of Joseph's sons (contrast A. Grabar, *RHR* 123 [1941], 168-69). Medieval Christian artists produced a parallel iconographic development based on Isa 11:1-10: the Tree of Jesse. See Arthur Watson, *The Early Iconography of the Tree of Jesse* (London, 1934). There are good reasons to hold that this parallel was entirely unconnected with the Dura reredos.

[59]Cf. Kraeling, *Synagogue*, pp. 321, 385-402; Heinz-Ludwig Hempel, "Zum Problem der Anfänge der AT-Illustration," *ZAW* 69 (1957), 120-29; Mary Lee Thompson, "Hypothetical Models of the Dura Paintings," in *The Dura-Europos Synagogue: a Re-evaluation (1932-1972)* ed. by Joseph Gutmann ("Religion and the Arts," 1; Missoula, Mont., 1973), pp. 31-77; André Grabar, *Martyrium* (Paris, 1946), II, 20, 116-17, 166-67, 233-34.

[60]Stern, *CRAI*, 1970, pp. 63-79, and "Orphée dans l'art paléochrétien," *CA* 23 (1974), 1-16; Barasch, *EI* 10 (1971), 94-99 (in Hebrew, with English summary on p. xi).

synagogue of Gaza. The mosaic is dated by an inscription to 508/9 C.E.[61] The Orpheus scene was fragmentary even when first discovered and photographed[62] and has suffered badly since. The royal lyre-player wears a jeweled diadem, a long, sleeved purple tunic, and a cloth-of-gold mantle. Around his head is a nimbus (halo). He sits upon an elaborate throne. The clothing, the throne, and the nimbus are typical of portrayals of Byzantine emperors. A Hebrew label, "David," identifies the king. To the right survive the front two thirds of a meekly listening lion and an undulating fragment which probably is an elephant's trunk but may perhaps be a snake.[63]

The mosaic of Gaza should be a decisive refutation of Kraeling's doubts[64] about the extent and integrity of the Orpheus composition in the Dura reredos.[65] Barasch rightly noted a peculiarity of the Gaza mosaic: numerous are artistic representations of Orpheus, a non-royal lyre-player, amid listening wild beasts; so are portrayals of enthroned kings and emperors playing musical instruments; rare indeed are portrayals of a royal lyre-player in the presence of listening beasts.[66] Stern took pains[67] (wrongly, I think) to dispute Kraeling's assertion that the "Orpheus" of the reredos is presented as a king. Barasch in his study made use of the article in which Stern presented this view. We may infer that Barasch agreed with Stern, and that is why he could assert that the Gaza mosaic is unusual as an "early example, perhaps the *only* one [italics mine]" in which the royal motif is mixed with what he calls the "pastoral," i.e., the (originally non-royal) Orpheus playing to beasts.[68] As we shall see, the Jewish, Christian, and Near Eastern parallels strongly confirm the view that the Dura "Orpheus," too, is royal. Scholars before me[69] have realized that a royal Orpheus

---

[61] Stern, *CRAI*, 1970, pp. 63-65.
[62] See fig. 7, reproduced from *Qadmoniot* 1 (1968), 124, with the permission of the Israel Exploration Society.
[63] Stern, *CRAI*, 1970, p. 70; Barasch, EI 10 (1971), 97.
[64] See above, 72-74, with n. 19.
[65] So Stern, *CRAI*, 1970, pp. 72-76, but see Sister Murray's view, cited in n. 19.
[66] *EI* 10 (1971), 95, with demonstration following in the remainder of the article.
[67] *JWCI* 21 (1958), 3-4; cf. Goodenough, IX, 93(last paragraph)-94.
[68] *EI* 10 (1971), 95.
[69] E.g., Du Mesnil, *Peintures*, p. 50; Stern, *JWCI* 21 (1958), 3. Furthermore, according to Stern (*ibid.*), the biblical David's instrument was the harp (Hebrew *kinnor*, Greek *kinyra*), not the lyre (Greek *lyra, kithara*). He is probably right about David in Byzantine iconography, but elsewhere the distinction cannot be pressed. At I Chron 25:1 the LXX renders Hebrew *kinnor* by *kinyra*; Aquila, by *kithara*; and Symmachus, by *lyra!* Similarly instructive are the differences of the three Greek translations at Psa. 90(91):3, 136(137):2, 146(147):7, and 150:3. See

playing to wild beasts cannot represent the "historical David" of the books of Samuel, Chronicles, and Psalms (including the apocryphal 11QPs^a 151A).[70] The David of those books is said to have played to God,[71] to men,[72] to sheep,[73] but not to wild beasts. Far from taming wild beasts, that David claims to have killed them.[74]

Hence, despite the label in the Gaza mosaic, the royal Orpheus there cannot represent the historical David. Rather, he is the Messiah predicted in Isa. 11.1-9.[75] The Messiah, too, will be called "David" and may indeed be the resurrected King David himself.[76] We shall find repeatedly, in the Jewish and Christian art from the third century C.E. well into the middle ages, important scenes that primarily depict, not the historical figures of the biblical narratives, but eschatological personalities.

It would, indeed, have been impolitic for Jews of Gaza, living under the Christian Eastern Roman Empire, to have labeled the mosaic depicting their Messiah with the Hebrew word *Māšīaḥ* ("Messiah"). The Messiah of the Jews was supposed to put an end to the Roman Empire! It was much safer to label him, correctly but ambiguously, as David. Thus, at provincial Dura in the mid-third century C.E., Jews were using the figure of the messianic royal Orpheus, and Jews at Gaza were still using that figure in the sixth. Clearly the persistent figure

---

also Paul Corby Finney, "Orpheus-David: a Connection in Iconography between Greco-Roman Judaism and Early Christianity?" *JJA* 5 (1978), 7, n. 5.

[70] For the text, see James A. Sanders (ed.), *The Psalms Scroll of Qumrqan Cave 11 (11QPs^a)* ("Discoveries in the Judaean Desert of Jordan," IV; Oxford, 1965), pp. 49, 54-60. The reading and meaning of vss. 2-3 are a matter of controversy. See my review of Sanders' edition, *JNES* 26 (1967); Finney, *JJA* 5 (1978), 13, n. 22; and Frank Moore Cross, "David, Orpheus, and Psalm 151:3-4," *BASOR* 231 (Oct., 1978), 69-71. Whatever the correct reading in vss. 2-3, there would still be nothing of Orpheus in the piece, any more than there is in Psa. 148:6-9. David, the shepherd, plays before sheep, not wild beasts. He tames nothing. The sheep do no more than the domestic animals in Psa. 148:9.

[71] Psa. 57:9, 71:22, 108:3.

[72] 1 Sam. 16:16-23.

[73] 11QPs^a 151A.

[74] 1 Sam. 17:34-36.

[75] See above, 79-80. One should not object to having the Messiah appear in two scenes of the reredos (cf. the objection of Stern *JWCI* 21 [1958], 3, par. 6, to Kraeling's suggestion that David appears twice). Isa. 11:1-9 and Isa. 11:11-13 are separated by a space in the Masoretic Text; even without the space, verses 1-9 and 11-13 easily lead to two separate scenes. Jacob, too, appears in two scenes of the reredos.

[76] Jer. 30:9, Ezek. 34:23-24; BT *Sanh.* 98b.

must have been created before the mid-third century at some more favored center of Judaism.

No other examples are known of the use of Orpheus in Jewish art, but Christians, too, saw messianic prophecy in Isa. 11.1-9. If Jews could use Orpheus to represent their Messiah, could not Christians do so, too, to represent their Christ? Indeed, they did!

A very important early piece of evidence has not been cited in this connection, probably because of Stern's mostly-correct reluctance to attribute Orpheus compositions of the fourth and fifth centuries to Christians unless there is positive evidence.[77] The Orpheus mosaic at Ptolemais in Cyrenaica shows the lyre-player surrounded by wild beasts. He wears the usual Phrygian cap, but around his head also is a blue nimbus. He wears a dark red chlamys, pinned over his right shoulder and falling to the ankles, and bright yellow slippers. R.M. Harrison, who published the mosaic,[78] remarked on how not only the costume and the nimbus but also the formal posture of the lyre-player (in contrast to his casual pose in all other Orpheus scenes known to Harrison) were identical to the costume and posture of Theodosius I and his sons on a silver diptych of 388 C.E.[79]

Indeed, the "dark red" of the chlamys is probably the imperial purple, and the bright yellow of the slippers probably represents cloth-of-gold. Harrison dates the mosaic to the late fourth or early fifth century.[80] The Orpheus of Ptolemais thus is an example of the royal or imperial Orpheus from the age of Theodosius I and his sons, when the Roman Empire was thoroughly Christian, including Cyrenaica. There are no other pagan examples of the royal Orpheus. I see no reason to doubt that the mosaic of Ptolemais is Christian.[81] Two and one half centuries younger than the Dura reredos, it is the earliest Christian example of the royal Orpheus known to me.

Despite the destruction that must have been perpetrated by iconoclasts, significant remnants survive of Christian representations of the messianic royal Orpheus, dating from the fifth through the early seventh century. Some of them bear captions which show conclusively

---

[77] See *CA* 23 (1974), 1, 14(last paragraph)-16.

[78] *JRS* 52 (1962), 13-18.

[79] *Ibid.*, pp. 16-17. On the imperial or royal connotations of the nimbus, see Adolf Krücke, *Der Nimbus und verwandte Attribute in der frühchristlichen Kunst* ("Zur Kunstgeschichte des Auslandes," Heft XXXV; Strassburg, 1905), pp. 72-73.

[80] *JRS* 52 (1962), 16.

[81] Cf. Harrison, *ibid.*, pp. 17-18.

that the figure is derived from Isa. 11.1-9.[82] David as the royal Orpheus charming the wild beasts is also attested in the Qur'ân and in the commentary on it by Tabari (838-923 C.E.) and, a century later, by the Persian author Hujviri.[83] We can assume that Muhammad and the Muslims took the figure from Christians.

Jewish and Christian use of the Orpheus figure has been a puzzle for scholars. The Jewish examples at Dura and Gaza both came as surprises. Specialists in early Christian art have long asked, "Why is Orpheus the only figure from Greek mythology that appears uninterpolated, without Christian window-dressing, in the pictorial repertoire of the third and fourth century Christianity?"[84]

For us, the question should be rephrased, because the Jewish Orpheus figure and many instances of the Christian one differ from the pagan in an important respect: those Jewish and Christian examples have a *royal* lyre-player. We have seen how Jews and Christians could come to adopt Orpheus and his beasts and transform him into the royal lyre-player to represent the Messiah of Isa. 11.1-9. This, indeed, is the sole pathway known to me by which Jews and Christians could come naturally to use Orpheus as they used no other figure in pagan mythology.[85]

There is a series of non-royal Christian Orpheus scenes, on walls of catacombs at Rome and on sculptured sarcophagi in Italy and Sardinia. The series begins ca. 220 C.E., before the time of the Dura synagogue, and extends down to ca. 400. On six of these nine pieces (including the earliest one, the catacomb painting of ca. 220) the lyre-player is shown only amid peaceful animals like sheep, goats, inoffensive birds, or a domestic dog. Two catacomb paintings show Orpheus amid the classical mixture of carnivorous beasts and peaceful herbivores and birds. Stern refused to commit himself on yet another catacomb painting, of which the section which probably contained quadrupeds has been destroyed, but since it shows a (carnivorous) eagle, we may assume that it had the classical mixture.[86]

---

[82]See Stern, *JWCI* 21 (1958), 4-6; for further details and dates, see R. de Vaux, "Une Mosaïque byzantine à Ma'in (Transjordanie)," *RB* 47 (1938), 227-58 and Plates, esp. pp. 223-34, 256, and Pl. XI, 1; Doro Levi, *Antioch Mosaic Pavements* (Princeton, 1947), pp. 359-60.

[83]Stern, *CRAI*, 1970, p. 77. On some medieval Byzantine texts and illuminations, see below.

[84]Finney, *JJA* 5 (1958), 15; cf. Stern, *CA* 23 (1974), 8, 15.

[85]On the unlikelihood of other proposed pathways of art and literature by which Jews and Christians might have come to use Orpheus, see Stern, *CA* 23 (1974), 8-12.

[86]Stern, *CA* 23 (1974), 1-8.

We ask again, why was early Christian art hospitable to Orpheus as it was to no other figure from pagan mythology? Furthermore, the tamed wild beasts could hardly be objectionable to peace-loving Christians. Why, then, are carnivores excluded from some of the scenes? These questions can be answered if the Orpheus scene first entered Christian art through the royal Messiah figure of Isa. 11.1-9. Once that had happened, even the non-royal Orpheus could represent the Messiah who tames the beasts. We have seen that the royal Orpheus for Jews could be David himself. For Christians, the non-royal Orpheus could be young David, ancestor of Jesus the Christ, prefiguring his glorious descendant. Young David was no king; he was both shepherd and musician. Scripture says nothing of his playing to wild beasts, and 11QPs^a 151A says he played to sheep; either or both of these facts would account for the absence of carnivores from six of the Christian scenes. If our reasoning is correct, the nine Christian scenes attest the existence of the royal messianic Orpheus from ca. 220, from a time earlier than the Dura synagogue.

The earliest example of the royal Orpheus known to us is the Jewish figure at Dura. The Christian non-royal examples allow us to push the origin of the figure back toward the late second century, a period at which it is extremely difficult to believe that Jews would borrow from the harried and despised Christians. Did Jews invent the royal Orpheus, and did Christians take him from them? Did the adherents of the two religions invent him independently? Stern argued well for the view that Christians took him from Jews.[87] We shall find clear signs that Christians borrowed from the Jewish artistic traditions which gave rise to the scene at the top of the reredos, and those borrowings would lend further plausibility to Stern's view. Nevertheless, there is no direct evidence. No examples of the royal Orpheus have been found in the catacombs or on the Christian sarcophagi. Stern's view is thus attractive but not proved.[88]

Once the Orpheus figure was naturalized in Christian art, it could be confused with that of the Good Shepherd or with that of the king-musician (who is not shown with wild beasts and was originally entirely distinct from Orpheus).[89] In this manner we can understand some Byzantine illuminations cited by Stern,[90] six of which show David playing to human figures and sheep and a dog, and three of which show Orpheus surrounded by the classical mixture of carnivorous

---

[87] *CA* 23 (1974), 12-15.
[88] Cf. Finney, *JJA* 8(1978), 8-15.
[89] Barasch, *EI* 10 (1971), 97-99.
[90] *CA* 23 (1974), 14.

The Central Composition of the West Wall

and harmless animals. The two musicians are similarly attired; each has a nimbus around his head and plays a harp, not a lyre. Similarly, Georgios Pisides, deacon of Saint Sophia in Constantinople in the early seventh century, addressing God in a poem calls the Psalmist David "Thy Orpheus," and five centuries later, Euthymios Zigabenos in his introduction to his commentary on the Psalms calls David "our Orpheus...the shepherd...and prophet and king."[91]

B. The Wing Panels and the Top of the Reredos

The theological and artistic schemes known to us through the topmost part of the Dura reredos and through the wing panels had still more vivid reverberations in Christian art, reverberations which enable us to identify enigmatic parts of the central composition. The paintings of the Christian building at Dura contribute nothing to the understanding of the central composition of the synagogue. Few are the early decorated churches which survived the ravages of time and iconoclasts. Outstanding among those survivors are a set of basilicas from the reign of Justinian in the sixth century C.E.: the church of St. Mary at the monastery of St. Catherine on Mount Sinai, that of San Vitale at Ravenna, and that of San Apollinare in Classe, which in the sixth century stood in a suburb of Ravenna.[92]

I am not the first to notice that in the church at the monastery on Mount Sinai there is a repetition of a pattern of the Dura synagogue which is too precise to be a coincidence: over the apse mosaic, to the left there is a mosaic of Moses at the burning bush, and to the right there is one of Moses receiving the Ten Commandments from the hand of God above.[93] The mutilated upper left panel at Dura is indeed easily

---

[91]*Ibid.*, pp. 12-14; the correct references to the sources are Georgios Pisides, *Hexaemeron* 90-91, *PG*, XCII, 1438, and Euthymios Zigabenos, *PG*, CXXVIII, 41.

[92]On the date, 549, of the apse-mosaic of San Apollinare in Classe, see Erich Dinkler, *Das Apsismosaik von S. Apollinare in Classe* ("Wissenschaftliche Abhandlungen der Arbeitsgemeinschaft für Forschung des Landes Nordrhein-Westfalen"; Köln und Opladen, 1964), 12-14, 21-22. Inscriptions date the apse-mosaic of Mount Sinai between 548 and 565 (*ibid.*, 26). Dinkler's book is excellent. Had he perceived the parallels between San Apollinare and the Dura synagogue, he might have left no room for my present article.

[93]See figs. 8 and 9, reproduced with the permission of the University of Michigan Press from George H. Forsyth and Kurt Weitzmann, *The Monastery of Saint Catherine at Mount Sinai: the Church and Fortress of Justinian* (Ann Arbor, 1973), Plates CXXVI and CXXVII. Previous recognition that the Moses panels of the church stand in the same tradition as the wing panels of Dura: André Grabar, *Martyrium: Recherches sur le culte des reliques et l'art chrétien antique* (2 vols.; Paris, 1943-46), II, 116-17, 166-67; *CA* 5 (1951), 10; Forsyth-Weitzmann, 15.

restorable as a picture of Moses receiving the Torah or the Ten Commandments.[94] Greek- and Coptic-speaking Christians read from left to right; the Aramaic-speaking Jews of Dura read from right to left. Hence, the reversal of left and right in the disposition of the scenes is just what one would expect.

Again, at Mount Sinai in both pictures Moses wears himation and striped chiton. As at Dura there is a partial symmetry: Moses at the bush stands at the left of the panel and looks to the right, while his arms slant down to the right toward his left foot, from which he is removing the shoe; Moses receiving the Commandments stands at the right of the panel and looks to the left, while his arms slant up to the left to receive the tables. As at Dura, the figure in the panel horizontally opposite to Moses at the burning bush is barefoot. Though nothing is said in Exod. 19.18-20.15 about the removal of shoes, one would assume that Moses learned from his experience reported in Exod. 3.2-5 to remove his shoes at the holy place of Mount Sinai.

There is another close parallel to this same pattern in the church of San Vitale.[95] The main body of the church is an octagon, to the eastern side of which is attached the U-shaped structure of the presbyterium (the space containing the altar) and apse. On the south wall of the presbyterium, by the pillar immediately adjoining the apse, is a picture of Moses (identified by a Latin label) removing his shoes at flaming Mount Sinai as he looks up leftward toward the hand of God. No burning bush is shown, so that the scene probably represents Exod 20.18 rather than, or in addition to, Exod. 3.2-5. Directly below this scene of Moses is another of him as a shepherd tending the flock of his father-in-law. On the north wall of the presbyterium, by the pillar immediately adjoining the apse, is a labeled picture of Moses on Mount Sinai receiving a scroll from the hand of God, which is above him to the right.[96] Directly below this scene of Moses is a depiction of white- and black-bearded men standing at the foot of the mountain; we may assume they represent the Israelites (Exod. 19.17-25). All three of these Moseses have a nimbus and wear the himation and the striped chiton.

---

[94]Kraeling, *Synagogue*, 230-33; Goodenough, IX, 112. At Sinai Moses received not only the tablets of the Ten Commandments (Exod. 32:15-16) but also the scroll of the Book of the Covenant, the Torah (Exod. 24:7).

[95]Noticed first by Georg Kretschmar, "Ein Beitrag zur Frage nach dem Verhältnis zwischen jüdischer und christlicher Kunst in der Antike" in *Abraham unser Vater: Festschrift für Otto Michel* (Leiden, 1963), 303-8, reprinted in *No Graven Images: Studies in Art and the Hebrew Bible*, ed. Joseph Gutmann (New York, 1971), 164-69. My description follows Kretschmar's.

[96]On the scroll, see n. 94.

The Central Composition of the West Wall

Should we not recognize at Dura, at Mount Sinai, and at Ravenna a shared tradition of religious art, one which frames the central composition with pictures of Moses? Should we not complete the headless picture in the upper left panel at Dura so as to make him a Moses receiving the tablets of the Ten Commandments or the scroll of the Torah from the hand of God? Should we not assume that the rectangular space around the head in the Dura wing panels has the same function as the nimbus at San Vitale?[97] Should we not assume that as at San Vitale, so at Dura, the four wing panels either show Moses or a scene associated with him?[98]

We should! But my predecessors have not observed the full extent of how the traditions exhibited in the synagogue of Dura controlled the central compositions of our three important sixth-century churches.[99] In fact, not only the framing Moses-scenes but also the main apse-mosaics of the churches stand in the same tradition as the central composition at Dura! There are good reasons why scholars have not perceived the connection. On the one hand, the apse-mosaics at Mount Sinai and at San Apollinare are clearly based upon the Transfiguration story from the New Testament (Matt. 17.1-9, Mark 9.2-10, Luke 9.28-36), so that one might not think of looking for a Jewish prototype. On the other hand, at San Vitale one cannot view the Moses-scenes on the walls of

---

[97] See n. 79.

[98] See Goodenough's arguments (IX, 110-18) for taking all four figures in the wing panels as Moses. I believe that at Dura figures in fringed himation and striped chiton are either angels or prophets; see for the present Goodenough, IX, 126-27, 159-62. The evidence at San Vitale is ambiguous, because at the west end of the north and south walls of the presbyterium appear labeled pictures of Jeremiah proffering an open scroll (cf. Jer. 36) and of Isaiah holding a closed one (cf. Isa. 8:16). Both prophets wear the himation and the striped chiton. Could not these scenes suggest that the men in the two lower wing panels of Dura are not Moses but some other prophet?

In fact, however, the evidence from San Vitale helps confirm Goodenough's arguments for identifying the men in the two lower wing panels as Moses. The scrolls in the hands of the Isaiah and the Jeremiah at San Vitale are quite different from the one in the lower right wing panel at Dura. Jeremiah proffers his scroll; the figure at Dura reads from his. Goodenough is wrong when he says (IX, 114) that Jeremiah at San Vitale reads his scroll "in the same mystic pose" as the man in the Dura wing panel. If the scroll in that panel does not fit Isaiah or Jeremiah or Ezekiel (who ate his: Ezek. 2:9-3:3), how can the prophet who holds it and reads from it be anyone but Moses? As Goodenough recognized (IX, 115-18), the fact that three of the four wing panels represent Moses makes it probable that the lower left panel, too, represents him, at the time of his death.

[99] Kretschmar in *Festschrift Michel*, 307-13, came closest; cf. A. Grabar, *Martyrium*, II, 164-67.

the presbyterium simultaneously with the apse-composition, which shows the Christ as *kosmokrator*, as king enthroned upon the world sphere, a type drawn from Roman imperial iconography, needing no Jewish antecedents.[100]

The strands of tradition which gave rise to the Transfiguration story are intricate and matter for controversy, and I cannot treat them in detail here.[101] Whatever other purposes the versions of the Transfiguration in the three Synoptic Gospels may serve, in their settings they have the function of validating the claim that Jesus was the Messiah against the evidence of events that might seem to prove otherwise.[102]

In Matthew and Mark Jesus strangely imposes temporary secrecy upon Peter, James, and John concerning what they have witnessed; in Luke, just as strangely, the three, without being so commanded, tell no one of what they have seen. In the passage which follows immediately in Matthew (17.10-13) and Mark (9.11-13), Jesus' own disciples seem to object to this imposition of silence, asking, "Why, then, do the scribes say that Elijah must first come?" Luke appears to have found the disciples' question and Jesus' answer superfluous and omitted both, very likely because he had already told in 1.17 of John the Baptist as a reincarnation of Elijah. The narrative in all three versions is very strange if it was not written against the background of a belief that when the Messiah came (surely a public event!), Elijah and Moses would be with him.[103] By the Transfiguration story, early Christians could claim that Elijah and Moses had indeed come with Jesus, but the witnesses to their coming long had said nothing of it, and, if that fact seemed strange, Matthew and Mark ascribed it to the Christ's own command.

The belief in the coming of Elijah to usher in the messianic age is well known and has its origin in Mal. 3.23. That prophecy itself surely drew on the fact that Elijah is not reported to have died but to have

---

[100]See Carl-Otto Nordström, *Ravennastudien* ("Figura," 4; Stockholm, 1953), Tafel 22b and 89 (with n. 3).

[101]See the commentaries to the passages in Matthew, Mark, and Luke and Morton Smith, "The Origin and History of the Transfiguration Story," *Union Seminary Quarterly Review* 35, 1 (Fall, 1980), 39-44.

[102]See the passages which immediately precede the story (Matt. 16:13-28, Mark 8:27-9:1, Luke 9:18-27).

[103]Cf. Rev. 11:3-15, where verse 6 shows that the two witnesses are Elijah, who shut up the sky and stopped the rain in the time of King Ahab, and Moses, who brought plagues upon Egypt, and see Howard M. Teeple, *The Mosaic Eschatological Prophet* ("JBL Monograph Series," Vol. X; Philadelphia, 1957), 8, 44, 108-9.

ridden up to heaven in a fiery chariot (1 Kgs. 2.1-11).[104] Moses' death and burial, however, are recorded in Deut. 34.5-6. But prophets had promised a miraculous Second Exodus, and surely someone would function as its Moses.[105] Believers in resurrection would have no trouble having Moses himself return to usher in the messianic era; doubters of resurrection could look forward to a second Moses just as they could to a second David.[106] The expectations that a Moses would be active in the messianic age could also find support in Deut. 18.15-18. Jews so much desired the first Moses to be able, like Elijah, to return without having to be resurrected, that they created stories about Moses' assumption alive into heaven.[107] Now let us look at the apses of Mount Sinai and San Apollinare. In the center at Mount Sinai[108] stands Jesus the Christ, shown in a radiant mandorla (almond-shaped enclosure),[109] with a radiant nimbus around his head. A set of medallions surrounds the entire scene of the apse. In the medallion directly above Jesus is a luminous cross. In the medallion directly below him are the head and shoulders of King David, Jesus' ancestor in Christian belief. King David is shown clothed as a Byzantine emperor, with the facial features of the emperor Justinian, who was reigning when the mosaic was made.[110] To say the least, then, Jesus the Christ is portrayed with splendor equal to the royal or the imperial. To the left of him stands a man in himation and striped chiton, labeled in Greek as Elijah. To the right of Jesus stands another, similarly dressed, labeled as Moses. Kneeling or crouching near Jesus' feet are John, Peter, and James, the three disciples who witnessed the Transfiguration.

More complicated is the apse-mosaic at San Apollinare.[111] Let us first consider its aspects which have obvious parallels at Mount Sinai. In the center of the apse at San Apollinare, where Jesus stands at Mount Sinai, is a jewel-studded Latin cross of gold, set upon a star-spangled night-sky-blue circular background which itself is surrounded by a red jewel-studded gloriole. At least the upper parts of the gloriole and its contents appear to be floating among clouds, though its bottom may touch the ground. At the junction of the beams of the cross is a bust of the

---

[104]See *ibid.*, 3-9 (sources cited from Apocrypha, Pseudepigrapha, Rabbinic Literature, and New Testament).
[105]See *ibid.*, 29-31.
[106]See *ibid.*, 43-48, 63-68, 74-93, 100-1, 107, 120-21, and above, n. 76.
[107]See *ibid.*, 41-43.
[108]See fig. 10, reproduced with the permission of the University of Michigan Press from Forsyth-Weitzmann, Pl. CIII. Cf. the description of Dinkler, 26-27.
[109]On the mandorla or aureole, see A. Grabar, *Martyrium*, II, 191-93.
[110]See Forsyth-Weitzmann, 15.
[111]See fig. 11, and cf. the description of Dinkler, 18-19.

Christ. Dinkler presents evidence that emperors and members of their families were the first to have their portraits set thus at the junction of the beams of a cross. He holds that there is no earlier example known of placing a picture of the Christ himself in that position.[112] Just above the top of the vertical beam is the Greek word *ICHTHYS* ("fish"), acronym in Greek for "Jesus Christ, Son of God, Savior." Just below the bottom of the vertical beam are the Latin words *Salus Mundi* ("Salvation of the World").[113] To the left and right of the horizontal beam of the cross are the alpha and omega of Rev. 22.13. Surely the cross is shown in more than royal splendor. High in the clouds above the cross is the hand of God.

To the left of the gloriole is a man shown only from the waist up, for the lower part of his body is immersed in the clouds. He wears a himation and a striped chiton and is labeled in Latin as Moses. To the right of the gloriole stands a similar figure, labeled as Elijah. Below, in a predominantly green landscape, studded with trees and flowering bushes, the three disciples who witnessed the Transfiguration are symbolized by three lambs. Such sheep-figures are common in Jewish biblical and post-biblical books, where human Israelites led by figures who are superhuman in some sense (kings by divine right, prophets speaking in God's name, or God Himself) are described as sheep under the care of a shepherd.[114] The image persists in the New Testament[115] and is quick to appear in early Christian art.[116]

Let us pause to assemble our clues. We know that Jews and early Christians believed that when the Messiah came, Moses and Elijah would accompany him. At both Dura and Mount Sinai we have Moses-scenes framing a depiction of a royal personality flanked by two figures in himation and striped chiton. At Mount Sinai the royal personality is the Messiah of the Christians. San Apollinare lacks the framing Moses-scenes, but the same two figures flank the royal cross. At both Mount Sinai and San Apollinare the flanking figures are labeled as Moses and Elijah. Surely then, in the synagogue of Dura, three centuries earlier than the two churches, the king is the Messiah of the Jews, and the flanking figures are Moses and Elijah. The same pattern seems to

---

[112]See Dinkler, 64-68. Grabar in his review of Dinkler, *CA* 15 (1965), 275-76, disputes these assertions.
[113]But see Dinkler, 68-71.
[114]E.g., Num. 27:17, Jer. 23:1-22, 50:6, Ezek. 34, Mic. 5:3, 7:14, Psa. 79:13, 95:7, 100:3, 1 Enoch 89:12-90:36.
[115]E.g., at Matt. 25:31-32, 26:31, Mark 14:27, Luke 12:32, John 10:1-16, 26-27, Rev. 7:17.
[116]See Dinkler, 73-75, esp. 75, n. 147.

Figure 11

Figure 12

Figure 13

have influenced the presbyterium and apse of San Vitale. There, too, Moses-scenes frame the apse, but the apse shows a royal Christ enthroned upon a world-sphere, flanked by nameless winged angels (wearing himation and striped chiton!), not by Moses and Elijah.

Here, then, is confirmation (if confirmation were needed) for identifying the king at the top of the Dura reredos with the Messiah of the Jews. We may guess that when the Dura reredos was complete the hand of God appeared above the Messiah as it does at San Apollinare. Here, too, we have the key allowing us to identify the flanking figures in himation and striped chiton at Dura as Moses and Elijah.

There is more to be learned from the apses of Mount Sinai and San Apollinare. In San Apollinare we have noted the tree-studded landscape in which stand the three white lambs who symbolize the disciples who witnessed the Transfiguration; nothing in the scene either at San Apollinare or at Mount Sinai suggests a mountain. In the Gospel accounts, however, the Transfiguration occurs on a mountain, and nothing is said of trees or bushes. At San Apollinare in the lowest level of the green landscape, axially below the jeweled cross, stands a man shown frontally, with a nimbus around his head, clothed as a bishop, in a pose of prayer, with his palms spread upward. A label identifies him as Saint Apollinaris, the saint over whose grave the church was built and for whom the church was named. Converging on the saint from the left and from the right stand symmetrically drawn lines of six lambs each. There would be no room for Saint Apollinaris in a literal representation of the Transfiguration, for he was not present at the event. There also would seem to be no room for a group of twelve at the Transfiguration, for only three disciples witnessed it. If the twelve lambs represented the disciples, Peter, John, and James would be shown twice, for no ascertainable reason.[117] We thus conclude that the lambs do not represent the disciples.

Now let us look at the apse on Mount Sinai. Clearly the artist knew how to show a mountainous background for his two Moses-scenes, yet he fails to show a mountain for the Transfiguration. This apse does not show a group of twelve, but it probably represents an extension of a tradition which displayed a twelve to accompany the scene of the royal Messiah: "It is a traditional feature of apse and bema compositions to depict the *twelve apostles* [italics mine] in framing medallion busts....In Sinai, the framing apostle series is very closely integrated thematically with the Metamorphosis [=Transfiguration] in that the three disciples of the Tabor scene are not repeated in the medallions but replaced by the two evangelists, Luke and Mark, and by

---

[117]See Dinkler, 73, n. 143.

Matthias. Moreover, the witnesses of the New Dispensation are supplemented at the bottom by those of the Old, i.e., by the major and minor prophets, to whom the bust of David is added in the center."[118]

Let us proceed to confront the puzzling aspects of the apses and to consider those puzzles in the light of the suggestive parallels between the apses and the central composition at Dura. Scholars have recognized that a long tradition must lie behind the artistic maturity and complicated symbolism even of the composition at Mount Sinai; all the more must a long tradition lie behind the much more complicated mosaic at San Apollinare.[119] Yet study of the remains of earlier and later Christian art reveals no clues to Christian antecedents adequate to produce the two apses.[120]

Here is a first puzzle. Another is the absence of any suggestion of a mountain from the two apses which purport to portray the Transfiguration; there is no trace of a mountain, either, in the Dura reredos. Is it possible that the tree-vine of the Dura reredos is paralleled by the tree- and bush-studded green landscape of San Apollinare, of which there is no suggestion in the Transfiguration narratives? The apses and the Dura reredos all have a group of twelve or thirteen associated with the messianic central scene. Again let us note that the Dura paintings are three centuries older than the apses. Should we not assume that the apses represent Christian adaptations of the Jewish iconographic tradition reflected at Dura and of the theological scheme symbolized by it? We should! But we should also pay due attention to some important insights of Erich Dinkler and correct an error of his.

For Jews the Messiah comes only once. The scene at the top of the Dura reredos is necessarily an eschatological one. Dinkler has demonstrated that the jeweled cross at San Apollinare, the luminous cross over the head of Jesus at Mount Sinai, indeed the Transfiguration scene in both churches with no hint of a mountain, and the Christ enthroned between two angels at San Vitale – all allude to the eschatological scene of the *Parousia*, the Second Coming of the Christ.[121] The partial immersion of Moses and Elijah in the clouds at San Apollinare also probably alludes more to the Messiah's final coming "with the clouds of heaven" (Dan 7.13 and its New Testament parallels), than to the total disappearance of Moses and Elijah in the

---

[118]Forsyth-Weitzmann, 13.
[119]See Dinkler, 28-29.
[120]*Ibid.*, 28-48, 112. For a refutation of the efforts of Grabar and Nordström to reconstruct Christian prototypes from surviving clues, see *ibid.*, 106-12.
[121]*Ibid.*, 87-100, 112-17.

cloud of the Transfiguration story. If there are allusions to the Transfiguration in San Apollinare and at Mount Sinai, it is because the Transfiguration prefigures the Second Coming. Thus, the royal Messiah and his attendants serve the same function at Dura and in the Christian apses. If Christians here borrowed an originally Jewish composition portraying the eschatological messianic king, they Christianized the scene by adding to it the three witnesses of the prefiguring Transfiguration.

Let us turn now to the group of twelve or thirteen portrayed at Dura and at San Apollinare and still hinted at in the apse on Mount Sinai. At Dura the assembled twelve or thirteen portray the fulfilment of Isa. 11.11-13. That prophecy did not loom so large for Christians as it did for Jews. Christians lacked the acute consciousness of being an exiled, dispersed, and bitterly divided nation consisting of twelve or thirteen tribes. Christians just might have symbolized the fulfilment of Isa. 11.11-13, but that passage mentions only Ephraim (i.e., the Northern Kingdom of Israel) and Judah, so that Christians might have used only two figures. We are about to see why they probably would not have used twelve.

A Christian eschatological source, Rev. 7.4-8, indeed was available to bring a depiction of the twelve tribes into a scene of the Second Coming. But Rev. 7.4-8 is only part of a longer description. In Rev. 7.4-9 a vast host of gentiles joins the surviving members of the twelve tribes. If Christian artists had created for themselves a depiction of Rev. 7.4-9, with or without allusions to Isa. 11.11-13, they would not have used twelve or thirteen figures but more. Indeed, a Christian artist of ca. 830 did precisely that in the Utrecht Psalter, where there is an illustration to accompany the "Psalm" of Isa. 12. The biblical text itself says that chapter is to be recited on the day of the fulfilment of Isa. 11.1-16! The artist showed the Christ standing in a mandorla high on the peak of a mountain, with a nimbus around his head, flanked by Moses and Elijah, with the three disciple-witnesses of the Transfiguration shown below, while large throngs of members of the True Israel converge on the scene from both sides.[122]

Parenthetically, let us observe that the Utrecht Psalter strongly suggests that the tradition known from the Dura reredos, which connects the scene of the messianic king and his two attendants with Isa. 11.11-13, was still alive in ca. 830.

Thus, the twelve lambs cannot represent the twelve apostles, nor, if the composition is originally Christian, could they represent the scene

---

[122] See *ibid.*, 44-46.

of Rev. 7.4-9.[123] However, if the composition already existed among Jews, Christians could take it and Christianize its interpretation by referring to Rev. 7.4-8. We must consider carefully alternative possibilities by which Christian artists could have produced the twelve in the apse-scene. Must they have borrowed the twelve from the Jewish iconography exemplified at Dura?

At Dura the twelve or thirteen stood by or even amid the branches of the tree-vine.[124] In our interpretation, the scene of the king and his subjects is a fruit of the tree-vine. The remains of early Christian art contain nothing to suggest that Christians used the tree-vine as a symbol. Rather, for Christians the vine symbolizes the Christ himself and thus can hardly represent the stock from which the Christ will sprout.[125] Trees are no part of the versions of the Transfiguration story. On the other hand, in Christian belief the Tree of Life will appear at the Great Consummation, near the "throne of God and of the Lamb"; there will be multiple Trees of Life, for they will grow "on this side and on that side" of the river of the Water of Life; they will bear "twelve kinds of fruit" yielding fruit every month, "and the leaves of the Tree are for the healing of the nations" (Rev. 22.2). The trees at San Apollinare show no fruit, and the sheep do not feed on them. Thus, the scene of Rev. 22.2 contributes nothing to an understanding of the trees in the apse of San Apollinare.

Dinkler, however, found a Christian text which connects the Transfiguration with a garden containing permanently-green trees and never-wilting flowers, in which dwell the departed souls of the righteous. The text is a pseudepigraphon, the Apocalypse of Peter, which has been dated to the mid-second century.[126] Of it a longer version survives in Greek, and a shorter version survives in Ethiopic. The Ethiopic text begins with a mention of how the eschatological cross will appear in heaven as a sign of the Second Coming.[127] Later,[128] the Ethiopic text turns to tell of the day of the Transfiguration. According to the Greek text, as the disciples (despite the three of the Synoptic Gospels, the Greek text of the Apocalypse of Peter gives their number

---

[123]Noteworthy is Dinkler's perplexity, at 102-3.

[124]The fact is no longer easy to see in fig. 1, and certainly is not shown in figs. 2, 3, 5, and 6, but it is implied by the proportions of fig. 4 and of Kraeling, *Synagogue*, Pl. XXXIII.

[125]John 15:1-16. See Goodenough, VI (1956), 53. On tree symbolism in early Christian art, see *ibid.*, VII (1958), 118-21.

[126]Dinkler, 90-95.

[127]Sec. 1, translated at Dinkler, 91.

[128]Secs. 15-16, translated at Dinkler, 92-93.

as twelve!)[129] were going up the mountain with Jesus, they asked him to show them their departed righteous brethren. Their request is not reported in the Ethiopic version. However, in both the Greek and the Ethiopic text, after the appearance of the two glorious figures (identified in the Ethiopic version as Moses and Elijah), Jesus showed the disciples a garden containing trees, and in it were dwelling throngs of the righteous dead.[130]

According to Dinkler, the Apocalypse of Peter has the Transfiguration, the eschatological cross, and a garden with trees: if it presents such striking parallels to the apse at San Apollinare, at the very least, it must be one of the sources for the apse of San Apollinare. But even if we follow the Greek version of the text, we cannot derive from it three plus twelve lambs. Dinkler himself notes that the Ethiopic version is the one which contains the most striking parallels to the apse of San Apollinare. Though we have evidence that the Apocalyse of Peter was being read in Italy in the sixth century, nothing tells us which version was known there.[131]

Dinkler himself views the twelve lambs as the righteous departed, resident in the garden.[132] But even if we invoke Rev. 7.4-8, it is hard to see why there should be twelve of them. Furthermore, they are displayed as lambs, in the same manner as the three witnesses of the Transfiguration. The three mortal witnesses were alive at the time of the Transfiguration and will be resurrected to view the Second Coming. It is thus difficult to regard the twelve lambs as the souls of the righteous departed. Moreover, Dinkler himself demonstrated that the figure of St. Apollinaris is an integral part of the composition, though it could have no place in a literal depiction of the Transfiguration: the saint is depicted as the intercessor for the faithful at the Last Judgment which will accompany the Second Coming.[133] The two rows of six lambs look to the saint. Surely the artist must have intended them to represent the living (or resurrected) faithful Christians at the time of the Second Coming, not the souls of the blessed departed. The lambs stand at the edge of the garden, either newly admitted inside through the saint's intercession or hoping to be.

---

[129]Their number is not specified in the Ethiopic text.
[130]In the Greek text the two figures with Jesus at the Transfiguration are not identified as Moses and Elijah but as the righteous departed brethren, and a more detailed description is given of the garden.
[131]See Dinkler, 90, 94-95.
[132]103.
[133]Dinkler, 100-2.

Neither the Ethiopic nor the Greek version of the Apocalypse of Peter says that the three disciple-witnesses entered the garden; they were only shown it, whereas the apse-mosaic has the three witness-lambs standing well within it. Thus, the portrayal of the three lambs is at variance with the Apocalypse of Peter, and the twelve lambs cannot represent the souls of the departed. The parallels between the apse and the Apocalypse can no longer be said to be striking. Indeed, though both versions of the Apocalypse say there were "blessed fruits" upon the trees, no fruits are shown in the mosaic. We are left with no Christian text which could have led a Christian artist to create the twelve lambs and their background.

But Jews long before had begun to portray twelve or thirteen subjects around the messianic king and the tree-vine, and Christian artists could adopt that pattern. Indeed, at Dura the twelve or thirteen at Dura are dressed as commoners, in contrast to the superhuman Messiah, Moses, and Elijah. Just so, the artist of San Apollinare portrayed the twelve representative Christian subjects of the returned Christ as lambs looking to the intercession of St. Apollinaris, in contrast to the saint, the Christ, Moses, and Elijah, who are shown as glorified human beings.

As for the garden, Dinkler takes for granted that it is Paradise,[134] but nothng proves that it is. The garden lacks the four rivers of Gen. 2.10-14 which elsewhere identify Paradise in Christian art,[135] and we have noted repeatedly that the trees show no fruit. The tree vine at Dura, too, has no grapes. In Christian symbolism there was no place for a tree-vine, with or without grapes. If Christians borrowed the iconographic tradition exemplified in the Dura reredos, they might transform the tree-vine into a garden with trees, as a place for the assembling of mankind at the feet of the Messiah at the Second Coming.[136] Whatever the meaning of the garden, the three witness-

---

[134] 19, 95, 103.

[135] See Dinkler, 53 (n. 90), 60, 115-16, and Abb. 22.

[136] Cf. 1 Enoch 90:20. Can the garden be Paradise after all, patterned after the Elysian Fields of Vergil and the Apocalypse of Peter (cf. Dinkler, 91, 93, 95), with the three lambs standing within it to represent the three resurrected witness-disciples at the Second Coming? I do not think so. One would have expected the resurrected Sts. Peter, John, and James to be shown, not as lambs, but with status at least equal to that of St. Apollinaris.

In the Ascension scene among the Salerno ivories (of ca. 1080), at the top four angels bear the aureole containing the enthroned and nimbed Christ. At the bottom stand the twelve apostles around the Virgin Mary, who has a nimbus around her head. Touching the top of that nimbus and growing up to touch the bottom of the aureole containing the Christ is a vine bearing grapes. See Robert P. Bergman, *The Salerno Ivories: Ars Sacra from Medieval Amalfi*

lambs stand in it only because it is not in heaven. They are shown perhaps for the purpose of Christianizing the scene and certainly for the purpose of alluding to the prefiguring event, the Transfiguration, which occurred when the witnesses were mere mortals; therefore they appear as lambs.

From our study of the Church mosaics and the reredos and wing panels of the Dura synagogue we can draw inferences about both the Christian and the Jewish compositions. Very strong are our inferences using the Christian parallels to identify mysterious or ambiguous figures at Dura. In the reredos, the king and his two attendants are the Messiah, Moses, and Elijah. All four figures in the wing panels represent Moses, as Goodenough argued.[137] In the upper right panel Moses stands at the burning bush; in the upper left, he receives the revelation (the tablets of the Ten Commandments or the scroll of the Torah); in the lower right, he reads the Torah to the Israelites (Exod. 24.7); in the lower left, he stands on the day of or at the very moment of his death.

Why do these scenes of Moses frame the picture of the tree-vine of Israel and its messianic fruit? More than one answer can be suggested. Does the scheme allude to the fact that Moses tended the vine of Israel during the crucial early stages of its growth?[138] Nothing in the pictures suggests that Moses was a vinedresser. Alternatively, the Moses-scenes may celebrate the divine revelations and promises which warned Israel away from sin and made it possible for the vine to grow: the promise of the departure from Egypt, the revelation of God's law to Moses, Moses' service of teaching it to Israel, and Moses' last admonitory prophecies (Deut. 32.1-47, 33.1-29). Perhaps the Moses-scenes in the wing panels are to be viewed as the protecting fence around Israel, God's vine.

Our comparative study of the central composition of the Dura synagogue and the Christian apses has certainly added to our understanding of the former. Can we not say that it has also added to

---

(Cambridge, MA, and London, England, 1980), fig. 38 (the Ascension scene) and 87-90 (the date). Interpreters have been hard put to explain the symbolism (see Josef Wilpert, *Die römischen Mosaiken und Malereien der kirchlichen Bauten vom IV. bis XIII. Jahrhundert* [2d ed.; Freiburg im Breisgau, 1917], II, 911; Goodenough, VII, 146-47; Bergman, 74). Can we see in this piece of mediaeval Christian art Christians still adopting the iconographic tradition exemplified in the Dura reredos and transforming the tree-vine, in this instance by giving it grapes because a grapeless vine seemed pointless?

[137] See n. 98.

[138] Cf. the prayer quoted above, n. 51.

our understanding of the latter? The great puzzle of the apses is finding how and where their complicated symbolism could have evolved. There are too many parallels between the apses and the tradition exemplified in the synagogue for the resemblance to be coincidental: Moses-scenes which frame, prominent trees, central subject with royal splendor flanked by prophets or angels in himation and chiton, and groups of twelve portrayed as of subordinate status. The synagogue was unquestionably earlier and built at a time when Jews could not have borrowed iconographic symbolism from Christians. In those cases where the apses differ from the Dura pattern, we have explained how the Christian artist could have proceeded to modify the Jewish scheme. We can thus propose with considerable confidence that the artists of the Christian apses drew upon the tradition exemplified in the Dura synagogue.

One piece of evidence is missing from our sources: nothing tells us how the Jewish pattern came to be adopted by Christians. André Grabar and Nordström indeed have argued that Palestinian Christian prototypes lie behind the Christian apses,[139] and Christians in Palestine are known to have learned from Jews; certainly Origen, Epiphanius, and Jerome did. Dinkler's arguments[140] discounting the evidence presented by Grabar and Nordström have weight, but their view may be true even if their evidence is questionable. Do the facts as we have them allow any inferences? Is it an accident of the chance survival of pieces of Christian art from the ravages of time and iconoclasts that the striking parallels for the central composition of the synagogue are in churches of the sixth century? Or that the earliest known Christian example of the royal Orpheus dates from the late fourth or early fifth century? One can imagine circumstances which could give rise to that chronology.

Figured art appears suddenly in the archaeological remains of Jewish Palestine. It hardly existed there among Jews during the first centuries B.C.E. and C.E. The Palestinian Talmud reports that wall-painting began in the times of Rabbi Yohanan (third century C.E.) and the making of floor mosaics in those of Rabbi Abbun (first half of the fourth century) and adds that both practices were tolerated.[141] Nothing tells us why Palestinian Jews began to have figured art or

---

[139] A. Grabar, *Martyrium*, II, 129-206; Nordström, 125-27.
[140] See above, n. 120.
[141] *'Abodah zarah* 3:3, 42d; 4:1, 43d, in the version published by J.N. Epstein ("Lisridey ha-yerušalmī," Tarbiẓ 3 [5692=1931-32], 20). I see no reason to doubt this testimony. Probably none of the synagogues in Jewish Palestine with figured carvings should be dated to the second century.

when and why Jews of Mesopotamia began to put paintings on the walls of their synagogues or whether Dura was one of the earliest examples there. There were iconoclasts even among the worshipers at the Dura synagogue, as one can tell from the fact that in the lowest rows of paintings eyes have been gouged out.[142] Iconoclasm eventually became the predominant view among Jews, though there were still synagogues with figured mosaics in the sixth century. Attractive symbols, rejected by Jews more and more in the fifth and sixth centuries, by that very fact might have become all the more attractive to Christians. Unemployed Jewish artists might become converts to Christianity and use their old iconography on behalf of their new faith. Strange as it seems, Jewish artists are known to have produced products for religious use by pagans,[143] so that even without being converted Jewish artists could have brought their own iconography into the decoration of Christian churches!

We have argued that Christians Christianized iconographic patterns that were originally Jewish. We are about to see how Jewish designers may have used the Moses-scenes to Judaize a reredos which, though Jewish in its entirety, still was composed of elements which were all originally pagan.

V. What Can the Royal Art of the Ancient Near East Tell Us about the Reredos?

Some problems of the reredos remain unsolved. What were the figures which originally stood in the space of the two blessings of Jacob, and why were they painted out? One can understand how Israel could be symbolized by a vine, but vines do not have the form of a tree. Why does the reredos have at its core the unnatural figure of a tree of which the branches and leaves are those of a vine? I believe we can solve these problems and confirm parts of our theory by studying the reredos in the context of ancient Near Eastern art.

My own research (now reinforced by articles of Dalia Levit-Tawil) has led me to an assumption which I believe to be very fruitful for understanding the paintings of the Dura synagogue: they draw heavily upon the matured patterns of the royal art of the *Sassanian* Persian dynasty.[144] This important path to understanding the paintings of the

---

[142]See Goodenough, IX, 23-24.

[143]See E.E. Urbach, "The Rabbinical Laws of Idolatry in the Second and Third Centuries in the Light of Archaeological and Historical Facts," *IEJ* 9 (1959), 158-65.

[144]Dalia Tawil, "The Purim Panel at Dura in the Light of Parthian and Sasanian Art," *JNES* 38 (1979), 93-109; Dalia Levit-Tawil, "The Enthroned King Ahasuerus

Dura synagogue has been largely neglected, but for seemingly good reasons. The Sassanian empire began in 226. The synagogue was built in 245/6. From 164 (long before 226!) until the destruction of Dura (probably in 257), with the possible exception of one brief interruption in 253, the city was a Roman army post, foreign to the Sassanian empire if not hostile to it. Rather than Sassanian patterns, would not one expect to see at Dura Greco-Roman ones and those of the Parthian empire, which held Dura before 164 and fell to the Sassanians as late as 226?[145]

The excavators were astonished at the extent to which those expectations are proved false. Within the Roman base of Dura there was considerable interest in the Sassanian empire and in its artistic patterns.[146] The synagogue is especially remarkable for the way it displays friendly interest in Persia. Jews long had good reason to look

---

at Dura in Light of the Iconography of Kingship in Iran," *BASOR* 250 (1983), 57-78. For one of the clues I myself discovered, see n. 49. I announced my assumption publicly on March 6, 1975, at the Oriental Institute of the University of Chicago when I presented my paper, "The Synagogue of Dura-Europos Reinterpreted: a Palace for God and for the Messiah," as a Lester Aronberg Judaica Lecture.

[145]On the history of Dura, see Hopkins, *Discovery*, 257-64; MacDonald, "Dating," *Historia* 35 (1986), 45-68. As an example of the prevailing view, see Ann Perkins, *The Art of Dura Europos* (Oxford, 1973), 62, 73 (n. 1), 121-26. For her, the art of Dura reflects mostly Parthian influence, with some admixture of Greek. She barely mentions Sassanian art and then only as a continuator of the Parthian, not as a precedent for Dura. Cf. Daniel Schlumberger, *L'Orient hellénisé* (Paris, 1970), p. 111; he holds that the artists of Dura followed the patterns of Parthian art and were insensible both to the currents of the Mediterranean world and to those of the rising Sassanian realm.

[146]See Michael I. Rostovtzeff, "Dura and the Problem of Parthian Art," *YCS* 5 (1935), 263-66, 272, 283-88, and especially B. Goldman and A.M.G. Little, "The Beginning of Sasanian Painting and Dura-Europos," *Iranica Antiqua* 15 (1980), 283-98. MacDonald ("Dating", *Historia*, 35 [1986], 54-61) raises valid points against the arguments which Rostovtzeff, Goldman, and Little base upon the "Battle Mural," but those points do not affect other evidence of Sassanian influences, especially that in the paintings of the synagogue.

toward Persia and her kings as liberators.[147] Benevolent King Ahasuerus is displayed prominently adjacent to the Torah niche of the synagogue. Rome and Persia were not constantly at war. Subjects of the Sassanian Shapur I visited the synagogue, and in Middle Persian they painted on its walls their approval of its pictures as late as 254.[148] Between 226 and the time in 245/6 when the walls of the synagogue were ready for decoration, there were enough intervals of peace to allow interested parties to learn the new patterns of Sassanian art.[149]

Those patterns were quick to mature, as we can tell from the rock reliefs and coins of Ardashir I (226-240) and Shapur I (240-72).[150] Our inadequate information and the fragmentary character of what survives can make it difficult to define what, beyond the rock reliefs and the coins, is Sassanian.[151] There is much to be learned about the synagogue paintings if we can assume that they reflect Sassanian rather than Parthian art. A distinctive feature of Sassanian royal art, marking it off from the Parthian, is the strong effort visible in the Sassanian to return to earlier patterns of Near Eastern (as opposed to Greek) art. In Daniel Schlumberger's felicitous expression, the Sassanian developments were a "renaissance."[152] The themes we are about to study will give abundant illustration of that fact.

Characteristic of the wall decoration of the synagogue and of the pagan painted temples of Dura is its organization in registers, in

---

[147]2 Chr. 36:32, Ezra, Neh., Isa. 44:28, 45:1-5; Josephus *BJ* 1.13.1(248)-16.6(317) and *AJ* 14.13.3(330)-15.7(434); *Ekha rabbati* (= *Lam. rabbah*) 1:41 to Lam. 1:3, BT *Sanhedrin* 98a-b. Though the scene of the "Battle of Gog and Magog" in the Dura synagogue (see above, n. 49) shows the Romans and the Persians destroying each other, it seems that the designer was not equally hostile to both sides. One horseman rides a black horse, very likely to symbolize the more disliked power (for Jews, even in Dura, that was Rome!), and one rides a white horse, very likely to symbolize more benevolent Persia (the Babylonian amora, Rab, a contemporary of the Dura synagogue, could find sins enough in Persia to justify her fall [BT *Yoma* 10a]). Can we believe that the Jews of Roman Dura could be so audacious as to show even relative favor to Persia? The subversive meaning of the scene would not be obvious to Romans unless explained to them.

[148]See n. 7.

[149]Cf. Hopkins, pp. 261-62.

[150]See Ghirshman, *Persian Art*, 122-66, 245-46.

[151]See Oleg Grabar, "An Introduction to the Art of Sasanian Silver," in *Sassanian Silver: Late Antique and Early Mediaeval Arts of Luxury from Iran* (Ann Arbor, MI, 1967), 19-84. Cf. Daniel Schlumberger, "Sur l'origine et sur la nature de l'art des Sassanides," in Huitième Congrès international d'archéologie classique (Paris, 1963), *Le Rayonnement des civilisations grecque et romaine sur les cultures périphériques* (Paris, 1965), 567, 576.

[152]*Ibid.*, 570-76.

multiple parallel bands. This is not the easiest scheme to use and is not found everywhere in the ancient world.[153] It does have significant parallels in the royal art of the ancient Near East, in which registered compositions were used to decorate palaces and temples and utensils made for the use of kings and utensils made for the use of commoners but depicting kings. The phenomenon goes back to the dynasties of Sumer (of the third millennium B.C.E.) and continues through the kings of Babylonia and Assyria and through the Achaemenian and Sassanian dynasties of Iran, with a very few examples known from the Parthian dynasty.[154]

Reliefs and murals are somewhat conspicuous by their absence from descriptions of ancient Near Eastern temples. There may have been many temple murals which could not survive the ravages of time. But in the monumental architecture of Assyria and Babylonia, temple architecture was identical or similar to palace architecture.[155] Moreover, the palace there was not a secular building. Indeed, an Assyrian palace was the residence of the king who was the high priest of the god Ashur.[156]

---

[153]See Kraeling, *Synagogue*, pp. 68-69; Rostovtzeff (*YCS* 5 [1935], 211-12, 242-47) is sure that it is not Greek in origin.

[154]For good surveys of the phenomenon of registered art, see Ann Perkins, "Narration in Babylonian Art," *AJA* 61 (1957), 54-62 and Plates 17-20 (includes Sumerian examples); Hans G. Güterbock, "Narration in Anatolian, Syrian, and Assyrian Art," *ibid.*, 62-71 and Plates 21-26. Güterbock rightly treats the bowls with concentric banded reliefs as a phenomenon parallel to the decoration of palace walls. Cf. Robert L. Alexander, "The Royal Hunt," *Archaeology* 16 (1963), 243-50. A good Assyrian example of registered palace reliefs is reconstructed in Pauline Albenda, "Landscape Bas-Reliefs in the *Bit-Hilani* of Ashurbanipal," *BASOR* 224 (Dec., 1976), 49-72, 225 (Feb., 1977), 29-48. Achaemenian examples: Roman Ghirshman, *The Arts of Ancient Iran From Its Origins to the Time of Alexander the Great* (New York, 1964), 160-65 (fig. 211), 198 (fig. 246), 201 (fig. 248), 204 (fig. 254), 231-32 (figs. 279-80). Few Parthian examples have been found; see Ghirshman, *Persian Art*, 48 (fig. 61; but is it Parthian?), 55 (fig. 68). Sassanian rock-reliefs: *ibid.*, pp. 153-54 (fig. 196), 158 (fig. 200), 184 (fig. 225), 192 (fig. 235); Sassanian silver: *ibid.*, 206 (fig. 245), and Ghirshman, "Notes iraniennes, V: Scènes de banquet sur l'argenterie sassanide," *Artibus Asiae* 16 (1953), 66-69 and figs. 16-17; painting in Sassanian style in house at Dura: Rostovtzeff, *YCS* 5 (1935), 285, in the context of 283-88. Even the dado below the three bands of narrative paintings in the Dura synagogue has Assyrian parallels. See F. Thureau-Dangin and Maurice Dunand, *Til-Barsib* (Paris, 1936), Plates XLVI, XLVII; André Parrot, *The Arts of Assyria* (New York, 1961), 4 (fig. 7), 99 (fig. 108).

[155]See A. Leo Oppenheim, *Ancient Mesopotamia: Portrait of a dead Civilization* (Chicago and London, 1964), 326-28.

[156]*Ibid.*, 99-100.

The Central Composition of the West Wall

Central to the Dura reredos is the tree-vine. There are parallels in the royal art of the ancient Near East. A sacred tree could occupy the center of the scene in the royal art of Assyria[157] and Achaemenian Persia,[158] as could a vine in that of the Sassanians.[159] Trees could also be important in framing symbolic royal scenes.[160] Vines, with or without supporting trees could be important parts of compositions in Assyrian, Achaemenian, and Sassanian art.[161] There are clear Sassanian examples of the unnatural tree-vine.[162]

From early dynastic Sumer down to the Muslim conquests and beyond, a small number of themes dominated the royal art of the empires of the Tigris-Euphrates valley. First, there was the legitimacy of the king, symbolized by scenes in which he receives the tokens of his office from divine figures. An Old Babylonian painting of an investiture survives from the eighteenth century B.C.E., as part of a composition in registers. It shows the king of Mari receiving the staff and circle, symbolic of rule, from the hands of the goddess Ishtar, in the presence of another god and goddess. The king stands *between* the two goddesses.[163]

An Assyrian painting of an investiture survives from the reign of Sargon II (721-705 B.C.E.), again as part of a composition in registers. It shows the god at the left handing the ring-sceptre to the king; the king stands *between* the god and a high official.[164] Before we leave the Semitic Assyro-Babylonians, we should look at another pattern of asserting the king's legitimacy, of which I can cite one example: two male figures (priests, I think), bring King Nabû-apla-iddina of

---

[157]Parrot, *Assyria*, 14 (fig. 16), 162 (fig. 205).
[158]See Samuel K. Eddy, *The King is Dead: Studies in the Near Eastern Resistance to Hellenism, 334-31 B.C.* (Lincoln, NE, 1961), 28-29.
[159]Edith Porada, *The Art of Ancient Iran: Pre-Islamic Cultures* (New York, 1965), 215 (Pl. 58), with description on p. 213.
[160]Trees frame the registered composition at Mari (Parrot, *Syria* 18 [1937], 341-45) and the cylinder seal of Darius I (Ghirshman, *Ancient Iran*, 268 [fig. 329]).
[161]On the tree-with-vine in the banqueting relief of Ashurbanipal and its later parallels, see below. See also *Sassanian Silver*, nos. 24 (discussed, p. 66), 45 (discussed, p. 73).
[162]*Ibid.*, no. 51 (described, p. 73); Ghirshman, *Artibus Asiae* 16 (1953), 67 (fig. 17).
[163]See André Parrot, "Les Peintures du palais de Mari," *Syria* 18 (1937), 335-39.
[164]Parrot, *Assyria*, 99 (fig. 108). The painting was found in Room 12 of Residence K at Khorsabad. The building was described as the house of the man second to the vizier in Gordon Loud and Charles B. Altman, *Khorsabad*, Part I: *The Citadel and the Town* (Chicago, 1938), 65, but Henri Frankfort, *The Art and Architecture of the Ancient Orient* (Harmondsworth, 1954), 84, called the location the throne room.

Babylon, who stands *between* them, into the presence of the god Shamash.[165]

Let us turn now to study scenes of investiture proper in the Iranian dynasties. The Parthians portrayed them, though I do not know of an example in which the king is shown between the god and another important personage.[166]

The theme was a favorite in Sassanian royal art, beginning with the first king of the dynasty.[167] For us, most important are the compositions which show the king between two deities or between a deity and an important personage. Let us call that arrangement the "sandwich pattern." From the reign of Ardashir I, from before the building of the synagogue, there is his poorly preserved investiture relief at Naqsh-i Rajab. Our evidence for the existence of a tradition of using the sandwich pattern to portray investitures allows us to infer that the relief at Naqsh-i Rajab represents an elaboration of that tradition. The relief shows Ardashir receiving the token from Ahuramazda. Behind the king stands, first, the eunuch flychaser so often portrayed with a Near Eastern King. If we are looking for instances of the sandwich pattern, we should disregard the presence of the flychaser. Next behind the king, however, stands a person in the robes of a Persian dignitary, so as to be the left member of the sandwich. Complicating the scene are two small figures inserted between Ahuramazda and the king. Their relative size allows us to infer that they have been added to the sandwich pattern, as an elaboration of it.[168]

Perhaps we can regard the investiture relief of King Narsah (293-302) as a somewhat similarly elaborated example of the sandwich pattern. The king receives the token from the goddess Anahita, and a bearded dignitary and another (now mutilated) figure stand behind him, but between the king and the goddess stands the small figure of his son.[169] Perhaps, then, we can also include here the investiture relief of Ardashir I at Firuzabad, where the king stands between Ahuramazda and three persons who are probably his own sons.[170]

---

[165] Parrot, *Assyria*, 168 (fig. 215).
[166] See Rostovtzeff, *YCS* 5 (1935), 172, 175; Ghirshman, *Persian Art*, 55.
[167] *Ibid.*, 131-33, 159, 167-68, 176, 190-93; Ghirshman, "Les Scènes d'investiture royale dans l'art rupestre des Sassanides et leur origine" *Syria* 52 (1975), 119-22.
[168] *Ibid.*, 120 (fig. 1) and Arthur Christensen, *L'Iran sous les Sassanides* (Copenhague, 1944), 90-91. On the small figures of the relief, see Ghirshman, *Syria* 52 (1975), 122-24. Eunuch flychasers: Parrot, *Assyria*, 41 (fig. 49), 51-52 (fig. 60), 69 (fig. 76), 103 (figs. 112-13).
[169] Ghirshman, *Persian Art*, 176 (fig. 218).
[170] *Ibid.*, 131 (fig. 167).

There are excellent Sassanian examples of the sandwich pattern in which both outer members are deities, in the investiture reliefs at Taq-i Bustan. One shows Shapur II[171] (309-379) standing between Mithras and Ahuramazda, and another shows Chosroes II[172] (591-628) standing between Anahita and Ahuramazda. Though these reliefs are later than the synagogue, the Near Eastern antecedents suggest that Shapur II knowingly resumed the old sandwich pattern with two deities; he did not reinvent it.

In a second theme, the ancient Near Eastern monarch's artists would portray his destructive might as he kills beasts in the hunt and crushes his enemies in battle or surveys them in their defeat, thus posing as the champion of man over beast, of truth and order over falsehood and rebellion, and as partner of his own great deity in vanquishing presumptuous opponents. This theme is absent from the reredos and is so common in Near Eastern art, from the Sumerians down through the Sassanians, that it need not detain us here.[173]

The king's destructive power should be used against foreign enemies and domestic rebels. Toward his own loyal subjects, who include docile conquered peoples of ethnic stock different from his own, the king should display his constructive might, as bringer of peaceful order and prosperity to his tamed subjects, who without his taming and protective power might be plagued by internecine strife. This fact brings a third theme into ancient Near Eastern royal art: the portrayal

---

[171]*Ibid.*, 190 (fig. 233), where the king is identified as Ardashir II (379-383); see, however, Guitty Azarpay, "The Role of Mithra in the Investiture and Triumph of Šāpūr II," *Iranica Antiqua* 17 (1982), 181-87.

[172]Ghirshman, *Persian Art*, 193 (fig. 235), where the king is identified as Peroz (459-484); see, however, M.C. Mackintosh, "Taq-i Bustan and Byzantine Art: a Case for Early Byzantine Influence on the Reliefs of Taq-i Bustan," *Iranica Antiqua* 13 (1978), 150-51.

[173]This ancient Near Eastern theme is seen on the north wall of the synagogue in the portrayal of the War of Gog and Magog; see n. 49. On the theme, see, e.g., Güterbock, *AJA* 61 (1957), 63. Scenes of hunts: Parrot, *Assyria*, 54-61 (figs. 62-65), 99 (fig. 108), 269-76 (fig. 345); Ghirshman, *Ancient Iran*, 202-3 (figs. 250-53), 268 (fig. 329), and *Persian Art*, 55-56, 173 (fig. 215), 187 (fig. 229), 194-99 (figs. 236-38), 206 (fig. 245), 207 (figs. 247-48), 212-13 (figs. 252-53); *Sassanian Silver*, nos. 1-10; Prudence Oliver Harper, *The Royal Hunter: Art of the Sassanian Empire* (New York, 1978), figs. 3-4, 6-7, 12, 17, 17b, 46, 47; eadem, *Silver Vessels of the Sassanian Period*, Vol. I: *Royal Imagery* (New York, 1981), x-xv, 40-98, and Plates 8-32, 37-38. Scenes of battle and victory: *ANEP*, figs. 298-301, 303, 309; Parrot, *Assyria*, 113-15 (figs. 121-29), 122-23 (figs. 138-46), etc.; Ghirshman, *Ancient Iran*, 235 (fig. 283), 268 (fig. 329), and *Persian Art*, 55, 125 (fig. 163), 132-33 (fig. 168), 152-61 (figs. 195-206), 179 (fig. 220), 184-85 (fig. 225), 190 (fig. 233); figs. 168, 202, and 233 show an investiture scene with trampled vanquished enemies); Harper, *Royal Hunter*, fig. 71.

of how the enthroned king's subjects peacefully accept his rule.[174] Sometimes the enthroned king and his deferential subjects are shown in a scene which includes battle or the postures of the defeated or slain enemy. Especially interesting for us are the examples, mostly Sassanian, which show the enthroned king in the center flanked by symmetrically arranged deferential subjects.[175] The king can even turn lions into peaceful subjects, though one might have thought that the realm of wild beasts was permanently foreign to man, and so we have the rare scenes showing the king with a tame pet lion.[176]

Related to the third theme is a fourth: the depiction of the pleasures, even the carousals, of peace and of the king, their bringer, as participant in them.[177] Especially important for us are some examples of this fourth theme. I shall henceforth use italics to call attention to features significant for understanding the Dura reredos.

First, there is the famous relief in the British Museum (fig. 12),[178] from the palace at Nineveh of the Assyrian King Ashurbanipal (668-631 B.C.E.). Part of an elaborate composition in registers, it shows the *king reclining* on a high *couch* as he drinks from a bowl. On a high throne to the left, at the foot of the couch, sits the queen, also drinking from a bowl. A tree stands to the right of the king, and another tree, to the left of the queen. Entwined in and supported by the branches of each *tree* is a *vine*. The vines extend toward one another; the shorter one from the left grows over the queen, and the longer one from the right grows *over the king*. In front of the middle of the king's couch is an elaborate *table* bearing banqueting equipment. Unfortunately, fig. 12

---

[174]See again Güterbock, *AJA* 61 (1957), 63. See also P.E. Botta and E. Flandin, *Monuments de Ninive* (Paris, 1849-), I, Plates 121 and 144; Parrot, *Assyria*, 103-4 (figs. 112-13); Ghirshman, *Ancient Iran*, 198 (fig. 246), 201 (fig. 248), 204-6 (figs. 254-55), and the docile tribute-bearers of 160-65 (fig. 211); Parthian examples: Ghirshman, *Persian Art*, 52 (figs. 64-65), 54-55 (figs. 67-68).
[175]Henri Frankfort, *The Art and Architecture of the Ancient Orient* (Baltimore, 1955), Pl. 89 (relief of Ashurnasirpal II of Assyria [883-859 B.C.E.]); Ghirshman, *Persian Art*, 169-72 (figs. 212-14; reliefs of Bahram II [276-293 C.E.]), 184 (figs. 225-26; relief of Shapur II), 206 (fig. 245; upper register of plate, depicting Chosroes I [531-579 C.E.]); *Sassanian Silver*, no. 12 (discussed by O. Grabar, ibid., 56-57); Harper, *Royal Hunter*, 80, fig. C, and *Silver*, Plates 19, 33-36.
[176]See Thureau-Dangin, *Til-Barsib*, pp. 54-55 and Pl. L. There are Roman compositions depicting royal hunts in which the lion is not killed; see Victorine von Gonzenbach, Review of *Sarcofagi romani di caccia al leone*, by Alessandra Vaccaro Melucco, *Archaeology* 23, 1 (Jan. 1970), 65.
[177]Sumer: *ANEP*, fig. 304 and p. 284. Assyria: Botta and Flandin, *Ninive*, I, Plates 52, 55, 57-68, 76.
[178]Reproduced with the permission of the Trustees of the British Museum from Parrot, *Assyria*, pp. 51-52 (fig. 60).

has been cropped and does not show the tree farther over to the left, from which hangs the *severed head* of the king's vanquished enemy.

The composition is all the more remarkable because it is "the earliest known example of the symposium motif, in which a male personage semi-reclines upon a couch,"[179] and because its finely worked vines entwined in the trees "show the full development of a motif for which there is, at present, no precedent."[180] Either Ashurbanipal's relief itself set the precedent or else the relief is an early reflection of a tradition which thereafter was strong in ancient Near Eastern royal art. The Achaemenian Persian kings held court under a golden representation of plane-tree-with-vine.[181] The Sassanians, too, portrayed the plane-tree-with-vine.[182] The Parthians and Sassanians displayed the king or prince in the reclining position upon a couch.[183]

We must pay particular attention to the charming Sassanian silver plate in the Walters Art Gallery of Baltimore,[184] which most vividly displays the survival of the tradition exemplified in the relief of Ashurbanipal with his queen. The plate shows a Sassanian king half-reclining on a high couch, holding a mirror in his left hand and offering a wreath of flowers in his right hand to his queen, who sits on the couch with him, at his feet. In front of the couch is a table bearing a bowl piled high with fruit. On the floor, under the couch or by it are three boar's heads. Above the royal couple instead of vines is a canopy decorated with figures which probably represent stars.[185] Tree and vine are absent, but we have couch, *king, king's posture, queen, table,* and *severed heads* in common with Ashurbanipal's relief, and the *canopy* of the plate and the *vines* of the relief can be viewed as serving the same purpose. The royal hunt is only the king's war against the hostile beast, by which he practices his skills for warfare against

---

[179]Albenda, *BASOR* 224 (Dec., 1976), 49.

[180]Albenda, "Grapevines in Ashurbanipal's Garden," *BASOR* 215 (1974), 14.

[181]See Eddy, *King,* 26-29.

[182]On a silver plate in the British Museum which shows a scene of investiture. The plate is mentioned by Andreas Alföldi, "Die Geschichte des Throntabernakels," *La Nouvelle Clio* 1-2 (1949-50), 553. I have not found a photograph or a clearer citation of it.

[183]Parthians: Ghirshman, *Persian Art,* 54 (fig. 67). Sassanians: Goldman and Little, *Iranica Antiqua,* 285 (with fig. 2), 286 (fig. 3), 287, and Plates V-VI; Ghirshman, *Artibus Asiae* 16 (1953), 63 (fig. 14 [= *Sassanian Silver,* no. 13]), 67 (fig. 17); *Sassanian Silver,* no. 14.

[184]*Sassanian Silver,* no. 13 (see above, n. 183); also published in Ghirshman, *Persian Art,* 218 (fig. 259). Another banqueting couple over a severed head: Harper, *Royal Hunter,* fig. 73; see also *ibid,* 74-75, fig. 25.

[185]Ghirshman, *Artibus Asiae* 16 (1953), 65; Alföldi, *La Nouvelle Clio* 1-2 (1949-50), 561.

human enemies, so that the boar's heads serve the same function as the head of Ashurbanipal's human foe.

The king in life was portrayed as enjoying a victory banquet. He could also be portrayed in death, on his sculptured sarcophagus, as enthroned and being served a similar banquet. A very important example for us is the sarcophagus (fig. 13) of Ahiram, king of Byblos in Phoenicia (tenth century B.C.E.).[186] The king sits upon an elaborate throne. In front of him is a peculiar *table*, the height of which rises well above the seat of the throne.

Two or more of these themes of royal art were often combined on a single monument. We may cite from the third millennium B.C.E. the two sides of the Standard of Ur, one displaying the king at war and the other, in victorious peace.[187] In the eighth century B.C.E. in the palace of Sargon II at Khorsabad war and victorious peace were visible simultaneously, war in a lower register and peace in an upper.[188] The *iwan* of Chosroes II of the seventh century C.E. on the back wall shows, in an upper register, a royal investiture and, in a lower, the king as a mounted warrior, and on the side walls are two royal hunts.[189] The Dura reredos combines a tree-vine with all four themes.

The planner of the scheme of paintings exemplified in the Dura synagogue surely worked in a more favored center of Judaism than that provincial border-fortress. He appears to have done his best, however, to make it easy for the available artists, whether they were Jews or non-Jews. The patterns of royal art were well known. Even provincial artists were accustomed to producing pieces of royal propaganda. Wherever possible, the planner used those stock motifs as the basic designs for expressing his Jewish ideas.

Without the ancient Near Eastern traditions, it might have been awkward to combine the *vine* of Israel[190] with the *tree*-imagery of Isa. 11.1, where "shoot," "stock," and perhaps "twig" both in the Hebrew and in English are terms appropriate for a tree, not a vine. The images

---

[186]Reproduced from the original photograph of James B. Pritchard (published as *ANEP*, fig. 458), with the permission of the University Museum, University of Pennsylvania.
[187]*ANEP*, figs. 303-4.
[188]Botta and Flandin, *Ninive*, I, Plates 52, 55, 57-68, 76.
[189]Ghirshman, *Persian Art*, pp. 192 (fig. 235), 193-99 (with figs. 236-37); Mackintosh, *Iranica Antiqua* 13 (1978), 149-52, 172-74. Mackintosh may be right, that the *iwan* of Chosroes II at Taq-i Bustan shows Byzantine influence, but he paid no attention to the continuity of the Near Eastern themes we have just traced and to their presence together in the organized composition of the Dura reredos.
[190]See n. 51.

of the Near Eastern tree-with-vine and tree-vine stood available for the Jewish designer. Gute thought he saw the tree-vine as emerging from a vase.[191] If the vase really was in the original composition, it, too has something of a parallel in the Sassanian silver plate which shows a tree-vine growing out of a body of water.[192] If the designer wished to portray a majestic dying Jacob blessing his descendants at the foot of the tree-vine and in its shade, all he had to do was draw upon the stock figure of the victorious king banqueting on his couch in the shade. At Dura, the painter of the blessing-scenes at first reproduced the stock figure with stolidly absolute fidelity. He showed,[193] in the left scene, a table with elaborate vertical legs somewhat like the one in the relief of Ashurbanipal. Atop that table is perhaps a banqueting bolster.[194] On the floor beneath the couch or beneath the table is a round object. Can we not guess that it was originally a severed head? In the blessing scene to the right, in front of the couch are the "rampant felines," but their shape is very like the outline of the table on the sarcophagus of Ahiram. Indeed, Pearson, who sketched the reredos when it was fresh, drew in the space of the "rampant felines" what can easily be interpreted as a table,[195] and Kraeling was tempted so to interpret it, but held back because he doubted that two different forms of table could be portrayed in the reredos.[196] He should have noted that the Dura artist practiced variation in the form of the ark[197] and of the royal throne.[198]

A banqueting table does not belong in a scene of Jacob's death, much less a severed head. Therefore, those figures were painted out. On the other hand, the original designer or perhaps the Jews of Dura themselves delighted in portraying Jacob's deathbed after the pattern of a royal couch-throne. Painted across each of the spaces in which the tables stood is the same footstool which accompanies the throne at the top of the reredos and the throne of the Pharaoh in the painting at the north end of the bottom register of the west wall of the synagogue.[199] Jews did not glorify hunting, but the designer could draw upon the

---

[191]See fig. 3 and n. 15.
[192]*Sassanian Silver*, no. 51 (discussed, p. 73).
[193]See figs. 3, 4, 6.
[194]See Goodenough, IX, 82; Kraeling, *Synagogue*, 63-64.
[195]See fig. 4.
[196]*Synagogue*, p. 64.
[197]Goodenough, XI, figs. 332, 334, 347.
[198]*Ibid.*, figs. 323, 329, 336, 338.
[199]See *ibid.*, fig. 338, and cf. *Sassanian Silver*, nos. 12, 16, and Ghirshman, *Persian Art*, 203 (fig. 242), 205-6 (figs. 244-45).

ancient Near Eastern theme of the king with his tame lion[200] and combine it with the Greek figure of Orpheus. We have seen how a tree was traditionally part of that scene.[201] And so we have the royal Orpheus as a "fruit" of the Dura tree-vine.

Finally, at the top of the reredos, we have a combination of the two ancient Near Eastern motifs of investiture and enthronement. In a pagan investiture scene on the sandwich pattern, the king stands *between* his great deity and another deity or another important person and receives from the great deity the tokens of royal power. Jews and Christians could not so portray their great God the Father on a level with another deity or with a human being. Instead, in the Transfiguration story, the voice of God confers power upon the Christ as he stands *between* the two superhuman prophets, and in the apse of San Apollinare the hand of God is shown above to confer power upon the similarly placed cross symbolizing the Christ. Christians could worship the Christ, but nothing indicates that Jews thought of worshiping their Messiah alongside their God. Yet the Messiah sits in the center of the composition of the reredos, in a position where a pagan or a Christian would expect to find a depictions of the deity to be worshiped. Therefore, I think we must assume that as at San Apollinare, so at Dura the hand of God appeared over the Messiah, who sits enthroned between the two superhuman prophets.[202] The Messiah himself is a glorious accomplishment of God, but God is the one to be worshiped.

At Dura, the investiture scene has been conflated with the enthronement scene, and therefore the Messiah in the upper reredos does not stand but sits. Even for this posture there are an ancient Near Eastern precedent and parallels, in the investiture scenes, beginning with Ardashir I, which portray the king on horseback.[203] Finally, we have seen how the symmetrically arranged obedient subjects and the presence of a tree are characteristic of ancient Near Eastern enthronement scenes. Thus the motifs of pagan royal art served to illustrate the Jewish message derived from Gen. 49 and Isa. 11! Though we have no way of reading the designer's mind, well may he have felt the need to have four pictures of Moses serve as the "fence" around the scene, to ensure that the Jewish onlookers would understand that the origin of the promise of Messianic felicity lay in the Torah revealed

---

[200] See n. 176.
[201] See n. 56.
[202] Cf. the putto who brings the diadem from on high to Shapur I (Ghirshman, *Persian Art*, 155-56 [fig. 197]).
[203] *Ibid.*, 132 (fig. 168), 159 (fig. 202), 167-68 (fig. 211), and cf. Ghirshman, *Ancient Iran*, 235 (fig. 283).

through Moses and that fulfilment of that promise depended upon faithful observance of that Torah.

We have now explained how all the stages of the painting of the central composition arose from the designer's use of stock motifs of pagan royal art and from the unimaginative procedure of the local artist (very likely, a non-Jew). The artist first completely reproduced the stock motif with all its inappropriate elements, which thereafter had to be painted out. The designer's scheme was complete in his mind before any paint was applied to the walls of the synagogue. Even the border-pattern crossing the middle of the reredos probably did not come as an intrusion into the designer's plan. The border-pattern and the painted pilasters and the ceiling tiles are meant to give the impression of a palatial trellised royal garden pavilion, with grapevines running through the trelliswork.[204] If two of the spaces framed by the trelliswork showed the continuous tree-vine, no harm was done. In fact, the framed spaces both showed the Messiah as fruit of the tree-vine though the lower space also depicted the much earlier scene of Jacob (in a real trellis, all framed spaces viewed by the observer belong to the present). The reredos in the context of the rest of the decoration of the synagogue thus proclaims the building to be a palatial pavilion, as it were, one to house God and the Messiah.

List of Abbreviations

AJ	*Antiquities of the Jews*
AJA	*American Journal of Archaeology*
ANEP	James B. Pritchard, *The Ancient Near East in Pictures Relating to the Old Testament* (Princeton, 1954)
BASOR	*Bulletin of the American Schools of Oriental Research*
BJ	*Bellum Judaicum* (= *Jewish War*)
BT	*Babylonian Talmud*
CA	*Cahiers archéologiques*
CRAI	*Comptes rendus de l'Académie des inscriptions et belles lettres*
EI	*Sefer Eretz Israel*
Forsyth-Weitzmann	George H. Forsyth and Kurt Weitzmann, *The Monastery of Saint Catherine at Mount Sinai: the Church*

---

[204]See Kraeling, *Synagogue*, 53; Goodenough, IX, 57-58.

	and *Fortress of Justinian* (Ann Arbor, 1973)
Goodenough	Erwin R. Goodenough, *Jewish Symbols in the Greco-Roman Period* (13 vols.; "Bollingen Series," XXXVII; New York, 1953-68)
IEJ	*Israel Exploration Journal*
JBL	*Journal of Biblical Literature*
JJA	*Journal of Jewish Art*
JNES	*Journal of Near Eastern Studies*
JRS	*Journal of Roman Studies*
JT	Palestinian (or "Jerusalem") Talmud
JWCI	*Journal of the Warburg and Courtauld Institutes*
Neusner	Jacob Neusner, *A History of the Jews in Babylonia* (5 vols.; Leiden,1965-1970)
PG	J.-P. Migne, *Patrologiae Cursus Completus, Series Graeco-Latina* (Paris, 1857-1934)
RB	*Revue biblique*
Report VI	*The Excavations at Dura Europos: Preliminary Report of the Sixth Season of Work, October 1932-March 1933*, ed. by M.I. Rostovtzeff, A.R. Bellinger, C. Hopkins, and C.B. Welles (New Haven: Yale University Press, 1936).
RHR	*Revue de l'histoire des religions*
YCS	*Yale Classical Studies*

5

Tales of the Tobiads

The stories of Joseph the Tobiad and his son Hyrcanus in Josephus *AJ* xii have long puzzled scholars. Morton Smith has done much to remove the puzzling from the records of the past. In gratitude for the help he gave me in my first stumblings toward teaching and scholarship, I take pleasure in dedicating to him my effort to solve the Tobiad puzzle.

When a historian writes a puzzling narrative, it is often because his own convictions drive him to consider the straightforward as embarrassing or incredible. Hence, one key to the puzzle may lie in Josephus' beliefs. First, then, let us list what were Josephus' own biases when he narrated the history of the third and second centuries B.C. Thereafter, let us summarize the Tobiad stories and the external evidence on the Tobiads so as to set forth the puzzling aspects of Josephus' narrative.

Josephus was proud that he was a descendant of Jonathan the Hasmonaean and defended the honor of the members of the Hasmonaean dynasty down through John Hyrcanus.[1] To defend the Hasmonaeans he would denigrate their rivals.[2] In particular, he took First Maccabees, a work of pro-Hasmonaean propaganda, as his basic source for the history of the rise of the Hasmonaean dynasty. He knew also the work of Jason of Cyrene or its abridgement, Second Maccabees; both the original and the abridgement were works of anti-Hasmonaean propaganda. Throughout his narrative, Josephus supports First Maccabees against Second Maccabees, except in the case of the story of Antiochus IV's atrocities at Jerusalem, where Josephus was forced by

---

[1]Vita I. 2-5; *AJ* xii. 6. 1. 265 – xiii. 10. 7. 300
[2]Even Pharisees, as at *BJ* i. 2. 8. 67 and *AJ* xiii. 10. 5. 288-92.

his belief in the veracity of the prophesies of Daniel to emend the text of First Maccabees.[3]

By the time he wrote the *Antiquities* and the *Life*, Josephus was a convinced Pharisee, but even when he was younger, he had been sympathetic to both the Pharisees and the Essenes.[4] Accordingly, he could not approve of breaches of Jewish law.

This pious Jewish historian first (*AJ* xii. 4. 1. 154) joins some other ancient authors[5] in interpreting a piece of Ptolemaic propaganda in such a way as to lead to a conclusion now known from both literary and numismatic evidence to be false:[6] that Antiochus III, on giving his daughter Cleopatra in marriage to Ptolemy V in 193 B.C., actually turned over to Ptolemy as a dowry "Coele-Syria, Samaria, Judaea, and Phoenicia." Since the good evidence of Polybius (xxviii. 1. 3; 20.9) was surely available to Josephus (see, e.g., *AJ* xii. 9. 1. 358), why should Josephus have accepted the false conclusion?

Josephus goes on to say (*AJ* xii. 4. 1. 155) that Ptolemy and Cleopatra[7] shared the revenues of this dowry, farming out the taxes to prominent natives of the subject territories. An apparently gratuitous reference follows (*AJ* xii. 4. 1. 156): that in this period, the high priesthood of Onias, the Jews suffered heavily from the plundering raids of the Samaritans.

Having thus introduced Onias II as a high priest of ill fortune, Josephus goes on to give the succession of high priests: Simon the Just, Eleazar, Manasses, and this Onias, son of Simon the Just. He characterizes this Onias II as small-minded and avaricious. At this point begins the tale of the Tobiads (*AJ* xii. 4. 1-11. 158-236). The whole tale presupposes that the Ptolemaic empire has complete control of southern Syria and of Palestine, contrary to what is known to have been true from 200 B.C., when Antiochus III conquered the area.[8]

---

[3]For proof, see my *I Maccabees* ("The Anchor Bible," vol. 41; Garden City, N.Y., 1976), pp. 55-61, 558-574, and my *II Maccabees* ("The Anchor Bible," vol. 41A: Garden City, N.Y., 1983), pp. 16-17 (n. 80), 185-86, 302-3.

[4]Morton Smith, "Palestinian Judaism in the First Century," in Moshe Davis (ed.), *Israel: Its Role in Civilization* (New York, 1956), pp. 74-77; J. *Vita* 2. 10-12, 5. 21; *BJ* ii. 8. 2-14, 119-66.

[5]Appian *Syr.* 5; Porphyry, *F. Gr. Hist.* 260, F 47.

[6]See Victor Tcherikover, *Hellenistic Civilization and the Jews* (Philadelphia, 1959), pp. 128, 458, n. 29.

[7]See Maurice Holleaux, "Sur un passage de Flavius Josèphe," *REJ*, XXXIX (1899), 161-76; revised edition printed in M. Holleaux, *Études d'épigraphie et d'histoire grecques* (Paris, 1942), pp. 337-55.

[8]See Tcherikover, p. 127.

When contemptible Onias II refused to pay the customary 20 talents of his own income on behalf of the people to Ptolemy, the king became angry and sent to Jerusalem an envoy bearing a threat to dispossess the Jews and distribute their land as lots to his soldiers if the money should not be paid. Ptolemy here at *AJ* xii. 4. 1. 158 is strangely identified as "Ptolemy [III] Euergetes, who was the father of [Ptolemy IV] Philopator," though Josephus has said that his narrative is set in the reign of Ptolemy V Epiphanes.

Brazen Onias, however, was not "put out of countenance" (*ibid.*, 1. 159). Young Joseph, son of Tobias and of the high priest's sister, rose to the occasion. He rebuked Onias, reminding him that his claim to be the chief spokesman of the nation *(prostasian)* and high priest rested on payment of the money he was withholding. Onias, unconcerned, left to Joseph the prerogative of being the people's spokesman before the king, who is here (*AJ* xii. 4. 2. 163) again strangely identified as "the Benefactor" *(Euergetes)*. Joseph undertook the task and immediately impressed Ptolemy's envoy by generously entertaining him. The envoy brought back to Ptolemy and Cleopatra a favorable report of Joseph, preparing the ground for the young man's own visit to court.

Joseph, with the help of friends in Samaria,[9] raised 20,000 drachmas with which he bought as rich equipment as he could, though he was ridiculed for his poor appearance by the others who had come to Alexandria to bid for tax-farming rights. Joseph made a special trip to Memphis to see the king and so impressed him there with his wit that he won the king's favor, to the point that when the king came to Alexandria, Joseph was the envy of the other bidders, and all the more when he out-bid them all by giving a figure which was double the current revenue and mentioned in addition the property he would confiscate from tax-evaders. When the king asked for the customary guarantors for so audacious a bid, the witty Joseph offered Ptolemy and Cleopatra each other. Pleased, the king let Joseph have the contract without guarantors, whereupon Joseph used a contingent from the royal army and rigorously collected the taxes in the gentile cities of Ptolemaic Syria, executing those who refused to pay.

Thus, Joseph grew very wealthy and used his wealth to purchase the favor of Ptolemy, Cleopatra, and all who were powerful at court. Joseph enjoyed this prosperity for 22 years. He begot seven sons by one wife, and then he begot an eighth son under very romantic

---

[9] If "Samaria" means the city, the friends were Greeks or Macedonians. If "Samaria" means the district, the friends may have been Samaritans. Joseph and the author, as we shall see (below, p. 140) could admit the sanctity of the Samaritan temple; cf. II Maccabees 5.23, 6.2.

circumstances. That is, when Joseph fell in love with a gentile dancing-girl, Joseph's brother, to preserve him from the sin of intercourse with a gentile woman, took his own daughter and gave her to the drunken Joseph, who fell in love with her instead and begot Hyrcanus. These events are narrated without apology, indeed proudly. Are these tales of bribery and wenching, which are romantic enough to suggest they are fiction, the sort of history one would expect from the pious Josephus?

Hyrcanus grew up to be a clever rascal, resourcefully able to carry out his father's orders, regardless of cost, and became his father's favorite son, much to the envy of his brothers. When a son was born to King Ptolemy and the aged Joseph was unable to go, of all the sons only Hyrcanus was willing to go to the royal festivities in Joseph's place. Hyrcanus asked only for a letter allowing him to draw from Joseph's steward in Alexandria whatever funds were needed for gifts. Characteristically, the clever young man used the letter to demand the vast sum of 1,000 talents from the steward and chained the steward when he refused to deliver the money. When the king himself objected to Hyrcanus' failure to present himself at court and to his treatment of the steward, Hyrcanus gave a witty reply. Back home, he said, there was a custom, that the child-of-a-father *(ton gennêthenta)*[10] was not to partake of the meat of a sacrifice until he himself had brought a sacrifice to God. As Joseph's benefactor,[11] Ptolemy was analogous to God. Hyrcanus had not presented himself to the king because he was still preparing his offerings to Ptolemy. Hyrcanus said he had punished the steward, his father's slave, for disobedience, just as the king himself had to punish disobedience. Already by his reply Hyrcanus won Ptolemy's favor.

On getting the thousand talents from the helpless steward, Hyrcanus used the money to purchase an extravagant gift for the king and queen. At a royal banquet, when rivals piled the bare bones left over from the meat in front of Hyrcanus, to illustrate (as they had the royal jester say to the king) how Hyrcanus' father Joseph had stripped Syria, Hyrcanus "wittily" replied that only he had bones before him because the others, like dogs, had eaten the meat with the bones, while he, as a man, had eaten only the meat.[12] Hyrcanus led his rivals

---

[10] This is the reading of the manuscripts at *AJ* xii. 4. 8. 206. Herwerden's emendation, *genethliazonta*, is not to be accepted.

[11] Greek *euergetêi*; again a play of Ptolemy III's cult-epithet "Euergetes," but the king in the passage should be Ptolemy IV!

[12] Neither the original author nor Josephus is dismayed at the possibility that Hyrcanus ate meat that was not kosher; contrast Daniel 1.5-16 and II Maccabees 6.18-26. There are two possible explanations. Hyrcanus' *abstention* from meat may have suggested the prank to the malicious rivals, for Hyrcanus'

to think that his gifts to the king would be modest, so that they would do little to compete, and then he dazzled all with his extravagant gift to the king and queen. He also bribed important courtiers, for already at this time his jealous brothers were trying to have him murdered. Having won the royal favor, Hyrcanus asked only that the king write back to his father and brothers.

On Hyrcanus' return home, however, the envious brothers tried to kill him, with the connivance of Joseph, who was angry over the extravagant use of his money. Hyrcanus escaped across the Jordan after killing two of his brothers. There the young man remained, "levying taxes" (*phorologôn*) on the natives. The last two sentences are surprisingly brief for such a violent episode in the drama. Nevertheless, Josephus' choice of words lets us know, first, that somehow Hyrcanus was safe in Transjordan from the vengeance of Joseph and Joseph's other sons. Surely the favor of Ptolemy protected him in territory still under Ptolemaic control. Indeed, young Hyrcanus is not described as an outlaw but as "levying taxes." Evidently, he became the official collector in his district of taxes for the Ptolemaic empire.

Joseph himself probably continued to hold the profitable post of tax-farmer of the rest of Ptolemaic Syria and Phoenicia. The fact is strange but hardly impossible. Josephus seems not to have considered the possibility.

At this point in the narrative (*AJ* xii. 4. 10. 223-24) comes a chronological note: "Around that time Seleucus [IV (187-175)][13] ...became king, and Joseph, Hyrcanus' father, died, a fine and high-minded man who had brought the Jewish people from poverty and political weakness to more splendid opportunities of life during his 22 years as farmer of the taxes of Syria, Phoenicia, and Samaria." Onias II also died, to be succeeded by Simon II and then by Onias III, who,

---

witty claim to have eaten the meat may be no more factual than his witty claim that the malicious rivals ate the bones. Alternatively, the original author may have held the view that the dietary laws were to be observed only in the Land of Israel (Deuteronomy 12.1 with 12.20-25 and 14.3-21) or at any rate that they were not binding in Egypt (see Leviticus 11.45 in the context of the whole of Chapter 11).

[13] The Seleucus here can be only Seleucus IV Philopator, for at *AJ* xii. 4.11. 234 he is said to have been succeeded by Antiochus IV Epiphanes. The narrative here at *AJ* xii. 4. 10. 223 wrongly gives the cult-epithet of Seleucus IV as "Soter," which was the cult-epithet of Seleucus III (225-223). Josephus may have found "Seleucus" without any cult-epithet in his source. If so, the error belongs to Josephus. However, as we shall see (below, n. 91), the original author could have made the slip, if, indeed, it was a slip; see below, p. 149.

Josephus says, received a letter from "Areios," king of Sparta, which Josephus quotes.

This chronological note teems with difficulties. Josephus, as if to leave no doubt as to the correctness of the figure, mentions twice Joseph's 22 years as tax-farmer (*AJ* xii. 4. 6. 186; 10. 224). But Josephus' own chronological framework leaves no room for the 22 years. Measuring the 22 years from the marriage of Ptolemy V to Cleopatra I in 193, we reach at least 172, long after the death of Seleucus IV in 175, whereas, Josephus placed the *accession* of Seleucus IV around the time of Joseph's death and held that Seleucus IV reigned at least several years (*AJ* xii. 4. 11. 234). Measuring even from Antiochus III's conquest of Syria and Palestine in 200, we reach at least 179, one year after the death of Ptolemy V, which Josephus places *after* the death of Joseph (*ibid.*, 235). Equally difficult is the end of Josephus' chronological note. Areus I, king of Sparta, died in 265, and even the child-king Areus II died in 254.[14] Moreover, Ben Sira's words strongly suggest that a Simon was high priest at the time of Antiochus III's conquest of Judaea, but on Josephus' chronology no Simon could have been so, since Simon I was succeeded by Eleazar, a contemporary of Ptolemy II (285-246 B.C.),[15] and Simon II became high priest in the reign of Seleucus IV. Why does Josephus assume so unlikely a chronology?

Josephus resumes the thread of the narrative with the death of Joseph, which was followed by violent struggles among the Jews. The majority backed the elder sons of Joseph against Hyrcanus, as did Simon, the high priest. The narrator explains that Simon's decision was based on his relationship *(syngeneian)* to the elder sons. This statement makes sense only if Simon, Joseph's first-cousin, was somehow more closely related to Joseph's first wife than to Hyrcanus' mother. Since the narrator, as we shall see, later condemns the elder brothers as wicked, he appears here to have gone out of his way to cast aspersions on the character of Simon II, associating him with the wicked. Why would he do so?

The story goes on to say that Hyrcanus remained in Transjordan as a robber-baron preying on the Arabs and built a fortress "Tyre," which is described in detail. Hyrcanus held power in the region "for seven years, through all the time that Seleucus was king of Syria." However, when the forceful Antiochus IV (175-164) replaced Seleucus IV and the

---

[14]Hans Volkmann, "Areus," *Der Kleine Pauly*, I (1964), 532.
[15]Ecclesiasticus 10.8, 50.1-24, and see Tcherikover, pp. 79-81; *AJ* xii. 2. 1. 11, 5. 40-44; 4. 1. 147. Cf. *Mishnah, Abot* 1.2, and Emil Schürer, *The History of the Jewish People in the Age of Jesus Christ* (New English Version, revised and edited by Geza Vermes, Fergus Millar, *et al.*; 3 vols. in 4; Edinburgh, 1973-87), II, 359-60.

Ptolemaic empire was left under a weak regime of child-heirs (Ptolemy VI Philometor, 180-145, and his younger brother), Hyrcanus committed suicide rather than fall into Antiochus' hands, and his property was seized by Antiochus. Suddenly here we find Syria and Palestine no longer in Ptolemaic but in Seleucid hands, and this situation is probably what Josephus understood by "through all the time that Seleucus was king of Syria." "Syria" in *AJ* xii means "Syria and Palestine," the territory conquered by Antiochus III in 100; in the *Antiquities* it begins to mean "the Seleucid empire" from xiii. 4. 1. 80. If so, we may acquit Josephus of underestimating the length of the reign of Seleucus IV (187-175); rather, he thought that Seleucus IV gained control of Syria and Palestine around 181. His source, however, as we shall see, knew that the region was under Seleucid rule from 200.

So end the tales of Joseph and Hyrcanus. The narrative goes on to say that in the struggles which broke out in Jerusalem between rival claimants to the high-priesthood,[16] the surviving Tobiads supported Menelaus, while the majority of the people supported Jason. We next read that it was Menelaus and the Tobiads who, hard pressed, then went to Antiochus IV and received his permission to follow Greek ways in Jerusalem. Strangely, nothing is said here of their having received the king's help to suppress their rivals. As we shall see, Josephus or his source had reasons for the silence.

When Josephus wrote his brief account of our period in his *Jewish War*, he had no other sources than are reflected by his account in his *Antiquities*. However, important books were not in his possession when he was writing his earlier work, so that he wrote from memory an account full of mistakes.[17] Thus, at *BJ* i. 1. 1. 31-32 he has Onias-Menelaus confused with Jason. He writes that Onias-Menelaus expelled the Tobiads from the city, and the Tobiads took refuge with Antiochus, who invaded Judaea, took and sacked Jerusalem and the temple, slaying a large number of Jews who were partisans of the Ptolemaic empire. If we substitute Jason for Onias-Menelaus in the foregoing sentence, we have the historical fact.[18]

Chance has preserved for us on papyrus in Egypt the archives of Zenon, an agent of Apollonius, *dioiketes* (finance minister) of Ptolemy

---

[16]Jason's coup against Menelaus occurred in 169 B.C. On the date and on the confusion in Josephus' narrative of Antiochus IV's activities in Jerusalem, see my *I Maccabees*, pp. 207, 558-68, and my *II Maccabees*, pp. 246-47.
[17]See my *I Maccabees*, pp. 60-61.
[18]Similar in origin is Josephus' confusion, at *BJ* vii. 10. 1. 423-24, of Onias III with Onias IV. Josephus had further troubles writing from memory: at *AJ* xx. 10. 3. 235 he turned Onias IV into a son of Onias-Menelaus!

II. Among the documents reflecting Zenon's extensive business contacts in Ptolemaic Syria are documents of 259 and 257 revealing that a certain Tubias was in command of a unit of Ptolemaic military colonists settled at Birta in the Ammanitis (i.e., the Biblical Land of Ammon in Transjordan) and that this Tubias wrote letters directly to the king and to his powerful minister.[19] Birta is probably identical with 'Arāq el-Emīr in Transjordan and with the place Josephus calls "Tyre." At the site are extensive ruins, as well as an inscription of the name *Tōbīyāh* in Hebrew characters of the sixth or early fifth century B.C.[20]

On the basis of the inscription and the clues in Josephus, in the archives of Zenon, in the Bible, and in other ancient documents, Mazar has been able to trace the Tobiad family well back into the time of the first temple.[21] Scholars agree that Josephus' Tobiad Joseph was a descendant, probably the son, of the Tubias in the Zenon papyri.[22]

Second Maccabees is an abridgement of a longer work, no longer extant, by Jason of Cyrene.[23] At Second Maccabees 3.11 the high priest Onias III protests to Heliodorus, the minister of Seleucus IV, that it would be wrong for him to confiscate the money on deposit in the temple. Onias informs Heliodorus that part of the money on deposit belongs to the very great personage Hyrcanus the Tobiad. This is very strange, since we learn from Josephus that Hyrcanus was a rebel against the Seleucid empire,[24] whose goods were forfeit to the king.[25] Why should Jason of Cyrene have thus presented Onias as weakening his own case?

The narrative of Second Maccabees probably touches upon Tobiad matters gain when we learn (Second Maccabees 4.26, 5.7) that Jason the Oniad, who supplanted his brother Onias III as high priest, on being driven from Jerusalem both in 171 and in 169 B.C.[26] fled to the Ammanitis, the area of the Tobiad stronghold. Jason the Oniad was a second-cousin of Hyrcanus and likely shared his political views.

Both books of Maccabees let us know that the "Tobiad Troop" of soldiers, many if not most of them Jews, continued to exist in the lands

---

[19] *Corpus Papyrorum Judaicarum*, ed. Victor A. Tcherikover and Alexander Fuks, Vol. I (Cambridge, Mass., 1957), Nos. 1-2, 4-5.
[20] B. Mazar, "The Tobiads," *Israel Exploration Journal*, VII (1957), 141-42; Paul Lapp, "The Second and Third campaigns at 'Arâq el-Emîr," *Bulletin of The American Schools of Oriental Research* 171 (Oct., 1963), 24-26, 38-39.
[21] *Israel Exploration Journal*, VII (1957), pp. 137-45, 229-38.
[22] *Corpus Papyrorum Judaicarum*, Vol. I, pp. 117-18.
[23] II Maccabees 2.19-23.
[24] *AJ* xii. 4. 11. 229-36.
[25] See Bickerman, *Institutions des Séleucides* (Paris, 1938), p. 121.
[26] See above, n. 16.

east of the Jordan long after Hyrcanus was dead. They are mentioned in connection with events of 163 B.C.[27]

We have, then a long list of puzzling questions:

1. Why does the pious Josephus tell the often unedifying stories of Onias II and the Tobiads, especially since in the narrative there is no apology for the unedifying aspects?
2. Why does Josephus accept Ptolemaic propaganda at *AJ* xii. 4. 1. 154 instead of following the reliable Polybius?
3. Why does Josephus at *AJ* xii. 4. 1. 156 bother to refer to Samaritan raids during the high-priesthood of Onias II?
4. Why does Josephus take the story of the Tobiads, which presupposes that the Ptolemies were ruling Palestine and southern Syria, and place it in a period too short to accommodate even Joseph's 22 years as tax-farmer, the reign of Ptolemy V and Cleopatra I, who ruled after the Seleucid conquest of the area?
5. Why does Josephus twice take a king, who he has said is Ptolemy V, husband of Cleopatra I, and identify him as Ptolemy III Euergetes, father of Ptolemy IV Philopator?
6. Why does Josephus at *AJ* xii. 4. 10. 224-27 move Simon II into the reign of Seleucus IV and date a letter of the third century B.C. in the reign of Seleucus IV?
7. Why does the narrative at *AJ* xii. 4. 11. 229 associate the high priest Simon II with wicked men?
8. Why does Josephus or his source at *AJ* xii. 5. 1. 240-41 say nothing of how Antiochus IV suppressed the rivals of Onias-Menelaus and of the Tobiads?
9. Why did Jason of Cyrene present Onias III as mentioning the deposits of Hyrcanus the rebel?

To these questions we may add two more:

10. The sensational and witty details of the Tobiad stories are so reminiscent of the Biblical tales of Joseph and of Hellenistic romances; can these details be true?
11. Pious Jews treasured stories of miracles. Second Maccabees Chapter 3 contains traces of two versions of the miracle of the repulse of Heliodorus.[28] Why does the pious Josephus say nothing of the miracle?

---

[27] I Maccabees 5.13; II Maccabees 12.17, 35; see my *I Maccabees*, pp. 298-99, and my *II Maccabees*, pp. 439-40, 446.
[28] See my commentary.

No author proceeding to write an account on the basis of his own knowledge would confront his reader with the spectacle of such problems. Two factors will suffice to explain how Josephus came to do so. First, Josephus' only source for the events was one which Josephus, having the biases we noted above, found incredible. On the basis of his own presuppositions and aims he tried to "correct" it. Second, the *Antiquities* is a huge work, written when Josephus was no longer young.[29] Large sections of the work Josephus turned over to his Greek secretaries to copy and restyle from existing Greek sources, reserving for himself the important tasks of translating Hebrew and Aramaic sources and of determining and revising content.[30] Sometimes he overlooked passages which needed to be revised, as in the numerous cross-references taken over from his sources which now have nothing to refer to in Josephus' work.[31] The Tobiad stories contain such overlooked passages.

To use these factors to solve our problems, we must first determine as accurately as possible what the original story of the Tobiads was. We are fortunate that in two instances Josephus overlooked words of the original which needed revision, so that his secretary copied the original, producing our Question 5.

Several facts guarantee that the words identifying the Ptolemy of the story as Ptolemy III Euergetes represent the original reading, overlooked by Josephus, rather than corrections by a later scribe. As Tcherikover has noted,[32] no later scribe would have felt the need to correct the passages since Josephus has already explained how Ptolemy V came to be ruler of Syria and Palestine after they had been conquered by Antiochus III.

Furthermore, a Jewish or Christian scribe would have identified Ptolemy III in the normal manner, as the son of his father, not as the father of Ptolemy IV Philopator, the more so as Ptolemy III's father was Ptolemy II Philadelphus, famous from *AJ* xii. 2. 1-15. 11-118, whereas Ptolemy IV Philopator otherwise is barely mentioned by Josephus (*AJ* xii. 3. 3. 130-31).

Another guarantee is the punning on Ptolemy III's cult epithet, *Euergetês* ("Benefactor"; *AJ* xii. 4. 2. 163 and 8.206).

Moreover, at *AJ* xii. 4. 3. 167 and 4. 178 the king and queen are referred to as "the king and his wife" rather than as "the king and

---

[29]*AJ* i. Prooem. 2. 7; Josephus was born in 37/8 of the Christian era (*Vita* 1. 5) and finished the *Antiquities* in 93/4 (*AJ* xx. 12. 1. 267).
[30]See H. St. John Thackeray, *Josephus* (New York, 1929), pp. 100-24.
[31]E.g., *AJ* xii. 5. 2. 244; xiii. 2. 1. 36 and 4. 6. 108.
[32]Pp. 129 and 458, n. 32; see also M. Stern, "Notes on the Story of Joseph the Tobiad," *Tarbiẓ*, XXXII (5723 = 1962), 42 (in Hebrew). Stern's study is superb.

queen." Not all Ptolemaic queens bore the title "the King's Wife." Berenice II, wife of Ptolemy III bore the title "Wife" as part of her official style.[33] On the other hand, Cleopatra I Syra, wife of Ptolemy V Epiphanes, bears the title only on a dedication of ca. 186.[34] Berenice I, wife of Ptolemy I Soter bears the title "Wife" on one dedication[35] but probably was not officially so styled. We thus may exclude from consideration Ptolemy II and his wives, Arsinoë I and Arsinoë II, as well as Ptolemy IV and his wife Arsinoë III, for these queens did not bear the title "Wife."[36] Since none of the Ptolemies after Ptolemy V had any claim to the taxes of Syria and Palestine, we need not consider later royal couples.

Josephus also overlooked in his source the need to correct the 22 years of Joseph's career as tax-farmer. They cannot be fitted into the reign of Ptolemy V, but they can easily be accommodated within the reigns of Ptolemies of the third century.

Indeed, if we take Ptolemy III and Berenice II to be the king and queen under whom Joseph became tax-farmer, the details of the story of the Tobiads fit better than with any other identification. Thus, we may exclude Ptolemy I, all of whose sons were born before he ever had secure control of Syria and Palestine so as to be able to turn the taxes over to tax-farmers,[37] contrary to *AJ* xii. 4. 7. 196. Nor could Joseph have become tax-farmer under Ptolemy I with part of his twenty-two-year tenure extending into the reign of Ptolemy II. Zenon, writing under Ptolemy II, knows nothing of the mighty tax-farmer Joseph or of the Transjordanian robber-baron Hyrcanus. Joseph's activities are incompatible with the policy of Ptolemy II,[38] and Transjordan was firmly held by Ptolemies I-III.[39] Moreover, any sons of Ptolemy II to correspond to *AJ* xii. 4. 7. 196 were probably born in the reign of Ptolemy I.[40]

Furthermore, so firm was the hold of Ptolemies I and II on Syria and Palestine after 301 B.C.,[41] that it is hard to see how the

---

[33]See Friedrich Priesigke and Emil Kiessling, *Wörterbuch der griechischen Papyrusurkunden* (Berlin, 1925), III, 34-35.
[34]*Sammelbuch griechischer Urkunden aus Ägypten*, ed. Preisigke and Kiessling (Strassburg and Göttingen, 1915-), 8927.
[35]*Sammelbuch* 10091.
[36]Preisigke, *Wörterbuch*, III, 33-35.
[37]Hans Volkmann, "Ptolemaios 18," *RE*, XXIII² (1959), 1611-13, 1615-16, 1623-25; "Ptolemaios 19, " *ibid.*, col. 1645; "Eurydike 3," *Der Kleine Pauly*, II (1967), 452.
[38]See Tcherikover, p. 460, n. 43.
[39]For the present, see Tcherikover, pp. 61, 64-65, 105-6.
[40]Volkmann, "Ptolemaios 20" and "Ptolemaios 21," *RE*, XXIII, 1666-67.
[41]For the present, see Tcherikover, pp. 57-74, 105-6.

parsimonious high priest Onias could have dared to refuse to pay tribute to either. The Seleucid empire did not relinquish its claim to the area, but never challenged Ptolemy I and in conflicts with Ptolemy II never got near Judaea.[42] The hold of the Ptolemies on Palestine weakened first under Ptolemy III.

Tcherikover[43] and Stern[44] try to date Onias' refusal of tribute in 242 or ca. 240, near the close of the Third Syrian War, when Seleucus II was counterattacking against Ptolemy III and threatening the Ptolemaic holdings in Asia. However, in that year Ptolemy III kept firm hold on Jerusalem. Seleucus II did capture Damascus and Orthosia and held out against vigorous Ptolemaic efforts to retake them in 242/1, but his attempt to push on into Ptolemaic territory in that year failed completely[45] Hence, in 242/1 there was little if any time in which a high priest in Jerusalem could decide it was safe to refuse tribute, receive a threatening message from a Ptolemy, and reject it. Moreover, the narrative of the Tobiad story at its outset reflects a time of peace: what king would harshly demand tribute in an insecure border-area? What tax-farmer would bid high in a time of insecurity? Rather, Onias' refusal to pay tribute probably came in the inactive last years of Ptolemy III, after 241.[46]

Joseph's clever son, Hyrcanus, went to Egypt to felicitate a Ptolemy on the birth of a son (AJ xii. 4. 7. 196-97). Leading men from the entire empire came to celebrate the birth; hence, it was the birth of a legitimate child. The child can be neither of the two sons of Ptolemy III. Ptolemy IV was about 17 years old at his accession late in 222,[47] and his brother Magas was old enough to be a menace to him.[48] Both, then, were born before 234, and Hyrcanus, who was begotten after 241, after his father became tax-farmer, cannot have come as a youth of over 13 (AJ xii. 4. 6-7. 190-97) in honor of the birth of either. The son born to a Ptolemy could be only Ptolemy V Epiphanes, the one son of Ptolemy IV, and he was born in 210.[49] Reckoning back again from Hyrcanus' age upon his visit to Alexandria, we find that Joseph must have become tax-farmer before 223.

---

[42]Volkmann, RE, XXIII, 1646-48, 1650-52, 1654-56.
[43]P. 129.
[44]Tarbiz, XXXII, 43.
[45]Justin xxvii. 2. 5; Daniel 11.9; Volkmann, RE, XXIII, 1671.
[46]A. Bouché-Leclercq, Histoire des Lagides (Paris, 1903-7), I, 264-85.
[47]Volkmann, "Ptolemaios 22," RE, XXXIII, 1678; Alan E. Samuel, Ptolemaic Chronology (München, 1962), pp. 106-8.
[48]Volkmann, RE, XXIII, 1679.
[49]Volkmann, "Ptolemaios 23," RE, XXIII, 1691; cf. Stern, Tarbiz, XXXII, 43-44.

A logical time for the end of Joseph's 22 prosperous years as tax-farmer would be the death of Ptolemy IV Philopator in 205 or 204.[50] In the troubled years which followed, no tax-farmer for the Ptolemies in Syria and Palestine would enjoy good fortune; after Syria and Palestine became the theater of the bitter fighting of the Fifth Syrian war in 202, any such tax-farmer lost heavily.[51] An end for the 22 years around 205 implies a beginning around 227.

The story of the Tobiads gives no reason why Onias II refused to pay tribute to Ptolemy III. As we shall see, the original author of the story was a pro-Ptolemaic Jewish propagandist. It was not to his interest to suggest that in the reign of Ptolemy III there was a pro-Seleucid plot among the Jews which involved the high priest himself. Hence, the original author ascribed the refusal of tribute to the stupidity, childish stubbornness, and avarice of an old man.

Onias, however, may have had good political reasons to refuse to pay tribute. By shortly after 230 Seleucus II had finally won his war with his brother Antiochus Hierax;[52] in 228/7 Antiochus Hierax was killed in Thrace.[53] With the threat from his brother removed, Seleucus II could think of expansion at the expense of his neighbors, the Ptolemaic and Attalid kingdoms. We know nothing of overt moves by Seleucus II before his death in 225. He may have encouraged Onias II to defy Ptolemy III. The next Seleucid, Seleucus III (225-223), did indeed proceed promptly against the Attalids, and Daniel 11:10 suggests that Seleucus III with his brother, the future Antiochus III, planned an attack on the Ptolemaic empire.[54] Thus, Onias II could have had good

---

[50]See Hermann Bengtson, *Griechische Geschichte* (4th ed.; München, 1969), p. 425, n. 5. Stern, *Tarbiẓ*, XXXII, 45-47, suggests that the 22 years ended in 218 when Joseph could have been driven by the brilliant but temporary victories of Antiochus III (Volkmann, *RE*, XXIII, 1680-84) to acts which lost him Ptolemaic favor. However, Josephus' narrative implies that Hyrcanus' mission to congratulate Ptolemy IV on the birth of his son in 210 fell within the 22 years (*AJ* xii. 4. 7. 196: Joseph was still one of the grandees of Syria and the territories subject to the Ptolemies; 10. 224). Also, the motive for Joseph's anger against his favorite son may have been fear that Hyrcanus had supplanted him as tax-farmer.

[51]Volkmann, *RE*, XXIII, 1692-95, 1699, 1702; J. *AJ* xii. 3. 3. 129-39.

[52]Bickerman, "Notes on Seleucid and Parthian Chronology," *Berytus*, VIII (1944), 78.

[53]Bengtson, p. 410.

[54]See Edwyn R. Bevan, *The House of Seleucus* (London, 1902), I, 204; Daniel 11.10 ($Q^e r\bar{e}$ and the Greek of Theodotion): "His sons shall wage war..." See, however, H.L. Ginsberg, *Studies in Daniel* (New York, 1948), p. 47. The seer in Daniel 11.10 may have begun with the plural, speaking of the two sons of Seleucus II, and gone on in the singular to speak only of Antiochus III. If so,

reason to refuse tribute either in the reign of Seleucus II or in the reign of Seleucus III.[55]

We still must account for the story of the king and queen both being involved in the giving of tax-farming contracts and for Joseph's witty suggestion that they each be his surety for the other. These strange facts do not presuppose Antiochus III's fictitious gift of Syria and Palestine as dowry upon the marriage of Cleopatra I to Ptolemy V. Many documents show how Ptolemies associated their wives with them in transactions and decrees. This was especially true beginning with the reign of Ptolemy VI Philometor,[56] but is well documented already under Ptolemy III.[57] Even if the strong-minded Berenice II did not hold land in Syria and Palestine in her own right, she could still have been involved with her husband in the negotiations for farming the taxes,[58] or else, if the original author wrote taking for granted the institutions existing from the reign of Ptolemy VI, the original author could have imagined she was so involved.

Thus, the only internal evidence against setting the story of the Tobiads in the reigns of Ptolemies III and IV is the queen's name, "Cleopatra." The first Ptolemaic Cleopatra was the wife of Ptolemy V. The treatment of the name is Josephus' text is strange. The queen is only mentioned in connection with the king, but wherever the queen is mentioned, her husband is mentioned only as "the king," never with his name "Ptolemy" or with his cult-epithet.[59] We shall see that Josephus found the original version of the story chronologically incredible. It is

---

read *wb' bnw*, "And then his one son will come...," for the ungrammatical *wb' bw'*.

[55] Onias may also have expected the imminent fulfilment of Daniel 2.44. I cannot deal here with the possibility.

[56] Ptolemy VI and Cleopatra II: *Sammelbuch* 9681; A.S. Hunt and C.C. Edgar, *Select Papyri*, Vol. II (Cambridge, Mass., and London, 1934), Nos. 272 and 273. Ptolemy VIII and Cleopatra II and/or Cleopatra III: *Sammelbuch* 8396, 8880, 9899, 100096.

[57] Volkmann, RE, XXIII, 1675-77.

[58] The formula in the document selling the taxes to a tax-farmer was "we sell" (*pôloumen*). In extant documents the subject of the verb is not expressed. It could as easily be the king and queen as the king alone. See Claire Préaux, *L'économie royale des Lagides* (Bruxelles, 1939), p. 451; Ulrich Wilcken, *Urkunden der Ptolemäerzeit*, I (Berlin and Leipzig, 1927), p. 509, on No. 112, Col. I, line 1.

[59] *AJ* xii. 4. 1. 154 is Josephus' own effort to give the chronological setting. At 3. 167, we have "the king and his wife, Cleopatra"; at 3. 171 and at 4. 178, neither is named; at 5. 185, we have "the king and Cleopatra"; at 8. 204, we have "Cleopatra...the king...Cleopatra"; at 9. 217, "the king...Cleopatra."

easy to understand how Josephus could have removed the king's name and cult-epithet in an effort to "correct" the narrative he found so incredible. If so, did he also alter the queen's name to "Cleopatra"? By Josephus' time, the belief had long been prevalent, that all Ptolemaic queens were Cleopatras.[60] However, it is more likely that Josephus did not so "emend" the text, for if he had, one would have expected him also to identify the king as Ptolemy V Epiphanes. As we shall see when we identify him, the original author had good reason to misname Berenice II and Arsinoë III as "Cleopatra," and good reason not to name the king.

We must now consider the subsequent career of Hyrcanus. As long as the Ptolemies held the region, he could remain uneventfully in Transjordan, as tax-collector. With the Seleucid conquest, he probably lost his office of tax-collector but may still have held an influential if precarious position in the area. The original author, if he was indeed a pro-Ptolemaic propagandist, would say little or nothing of his hero Hyrcanus' accommodations with the rival Seleucids. For their part, the Seleucids may have been content to leave Hyrcanus unmolested for many years in Transjordan, on the principle, "Let sleeping dogs lie." With the death of Joseph, some time after the accession of Seleucus IV in 187, Hyrcanus attempted to return by force to Jerusalem, but he was repulsed and thereafter became a "robber-baron" in the old Tobiad stronghold. We may be able to date Hyrcanus' attempt and repulse more accurately, but first we must survey this entire phase of his career.

Hyrcanus' policy as a robber-baron in Transjordan surely looked to the Ptolemaic empire. A petty chieftain preying on border territories claimed by one empire can hardly help looking for support and safety to the near-by rival empire, especially if he enjoyed Hyrcanus' earlier close ties of friendship with the reigning dynasty of the rival empire. The high priest Simon II probably led the Jews to change their allegiance from the Ptolemaic to the Seleucid empire.[61] Simon II supported Hyrcanus' "wicked" brothers, surely because both Simon and the brothers had a pro-Seleucid policy. Indeed, Hyrcanus was regarded as a rebel by the Seleucid kings, and his brothers had the favor and support of Antiochus IV, who at their behest massacred the pro-Ptolemaic faction in Jerusalem (*BJ* i. 1. 1. 31-32; cf. *AJ* xii. 5. 3. 247).

---

[60]Thus Livy at xxvii. 4. 10 calls Arsinoë III, the wife of Ptolemy IV, "Cleopatra." So prevalent was the name among the females of the later Ptolemaic dynasty, that even Berenice III bore the name after 89 B.C. See Stähelin, "Kleopatra 21," *RE*, XI (1922), 782. The brief reign of Berenice IV and the brief prominence of Arsinoë, sister of Cleopatra IV, left little impression.

[61]See above, n. 15.

Hyrcanus won a minor victory when the high priest Onias III sympathized with him enough to accept his deposits at the temple (Second Maccabees 3:11), but the death of Ptolemy V in 180 and the bungling regime of the guardians of his child-heirs left Hyrcanus with small hope of support. Hyrcanus' death can be placed with considerable confidence late in 170 or in 169, when Antiochus IV's victories in Egypt seemed to end all hope that the Ptolemies would reconquer Syria and Palestine.[62]

Against this dating stands the note at *AJ* xii. 4. 11. 234, that Hyrcanus' career as robber-baron lasted "seven years, through all the time that Seleucus was king of Syria." The natural interpretation of the words is that Hyrcanus was a robber-baron for no longer than seven years, and that his career came to an end only a short time after the death of Seleucus IV. If so, the seven years would extend from 182/1 to 175 or 174. This would be in harmony with the implication of *AJ* xii. 4. 11. 234-35, that Ptolemy V (died 180) died after Hyrcanus became a robber-baron. However, Josephus appears not to have understood his sources properly. The same passage has Ptolemy V dying at the same time as Seleucus IV, or later. Moreover, Josephus' own account puts Hyrcanus' suicide in the reign of Antiochus IV and suggests that Ptolemaic weakness had as much to do with Hyrcanus' suicide as had Seleucid power.[63] Antiochus IV is not reported to have invaded Transjordan. Hence, his reported confiscation of Hyrcanus' property probably took place when he sacked the temple in 169: Antiochus IV accomplished what Heliodorus failed to do (cf. Second Maccabees 5.18). If so, reckoning the seven years as ending in 170 or 169, we have them beginning in 177/6 at the earliest. We might disregard, as a mistake of Josephus', the questionable implication at *AJ* xii. 4. 11. 234-35, that Ptolemy V died after Hyrcanus became a robber-baron. Alternatively, we might regard the number "seven" as corrupt. Then, though there would be no way of being sure what the original number was, one could suggest a plausible guess. If in Josephus' source numbers were expressed not in words but in figures, "17" (ιζ) could easily have become "7" (ζ). If so, the 17 years began near the beginning of the reign of Seleucus IV, between 187 and 185.

Thus, the original account of the Tobiads made sense and had a consistent chronology, which we may summarize as follows:

---

[62]Volkmann, "Ptolemaios 24," *RE*, XXIII, 1704-9, and for the present, see especially Otto Mørkholm, *Antiochus IV of Syria* (København, 1966), pp. 64-87. I shall treat the subject in a later study.
[63]*AJ* xii. 4. 11. 234-36.

Between 227 and 224	Seleucid ambitions threaten Ptolemaic hold on Syria and Palestine. Onias II refuses to pay tribute to Ptolemy III Euergetes. Joseph the Tobiad becomes tax-farmer.
Between 226 and 223	Hyrcanus born.
221	Accession of Ptolemy IV Philopator.
210	Birth of Ptolemy V Epiphanes. Hyrcanus wins favor of Ptolemy IV, but his jealous brothers drive Hyrcanus to flee to Transjordan, where he becomes a tax-collector.
205 or 204	Death of Ptolemy IV, leaving Ptolemaic empire weak under the child-king, Ptolemy V.
Between 205 and 202	End of Joseph's 22 prosperous years as tax-farmer.
202-197	Fifth Syrian War. Antiochus III conquers Syria and Palestine. High priest Simon II and Tobiads of Jerusalem turn pro-Seleucid.
187-165	Reign of Seleucus IV. Joseph dies. Hyrcanus fails in attempt to return to Jerusalem and becomes independent robber-baron in Transjordan. Onias III accepts Hyrcanus' deposits at the temple in Jerusalem. Heliodorus fails to seize the deposits.
Between November 170 and summer, 169	Sixth Syrian War begins. Antiochus IV overruns most of Egypt. Hyrcanus commits suicide.
Late summer or early autumn, 169	Jason the Oniad fails in pro-Ptolemaic coup at Jerusalem.[64] Antiochus IV sacks the temple. Jason withdraws to Ammanitis.

As for the sensational details of the story which appeared so incredible as to provoke our Question 10, only the figure for the taxes of Syria and Palestine at *AJ* xii. 4. 4. 175 need be fictitious.[65] Ancient authors writing of a past generation famous for its prosperity were prone to such exaggerations even when they aimed to write the sober

---

[64]See my *I Maccabees*, p. 207, and my *II Maccabees*, pp. 246-54. Rejected by Antiochus IV, who let Menelaus supplant him, Jason could easily have turned to the pro-Ptolemaic side. Indeed, Jason's coup is described as pro-Ptolemaic at *BJ* i. 1. 1. 32, as we saw above. Further confirmation of Jason's position can be found in the fact that after the failure of his coup he fled first to the Ammanitis (II Maccabees 5.7), stronghold of the pro-Ptolemaic Hyrcanus, who probably committed suicide shortly before.

[65]See Tcherikover, p. 460, n. 42.

truth.[66] Youthful wit at royal courts and teenagers undertaking military enterprises were commonplace phenomena in the Hellenistic age.[67]

Though we have established the original chronology, the story of the Tobiads in Josephus remains a puzzle. The narrator is sympathetic to the Ptolemies. He approves of, indeed takes pride in, the heroes Joseph and Hyrcanus.[68] But the Ptolemies lost their hold on Syria and Palestine and their defeat meant the ultimate failure of Joseph and Hyrcanus; the surviving members of the family, according to the story itself, were traitors to the Jews, implicated in the atrocities of Antiochus IV. What Jew would tell proudly of the temporary financial and diplomatic successes of a father and son from such a family? Yet the narrator gloats in such a way over the discomfiture of gentiles that he cannot have been a non-Jew.[69]

The story could hardly have come from a larger work on the history of the Jews, or Josephus would have drawn on the larger work to give a better picture of the period. In its setting in Josephus, the tale of the family of tax-farmers makes a poor substitute for national history. Surely more occurred in the years between Ptolemy V's marriage to Cleopatra in 197 and Antiochus IV's sack of Jerusalem in 169 than the careers of the Tobiads which Josephus forces into the period. Ben Sira informs us of many undertakings, especially the activity of the high priest Simon II.[70] The focus of our story is so closely on the cleverness of Joseph and Hyrcanus and on the relations with the Ptolemies that it is hard to see how it could come from a national history. No specifics are given as to how Joseph improved the lot of his people (*AJ* xii. 4. 10. 224), and the tale of the begetting of Hyrcanus and the details of Hyrcanus' conduct in Alexandria were surely not the stuff of history for a Greek, much less for a Jew. Such stories could be used as illustrations

---

[66]Cf. I Kings 10.14-21.

[67]See, e.g., Plutarch *Alexander* 5-9, *Demetrius* 4-5, *Eumenes* 1, and *Pyrrhus* 4; cf. Tcherikover, p. 461, n. 50.

[68]*AJ* xii. 4. 2. 160, 166; 3. 167, 173; 5. 182; 6. 186, 189-95; 8. 207; 9. 214, 219-20; 10. 224.

[69]See *AJ* xii. 4. 3. 174; 4. 179; 5. 180-83 with 6. 186; 9. 211-14, 217-18; 10. 224.

[70]Josephus probably knew of Ben Sira's work, copies of which have been found at Masada and Qumran. Josephus may have followed his own chronological theories to date Ben Sira in the third century and to regard Ben Sira's high priest Simon as Simon I "the Just." More likely, however, the pro-Hasmonaean Josephus may have discounted Ben Sira's book as propaganda favoring the high-priestly line of Simon II and Onias III and Onias IV, the challenger of Hasmonaean high-priestly legitimacy. Ben Sira is, indeed, a pro-Oniad propagandist.

Tales of the Tobiads 133

of national decadence, but the author on the contrary takes pride in them.

The narrative does not serve the purposes of family history, either, for it completely ignores the earlier glories of the Tobiads[71] to assert that Joseph rose purely through winning the favor of the Ptolemies. And then the author goes to great lengths in describing how Hyrcanus duplicated his father's feat of winning Ptolemaic favor, an achievement which was not only sterile but cost Hyrcanus and his family dearly.[72]

Could Josephus' source have been a biography or a fictional romance? The Biblical stories of the Patriarchs and of Moses, Samson, Saul, and David might have served a Jewish writer as precedents for a biography. Works like Tobit, Esther, Judith, and Third Maccabees could have served as examples of Jewish romances. The little that is known of Hellenistic biography – its interest in scandalous and spectacular exploits and reversals of fate – suggests that a Hellenized Jew might have written our story as biography.[73] However, such a biography surely would have had considerable detail on the character and deeds of Joseph and Hyrcanus, including their religious practice and Hyrcanus' relations with his fellow-Jews while in exile in Transjordan. Hellenistic biography and fictional romance give much attention to the hero's piety and group loyalty.[74] Surely the pious Josephus would not have omitted such details so as to leave the narrative with its present remarkably unedifying character. Hence, Josephus' source could hardly have been a biography, whether after the Greek or after the Jewish pattern.

Still less could it have been a fictional romance. The historical fiction produced by Jews in the Hellenistic period (e.g., *Aristeas to Philocrates*, the Hebrew and Greek books of Esther, Judith, and Third Maccabees) all had both a happy ending and an edifying message. Both are conspicuously absent from the Tobiad story in Josephus. If our story was extracted from a larger work of fiction, one could ask, what came after the end of our extract? Moralizing on Hyrcanus' bad end? That would be strange in view of the sympathy shown him in the narrative and would still leave the ending sad. More events about the Tobiads? The surviving members of the family were wicked and came to

---

[71] Mazar, *IEJ*, VII, 137-45, 229-38.
[72] Cf. Stern, *Tarbiz*, XXXII, 37-38.
[73] See Albin Lesky, *Geschichte der griechischen Literatur* (2d ed.; Bern and München, 1963), pp. 741-42.
[74] See Moses Hadas (ed.), *The Third and Fourth Books of Maccabees* (New York, 1953), pp. 13-15.

a bad end. Moreover, the accurate historical allusions and the date of composition, as we shall see, put the story too close to the events to leave it likely that here is a historical romance. The ancients did not write romances about the recent past.[75]

If the story is not history and is not fiction, what is it? There is at least one other possibility. The story could be propaganda. It does indeed have a message and a moral: that it pays for a Jew to cooperate with the Ptolemies. Joseph, who did so, prospered and was the benefactor of his nation. This Joseph might succumb to sexual temptation, as Judah did with Tamar and King David did with Bathsheba, but the Tobiad's brother saved him from sinning thereby. The offspring of the brother's virtuous trickery was Hyrcanus. Talented young Hyrcanus would have continued the policy of collaboration with the Ptolemies which had such beneficial results. The Jewish nation, however, was robbed of enjoying Hyrcanus' talents. Hyrcanus' envious brothers, aided by the high priest Simon II, drove him out of Jerusalem and turned to a policy of collaboration with the wicked Seleucids. Finally wicked Antiochus IV drove Hyrcanus to suicide.[76]

As far as we can tell, Pro-Ptolemaic-anti-Seleucid policy in the Tobiad family ended with Hyrcanus' death. But Jewish collaboration with the Ptolemies against the Seleucids was a live issue into the first century B.C. The original author obviously survived Hyrcanus' death. A pro-Ptolemaic propagandist among the Jews could not have allowed his work to conclude with the disastrous fate of Hyrcanus. In fact, the account in Josephus presents more information on the Tobiads, information which serves the same propagandistic purpose: Menelaus and the surviving, pro-Seleucid Tobiads, rejected by the majority of their people, bought Antiochus IV's support by toadying to the mad enthusiasms of the Seleucid king and thus brought first the "Hellenization of Jerusalem" and then the atrocious persecution.

This view Josephus could have derived from no other source known to us. The author of First Maccabees 1.11-64 does not name the wicked, nor does he say that the Hellenizers were driven by any domestic pressures. To him their wickedness was deliberate perversity; and divine wrath, not the advice of Tobiad renegades or the rebellion of pro-Ptolemaic Jews, turned Antiochus IV into a persecutor (*ibid.*, verse 64). Jason of Cyrene never blames the Tobiads but with great emphasis lays the guilt upon the Oniad Jason and upon Menelaus and secondarily

---

[75] Cf. Stern, *Tarbiz*, XXXII, 38. On Greek romances in the second century B.C., see Ben Edward Perry, *The Ancient Romances* (Berkeley and Los Angeles, 1967), pp. 153-77.
[76] Cf. Stern, *Tarbiz*, XXXII, 39-40.

upon their followers and again ascribes the persecution to God's wrath (Second Maccabees 4.7-17; 6.12-16; 13.3-8).

To give bribes against the interests of justice and against the interests of one's countrymen is normally considered discreditable. Jason and Menelaus both bribed Antiochus IV in order to usurp the highpriesthood (Second Maccabees 4.8-9, 24), and Menelaus gave further bribes to the king's officials in order to obstruct justice (*ibid.*, 4.34, 45). The Tobiads, too, surely offered incentives to Antiochus. All these bribes could be shown to have disastrous results for the Jews. Hence, an impartial observer writing a history of the Jews (e.g., Herod's friend, the historian Nicolaus of Damascus) probably would have named all three groups of bribers, or, like First Maccabees, he would have named none. We can understand why Jason of Cyrene (or the abridger), writing long after the events, cares nothing for the guilt of the Tobiads, an extinct wicked family but goes to great lengths to condemn the impious high priests. In Second Maccabees, Jason the Oniad, the eventual partisan of the Ptolemies, receives at least as much condemnation as Menelaus, the loyal creature of the Seleucids. Indeed, though Jason of Cyrene quotes a speech complimentary to Hyrcanus the Tobiad (II Maccabees 3.11), he nowhere shows us any pro-Ptolemaic bias. The account in Josephus' *Antiquities*, on the other hand, shifts all blame from Jason to the surviving Tobiads, and to Menelaus and Antiochus. To blame the surviving Tobiads and Menelaus and Antiochus fits the propaganda message of the story of Joseph and Hyrcanus, and hence we are correct in assuming that *AJ* xii. 5. 1. 239-41 as well as *BJ* i. 1. 1. 31-32 came from that same source. The account at *AJ* xii. 5. 1. 239-41 does a strange thing: it exonerates Jason, who has the support of the majority of the people. Does it do so because of his pro-Ptolemaic position? We might also ask, does Josephus' history contain any further sections which might be ascribed to this same source? To answer these questions we must first establish the identity of the author of our story and the date of its composition, a task which Josephus' carelessness has made easy.

The *terminus post quem* is given by *AJ* xii. 4. 1. 158, where the writer finds it necessary to say that this Ptolemy Euergetes is the father of Ptolemy Philopator, implying that by his time there had been more than one Ptolemy Euergetes. Hence, he wrote sometime after Ptolemy VIII assumed the cult-epithet "Euergetes." Ptolemaic kings assumed cult-epithets upon their accession, and there is no reason to assume that Ptolemy VIII did otherwise. The only question is, when did Ptolemy VIII consider he had "acceded"? He counted his regnal years from his joint reign with Ptolemy VI, which began in 170. He arrived in Egypt as a rival claimant against Cleopatra II and Ptolemy VII by late

September, 145. He certainly had "acceded" by the time he married Cleopatra II, by late spring, 144, and an inscription shows him bearing his cult-epithet while married only to Cleopatra II, hence before his marriage to Cleopatra III in 142; another inscription probably shows him bearing the cult-epithet while courting Cleopatra II.[77]

Who was the pro-Ptolemaic, anti-Seleucid Jewish propagandist? He wrote after summer, 145. He believed that there could be sympathetic mutual respect between Greeks and Jews. In particular, he admired clever Jews who succeeded in the Greco-Macedonian world through loyal service to the Ptolemies. He believed that the Torah should be obeyed, but his moral sense was not much offended by the sexual lapses of Joseph and the sharp practices of Joseph and Hyrcanus. He hated the pro-Seleucid Tobiads and Menelaus, the first usurper to

---

[77]Cf. Volkmann, "Ptolemaios 27," *RE*, XXIII, 1721, 1725-26. First inscription: Wilhelm Dittenberger, *Orientis Graeci Inscriptiones Selectae* 130. In the inscription Cleopatra II as was customary shares her husband's cult-epithet. The inscription of a statue-base from Crete, however, records that King Ptolemy VIII, already bearing the cult-epithet "Euergetes," set up a statue of his sister, Cleopatra II *Philometor*, naming her with the cult-epithet she got from her first husband, Ptolemy VI. The statue was probably a conciliatory gesture by Ptolemy VIII, already recognized by some as Ptolemaic king, during his negotiations with Cleopatra II in 145 or 144 and before their marriage. Hence, we would know that Ptolemy VIII assumed the cult-epithet before the marriage. The inscription was published by Margherita Guarducci (*Miscellanea di studi alessandrini in memoria di Augusto Rostagni* [Torino: Bottega d'Erasmo, 1963], pp. 214-221), who dated it between 124 and 116, viewing the statue as a conciliatory gesture at the end of the war of 131-124 between Ptolemy VIII and Cleopatra II. Apparently she never considered the possibility of dating it in 145-144. The later date is unlikely for several reasons. In 145-144 "Philometor" was an innocuous part of Cleopatra II's official name. In 131 it became a piece of propaganda against Ptolemy VIII, stressing that only the line of Ptolemy VI had the right to rule; see below, n. 113. No other document of 124-116 shows Ptolemy VIII allowing the use of the provocative epithet. Finally, though the Ptolemaic empire had a garrison at Itanos on Crete in the reign of Ptolemy VI and perhaps for a short time after his sudden death, thereafter there is no trace of a Ptolemaic foothold on Crete; see Guarducci, *ibid.*, p. 219, and *Inscriptiones Creticae*, Vol. III, p. 77, and Stylianos Spyridakis, *Ptolemaic Itanos and Hellenistic Crete* ("University of California Publications in History," Vol. LXXXII; Berkeley and Los Angeles, 1970), pp. 82-83, 86, 98; Walter Otto, *Zur Geschichte der Zeit des, 6. Ptolemäers* ("Abhandlungen der Bayerischen Akademie der Wissenschaften, Philosophisch-historische Abteilung," Neue Folge, Heft XI [1934]; München, 1934), p. 133. See now Wehrli, *ZPE*, XV (1974), 8-10. On the date of the marriage of Ptolemy VIII to Cleopatra III, see Heinz Heinen, "Les mariages de Ptolémée VIII et leur chronologie," *Akten des XIII. Internationalen Papyrologenkongresses* ("Münchener Beiträge zur Papyrusforschung und antiken Rechtsgeschichte," LXVI; München, 1974), pp. 147-55.

break the line of Oniad high priests.[78] As Stern has noticed,[79] the author was so attached to the Ptolemaic system that he uses Ptolemaic terminology, calling the huge province in which Joseph was active "Syria and Phoenicia"[80] or simply "Syria,"[81] rather than using the Seleucid names "Coele-Syria and Phoenicia" or simply "Coele-Syria."[82]

There is an obvious candidate fitting this description: Onias IV, son of the high priest Onias III, trusted and loyal military commander for Ptolemy VI and for his sister-wife and successor Cleopatra II. Onias IV was also the disappointed legitimate Oniad pretender to the high-priesthood and the founder of the Jewish temple of Leontopolis in Egypt.[83] Onias IV could have written his propagandistic memoirs (*hypomnēmata*).[84] The strange manner in which the high priest Jason is exonerated at *AJ* xii. 4. 1. 158 serves to confirm the identification of the author with Onias IV. His uncle Jason, though a usurper and a Hellenizer and a temporary collaborator with the Seleucids, had had nothing to do with *forcing* Jews to violate the Torah and was a legitimate member of the Oniad line. His pro-Ptolemaic coup, though unsuccessful and regarded by Jason of Cyrene as murderously cruel, served to atone for his collaboration with the Seleucids. Onias IV moved in the Hellenistic world as much as his uncle Jason had. Probably, so did Onias III, who was highly esteemed by gentiles when he was murdered after long residing at Antioch. Perhaps even Ben

---

[78]The Oniads traced their descent from the high priest Jeshua of the priestly clan of Yeda'yah. See Ezra 2.36; Nehemiah 7.39, 12.1, 6, 10-11; I Chronicles 9.10, 24.7; and R. de Vaux, *Ancient Israel* (New York, 1961), pp. 388-403, and J. Liver, "The 'Sons of Zadok the Priests' in the Dead Sea Sect," *Revue de Qumran*, VI (1967), 18-28. Menelaus came from the priestly clan of Bilgah; see II Maccabees 4.23-25 and 3.4, reading Balgea with the Latin versions. Josephus' effort to represent Menelaus as an Oniad is a piece of pro-Hasmonaean, anti-Oniad propaganda, whether due to Josephus himself or to his source.

[79]*Tarbiz*, XXXII, 39.

[80]*AJ* xii. 4. 3. 169.

[81]*Ibid.*, 3. 174; 5. 180; 7. 196, 201; 9. 212. Josephus did not understand the terminology and mistakenly tried to correct it at *AJ* xii. 4. 1. 154, at 4. 175, and at 10. 224.

[82]Josephus found the Ptolemaic terminology in his source puzzling. Probably he was not even acquainted with Seleucid terminology, as is indicated by his own introductory paragraph at *AJ* xii. 4. 1. 154, where he feels it necessary to mention Samaria and Judaea though the Seleucid province of Coele-Syria and Phoenicia included them.

[83]*AJ* xii. 5. 1. 237; 7. 387-88; xiii. 3. 1. 62-73 (and cf. 10. 4. 285-87 and 13. 1-2. 351-54); xx. 10. 3. 236; *BJ* i. 1. 1. 33; vii. 10. 2. 421-32; *Ap.* ii. 5. 49-53. See also Uriel Rapaport, "Les Iduméens en Égypte," *Revue de philologie*, 3d series, XLIII (1969), 79-81.

[84]See my *II Maccabees*, pp. 35-36.

Sira's revered Simon II had been something of a moderate Hellenizer.[85] Onias IV surely held against Jason the supplanting of Onias III. But he would tend to pass over in silence any pro-Seleucid tendencies of his ambiguous uncle as well as any role of Jason's in the atrocious persecutions inflicted on the Jews by Antiochus IV. On the other hand, Onias IV could well be proud that Joseph and Hyrcanus, the earlier distinguished Jewish supporters of the Ptolemaic cause, were his close kin, and could well stress the fact in his narrative.[86]

Even errors in the account as presented by Josephus are partly explained by the assumption that Onias IV was the author, in particular, the naming of the queen as Cleopatra rather than Berenice or Arsinoe. Onias IV and his heirs owed their successes especially to the female sovereigns of the Ptolemaic line, Cleopatras II and III.[87] Onias IV was a clever soldier but hardly a professional writer of propagandistic history intent on giving an impression of accuracy. Writing after summer, 145, he was late enough to imagine that early Ptolemaic queens were also Cleopatras; and wishing to flatter his energetic patroness, Cleopatra II, Onias IV may have deliberately singled out an imagined earlier Cleopatra as the patroness of his kinsman. Cleopatra II hated her second husband, Ptolemy VIII Euergetes II. She also bitterly hated her daughter, Cleopatra III, after Euergetes II marred Cleopatra III in 142, though a strange compromise by 139 saw the Ptolemaic empire with two queens. Thereafter the official style distinguished the two Queens Cleopatra by giving Cleopatra II the title "Sister" and Cleopatra III the title "Wife," of Ptolemy VIII.[88] It may have been Onias IV, not Josephus, who refrained from naming the king in our story after twice identifying him at *AJ* xii. 4. 1. 158 and 2. 163. Thereafter, the name and cult-epithet might have irritated his patroness by reminding her of the hated Euergetes II. In fact, Euergetes II strove mightily in his propaganda to

---

[85]Onias III: II Maccabees 4:5, 33-35; Simon II: see above, n. 15. With considerable probability, one may trace back farther the family heritage of the Oniads, to seek relations of mutual respect between Greeks and Jews. Chronologically, the Onias to whom Areus I of Sparta addressed a letter can have been only Onias II. The letter is authentic and probably was preserved in an archive at Jerusalem. See my *I Maccabees*, pp. 455-59, and my *II Maccabees*, p. 29.

[86]One who intended to discredit the Oniads might also stress their kinship with the Tobiads (as did Josephus), but he would not have *written* a narrative proudly sympathetic to Joseph and Hyrcanus. Josephus *borrowed a previously-written narrative.*

[87]See above, n. 83.

[88]See Volkmann, *RE*, XXIII, 1725-28.

identify himself with Euergetes I and his wife, Cleopatra III, with Berenice II.[89] On the other hand, Onias IV's narrative emphasizes the merits of the *real* Benefactor King, Euergetes I, and his queen-wife, who benefited the Jews in contrast to the poor sham of the reigning Euergetes II and Cleopatra III, who were hostile or indifferent to the Jews.[90] For the sake of the contrast Onias IV could have displayed the name "Cleopatra" prominently in his narrative. Onias IV lived late enough to know little or nothing of the Tubias who dealt with Ptolemy II. Onias IV was glad to portray Tubias' son Joseph, offspring of an Oniad mother, as a self-made man like himself.[91]

Another peculiarity of our story becomes understandable if Onias IV was the author, the identification of Ptolemy III Euergetes at *AJ* xii. 4. 1. 158 as the father of Ptolemy IV Philopator rather than in the normal way, as the son of Ptolemy II Philadelphus. Onias IV had good reason to identify the real benefactor king as the father of Ptolemy Philopator. After the death of Ptolemy VI in the late summer of 145, his young child by Cleopatra II, Ptolemy VII Neos Philopator, was the heir to the throne, but the Alexandrians rebelled against Cleopatra II and her son and offered the throne to Ptolemy VIII. Though Cleopatra's cause was supported by her Jewish army-commanders, one of whom was Onias IV, she was unable to prevail. As a compromise, she let Ptolemy VIII take the throne and married him. However, on the wedding day Ptolemy VIII had the young Philopator murdered.[92] Thereafter, Cleopatra II and her supporters could appreciate allusions suggesting that a real benefactor king would be the father, not the murderer, of a Philopator.

If propagandistic memoirs by Onias IV were Josephus' source for the account of the Tobiads in Book xii of the *Antiquities*, two other sections of the *Antiquities* surely draw on the same source. One is Josephus' detailed account of the origins of Onias IV's temple at Leontopolis (*AJ* xiii. 3. 1-3. 62-73). The other is *AJ* xiii. 4. 5-9. 103-20. There Josephus suddenly ceases to paraphrase First Maccabees and substitutes a

---

[89]See Walter Otto and Hermann Bengtson, *Zur Geschichte des Niederganges des Ptolemäerreiches* ("Abhandlungen der Bayerischen Akademie der Wissenschaften, Philosophisch-historische Abteilung," new series, XVII [1938]), pp. 44. 47-56, 76-87.
[90]Volkmann, *RE*, XXIII, 1726, 1730; Bickerman, "Ein jüdischer Festbrief vom Jahre 124 v. Chr.," *Zeitschrift für die neutestamentliche Wissenschaft*, XXXII (1933), 246-54.
[91]Onias IV, remembering only that Seleucus IV used a cult-epithet also found among the Ptolemies, could have made the error of calling him "Soter" instead of "Philopator." See above, n. 13.
[92]Volkmann, *RE*, XXIII, 1725-26

narrative from another source, markedly favorable to Ptolemy VI Philometor where First Maccabees 11 is hostile and markedly hostile to Alexander Balas where First Maccabees 11 is favorable. As the beneficiary of Ptolemy VI Philometor and his queen, Cleopatra II, Onias IV could well be the author, describing how Ptolemy VI's untimely death prevented a new golden age of Ptolemaic benevolent rule over Judaea and how Seleucid treachery sent the survivors of the Ptolemaic expeditionary force fleeing back to Alexandria. We may imagine that Onias' narrative went on to report how the returning survivors put the wicked Ptolemy VIII in power,[93] so that the death of Ptolemy VI and the ensuing Seleucid treachery brought evil results both for the Jews and for the Ptolemaic empire. Josephus omitted such propaganda as uninteresting, but he probably preferred Onias' account of Ptolemy VI's struggle with Alexander Balas because Greco-Roman opinion of Ptolemy VI and Alexander Balas coincided with Onias'.[94] Josephus was writing for a Greco-Roman audience.

From Onias IV's propaganda as the founder of the temple of Leontopolis (AJ xiii. 3. 1-2. 66-68, 70-71), we can infer one cardinal point of his ideology: the temple at Jerusalem is no longer (or not yet) "the place which the Lord hath chosen."[95] Hence the sole unbroken earthly link to the cult prescribed by God in the Torah is the Aaronid-Zadokite-Oniad line of high priests, of which Onias IV was the heir.[96] From Ben Sira's praise of this high-priestly dynasty[97] we can infer that Ben Sira was their eager propagandist and shared their views. Along with praising the Zadokite priesthood and the present representative of it, the high priest Simon II, Ben Sira also strongly denies the possibility of immortality and resurrection,[98] probably in agreement with the Oniad position. Hence, Onias IV and his followers probably denied the doctrines of immortality and resurrection, and as

---

[93] *Ibid.* On the possibility of a Ptolemaic golden age, see John J. Collins, *Studies in the Sibylline Oracles* (Diss. Harvard, 1972), summarized at *Journal for the Study of Judaism*, III (1972), 182-83.

[94] See Polybius xxviii. 21. 4-5; Diodorus xxxiii. 1. 3. 12. 1; Justin xxxv. 2. 2; Athenaeus v. 211a.

[95] Deuteronomy 12.5-7 etc.; Jeremiah 7.3-15, Ezekiel 24.21, Lamentations 2.7, etc. Onias IV could claim that no miracle had as yet attested God's presence in the second temple. See my *I Maccabees*, pp. 546-47, and my *II Maccabees*, pp. 13-16.

[96] See I Chronicles 6.1-15 and above, n. 78.

[97] Ecclesiasticus 45.6-26, 50.1-24, 51.12 ix.

[98] *Ibid.*, 17.27-28, 22.11, 28.6, 41.11-13, and the lack of any utterance to support the doctrines.

Tales of the Tobiads 141

partisans of the Zadokite line they could well have been the first to be called "Sadducees" (= "Zadokites").[99]

If Onias IV pressed the claims of his family to be the sole unbroken earthly link to the cult prescribed by God in the Torah, how could he prove his point? The strongest proof he could produce to show that God's favor still rested upon the family would be a miracle on behalf of an Oniad high priest in the age of the second temple, when miracles were rare or absent. We read in Second Maccabees 3 that such a miracle did occur, through the merit of Onias IV's own father Onias III. If Onias IV knew of the miracle, surely he must have told of it. Jason of Cyrene, who wrote around 90 B.C. in the reign of Alexander Jannaeus,[100] could draw on the work of Onias IV. Indeed, Jason did draw on it, as can be seen from clues in the narrative of Second Maccabees. Two of these clues are most conspicuous.

The sanctity of the second temple is an unquestionable fact both for Jason of Cyrene and for his abridger: God himself protects the temple, except when Israel sins.[101] Yet the abridged history in Second Maccabees begins with the strange assertion (3.1) that only the piety of Onias III (not God's providence!) gave the Holy City the blessings of peace. This reflects a view like that of Onias IV, that the second temple is not, or is not yet, the place which the Lord hath chosen.

Still more conclusive a clue is the mention of Hyrcanus the Tobiad at Second Maccabees 3.11, which was so puzzling as to produce our Question 9. Indeed, Hyrcanus is nowhere else mentioned in Second Maccabees and need not have been mentioned at 3.11, where by mentioning the deposits of an outlaw Onias III impairs his own plea that the deposits in the temple were inviolable. Onias IV could well have presented Onias III as having done so, for thus he was able to show that divine providence protected both his father Onias III and his hero Hyrcanus. By associating Onias III with Hyrcanus, Onias IV was also able to show that his scrupulous father, too, had pro-Ptolemaic leanings. Jason of Cyrene, who had no such motives, must have taken this part of his story from one of his sources.[102] Who but Onias IV would both ascribe a miracle to the merit of Onias III and regard Hyrcanus as a hero?

Let us now try to determine more precisely the date at which Onias IV wrote. The convergence of the evidence allows us now to state more

---

[99]Cf. J. *BJ* ii. 8. 14. 165 and *AJ* xviii. 1. 4. 16, and see my *II Maccabees*, p. 167.
[100]For proof, see my *II Maccabees*, pp. 82-83.
[101]II Maccabees 2.19-22; 3.12, 18, 30, 38-39; 5.17-20.
[102]See above, n. 28, and M. Stern, "The Death of Onias III," *Zion*, XXV (1960), 5 (in Hebrew)

confidently that Onias wrote propaganda stressing that the Ptolemaic dynasty is normally good to the Jews and that Ptolemy III Euergetes I and his wife "Cleopatra" were the real benefactor couple. Onias might need to write such propaganda as soon as a reigning Ptolemy showed hostility to the Jews, as did Ptolemy VIII Euergetes II around the beginning of his reign in 145.[103] Onias could argue about who were the real benefactor couple only when there was a rival "benefactor couple" to whom Onias and his patroness, Cleopatra II, were hostile. Such a couple existed only after the marriage of Ptolemy VIII to Cleopatra III in 142.

At what Jewish audience did Onias aim his propaganda? The use of Ptolemaic terminology might suggest that it was the Jewry of the Ptolemaic empire, but the interests of the Oniad dynasty surely included winning the support of the Jews of Judaea for the return of the dynasty to the high-priesthood. We ought therefore to look for times at which it would be possible and desirable for Onias to direct such propaganda toward both Jewish audiences.

Onias was a soldier who could be punished for propaganda against the reigning Ptolemy. He would risk such propaganda only when he found it necessary to rally Jewish support around Cleopatra II and only when there was hope that Cleopatra's cause could prevail and only when there was some hope of convincing his Jewish audiences. The years immediately following the marriage in 142 were hardly conducive to such propaganda. The Jews in the Ptolemaic empire must have been impressed by Simon the Hasmonaean's achievement of independence for Judaea in that same year of 142.[104] Simon had won without Ptolemaic aid. Jews in the Ptolemaic empire still remembered how Ptolemy VIII's hostility had menaced them. It would have been difficult to convince even Jews within the Ptolemaic empire that collaboration with the Ptolemies was the best course for Jews everywhere, and it would have been quite impossible to argue that case successfully to Jews of Judaea.

For about a decade after 142 it would appear that Jews and Onias himself had nothing to fear from the regime of Ptolemy VIII. In 145/4 Ptolemy VIII proclaimed a sweeping amnesty for his opponents;[105] and even if the story in Josephus of the miraculously foiled massacre of the

---

[103] J. Ap. ii. 5. 51-56; Bickerman, *Zeitschrift für die neutestamentliche Wissenschaft* XXXII, 253-54.
[104] I Maccabees 13.41.
[105] Marie-Thérèse Lenger, "Décret d'amnistie de Ptolemée Évergète II et lettre aux forces armées de Chypre," *Bulletin de correspondence hellénique*, LXXX (1956), 438-56; Volkmann, *RE*, XXIII, 1726.

Jews of Alexandria is true and belongs in 145/4, the end result saw Ptolemy VIII desisting from anti-Jewish measures.[106] Cleopatra II in 142 did break with her hated husband, and Galaistes, a Greek commander who had served Ptolemy VI, did come from abroad and try to rally rebels around a supposed son of Ptolemy VI. However, no evidence involves either Cleopatra II or Jews in Galaistes' effort; indeed, we are not even told that Galaistes landed in Egypt. Ptolemy VIII's sole difficulties in holding the loyalty of his army were financial. With the help of a wealthy friend he paid the soldiers and kept firm hold of the Ptolemaic empire.[107] Under such circumstances it would not have been safe for Onias IV to circulate his propaganda against Ptolemy VIII, and the Jews, then unmolested, would not have paid it any heed.

Cleopatra II's name reappears in the date-formulas of Ptolemaic documents in 139, clearly showing that some sort of accommodation had been worked out between her and Ptolemy VIII.[108] The period which followed, down to 132, again was unpropitious for the publication of a work like that of Onias IV. Cleopatra II herself had made peace with the false "benefactor couple," and the Jews were unmolested.

---

[106] J. *Ap.* ii. 5. 50-55. Our only source for the events is Josephus' propagandistic reply to Apion's anti-Jewish propaganda. Neither Apion nor Josephus in such polemics was much concerned about precise chronology. Josephus first reports that the Jewish commanders Onias and Dositheus ended a war between the Alexandrians and Cleopatra II and thus saved the Alexandrians from annihilation. The war can hardly be other than the rebellion of the Alexandrians against Cleopatra which followed the death of Ptolemy VI in 145 (Volkmann, *RE*, XXIII, 1725-26). Then Josephus quotes Apion's charge, that Onias "thereafter" marched on Alexandria. How long thereafter? Josephus' reply, that Onias was then protecting the interests of Cleopatra II and of her sons by Ptolemy VI, assumes that the march occurred shortly thereafter, but Josephus himself has just said that Onias and Dositheus had saved the Alexandrians from a disastrous war by *ending* it. Apion's "thereafter" might refer to a march by Onias on Alexandria during Cleopatra II's coup against Ptolemy VIII in 131. Then, indeed, Ptolemy VIII fled, not daring to face the forces fighting for Cleopatra II, as suggested at J. *Ap.* ii. 5. 53; and after his victory Ptolemy VIII proceeded against his non-Jewish opponents with brutality equal to that against the Jews in Josephus' story (*ibid.*). See Volkmann, *RE*, XXIII, 1729-32. If Josephus' story of the foiled massacre belongs to the 120's, we are left to infer the dangers faced by the Jews in the 140's at the hands of Ptolemy VIII from other sources: from Onias IV's steadfast support of Cleopatra II and from Bickerman's interpretation of II Maccabees 1. 1-8; see above, n. 103.

[107] See Volkmann, *RE*, XXIII, 1728.

[108] *Ibid.*

However, Antiochus VII brought the Hasmonaean prince John Hyrcanus and Judaea back under Seleucid domination after a protracted siege of Jerusalem; the campaign probably lasted from 134 or 133 to 132 or 131.[109] Thereupon, Onias IV's case for Jewish collaboration with the Ptolemies became stronger: perhaps God's sentence upon the Jews condemning them to foreign rule still had some time to run.[110]

At this very time, events in the Ptolemaic empire brought about a situation which exactly fits Onias IV's propaganda. In 132/1 Ptolemy VIII began to stress his own identification with Ptolemy III and the identification of his wife Cleopatra III with Berenice II. There is good reason to believe that at least in part Ptolemy VIII did so in order to reassert the Ptolemaic claims to Syria and Palestine,[111] once firmly held by Ptolemy III. These Ptolemaic claims included Judaea. In the same year, in April or May of 131, a new civil war broke out between Ptolemy VIII and Cleopatra III on the one side and Cleopatra II on the other.[112] From the outset of the struggle Cleopatra II took as her cult-epithet "Thea Philometor Soteira," thereby stressing her identification both with her dead husband Ptolemy VI Philometor, a benefactor of the Jews, and with the early origins of the Ptolemaic dynasty ("Soter" was the cult-epithet of Ptolemy I).[113] Onias IV surely wished to rally Jews to the cause of Cleopatra II. It would take considerable effort at this time to persuade Jews that their interests lay with the Ptolemaic dynasty as represented by Cleopatra II. Jews had been scared by Ptolemy VIII in the 140's and had seen even pro-Jewish Cleopatra II join forces with him in a coalition government. If God still willed that the Jews should be subjected to a foreign empire, perhaps that empire was that of the Seleucids, whose king, Antiochus VII, had spared Jerusalem and shown respect to the God of Israel.[114] Hence, well might Onias circulate propaganda to Jews, stressing (1) Onias' links through his kinsmen to the real benefactor couple, Ptolemy III and Berenice II; (2) the merits of Ptolemy VI Philometor and his widow Cleopatra II as opposed to the "false benefactor couple"; and (3) the benevolence of the Ptolemies as against the wickedness of the Seleucids.

There is a firm *terminus ante quem* beyond which Onias IV's propaganda would have been absolutely useless: early in 129 Cleopatra

---

[109] J. *AJ* xiii. 8. 2-3. 236-48; Ralph Marcus, *Josephus*, Vol. IX (London and Cambridge, Mass., 1943), pp. 346-47, n. *c*.
[110] Cf. Daniel 9.4-24.
[111] Otto and Bengtson, pp. 47-56, 76-87.
[112] Volkmann, *RE*, XXIII, 1729-31.
[113] *Ibid.*, col. 1730.
[114] J. *AJ* xiii. 8. 2-3. 242-48; Diodorus xxxiv. i.

II herself was so hard pressed that she, the Ptolemaic queen, betrayed the Ptolemaic cause and sought the aid of her son-in-law, the reigning Seleucid Demetrius II, by offering him rule over Egypt.[115] In that same year, 129, John Hyrcanus and Judaea had become free of Seleucid domination with the death in battle of Antiochus VII.[116] Even Ptolemy VIII was backing a Seleucid pretender, Alexander Zabinas.[117] No longer could Onias present to the Jews the spectacle of the righteous Ptolemies as opposed to the wicked Seleucids. Jews in Judaea again could think of a policy independent of foreign empires, and Jews in the Ptolemaic empire had reason to desert the cause of Cleopatra II as Ptolemy VIII increasingly won the upper hand. Thus, long before Cleopatra II became reconciled in 124 to her enemies Ptolemy VIII and Cleopatra III,[118] it had already become impossible to write the propaganda of Onias IV. We may confidently date Onias' work between the outbreak of the civil war in April or May, 131, and Cleopatra II's offer to Demetrius II in 129.

We turn now to Josephus' use of Onias' work. Josephus' pro-Hasmonaean bias is the key to solving all the remaining problems concerning the strange way in which Josephus presents the stories of the Tobiads.

The supporters of the Zadokite-Oniad line of high priests could claim that the upstart Hasmonaeans, whatever their virtues, had no right to ignore the legitimacy of the earlier dynasty: just before being deposed by the wicked Seleucid kings, the Zadokite-Oniad line had produced the great figures, Simon II the Just[119] and Onias III. Josephus' account removes great Zadokite-Oniad priests from the period of the rise of the Hasmonaeans. Discounting the evidence of Ben Sira and of other Jewish traditions, Josephus asserts that Simon I, of the early third century B.C., was Simon the Just, and with the help of Onias IV leaves Simon II as an ephemeral supporter of wicked Tobiads.[120] Onias III in fact was high priest for an extended period under Seleucus IV, was held to have merited a divine miracle, and later lost his life for a sacred cause.[121] Discounting the evidence for these facts, Josephus reduces Onias III to a nonentity.[122]

---

[115] Volkmann, *RE*, XXIII, 1731.
[116] J. *AJ* xiii. 9. 1. 254-10. 1. 273.
[117] Volkmann, *RE*, XXIII, 1731.
[118] *Ibid.*, cols. 1732-34.
[119] See above, n. 15.
[120] *AJ* xii. 2. 5. 43; 4. 1. 157-58; 10. 224-25, 229.
[121] II Maccabees, 3, 4. 1-38.
[122] *AJ* xii. 4. 10. 225; 5. 1. 237-38.

Josephus wrote at a time when both Simon I and Simon II were little more than names, but Onias III figured prominently both in the work of Onias IV and in the Maccabaean history of Jason of Cyrene. How did Josephus manage to eliminate Onias III as a religiously important figure? Though the narrative of the repulse of Heliodorus as presented by Jason of Cyrene might in itself be unassailable, Josephus perceived that it drew on Onias' work. Attacking Onias' work in the manner of a nineteenth-century German "scientific" critic, Josephus found it to be a very systematic distortion of history for the purposes of Zadokite-Oniad propaganda. By removing the "distortions," Josephus found he could produce the pro-Hasmonaean "truth." An earlier pro-Hasmonaean writer could have produced his "corrected" version of Onias' work, but no evidence suggests that the "scientific critic" was other than Josephus himself.

Josephus found strange historical errors in Onias' original narrative. When Joseph the Tobiad became tax-farmer, both king and queen of the Ptolemaic empire drew revenues in their own right from Syria and Palestine. Josephus could not see how that could be the situation, unless the queen held her rights as part of her dowry. The only Ptolemaic queen who was even reported to have received such a dowry was Cleopatra I.[123] Josephus may have known that the report was suspect as Ptolemaic propaganda, but Onias IV, the author of the work lying before him, was a loyal servant of the Ptolemies, who could not have written contrary to the claims of the dynasty. There was nothing to make Josephus consider the possibility that the Ptolemies claimed Syria and Palestine de jure, on the basis of a dowry which had never been conveyed de facto. Hence, Josephus assumed that Onias placed his narrative in the reign of Ptolemy V and Cleopatra I. If Josephus at all noticed the occurrence of "Euergetes," the cult-epithet of Ptolemy III, he took it to be the common noun, "benefactor."[124]

As soon as Josephus could place the beginning of Joseph the Tobiad's career as tax-farmer in the 190's, several stories involving Zadokite-Oniad high priests immediately roused his suspicions. Onias IV reported that a miraculous apparition, through the merit of Onias III, delivered the temple from Heliodorus, the minister of Seleucus IV. Unlike Onias IV, Josephus believed that the temple in Jerusalem was under the direct protection of God; God did not need to be prompted by any human merit, and Onias III in any case was undistinguished. In another story probably known to Josephus, a suspiciously similar apparition in answer to the prayers of the high priest Simon II

---

[123]Polybius xxviii. 20. 9 and see above, n. 5.
[124]Cf. Luke 22.25.

Tales of the Tobiads 147

delivered the temple from Ptolemy IV.[125] On studying Onias IV's narrative, Josephus found reason to consider all such "Oniad propaganda" a tissue of lies.

At *AJ* xii. 4. 1. 159 Josephus reproduces the crucial passage from Onias IV's work: the dangerous threats of Ptolemy against Judaea, provoked by Onias II's failure to pay tribute "did not at all *discountenance*" (*edysôpei...ouden*) Onias II. Jason of Cyrene's narrative, partly derived from the work of Onias IV, goes to great lengths to portray how Heliodorus' threats *discountenanced* Onias III (Second Maccabees 2.16-17, 21). Josephus could read of both episodes in his copy of the work of Onias IV. Of the earlier episode, Onias IV told how at the dark moment for the Jews, surprisingly though not miraculously, the cleverness of Joseph the Tobiad came to the rescue. Of the later episode, Onias IV told how at the dark moment for the Jews the miraculous apparition came to the rescue. On Josephus' chronology, the events, if real, were separated by only a few years. The similarity of the two events, so close together in time, was incredible to Josephus. He could easily see that Onias IV told of both for the purposes of Oniad propaganda. Josephus knew that even in propaganda there could be some truth. It was not difficult to decide which of the two events to condemn as a propagandistic fabrication. Surely not the earlier one: Joseph the Tobiad stood outside the direct line of the high-priestly dynasty and the Oniad priest involved was contemptible. Surely Onias IV must have fabricated the later "doublet." The "doublet" glorified Onias IV's own father, compensated for the contemptible character of Onias II, and showed that real threats to the Jews and their temple come not from the Ptolemaic empire served by Onias IV but from the hated Seleucid empire. If there had been a miracle in the time of Seleucus IV, Daniel would have alluded to it in the prophesy at Dan. 11.20; but though Daniel mentions there the attempt to levy funds, he says nothing of a miracle. Josephus "saw clearly" what Onias IV had done: on the basis of events from the lifetime of Onias II, Onias IV had fabricated events for a laudatory account describing Onias III. To "correct" the "distortion," Josephus eliminated the "doublet."

Josephus would not have minded leaving Onias III as a mere name in the succession of high priests.[126] However, he knew from Jason of Cyrene and perhaps from Onias IV that the Oniad high priest Jason

---

[125] III Maccabees 1. 10-2. 24; I shall show elsewhere that III Maccabees is a refutation of the work of Onias IV, written not long after that work was published.
[126] On the difficulties of Josephus' account of the death of Onias III (*AJ* xii. 5. 1. 237), see my *II Maccabees* pp. 219-220.

upon the failure of his coup at Jerusalem finally found refuge at Sparta, having gone there "because of the ties of kinship" *(dia tên syngeneian)* between the Spartans and the Jews. The only source Josephus knew from which Jason the Oniad could learn of the ties of kinship was the letter of the Spartan King Areus to a high priest Onias.[127] As far as Josephus knew, Jason the Oniad was the first Jew to take note of the ties of kinship, later to be exploited by Josephus' own ancestor, Jonathan the Hasmonaean.[128] Philhellenic Onias IV may very well have quoted the letter in his work, drawing its text from Oniad family archives, and may have correctly indicated that the recipient was Onias II, but see my *I Maccabees*, pp. 459-60. Josephus would not take such an assertion uncritically. Did Jason the Oniad and Jonathan the Hasmonaean act on the basis of a long neglected letter to Onias II or on the basis of a more recent letter to Onias III? Josephus himself cherished indications of amity and kinship between Jews and virtuous Greeks.[129] It was incredible to him that a letter of Areus could have been unanswered and ignored for decades, especially since the text of Areus' letter invited the high priest to send back a reply with the letter-bearer. Unable or unwilling to check the chronology of the Spartan kings, Josephus jumped at the "most probable" assumption: Onias III was the recipient of the letter from Sparta. If Onias IV said it had come to Onias II, Josephus had no difficulty regarding the fact as one more piece of propagandistic "distortion." Josephus would think that Onias IV would strive to make the date of cordial and disinterested overtures of Greeks to Jews as early as possible, for then Onias IV could say that long experience in his family proved that such cordial relations could exist and that Jewish-Greek cooperation could last beyond the dire emergency faced by Onias IV's patroness, Cleopatra II. As Josephus probably saw it, Onias IV had attributed to Onias III a doublet of an event which occurred under Onias II and had attributed to Onias II the receipt of a letter sent to Onias III. By removing the "distortions," Josephus produced the narrative as we have it in *AJ* xii. Having proved to his own satisfaction that Onias' chronology was wrong, Josephus altered it. He set the beginning of Joseph's career in the reign of Ptolemy V (*AJ* xii. 4. 1-2. 154-60). He set the death of Onias II in the reign of Seleucus IV (*AJ* xii. 4. 10. 223-25). Old already at the outset of Joseph's career, Onias II may well have died in the reign of Seleucus II (died 225) or Seleucus III Soter (225-223). Did Josephus find such a note in Onias' work? It is hard to see how Onias IV could have connected

---

[127] See II Maccabees 5.9 and above, n. 85.
[128] *Ibid.*
[129] J. *Ap.* i. 22. 162-204; ii. 38. 281-85.

Onias II's death with the reign of a third-century Seleucid rather than a Ptolemy, unless Onias IV did tell something of Onias II's pro-Seleucid plots.[130] Perhaps he did. On the other hand, Onias IV himself may well have recorded the death of Joseph as occurring early in the reign of Seleucus IV, who then ruled Judaea. If Josephus was at all aware of the difficulties of his own chronology, he decided that he did not have the time to solve them. His readers might not notice them, and perhaps he himself could solve them in a later edition. Josephus and his readers lacked the advantage of having a standard era according to which the dates could be assigned and easily lined up for comparison in a table. It is possible that neither he nor they perceived the difficulties.

With more leisure than Josephus and unfettered by his presuppositions, we can now solve all the problems we found in Josephus' narrative:

1. To Josephus' source, Onias IV, the exploits of Joseph and Hyrcanus were matter for pride. They were indeed repugnant to Josephus' moral code, and as a partisan of the Hasmonaeans Josephus included the stories to blacken the reputation of the Zadokite-Oniad line.

2, 4, 6, 7, 11. Josephus assumed that Onias IV could not have failed to write according to the Ptolemaic point of view, and that the participation of the queen in farming out the taxes presupposed the marriage of Ptolemy V and Cleopatra I. Josephus welcomed the chronology which resulted, since it allowed him to disprove Zadokite-Oniad claims to excellence and divine favor. Either he was unaware of the chronological difficulties of his own account, or he believed that they could be safely passed over in silence.

3. Josephus may have found in Onias' work the information that Samaritans had harassed the Jews during the high-priesthood of an Oniad when the Seleucids ruled Judaea. Whatever the source, for Josephus it served to refute the claims of supporters of the Zadokite-Oniad line that under the Seleucids the merit of an Oniad high priest had kept Jerusalem in perfect peace (Second Maccabees 3.1-3).

5. Josephus left to his secretaries the copying of the passages containing the name "Euergetes," failing to perceive the necessity of correcting them.

8. The preconceptions of both Onias IV and Josephus operated in succession to produce the strange story which mentions how Onias-Menelaus and the Tobiads curried favor with Antiochus IV yet omits any reference as to how Antiochus IV suppressed their enemies. The

---

[130]See above, pp. 127-28 and nn. 13, 91.

first Hellenization of Jerusalem was carried through, apparently without resistance, by the high priest Jason the Oniad at the beginning of the reign of Antiochus IV.[131] However, Onias IV wished to present an account in which his uncle Jason played no role in the Hellenization of Jerusalem. He jumped at the opportunity to suggest that the Hellenization was the work of Jason's violent political opponents, who thus purchased the favor of Antiochus IV when worsted at Jerusalem by Jason. He was glad to omit all reference to the disgraceful efforts of Jason and Onias-Menelaus to outbid one another for the high-priesthood.[132] It was, indeed, true that Onias-Menelaus and his partisans brought ruin upon the Jews by getting Antiochus' aid in 169, when Jason had worsted them.[133] Hence, Onias IV probably dated the first Hellenization of Jerusalem at the same time as Antiochus IV's sack of Jerusalem. If so, Onias' account did tell immediately how Antiochus IV suppressed the partisans of Jason.

Josephus was firmly convinced that the mass of Jews could not have allowed the introduction of Hellenic practices to Jerusalem without some resistance.[134] Hence, he rejected the account of Jason of Cyrene which told of the peaceful voluntary Hellenization carried through by Jason the Oniad. Onias IV's account, as we have reconstructed it, placed the introduction of Hellenic practices at a time when Antiochus IV was not only intimidating the Jews but subjecting them to physical violence. Yet Josephus could not accept Onias IV's version, either, because he was firmly convinced that when Antiochus IV sacked Jerusalem he sacked a totally innocent city.[135] Both Jason of Cyrene and Onias IV admit that Antiochus IV had reason to believe he was suppressing rebels against Onias-Menelaus, the man he himself had appointed high priest.[136] Furthermore, Josephus knew that the reliable author of First Maccabees dated the Hellenization of Jerusalem well before the sack.[137] Hence, Josephus separated the Hellenization from the sack. Perhaps he believed that Onias-Menelaus and the Tobiads had purchased Antiochus' moral support by offering to introduce Hellenic practices and that then Antiochus without physical violence intimidated the Jewish opposition, so that Onias-Menelaus and his partisans temporarily prevailed. With no other sources to help him,

---

[131] II Maccabees 4.7-17.
[132] *Ibid.*, 4.7-9, 24-25.
[133] II Maccabees 5. 5-21; see above, n. 16.
[134] J. *Ap.* ii. 37-38. 271-78.
[135] J. *Ap.* ii. 7. 83-84, 8. 90; cf. *AJ* xii. 9. 1. 357-59.
[136] II Maccabees 5.11; Onias' account as we have just reconstructed it.
[137] I Maccabees 1.10-24.

Tales of the Tobiads 151

Josephus decided silence was better than the expression of conjectures. His narrative went on to show that only later, out of sheer greed, Antiochus did sack Jerusalem and violently crush the opposition.[138]

9. Jason of Cyrene took over from Onias IV the mention of Hyrcanus' deposits.

10. Except for the exaggerated figure for the Ptolemaic revenues, the stories of Joseph and Hyrcanus are entirely true.

---

[138] *AJ* xii. 5. 3-4. 246-50; see my *I Maccabees*, pp. 558-68.

Part Two

RELIGIOUS RESISTANCE TO FOREIGN RULE

6

Uruk Prophecy

The fragmentary Uruk Prophecy is preserved on a damaged clay tablet found in Uruk in 1969 by the German Warka expedition. It is one of a group of tablets discovered in a residential area of a level of the early Achaemenid period. The tablets probably were part of the private library of the magician and diviner, Anu-ikṣur.[1]

The obverse of the tablet bearing the Uruk Prophecy is badly broken. Enough survives to suggest that it was written in the first person[2] and that it speaks of a hard time in the land, of failure of a rightful heir to succeed to the throne of his father, of a usurper from Uruk, and of a king who will be shut up in his palace for several months.

---

[1] Stephen A. Kaufman, "Prediction, Prophecy, and Apocalypse in the Light of New Akkadian Texts," *Proceedings of the Sixth World Congress of Jewish Studies, Held at the Hebrew University of Jerusalem, 13-19 August, 1973* (Jerusalem, 1977), vol. 1, pp. 223-27; Hermann Hunger and Stephen A. Kaufman, "A New Akkadian Prophecy Text," *JAOS* 95 (1975): 371-75; Hunger, *Spätbabylonische Texte aus Uruk*, vol. 1 (Berlin, 1976), pp. 21-23; Wilfred G. Lambert, *The Background of Jewish Apocalyptic* (London, 1978), pp. 10-12, 18-19; Jean-Georges Heintz, "Note sur les origines de l'apocalyptique judaïque á la lumière des prophéties akkadiennes," in *L'Apocalyptique*, Etudes d'histoire des religions, no. 3 (Paris, 1977), pp. 73-87; Helmer Ringgren, "Akkadian Apocalypses," in David Hellholm, ed., *Apocalypticism in the Mediterranean World and the Near East* (Tübingen, 1983), pp. 380-81, 385; Robert D. Biggs, "The Babylonian Prophecies and the Astrological Traditions of Mesopotamia," *JCS* 37 (1985): 86-90; Tremper Longman II, "Fictional Akkadian Royal Autobiography: A Generic and Comparative Study" (Ph.D. diss., Yale University, 1983), pp. 330-32, 349-53, 373-92. See also Robert D. Biggs, in Francesca Rochberg-Halton, ed., *Language, Literature, and History: Philological and Historical Studies Presented to Erica Reiner*, AOS Monograph, no. 67 (New Haven, 1987), pp. 1-14.

[2] Longman, "Fictional Akkadian Royal Autobiography," pp. 350-51.

The reverse of the tablet is better preserved. On it, a series of kings is predicted. First, a king from the Sealand who ruled in Babylon will come to reign over the devastated part of the land (lines 1-2). Then there will be an unjust king who will remove the ancient protective goddess of Uruk and make her dwell in Babylon, placing in her sanctuary in Uruk another, improper goddess. The unjust king will impose heavy taxes upon Uruk and devastate her; next, another unjust king will arise (lines 3-7). Line 8 begins with KI.MIN ("ditto") written five times and ends with the statement, surely about a king, "He will take the property of Babylonia to Assyria." Next, an unjust king will arise who will subdue and terrorize the whole world (lines 9-10). But finally a just king will arise who will establish the rites of Anu in Uruk and restore Uruk's protective goddess to her own sanctuary; he will renew and glorify Uruk, and after him his son will be king in Uruk and become master over the world (lines 11-16).

S.A. Kaufman, who wrote the first detailed commentary to the text, recognized that its formulas show it to be one example of a recently discovered genre of Babylonian literature[3] called "Akkadian prophecy" by A.K. Grayson and W.G. Lambert and "Akkadian apocalypse" by W.W. Hallo.[4] I prefer to use a different terminology for the following reasons. The peoples who used Akkadian had other types of prophetic literature than the one represented by the Uruk Prophecy. As for this type, it is found among other peoples besides those who used Akkadian.[5] The terms "apocalypse" and "apocalyptic" are derived from the Greek name of the book of Revelation in the New Testament. Scholars have tried in vain to give a consistent definition of those terms, as applied to literature earlier than the book of Revelation. The fact is not surprising, since even if earlier literary forms gave rise to the book of Revelation, to define the genre of those earlier forms by using the characteristics of Revelation is to risk reading history backwards.[6] I prefer, therefore, to call the type to which the Uruk Prophecy belongs "present-future prophecy."

---

[3]Hunger and Kaufman, "A New Akkadian Prophecy Text," pp. 373-75.
[4]Albert Kirk Grayson and Wilfred G. Lambert, "Akkadian Prophecies," *JCS* 18 (1964): 7-30; Grayson, *Babylonian Historical-Literary Tests* (Toronto and Buffalo, 1975), pp. 6-7, 13-22; W.W. Hallo, "Akkadian Apocalypses," *IEJ* 16 (1966): 231-42.
[5]Notably the Jews; in my book *Chosen Peoples*, I hope to treat the phenomenon as exhibited by Jews, Babylonians, Egyptians, and Zoroastrian Persians.
[6]In my book *Chosen Peoples*, I shall abstain from using the terms" apocalypse" and "apocalyptic." On the inadequacy of the terms, see, for the present, T.

In a present-future prophecy, the writer does not write in his own name or as a person of his own time. Rather, the real writer pretends that the author is a god who gave a revelation in the past or an ancient worthy who received revelations or omens in the past. Sometimes the composition really will be based on old material. Always, however, the writer will present his god or his ancient worthy as surveying the course of history through the relevant past down into the (often dreadful) present. To impress his audience with the prophetic power of the god or of the ancient worthy, the writer will give vivid details concerning the relevant past and the present. Then he goes on to predict a glorious future, which he is confident will come *soon* upon his real audience, though in some cases he will first predict a final peak of adversity to precede the glorious future.

The real interest of the writer is in the *present* which his pretended ancient worthy foresaw and in the near *future* which he himself believes he can foresee. Hence, I call these compositions "present-future prophecies," even though they frequently also involve the relevant past. The writer's details on the present are so vivid and his predictions of the future so impossibly glorious that a modern trained historian has no trouble identifying the writer's own present – if he has good enough sources on the writer's period. Indeed, S.A. Kaufman and others have tried to use this fact to determine the historical setting of the Uruk prophecy, but no one has yet found a convincing solution to the problem.

I believe that the reason for this perplexity is that it can be difficult to determine the point at which the text of a present-future prophecy leaves the author's present and turns to events which still have not happened in his time. Thus, in the Babylonian present-future prophecy called the Speech of Marduk,[7] written in the reign of Nebuchadnezzar I (1124-1103), Marduk predicts that Nebuchadnezzar I will show great and expensive honor to him and to his city, Babylon. An unwary modern reader might assume that the king had already displayed his munificence when the text was written, but it is far more likely that the writer hoped the text would induce the king to do so in the future.

My predecessors in interpreting the Uruk Prophecy have taken for granted that the restoration of the statue of the protective goddess of

---

Francis Glasson, "What is Apocalyptic?," *New Testament Studies* 27 (1980): 98-105.
[7]Rykle Borger, "Gott Marduk und Gott-König Shulgi als Propheten: Zwei prophetische Texte," *Bibliotheca Orientalis* 28 (1971): 3-13, 16-20.

Uruk to her city (mentioned at reverse, line 13) had already taken place when the author wrote. Nabopolassar or Nebuchadnezzar II is reported to have restored such a statue to Uruk. Hunger, Kaufman, and Lambert, therefore, put the writer's present in or after those reigns.[8] Let us consider the difficulties involved.[9]

Kaufman rightly noted, first, that the statue of the protective goddess of Uruk was removed in the reign of the Babylonian king Erîba-Marduk (mid-eighth century B.C.E.); second, that the five-fold KI.MIN ("ditto") in reverse, line 8, if construed according to normal usage, serves to repeat the previous sentence, "After him a king will arise, but he will not provide justice in the land, he will not give the right decisions for the land." That sentence would speak of an evil ruler after Erîba-Marduk, and the five dittos would bring the reader down through the reigns of the four later Babylonian successors of Erîba-Marduk into that of Tiglath-pileser III (745-727), who took the throne of Babylon for himself in 728, creating a personal union of the two kingdoms. But then, the good ruler of reverse line 11 is only the second to reign after Tiglath-pileser, and there is no legitimate way to construe the text so as to make that good ruler be either Nabopolassar (626-605) or Nebuchadnezzar II (605-562).[10]

Lambert questioned whether the statue of the deity referred to in the Uruk Prophecy was the same as the one reportedly removed by Erîba-Marduk and implicitly objected to the huge gaps in the series of kings as interpreted by Kaufman.[11] Lambert sought rather to ascertain what uninterrupted sequence of Assyrian and Babylonian kings could be made to fit the descriptions in reverse, lines 8-16. He found a different interpretation for the five-fold KI.MIN in line 8. For him, each KI.MIN repeated one word or phrase from the previous sentence: (1) *arkišu* ("after him"), (2) *šarru* ("a king"), (3) *illâma* ("will arise"), (4) *dīni māti ul idânu* ("he will not provide justice in the land"), (5) *purussê māti ul iparras* ("he will not give right decisions for the land").[12] But the sentence contains eleven words, which can be grouped in various ways, so that Lambert's procedure is already arbitrary.[13]

Proceeding on this basis, Lambert found that the last lines of the Uruk Prophecy (reverse, lines 8-16) tell, in order, of a bad king who

---

[8]Hunger and Kaufman, "A New Akkadian Prophecy Text," pp. 373-74; Lambert, *Background*, p. 11.
[9]Cf. Longman, "Fictional Akkadian Royal Biography," pp. 351-53.
[10]Hunger and Kaufman, "A New Akkadian Prophecy Text," pp. 374.
[11]Lambert, *Background*, p. 11.
[12]*Ibid.*, pp. 18-19, n. 16.
[13]C.F. Longman, "Fictional Akkadian Royal Biography," pp. 352-53.

will take the property of Babylonia to Assyria, a bad king who will subdue the world, a good king who will restore Uruk and bring back to her the statue of her protective goddess, and his son who will rule the world. Lambert took the last four kings to be Esarhaddon and Ashurbanipal of Assyria and Nabopolassar and Nebuchadnezzar of Babylon. He thus ignores the ephemeral Assyrian successors of Ashurbanipal and mixes Assyrian and Babylonian kings. The procedure might be admissible: a writer from Uruk might have regarded the Babylonian kings before Nabopolassar as mere puppets of Assyria and might have also disregarded the last Assyrian rulers. But what inhabitant of Babylonia would characterize Esarhaddon, the great restorer of ruined Babylon and the great conqueror of Egypt, merely as a bad king who took the property of Babylonia to Assyria? Thus, Lambert's theory uses arbitrary procedures and involves an absurdity.

I suggest, rather, that one should build upon Kaufman's method but on the assumption that when the author wrote, the restoration to Uruk of the statue of the goddess still lay in the future. The king who removed her image was Erîba-Marduk. The last king in reverse, line 8, who took the property of Babylonia to Assyria (through taxation if not through looting) was Tiglath-pileser III; for the writer, that fact was more important than Tiglath-pileser's vast conquests. The bad king in reverse, lines 9-10, who ruled the world, would then be Shalmaneser V (726-722); he continued to hold Babylonia in personal union and retained the vast empire of Tiglath-pileser III, crushing the last revolt of the kingdom of Israel. Perhaps, unlike his predecessor, he did not take tax-money or loot from Babylonia to Assyria, so that the writer could instead identify him by the size of his empire. Then, the first good king would indeed be Marduk-apla-iddina II, under whom Babylonians, who hated Assyrian rule, refused to recognize the overlordship of Sargon II, successor of Shalmaneser V. Marduk-apla-iddina did associate himself with Uruk as her benefactor, and he claimed that Marduk had picked him to end the evils caused by Assyrian domination and to restore Babylonia.[14]

Accordingly, the Uruk prophecy would be addressed to and propaganda for Marduk-apla-iddina II. The writer believed the king would be the successful liberator of Babylonia and the restorer of the goddess of Uruk to her sanctuary and would then found a dynasty which would rule the world. Marduk-apla-iddina II could claim to be king of

---

[14]C.J. Gadd, "Inscribed Barrel Cylinder of Marduk-apla-iddina II," *Iraq* 15 (1953): 123-34; and J.A. Brinkman, "Merodach-Baladan II," in R.D. Biggs and J.A. Brinkman, eds., *Studies Presented to A. Leo Oppenheim* (Chicago, 1964). pp. 28-31.

Babylon from 721 to 710. He abandoned the city without a struggle in 710 but continued to resist the Assyrian kings Sargon and Sennacherib down to 700.[15] However, the bright hopes expressed in the Uruk Prophecy are hardly likely after 710, and we may thus date its writing between 721 and 710.

---

[15]Brinkman, "Merodach-Baladan II," p. 12-27.

7

The Date of the Book of Jubilees

The book of Jubilees purports to be a divine revelation to Moses. Its contents run parallel to Genesis and the first twelve chapters of Exodus, occasionally rearranging material and especially making additions to confirm the doctrines of the author's Jewish sect. It contains bitter polemics against the holders of opposing views. The author was at least a spiritual and perhaps also a physical ancestor of the Qumran sect.[1]

His polemics give a vivid reflection of the live issues of his time as seen by him. If only one could be sure of the date of the book, one would have valuable insight into the sectarian movements among the Jews at that time, and one would have a clearer picture of the origins of the doctrines of the Qumran sect.

Some scholars have proposed that the book dates from shortly before Antiochus IV, in 167 B.C.E., forbade the Jews to observe their religion and imposed upon them the observance of another cult.[2] Others, however, have suggested later dates. The view of Robert H. Charles,[3] that the book was written during the reign of John Hyrcanus I (134-104 B.C.E.), long dominated the field. Recently, James VanderKam

---

[1] See Otto Eissfeldt, *The Old Testament: An Introduction* (New York and Evanston: Harper & Row, 1965), pp. 606-8; George W.E. Nickelsburg, *Jewish Literature between the Bible and the Mishnah* (Philadelphia: Fortress Press, 1981), pp. 73-80.

[2] Louis Finkelstein, "Pre-Maccabean Documents in the Passover Haggadah," *Harvard Theological Review* 36 (1943), 21, 24; Nickelsburg, *Resurrection, Immortality, and Eternal Life in Intertestamental Judaism* ("Harvard Theological Studies," 26; Cambridge: Harvard University Press, 1972), pp. 46-47, and Review of VanderKam (see n. 4), *Journal of the American Oriental Society* 100 (1980), 83-84.

[3] *The Book of Jubilees* (London: A. and C. Black, 1902), pp. lviii-lxiii.

argued that Charles' date was much too late, but he himself put the writing of the book between ca. 163-161 and 140 B.C.E.[4]

I propose here to give a detailed demonstration that the book dates from the years between 175 and 167 B.C.E. and probably from between 169 and 167 B.C.E. I shall also refute the arguments of Charles and VanderKam for a later date. I shall begin by presenting arguments to show that the book was written in the Hellenistic era.

I. The Book of Jubilees was Written After Alexander the Great Conquered Syria and Palestine and Before 100 B.C.E.

Though the author of Jubilees wrote in Hebrew,[5] in 8.12-30 he draws on the geographic terminology and concepts of the Greeks.[6] He preaches on issues which became pressing only when Greeks flooded into the neighborhood of Judaea, after the conquests of Alexander the Great. Only Greeks had the habit of exercising nude. The pagan non-Greek peoples regarded nudity with much the same horror as did the Jews.[7] If the author of Jubilees insists that a law inscribed on tablets in heaven forbids "going naked as the gentiles uncover themselves" (3.31), his gentile targets could have been only Greeks. Moreover, circumcision was practiced by all the non-Greek pagan peoples bordering on Judaea, but not by the Greeks.[8] The author of Jubilees "predicts" the time when Israelites will leave their sons uncircumcised, like the gentiles (15.33-34). The author could have had no occasion to forbid nudity and to speak of widespread failure to observe the commandment of circumcision unless he wrote when Greek influence had pervaded the Holy Land. That fact brings the date of his book down well into the third century B.C.E. On the other hand, a published fragment of a 170

---

[4]*Textual and Historical Studies in the Book of Jubilees* (Missoula, Mont.: Scholars Press, 1977), pp. 207-85.

[5]On the Hebrew fragments from Qumran and on the surviving translations, see VanderKam, pp. 1-18. On the clues in the versions pointing to Hebrew as the language of the original, see Charles, *Book of Jubilees*, pp. xxx-xxxiii.

[6]The use of Gādīr (Gades, modern Cadiz), the Sea of 'Atēl (the Atlantic), the Sea of Mē'āt (Lake Maeotis, the modern Sea of Azov), and the Tīnā River (the Tanais, the modern Don) as extremes, or boundary points, is found in Herodotus, and the three regions of Noah's sons come close to fitting the Greeks' three continents. See Henry F. Tozer, *A History of Ancient Geography* (2d ed., New York: Biblo and Tannen, 1964), pp. 67-69, 72, 80-85. The division of the inhabited earth into zones (vs. 30) is also Greek; the Greeks held that *their* zone was the moderate one (Aristotle, *Politics*, 7.7.2; Tozer, *History*, pp. 66, 179-80, 205-6).

[7]See Herodotus 1.10, Thucydides 1.6.

[8]See Herodotus 1.104.3.

Hebrew manuscript of Jubilees, found at Qumran, has been dated palaeographically a bit before 100 B.C.E.[9]

II. The Stress in Jubilees on Shunning All Gentiles Indicates the Book was Written After Late 175 B.C.E.

The main thrust of the book of Jubilees is to prove that the Jewish laws followed by the author and his sect are not a matter of fairly recent interpretation and legislation. Those Jewish laws included the use of a calendar with a 364-day solar year and the strict observance of peculiar regulations on the celebration of festivals and on the conduct of life, as well as a requirement to shun *all* gentiles. According to the book, these principles were revealed already before Moses to the patriarchs of the stories in Genesis.[10]

Abraham's insistence, at Jub. 22.16-22, that the Chosen Stock must shun all gentiles is peculiar and datable. One might have thought that the principle, that the Jews of Judaea should shun gentiles, was beyond question after the times of Ezra and Nehemiah, and that it was based on texts from the books of the Torah from Exodus through Deuteronomy.[11] The authority of the Persian king stood behind Ezra[12] and Nehemiah[13] and gave their interpretations of the Torah the force of royal law. Alexander the Great seems to have ratified the existing situation when he conquered the area from the Persian empire,[14] and so did his successors; for King Antiochus III of the Seleucid empire we have documentary evidence that he did so.[15] The self-separation of

---

[9]J.T. Milik, "Fragment d'une source du Psautier (4Q Ps 89) et fragments des Jubilés...," *Revue biblique* 73 (1966), 102-4. I owe the arguments in this paragraph of text to a now-lost manuscript version, complete with notes, of Elias Bickerman's book, *The Jews in the Greek Age*. See the published version (Cambridge, Mass., and London: Harvard University Press, 1988), p. 216.

[10]Cf. Eissfeldt, *Old Testament*, pp. 606-8.

[11]In the books of Ezra and Nehemiah, the Jews in Judaea are required to *separate* (Hebrew root: *bdl*) themselves from *all* gentiles (Ezra 9.1-2, 10.11, 16-17; Neh 9.2, 10.29, 13.1-3; I Esdr 8.69-70; cf. Ezra 6.21, I Esdr 7.13). Despite Deut 23.8-9, Jews are required also to separate themselves from Egyptians and Edomites. The use of the root *bdl* suggests that the source for the requirement is Lev 20.24-26, where God is said to have *separated* (Hebrew root: *bdl*) Israel from the *gentiles*, not merely from "the nation which I am casting out before you" (Lev 20.23). Neh 13.1-3, in which separation only from Ammonites and Moabites is mentioned, is based on Deut 23.3-7.

[12]Ezra 7.11-12, 25.

[13]Neh 5.14, 13.6-7.

[14]See Josephus *Ant.* 11.8.5 §338; on the legends at Josephus *Ant.* 11.8.2-5 §§ 306-45, see Abraham Schalit, "Alexander the Great," *Enc. Jud.* 2 (1972), 577-79.

[15]Josephus *Ant.* 12.3.3 §§138-44; II Macc 4.11

the Jews of Judaea from gentiles impressed Hecataeus of Abdera, who wrote in the reign of Ptolemy I, around the end of the fourth century B.C.E.[16] Few if any gentiles resided in Judaea between the time of Nehemiah and the 170's B.C.E.[17]

Ben Sira, writing ca. 180 B.C.E., finds it unnecessary to preach against association with gentiles. Though he regards Nehemiah as a hero, he says nothing about Nehemiah's efforts to separate Jews from gentiles. In Ben Sira's time, the point, that the Jews of Judaea should shun gentiles, still could be taken for granted.[18]

The interpretations by Ezra and Nehemiah, which required rigorous separation of Jews from gentiles, were not the only way to construe the texts. A case could have been made for a more lenient view, that the words of the Torah required Jews to keep separate only from the seven "Canaanite" nations (all of whom could have been regarded as extinct in the Hellenistic age) and from the Ammonites and Moabites.[19] There is, however, no trace that anyone in Judaea before the 170's B.C.E. acted against the rigorist interpretation of the requirement for separation, not even the notorious Tobiads.[20]

Indeed, the accounts in First and Second Maccabees imply that the rigorist interpretation prevailed until the beginning of the reign of

---

[16] *Apud* Diodorus 40.3.4.
[17] See my article, "Jewish Acceptance and Rejection of Hellenism," in this volume, pp. 15-17.
[18] See *ibid*. and Ben Sira 49:13.
[19] See above, pp. 7-8.
[20] The Toubias who is known from papyri resided, not in Judaea, but in Transjordan. We know nothing of his religious views. The "syncretism" displayed in his surviving letters may be only the perfunctory mannerisms of his Greek scribe. See Victor A. Tcherikover and Alexander Fuks, *Corpus Papyrorum Judaicarum*, Vol. I (Cambridge, Mass.: Harvard University Press, 1957), Nos. 1, 2, 4, 5.

Joseph the Tobiad, in entertaining the ambassador of Ptolemy at Jerusalem (Josephus *Ant*. 12.4.3 § 165), was only doing what was proper, as is shown by the examples of the pious Onias III (II Macc. 3.9) and Simon the Hasmonaean (I Macc. 15.32). Joseph was tempted to have an affair with a gentile dancing-girl *in Alexandria* but recognized from the first that to do so would be a sin, and he was saved from committing that sin by his brother. On the behavior of Joseph's son Hyrcanus at Ptolemy's banquet *in Alexandria*, see my article, "The Tales of the Tobiads," above, pp. 118-19, n. 12.

Josephus asserts that Joseph's sons, other than Hyrcanus, were instigators of the "Hellenistic Reform" at Jerusalem (*Ant*. 12.5.1 §240). The charge may well be false; see my article above, pp. 150-51. Even if it were true, the same Tobiads had earlier received the support of the pious high priest Simon II the Just and that of the majority of the Jews of Judaea (*Ant*. 12.5.1 §239; on Simon II, see my article above, pp. 120, 145).

Antiochus IV.[21] Only the successful petition then to Antiochus IV, of Jason the Oniad, brother of the high priest Onias III, late in 175 or early in 174 B.C.E., brought a change. Down to that point, Onias III is reported to have enforced Jewish law with rigor (II Macc 3.1). Thereafter, however, Antiochus IV deposed Onias III and made Jason high priest in his place and repealed the royal decrees enforcing the rigorist interpretation of the Jewish laws on separation.[22] Preserved at I Macc 1.11 is a summary of some of the arguments used by those who sought to relax the rules of separation: "Come, let us make a covenant with the gentiles around us, because ever since we have kept ourselves separated from them we have suffered many evils."

What is the meaning of the clause which begins "ever since?" Both the author of First Maccabees and the speakers he quotes knew the historical books of the Bible, from Genesis through Nehemiah. They knew that the patriarchs in Genesis associated freely with gentiles. They also knew that Moses and Joshua and Solomon (I Kgs 9.20-21) had kept the Chosen People separate from the gentiles, and that surely the righteous kings Hezekiah (I Kgs 18.6) and Josiah (I Kgs 23.25) did so, too. It is thus unlikely that the clause beginning "ever since" refers to the enactments of Ezra and Nehemiah. Rather, it alludes to the revelations through Moses which separated the Chosen People from the gentiles. The "lawless men" quoted by the author of First Maccabees held that those revelations had brought only trouble upon the Jews.

The argument of the "lawless men" at I Macc 1.11 had much in common with the views of Greek intellectuals who admired Jewish "philosophy" but deplored Jewish aversion toward gentiles. Hecataeus of Abdera blamed the aversion on Moses' own reaction to Egyptian mistreatment of Jews.[23] Others ascribed it to the superstition and "tyranny" of later Jewish leaders.[24] The account in Jub. 22.7-18 seems directly to counter reasoning like that of Hecataeus of Abdera: Abraham gives thanks for having lived his entire life in peace and then turns to instruct Jacob to shun all gentiles. Clearly, Abraham's instruction to Jacob was not in reaction to mistreatment by gentiles!

For an author writing to influence Jews who believed in the validity of the books of the Torah from Exodus through Deuteronomy, there was no need to insist, contrary to the implications of the stories in Genesis, that the patriarchs already observed the regulations later

---

[21] I Macc 1.11-14, II Macc 4.7-11.
[22] II Macc 4.7-11.
[23] *Apud* Diodorus 40.3.4.
[24] Strabo 16.2.37, C761.

revealed to Moses. The insistence, that the patriarchs observed the full rigor of the laws, including those requiring separation from the gentiles, is explainable only on the supposition that the rigorist author faced a situation in which it was easy for Jews to violate the laws of separation and in which it was argued that those laws were a detrimental addition to the pristine religion of the patriarchs. Hence, the author of Jubilees must have written after late 175 B.C.E.

III. The Book Knows of the Sack of Jerusalem in 169, but Not of the Royal Decrees Against the Religion of the Jews in 167 B.C.E.

We can further narrow the limits between which the book must have been written. In at least two instances, the book of Jubilees should have reflected the changes which King Antiochus IV tried to impose upon the religion of the Jews in 167 B.C.E.,[25] yet the book fails to do so and hence must have been written before the king's attempt to impose the changes.

Where the language of Genesis lent itself to interpretations which ran counter to his own beliefs, the author of Jubilees rewrote the passage to exclude those interpretations.[26] For example, the author at Jubilees 2.8-10 rewrote Gen 1.16-18 to exclude the possibility of a lunar calendar. Antiochus IV, in his decrees of 167 B.C.E. claimed he was restoring the original patterns of Jewish religion, not least in requiring the worship of the "Abomination of Desolation," a framework containing *maṣṣēbōt* (pillars"), erect cult-stones which represented the deity or contained his presence.[27] The king's agents are known to have cited texts from the Torah to prove the point.[28] Among those texts surely stood Gen 28.16-22, 31.13, and 35.7, passages in which Jacob shows reverence to a stone *maṣṣēbāh* which is said to contain God's presence.[29]

Even before the decrees of Antiochus IV, these passages were embarrassing to Jews who followed the Torah: explicit commandments forbade them to use such cult-stones.[30] Accordingly, the author of Jubilees (at 27.26-27) adjusted the content of Gen 28.18-22 to make it conform to the prohibitions of the Torah against *maṣṣēbōt* : he specified that Jacob's *maṣṣēbāh* was"for a sign," implying that it was not itself a

---

[25]See Jonathan A. Goldstein, *I Maccabees* ("The Anchor Bible," vol. 41; Garden City, N.Y.: Doubleday, 1976), pp. 125-60.
[26]Cf. Charles, *Book of Jubilees*, pp. xlviii-xlix.
[27]Goldstein, *I Maccabees*, pp. 142-52.
[28]*Ibid.*, pp. 261-62.
[29]See *ibid.*, p. 148.
[30]Lev 26.1; Deut 12.3, 16.21-22; see also Exod 23.24, 34.13-14, and Deut 7.5.

god. But the author of Jubilees says nothing to exclude the use of Jacob's *maṣṣēbāh* as a precedent for Jewish worship of the stone in the Abomination of Desolation which was supposed to contain God's presence. Indeed, he allows Jacob to set the extremely dangerous precedent of anointing the stone and of regarding it as a container of God's presence. Surely, then, the author wrote before Antiochus' decrees of 167 B.C.E.!

Another passage of Jubilees must have been written before the decrees of 167 but after late summer, 169 B.C.E. The author of Jub. 23.11-31 was a typical example of a person in the age of the cessation of prophecy who nevertheless believed he had prophetic inspiration. Like the authors of Daniel 7-12, I Enoch 85-90, and the Testament of Moses,[31] he wrote a piece surveying Jewish history from the death of Abraham down to his own time of troubles and predicting an imminent miraculous transforming intervention by God. In Jubilees, the miracle is a lengthening of the human life span (derived from Isa 65.20). Before the great miracle, which never happened, the author first speaks of vain efforts by pious young Israelites to use the sword to turn sinning Jews back into the path of righteousness; then he says some wicked Jews will "escape" from these bloody clashes and will go on to "exalt themselves to deceit and wealth, that they may each take all that is his fellow-Jew's" and will defile the holy of holies; then he speaks of cruel punishment of Israel by the gentiles; never does he say that gentiles will force Israel to violate the Torah; unlike the author of Dan 11.36, he makes no reference to a king who would "speak things past belief concerning the God of gods."

A pious Jew writing between 299 and 100 B.C.E. could have expressed himself thus only within the narrow period between autumn 169 and spring 167 B.C.E. Jews are not reported to have taken arms against one another on religious issues during the third century or in the first three decades of the second century B.C.E. The first such religious civil strife of the Hellenistic period was the riot against Lysimachus, brother of the high priest Menelaus, in autumn 170 B.C.E.[32] No more than a year later came the armed resistance of the pious both to the coup of the deposed high priest Jason and to his rival, the incumbent

---

[31]See Goldstein, *I Maccabees*, pp. 38-44.

[32]II Macc 4.39-42; Goldstein, *I Maccabees*, p. 162. At Dan 11.14 there probably is an allusion to an uprising in which Jewish interpreters of old prophecies sought to end Ptolemaic rule over the Chosen People; but the uprising is not portrayed as a civil conflict or as one in which the issue was righteousness versus wickedness. On the family strife among the Tobiads, see my article above, pp. 118-20, 129-31.

high priest Menelaus.³³ The pious drove Jason out of the holy city, and Menelaus *escaped* to the citadel of Jerusalem. Upon hearing of the disorders, King Antiochus IV marched to Jerusalem and cruelly punished the Jews there.³⁴ The king's intervention enabled Menelaus to retain power as high priest. Menelaus went on to *defile the holy of holies*, at least by conducting Antiochus into it,³⁵ and he also *exalted himself* oppressively over his fellow Jews.³⁶ Thus, the author of Jub 23.11-31 knows of the riot against Lysimachus, the resistance of the pious to Jason and Menelaus, the punishment of the Jews by Antiochus IV, and the behavior immediately thereafter the Menelaus. He knows of the events of 170 and 169 B.C.E., but he knows nothing of Antiochus' decrees forbidding obedience to the Torah, which came in spring 167 B.C.E.³⁷ He must therefore have written between 169 and 167 B.C.E.³⁸

---

³³II Macc 5.5-7; Goldstein, *I Maccabees*, p. 163. According to II Macc. 4.39, the riot against Lysimachus grew out of mass indignation against Lysimachus' robbery of temple property. At Jub 23.17-19 nothing is said of temple robbery. But the sect of the author of Jubilees may have had its own motives for participating in acts of protest, different from those of the sect favored by the historian in Second Maccabees. The author of Jubilees may not have been thinking primarily of the riot against Lysimachus. Foremost in his mind may have been the armed resistance of the pious in 169 B.C.E., where the pious may have risen against the Hellenizing high priests from a broad array of religious motives.
³⁴II Macc 5.11-16, I Macc 1.20-24; Goldstein, *I Maccabees*, p. 163.
³⁵II Macc 5.15, Diodorus 34-35.1.3; cf. II Macc 13.8, I Macc 1.21, 4.42-43 (the priests appointed by Judas are in contrast to Menelaus).
³⁶II Macc 5.23.
³⁷I Macc 1.44-51, II Macc 6.1-7; Goldstein, *I Maccabees*, p. 163; see also Jonathan A. Goldstein, "The Apocryphal Book of I Baruch," *PAAJR* 46-47 (1979-80), 183, n. 13.
³⁸As a whole, the book of Jubilees is a straightforward narrative sequence. The events of 170-169 B.C.E. in their order fit the account of Jub 23.19-24. Jub 23.25 should be viewed as rhetorical hyperbole, describing Israel under the oppressive acts of Antiochus IV between 169 and 167 B.C.E. Jub 23.26 would reflect a great movement of repentance carried out by the author's sect in response to the thought, "If God in his wrath has sent against us the sinners, the gentiles, we must try to appease Him by doing His will." Verses 26-31 then predict the miraculous divine intervention which will follow. Accordingly, the burden of proof is on anyone who would assert that the verses of our passage do not narrate a sequence of events in chronological order. Contrast Gene L. Davenport, *The Eschatology of the Book of Jubilees* (Leiden: Brill, 1971), 32-46, esp. 41, n. 1, and 43, n. 2.
The stress at Jub 15.11-13, 23-24, on circumcision, and the severe condemnation of failure to circumcise, can be used to show that the book was written at the latest in 152 B.C.E. Even as guerrilla warriors, the Hasmonaeans succeeded in enforcing adherence to circumcision (I Macc 2.46), and as princes of the nation they must have seen to it that every new-born male was

IV. The Date of Jubilees 23.11-31 Is Probably the Date of the Entire Book

Can we then say that the entire book of Jubilees was written between 169 and 167 B.C.E.? Surely, it is possible that the author of Jub 23.11-31 is different from the author of the rest of the book and that the passage was later added to it.[39] On the other hand, our passage, written between 169 and 167 B.C.E., now stands embedded in a book written between 175 and 167 B.C.E. There are two problems which could well have perplexed the author of the entire book:

1. How is it that Abraham, most righteous of the men who lived down to his time, had the shortest life?[40]
2. What of truly saintly members of the author's own sect in his own time? Would they, too, be limited to a short span of life?

In its setting Jub 23.11-31 with verses 9-10 serves to solve both problems. The wickedness of the wicked shortened the human life span, but God will soon restore it to full length. Thus, I think there is good reason to assume that the passage is not a later addition to the book. Even if it is an interpolation, it was written, at most, some six years later than the rest of Jubilees.

V. Refutation of the Arguments of Charles and VanderKam

Although VanderKam disposed of many of the arguments for a later date for the book of Jubilees, especially those of Charles, VanderKam himself would date the writing of the book later than we, placing it between ca. 163-161 and 140 B.C.E.[41] We proceed now not only

---

initiated into the Covenant of Abraham. The later Hasmonaeans imposed circumcision on conquered gentiles (Josephus, *Ant.* 12.9.1 §§257-58, 11.3 §319). Surely, such loud propaganda for circumcision as that in Jubilees became unnecessary from the time that Jonathan became high priest in 152 B.C.E. I learned this argument for giving the book of Jubilees an early date by reading the lost manuscript version of Elias Bickerman, *The Jews in the Greek Age.* Cf. the published version, p. 216.

[39]Cf. Davenport, *Eschatology*, pp. 10-19, 32-46, though the arguments presented there are not convincing.

[40]According to the Masoretic text of Gen 11.24-25, Abraham's grandfather Nahor had a shorter life of 148 years, but the Septuagint gives Nahor 204 or even 304 years. On the closeness of the text of the Torah used by the author of Jubilees to that represented by the Septuagint, see VanderKam, *Studies*, p. 103-38.

[41]*Ibid.*, pp. 207-85.

to present considerations even stronger than those brought by VanderKam against Charles' arguments, but also to show that VanderKam's own evidence for the date between ca. 163-161 and 140 B.C.E. does not prove his point.

1. Charles wrongly assumed that the author was a Pharisee who could approve of Hasmonaeans.[42] We can now show that the author was a spiritual ancestor of the Qumran sect, members of which called even early Hasmonaeans "the Wicked Priest," "the Cursed Man of Belial," and "the False Preacher."[43] Hence, passages in Jubilees cannot be interpreted as approving allusions to acts of the Hasmonaeans Jonathan, Simon, and John Hyrcanus.

2. Jub 31.15, with its reference to the preeminence of the tribe of Levi, alludes, not to Simon the Hasmonaean and his successors, but to the great pre-Hasmonaean Zadokite high priests and their anticipated heirs.[44] Indeed, only by emending the text of Jub 31.15 could Charles make it conform to the pattern of the "Hasmonaean propaganda" at Testament of Levi 8.11-17.[45] My colleague, George Nickelsburg, has studied the Ethiopic text of the passage for me. It has *wamakwānenta wamasāfenta wamalā'ekta yekawenu lakwellu zar'a weluda yā'eqob*, where the Latin has *et principes et judices erunt omni semini Jacob*. Ethiopic *mal'ak* normally translates Greek *angelos*, "angel" or "messenger." The Latin translator probably was at a loss to see how a high priest could *be* an angel, especially since the priests are only *compared* to angels at Jub 31.14; therefore, he omitted the word. Hence, the astonishing statement present in the Ethiopic text probably represents the original author's intentions: "They shall be princes and judges and angels [i.e., messengers of God] to all the seed of the sons of Jacob."

The author of Jubilees did not invent his list of the glories of Levi's high priestly descendants. In part they are derived from Mal 2.4, including the office of "angel." Ethiopic *makwanen* (literally "judge") frequently translates words for "ruler," including Greek *archōn* and *hēgoumenos*, the equivalents of Hebrew *śār, rōš, nāśī', and nāgīd* ("prince," "head," "chief"), and at Jub 31.18 the Ethiopic word refers to

---

[42]Charles, *Book of Jubilees*, p. li-lvi, lviii-lix.
[43]Cf. VanderKam, *Studies*, pp. 249-52. On the book of Jubilees and the Qumran sect, see VanderKam, *Studies*, pp. 258-83. On epithets used by the Qumran sect for the early Hasmonaeans, see J.T. Milik, *Ten Years of Discovery in the Wilderness of Judaea* (SBT 26; Naperville, Ill.: Allenson, 1959), pp. 64-72, 84-89, and Frank Moore Cross, Jr., *The Ancient Library of Qumran* (Garden City, N.Y.: Doubleday, 1961), pp. 144-52, and Goldstein, *I Maccabees*, p. 66, n. 21.
[44]Cf. VanderKam, *Studies*, pp. 247-52.
[45]*Book of Jubilees*, p. 187.

The Date of the Book of Jubilees

the prince descended from Judah (David or the Messiah). Nowhere in the Hebrew Bible is the high priest said to be such a prince or head of the nation. But the high priests of the Hellenistic period down into the second century B.C.E. certainly had the triple prerogatives predicted at Jub 31.15. Writing in the late fourth century B.C.E., Hecataeus of Abdera describes the priestly office as follows:[46]

> Moses took the men of greatest accomplishment and ability to be *heads (proistasthai)* of the nation and made them priests....He also made them *judges* of the most important cases and entrusted to them the guardianship of the laws and customs. Therefore, the Jews never have a king. Rather, the office of *head (prostasian)* of the people is given to that priest who is regarded as preeminent in wisdom and virtue. Him they call the high priest, and they look upon him as the *messenger (angelos)* to them of God's commandments...; as regards this last prerogative, the Jews are so ready to obey that they immediately prostrate themselves upon the ground when he expounds the commandments to them.

In the early second century B.C.E., the same picture of the high priestly office is drawn under the high priest Simon II by Ben Sira.[47] Though Ben Sira does not call the high priest a "messenger" or "angel," he still may have the Jews prostrating themselves before him.[48]

At Mal 2.7 the ideal priest is described in a context reproving sinful priests. The period of the great Zadokite-Oniad high priests, including Simon II the Just, could evoke the enthusiasm of the author of Jub 31.15 for the high priestly office and its legitimate occupant. But in the reign of Antiochus IV, the line held to be legitimate by the author of Jubilees was deposed forever, and the high priesthood fell first to wicked usurpers and then to the Hasmonaeans. To the author of Jubilees, those were sinful priests worthy of reproof. Since that author could only have hated the Hasmonaeans, it does not matter that John Hyrcanus I was high priest (134-104 B.C.E.) and had claims to be a prophet[49] and thus might have been described as a messenger.[50]

3. "Priest of the Most High God" at Jub 32.1 cannot be shown to have been derived from an official title of John Hyrcanus I.[51] As an official title it is attested among Hasmonaeans only for John Hyrcanus

---

[46] *Apud* Diodorus 40.3.4-6.
[47] Greek Sir 45.24-26.
[48] Hebrew Sir 50.21. See also Josephus *Ant.* 11.4.8 §§111-12, 12.4.2 §161; 20.10.3 §238, 4 §244, 5 §251, and *Ag. Ap.* 2.23 §§193-94.
[49] Josephus *J.W.* 1.2.7 §§68-69; *Ant.* 13.10.3 §282, 7 §§299-300; t. *Soṭa* 13.5 and parallels; cf. *T. Levi* 8.15, 18.6.
[50] See Hag. 1.13, II Chr 36.15-16.
[51] Contrast Charles, *Book of Jubilees*, p. lix.

II, not for John Hyrcanus I,[52] and Charles admitted[53] that the time of John Hyrcanus II was too late for the composition of Jubilees. "Most High God" as a name for the Lord is well attested in the first half of the second century B.C.E. and earlier, in Ben Sira and in Daniel.[54] How else would one refer to His high priest?

4. Charles held[55] that the victory of Jacob and his sons over Esau and his sons (Jubilees 38) reflects John Hyrcanus' conquest of Idumaea. On the contrary, the story reflects no historical event whatever. Rather, it is a demonstration that the fulfillment of the promises in Amos 9.12, Isa 11.14, and Obadiah will merely reestablish the conquests of Jacob. Jacob's descendants have a right, not only from Isaac's blessing, but also through conquest in war, to rule over Edom. According to Jub 38.13-14, from the time that Israel went down to Egypt, Edom has not been made to pay annual tribute, but Israel in the time of Moses still has the right to demand it. The passage does not reflect John Hyrcanus' conquest of Idumaea because Edom in Jubilees 38 is not only Idumaea (west of the Jordan rift, which in fact was conquered by John Hyrcanus) but also Mount Seir (in Transjordan, which no Hasmonaean ever conquered).

VanderKam holds[56] that the victory over Esau and his sons and their allies in Jubilees 38 reflects the victories of Judas Maccabaeus and his brothers over the Idumaeans and other neighboring peoples.[57] VanderKam was so intent on enumerating the similarities between the struggle in Jubilees and the campaigns reported in the books of Maccabees, that he neglected the profound and significant differences. We may note, first, that Judas and his brothers fought "Edom" only west of the Jordan. Charles' case in one point is stronger than VanderKam's: John Hyrcanus as well as Jacob and his sons conquered Edom,[58] but Judas and his brothers only passed through Idumaea on a punitive campaign, without conquering it. In the books of Maccabees, the hostile neighbors of the Jews are not said to have conspired

---

[52]Josephus, *Ant.* 16.6.2 §163. The dating formula at *b. Rosh ha-shanah* 18b is probably also of John Hyrcanus II. *Testament of Moses* 6.1 is a post-Herodian interpolation: see George W.E. Nickelsburg, Jr. (ed.), *Studies on the Testament of Moses* ("Septuagint and Cognate Studies," 4; Cambridge, Mass.: Society of Biblical Literature, 1973), pp. 5-58. Hence, that passage, too, need refer only to Hasmonaeans of the mid-first century B.C.E.

[53]*Book of Jubilees*, pp. lix, lxiv.

[54]Greek Sir 7.9, 24.23, 41.8; Hebrew Sir 46.5; Dan 3.26, 32, and 5.18, 21.

[55]*Book of Jubilees*, p. lxii; cf. VanderKam, *Studies*, pp. 238-39, n. 56.

[56]*Ibid.*, pp. 230-38.

[57]I Maccabees 5, II Macc 10.14-38, 12.10-37.

[58]Josephus *Ant.* 13.9.1 §257, *J.W.* 1.2.6. §63; Jub 38.8-14.

together, and with one exception,[59] they do not attack the Jews' home territory. In Jubilees, Edom takes the lead in building up a great alliance which together marches upon Jacob and his sons, who have their home at the tower near Hebron. The picture of Edom as the ringleader of Israel's enemies was a view prevalent among Jews for centuries after the role played by the Edomites in approving and profiting from the destruction of the kingdom of Judah by the Babylonians in 586 B.C.E.[60] This picture, however, does not reflect the Edomites in the time of Maccabaeus, for then the Idumaeans were but one enemy among may and neither incited others to attack the Jews nor profited from such attacks.

Let us examine the similarities which VanderKam considers "striking."[61]

(a) In the books of Maccabees,[62] Judas leads his brothers and the Jewish forces against Edom and the other nations; and, at Jub 38.5, Judah goes into battle in front of his brothers. The parallelism is much less striking than VanderKam thinks. It is not clear that Judah in Jubilees is analogous to Judas Maccabaeus in serving as commander. True, the expression "in front" occurs in Jub 38.5, but Judah there leads only Naphtali and Gad in fighting the enemies on the south side of the tower of Hebron. After writing "in front" in Jub 38.5 to explain Judah's role at the south wall, the author could leave the words unexpressed in Jub 38.6-8, for the reader would infer that Levi, Reuben, and Simeon, the sons of Jacob named first in the author's description of the eastern, northern, and western sectors, led the fighting in each of the other directions. In fact, Judah has no preeminent role in Jubilees 38. The great victors are first Jacob, who slays Esau and Adoran the Aramaean (Jub 38.2), and then Simeon and Benjamin and Reuben's son, Enoch, who slaughter and rout the Edomites and Horites (*ibid.*, 38.8).

(b) Almost the same nations appear in the lists of enemies confronting Jacob and his sons in Jubilees 38 and confronting Judas and his brothers in the books of Maccabees in the period after the purification of the temple. Indeed, one can make an even stronger case than VanderKam did, that the parallelism is too striking to be accidental. At Jub 37.6, 9-10, Esau's sons seek and get forces from Aram, Philistia,

---

[59]II Macc 10.24-31. The historian in Second Maccabees was mistaken. The campaign is the same as the one narrated at I Macc 5.6-8; see the Note on II Macc 10.24-38 in my *II Maccabees* (AB 41A; Garden City, N.Y.: Doubleday, 1983).
[60]Cf. VanderKam, *Studies*, p. 233.
[61]*Ibid.*, pp. 234-48.
[62]See n. 57.

Moab, Ammon, Edom, the Horites and the "Kittim," yet in the narrative of the battle at Jub 38.6-8 only the men of Moab, Ammon, the Philistines, Edom, and the Horites are mentioned. "Aram" is the equivalent of the Greek word "Syria"[63] and thus could mean "the Seleucid empire."[64] "Kittim" might mean Greek or Macedonian soldiers.[65] In I Maccabees 5, the campaigns of Judas and his brothers are indeed presented as wars against neighboring peoples, not as conflicts with the Seleucid empire and its armies. Furthermore, the Horites are not mentioned in the Hebrew Bible as enemies of the Israelites, but Seir is said to have been a Horite,[66] and the Baianites (or Sabaanites) defeated by Judas Maccabaeus were said to be descendants of Seir.[67] Can all this be coincidence? Should we not conclude that the passages in Jubilees 37-38 reflect the campaigns described in I Maccabees 5?

We should not. The "Horites" for the author of Jubilees are probably the inhabitants of Mount Seir, the original homeland of the Edomites.[68] By the author's time, the bulk of the Edomites lived in Idumaea, west of the Jordan rift, in territory which had been the southern part of Judah.[69] For him there were two names to designate the ethnic groups most closely related to Esau: Edomites (i.e., Idumaeans) and Horites; he never mentions Horites separately from Edomites. Hence, his allusions to Horites need only reflect the migration of the bulk of the Edomites to Idumaea; it need have no connection with Judas Maccabaeus' victory over the Baianites.

As for the "Kittim," the author's Hebrew may well have had "Hittites." The word in the preserved Ethiopic version is used to render in Ethiopic the Greek equivalents of both "Kittim" and "Hittites."[70] Hittites would, indeed, have been suitable allies for Esau and his sons, and enemies for Jacob and his. Even if the author wrote "Kittim" and meant Greeks or Macedonians, we would still have no proof that the passage reflects the campaigns of Judas Maccabaeus. "Kittim" had been harassing "Hebrews" for centuries before Maccabaean times and could long have been viewed as potential allies of Edomite haters of Israel.[71]

---

[63]Very frequently in Greek translations of the Hebrew Bible.
[64]See Élie Bikerman, *Institutions des Séleucides* (Paris: Geuthner, 1938), pp. 4-5.
[65]See Goldstein, *I Maccabees*, pp. 191-92.
[66]Gen 36.20; cf. Deut 2.12.
[67]See Goldstein, *I Maccabees*, pp. 294-95.
[68]See Deut 2.12.
[69]Michael Avi-Yonah, *The Holy Land* (revised ed.; Grand Rapids, Mi.: Baker, 1977), pp. 25-26.
[70]Charles, *Book of Jubilees*, p. 216.
[71]See Num 24.24, I Macc 1.1-9.

Far from being a significant reflection of Judas Maccabaeus' campaigns, the absence of the names of Aram and the "Kittim" from the description of the battle at Jub 38.5-10 is probably an accident. The first contingent of allies to come to join the sons of Esau was from Aram, with Adurām the Aramaean (Jub 37.9). At the beginning of hostilities, Jacob slew Esau and Adōrān (= Adurām); and Jacob's sons – Judah, Naphtali, and Gad – went forth against unnamed enemies in the south. But by subtracting from the list in Jub 37.9-10 the enemies named in Jub 38.6-8 as fighting on the east, north, and west, we are left with Aram and the "Kittim" for the south.

The enemies of Jacob listed in Jubilees 37-38 are simply the neighbors of the Promised Land and would fit any period in which an army of the patriarchs of Genesis, or an army of Israel or Judah or Judaea, fought all neighbors.[72] Moreover, nothing in Jubilees 37-38 reflects the Nabataeans (I Macc 5.25, II Macc 12.10-12) or the other Arabs (I Macc 5.31). The author of Jubilees could have represented the peoples of heathen "Gilead" (I Macc 5.9, 25-45) by Amorites,[73] but Amorites are not mentioned in Jubilees 37-38. Moreover, nothing there reflects Simon's victories over the heathens in Galilee (I Macc 5.21-23).

(c) At I Mac 5.65, Hebron is the site of the victory of Judas Maccabaeus and his brothers over the Idumaeans to the south of Judaea; at Jub 36.20 and 37.15-17, the tower near Hebron is Jacob's home and the site of the victory of Jacob and his sons over Esau and his. Again, however, the contrasts between the two narratives are more significant than the parallels. Judas Maccabaeus does not capture the *Idumaean* city of Hebron but attacks its fortifications and destroys its *towers*. Jacob in Jubilees 37-38 has the *tower* near Hebron as his *own* throughout. As a punitive expedition, Maccabaeus' campaign asserted no Israelite rights over Idumaean Hebron. The story in Jubilees probably is meant to assert that the territory of Hebron is rightfully Israelite, a claim which Jews made from the time that the Edomites encroached on southern Judah in the sixth century B.C.E.

(d) According to I Macc 5.17-18, Judas Maccabaeus divided his men into three forces to fight the many-sided peril which threatened his people, and the chapter tells of campaigns to the north, south, east, and west of Jerusalem; according to Jub 38.4-8, Judah and his brothers, divided into four groups, went out from the tower near Hebron in four

---

[72]David fought the Philistines, Moab, Aram, Edom, Amalek, and Ammon (II Sam 8.1-14, 10.1-14). Jehoshaphat fought Philistines (II Chr 18.11), Aram (II Chr 18.10, 30), Moab and Ammon (II Chr 20.1), Edom and Aram (II Chr 20.2), and Seir (II Chr 20.10, 22-23; identical with Edom?).
[73]See Num 32.29-40.

directions to fight against the several gentile nations. Here, too, the contrasts are more significant than the parallels. Twelve is divisible by three. If the author of Jubilees had wished to reflect Maccabaeus' three forces, he would have divided Jacob's sons into three groups of four, not into four groups of three. Furthermore, unlike the battle in Jubilees 38, the campaigns of Maccabaeus' forces are fought on widely separated fronts, and his third detachment fights without authorization and is defeated. Had the author of Jubilees 38 wished to reflect the great campaigns which Judas Maccabaeus and his brother Simon fought simultaneously in two widely separated sectors, he would have told of their namesakes' actions in an altogether different manner from what we have: he would have put Judah on the east, not on the south, and Simeon on the north, not on the west.

Thus, there is no reason to assume that the victory of Jacob and his sons over Esau and his in Jubilees 37-38 reflects Hasmonaean victories.

5. Similarly, the victory of Jacob and his sons over the Amorites in Jub 34.1-9 need not reflect Hasmonaean victories.[74] VanderKam admits that the parallels are weak,[75] and Charles himself recognized that the passage is an expansion of a much older legend about Jacob's conquest of Shechem, based on Gen 48.22.[76] Most of the names in the narrative have no significance in Hasmonaean history. The names were probably added to "Shechem" by an author familiar with the book of Joshua.[77]

6. The curse upon the Philistines at Jub 24.28-32 shows the author knew that the Greco-Macedonian empires (Kittim) ruled over Philistia (verse 28), but verses 29-32 need not reflect Hasmonaean conquests,[78] but only the anti-Philistine prophecies at Isa 11.14, Obad 19, Zeph 2.4-7, and Zech 9.5-7, as well as the hatred felt by Jews of the second century B.C.E. toward the inhabitants of Philistia.[79]

We may thus conclude that the author of Jubilees wrote between autumn 169, and spring 167 B.C.E.[80]

---

[74]Contrast Charles, *Book of Jubilees*, pp. lxii-lxiii.
[75]P. 229.
[76]P. 200.
[77]See Appendix.
[78]Contrast Charles, *Book of Jubilees*, p. lxiii.
[79]See Sir 50.25-26.
[80]For other arguments for a similar dating, see Finkelstein, *HTR* 36 (1943) 20(last paragraph)-24

Appendix: The Place-Names in Jubilees 34.4, 7-8

In their present form, as they stand in the Ethiopic text of Jub 34.4, 7-8, only Bēthōrōn (Beth-Horon) and Tāphū (Tephō, Tappûaḥ) are mentioned at all in the books of Maccabees. Beth-Horon is an important site in the career of Maccabaeus (I Macc 3.16-24, 7.39) and appears also in the list of points fortified by Bacchides in 160 or 159 B.C.E. (I Macc 9.50). Tappuah in the books of Maccabees occurs only in the list of points fortified by Bacchides. One should add that Tamnāt ārēs, mentioned at Jub 34.8 as having been fortified by Jacob, is surely Timnath-heres (Judg 2.9) and is probably identical to Thamnatha in the list at I Macc 9.50. One must concede that a Jewish patriot, after Bacchides fortified the sites, could have been interested in asserting that Jews had a prior claim to them, based upon earlier conquest or fortification of them by Jacob. But, if so, why do we not find the whole list from I Macc 9.50 reproduced in Jubilees 34? When we get probable identification of the places mentioned in Jubilees 34, we shall find that all but Beth-Horon lay outside the borders of Judaea in the Hellenistic period down to the middle of the reign of John Hyrcanus (Avi-Yonah, *Holy Land*, pp. 11-67). Beth-Horon was at least not securely held by the Jews during the Hellenistic period down through the career of Judas Maccabaeus and the early career of his brother Jonathan (*ibid.*, p. 17). Thus, a Jewish patriot could have written our passage at any time during the Hellenistic period down to the middle of the reign of John Hyrcanus.

The presence of at most one name, important in the victories of the Hasmonaeans, is hardly impressive. One should, rather, note that of the names as they stand, four are important in the book of Joshua (Tappuah: Josh 15.34, 53, 16.8 17.8; Sēlō = Shiloh: Josh 18.1, 8-10, 31, 19.51, 21.1-2, 12, 22.9; Beth-Horon: Josh 10.10-11, 16.3, 5, 18.13-14, 21.22; and Timnath-heres [= Timnath-serah]: Josh 19.50 [cf. Judg 2.9]), and one, Gā'as (= Gaash) is mentioned there (Josh 24.30). Scholars have been quick to assume that names in the list have been corrupted, and by emendation they have added to the list names supposedly important in Hasmonaean history. Should we not assume, rather, that names from the book of Joshua have been corrupted? (On the wish of the author of I Maccabees 9 to echo the book of Joshua, see Goldstein, *I Maccabees*, pp. 381, 385-86.)

Let us examine the remaining names from Jub 34.4, 7-8.

1. Charles read the third name in the list as *Sērāgān* or *Sarēgān*. VanderKam cites also the reading of ms. C *(Sarāgān)*, and of the Latin Jubilees *(Saragon)*. The parallel at *T. Judah* 5.1 has *Aretan*, and

Midrash Wayyissā'û has *srṭn,* and *Sēper Hayyāšār* has *Srṭwn.* VanderKam himself noted (p. 222) that the g could well have come from the misreading of a Greek tau as gamma. He wanted to read the word as "Pirathon." Pirathon (Pharathon) does appear in the list at I Macc 9.50. But, by following VanderKam's own method and by merely reading *t* for *g* (as is suggested by the parallel texts), we get *Sarēt ān* and an original Hebrew *Ṣarēt ān* or *Ṣarĕtan* (= Zarethan), the place mentioned at Josh 3.16 (cf. I Kgs 7.46) as being by the Jordan, near Adam, upstream from Jericho. On the difficulties of locating Zarethan, see Bustanay Oded,"*Ṣĕrēdâ, Ṣĕrērâ, Ṣārĕtan,*" *Encyclopaedia Biblica* 6 (Jerusalem: Bialik Institute, 1971), 765-68 (in Hebrew).

2. The second name in the list of Jubilees is *Arēsa*. The various Greek witnesses at T. Judah 3.1 have *Asour, Sour, Assyriōn,* and *Zour*. *Midrash Wayyissā'û* has *ḥṣr,* and *Sēper Hayyāšār* has *ḥzr*. To judge by the parallels, the Hebrew original had *Ḥāṣôr* = Hazor, the site of a great victory of Joshua (Josh 11.1, 10, 11, 13; 12.19). Admittedly, Hazor was also the site of a great victory by Jonathan the Hasmonaean (I Macc 11.67-74), but that victory came between September 145, and summer 143 B.C.E. (Goldstein, *I Maccabees,* p. 170), far too late to be known to the writer of Jubilees (see n. 168-69). VanderKam (p. 221) would see in *Arēsa* a corruption of "Adasa" (*Ḥăd āšâ*), the site of Maccabaeus' victory over Nicanor (I Macc 4.40-45). Even if VanderKam's emendation is correct, Hadashah is mentioned at Josh 15.37.

3. The last name in the list of enemy cities was read by Charles as Ma'anīsākīr. According to VanderKam, ms. A reads *Mā'anisakēr,* and mss. C and D, *Mā'anisākir*. The Latin Jubilees was *Manesacer.* T. *Judah* 6.3 has *Machēr* or *Machir*. *Midrash Wayyissā'û* has *m ḥnh šbyr* and *šbyr mlk mḥnym,* and *Sēper Hayyāšār* has *šbyr mlk mḥnymh.* The other kings in Jub 34.4 and 7 are designated only by their cities and not by their own names, so that it is not likely that *Mā'anisākir* is a corrupt combination of the name of a king with the name of his city (contrast Charles, *Book of Jubilees,* pp. 202-3). Later writers tried to bring the personal names of the kings into the story, as we find in *Midrash Wayyissā'û* and *Sēper Hayyāšār*. A writer like the author of Jubilees is unlikely to have invented place-names: he either took them from scripture or from events of his own times. We can only guess what he wrote here. The parallel texts suggest that he wrote at least one word beginning with the phonetic equivalent of *Ma'ani-* and another word ending in *-ir*. No such pair of place names occurs in Hasmonaean history. But *Ma'ani-* immediately suggests Hebrew *Maḥanayim,* and Mahanayim at Josh 13.26 in the Hebrew and in the Greek is associated with Debir. Perhaps the Hebrew original of Jub 34.4 had *wmlk mḥnym*

wdbyr (and the King of Mahanayim-and-Debir") or *wmlk mḥnym wmlk dbyr* ("and the king of Mahanayim and the king of Debir").

4. In Jub 34.8, Rōbēl is mentioned as a city "built" (i.e., fortified) by Jacob. Here, too, the author surely is asserting that the Jews have rights to a strategic site which go back to the time of Jacob. One would assume that the site was a strong point in his own day. VanderKam, following the *'rb'l* of *Midrash Wayyisā'û* and *'rbln* of *Sēper Hayyāšār*, would identify Rōbēl with Arbela in Galilee, the site of a massacre of Jews in 160 B.C.E. by a Seleucid army at a time when the Hasmonean force was far away (I Macc 9.2). Though the area has steep cliffs and caves, we do not hear of its being regarded as a strong point in the second century B.C.E. (but cf. Josephus *Ant.* 14.15.4 §§415-17). Though Arbela in Galilee is not mentioned in the book of Joshua, VanderKam's identification at present seems to be the best available. One might still think of the fountain of *Rōgēl* near Jerusalem (Josh 15.7, 18.16), of *Har Habba'al* or *Har Habba'alâ* (Josh 15.11) and *Ḥărabbâ* (Josh 15.60) in the territory of the tribe of Judah, and of *Har 'Ēbāl* (Mount Ebal; Josh 8.30, 33), but not one of them is known to have been a fortified point. The author of Jubilees may have taken all the other names from Joshua and still have brought in Arbela. Knowing that Hazor lay in the far north and that Jews had claims to Arbela, which lay on the road between Hazor and the territory around Shechem used by Jacob, the author may have liked the idea that Jacob fortified Arbela against future menaces from the north.

8

The Testament of Moses: Its Content, Its Origin, and Its Attestation in Josephus

I. The Original Content

In periods when God seems to hide himself precious indeed is the word of God to the pious. They are then apt to take their own wishful thinking for divine revelation. False prophecies have often had profound influence in history, and texts of them have much to teach the historian. Disappointed believers, however, tend to suppress the memory of prophecies which prove too obviously to be false. The Testament of Moses, a false prophecy, survives miraculously only in Latin on a corrupt nearly-illegible palimpsest. By suggesting that chs. 6 and 7 are probably an interpolation dating from post-Herodian times, Jacob Licht has provided the key to seeing this text as originally an apocalypse of the time of the persecution of the Jews by Antiochus IV.[1] Licht made his suggestion with the diffidence which is appropriate when one deals with a text so illegible and so obscure. Nevertheless, he is probably right.

The seer of the Testament of Moses proceeded as did the authors of the apocalypses at Enoch 85-90 and Dan 7, 8, and 11, which also come from the time of Antiochus IV:[2] he gave a synoptic view of history

---

[1] J. Licht, "Taxo, or the Apocalyptic Doctrine of Vengeance," *JJS* 12 (1961) 95-103. See also George W.E. Nickelsburg, Jr., *Resurrection, Immortality, and Eternal Life in Intertestamental Judaism* (HTS 26; Cambridge: Harvard University Press, 1972).

[2] See my *I Maccabees* ("The Anchor Bible," vol. 41; Garden City, N.Y., 1976), pp. 40-42.

down to the time of the persecution. The events immediately preceding and during the persecution are described with such detail as to suggest strongly that these are the events of the situation confronting the author and his intended audience. The authors of the apocalypses in Enoch and Daniel did not invent their predictions. They derived them from "scientific" study of the words of earlier, "true prophets," especially Isaiah.[3] Similarly, the author of the Testament of Moses did not invent but derived his predictions especially from Deut 32, Joel, and Isaiah.

All three apocalypses failed to be fulfilled. The apocalypses in Daniel and Enoch were being supplemented, to keep them up-to-date with unexpected events, already during the persecutions and during the career of Judas Maccabaeus.[4] Nevertheless those apocalypses proved to be obscure enough so that some of the faithful could preserve them as they were in the lifetime of Judas Maccabaeus, and later believers could interpret the wicked empire as Rome, without changing the text.[5] On the other hand, the Testament of Moses probably was too specific. Taxo the martyr and his seven sons may well have been real persons who were remembered. Their deaths obviously did not bring the predicted miraculous consummation of history. Believers might hold that the victories of the Hasmonaeans were a prelude to the predicted consummation; but when a century elapsed and the Jews were "enslaved" to Rome and the Herodian dynasty, believers could preserve the Testament of Moses as a true prophesy only by altering its text to take account of the unexpected events. A pious reviser could believe that his alterations of the text represented the intent of the original author, but he would have known that not everyone had to agree with him. Suspicious skeptics can exist in any period. To minimize the challenges of skeptics, a pious reviser must make his additions and alterations as slight as possible. He will prefer to place them at positions where it is conceivable that material could have

---

[3] See Nickelsburg, *Resurrection*, pp. 17-26; on Enoch 90.20-42, for the present see R.H. Charles, *The Book of Enoch* (Oxford, 1893), *ad loc.*, and the *Apocrypha and Pseudepigrapha of the Old Testament* (Oxford, 1913), II, 259-60.

[4] Licht's theory of interpolation becomes all the more certain when the development of the Testament of Moses is compared with that of the apocalypses in Enoch and Daniel.

[5] E.g., Jerome to Dan 7.7; Babylonian Talmud, '*Abodah zarah* 2b. The new temple brought by God (Enoch 90.28-29) is the probable source of a long chain of texts; see those collected by V. Aptowitzer, "The Heavenly Temple in the Agada," *Tarbiz* 2 (1930-31) 270-72 (Hebrew). Perhaps the falsity of the bulk of Enoch eventually proved to be so blatant that Jews and most Christians abandoned the book and did not attempt to preserve it by interpolation.

been misread or lost from an original manuscript, such as at the beginning or the end of a scroll or at the foot or the head of a column of writing.[6] Licht suggests that all of the material in chs. 6 and 7 is interpolated. Always bearing in mind the tenuous preservation of the text, we are entitled to ask whether the reviser would have dared to add so much.

Indeed, if all of chs. 6 and 7 represents a later interpolation, a difficulty arises: the seer jumps from describing the impious regime (ca. 175-169) of the corrupt and unjust high priests Jason and Menelaus (ch. 5)[7] to tell of the persecution (ch. 8), without mentioning either Antiochus IV's rapid march in 169 from Egypt to capture Jerusalem and sack the temple or the murderous expedition of Apollonius the Mysarch in 167.[8] The seer's interest in Jerusalem and the temple is such[9] that it is inconceivable that he could have omitted these events. It is likely that the seer alluded to them in his own original version of ch. 6. If our dating of the Testament of Moses is correct, 6.1 is certainly a post-Hasmonaean interpolation. The rest of the chapter, however, may contain the original words of the seer amid post-Herodian alterations. After speaking of the sinful leadership of the high priests in ch. 5, the seer may have gone on in ch. 6 to write,[10]

---

[6]Thus, the author of Dan 12.4-end appended the passage to Daniel 11.1-12.3 when it became clear that the death of Antiochus IV did not conform to 11.40-45 and was not followed by the resurrection.

[7]2 Macc 4.7-50..

[8]Charles noticed the omission (*AP*, II, 420).

[9]See 2.4, 6; 3.2; 4.7-8; 5.3-4, 6, 9; 8.5. Dan 7 probably does not mention the events before the persecution, but that apocalypse is a reworking of an earlier prophesy which mentioned neither Jerusalem nor the temple, as I shall show. The author of the apocalypse in Enoch had a negative attitude toward the second temple. See below.

[10]The Latin text would be as follows, with brackets around the probable interpolations: *Et succedit illis rex petulans [qui non erit de genere sacerdotum], homo temerarius et improbus, qui elidit principales eorum gladio [et locis ignotis singuli et corpora illorum, ut nemo sciat, ubi sint corpora illorum]. Occidit maiores natu et iuuenes non parcet. [Tunc timor erit illius aceruus in eis in terram eorum] et faciet in eis iudicia, quomodo fecit in Aegyptiis.* For the last three words, the palimpsest has *fecerunt in illis Aegypti*, which I take to be the reviser's effort to make my hypothetical original text fit Herod. Cf. Ezek. 11.9-10, 16.39-41, 30.19.

The Latin continues: *[per xxx et iiii annos et puniunt eos et producit natos...ecedentes sibi breuiora tempora dominarent* (palimpsest: *donarent*)]. I omit here the next words, which may refer to the expedition of the Mysarch (see below, n. 16) and pass to words which may have been transposed from their original position by the reviser: *et partem aedis ipsorum igni incendit.*

There shall come upon them an insolent king, a man rash and wicked,[11] and he shall cut off their chief men with the sword. He shall slay old and young, sparing none.[12] He shall inflict punishment upon them as he did upon the Egyptians.[13] He shall burn a part of their temple with fire.[14]

Thus, the seer, like the authors of 1 and 2 Maccabees, would have viewed Antiochus' sack of Jerusalem as punishment for the sins of Jason and Menelaus and the members of their factions.[15] In 6.9 the seer may have gone on to speak of the expedition of the Mysarch,

Into their country the murdering troops of a powerful king shall come, who shall conquer them and carry off captives.[16]

Even if all of 6.1-7 might belong to the interpolator, v. 9 might still be read as referring to Antiochus IV's capture and sack of Jerusalem:

Into their country murdering troops shall come and a powerful king, who shall conquer them and carry off captives and burn part of their temple.[17]

---

[11]Cf. 1 Macc 1.10; 2 Macc 5.15, 17, 21; 9.4, 7-8; Dan 8.23; Deut 28.50.
[12]Cf. 1 Macc 1.20; 2 Macc 5.11-14; Dan 11.28; Deut 28.50. 1 Macc 1.20 is defective and can be restored from Josephus *Ant.* 12.5, 3-4 (246b-247a, 249). The meaning of Dan 11.28 is not obvious but can be shown to be relevant. I prove these assertions in my commentary to 1 Macc 1.20.
[13]See 1 Macc 1.17, to be compared with 1.20 as restored from Josephus (see above, n. 12); and Dan 11.25-26, to be compared with 11.28 as interpreted above in n. 12.
[14]See 2 Macc 1.8 and 8.33. Though the pious authors in 2 Maccabees blamed Jason and his men for the fire, clearly it was set in the course of Antiochus IV's attack, so he, too, could be blamed for it.
[15]1 Macc 1.11-15, 28; 2 Macc 1.7; 4.10-17; 5.17-20.
[16]*In partes* (palimpsest: *pares*) *eorum cohortes* (Palimpsest: *mortis*) *uenient occidentes* (palimpsest: *et occidentes*) *regis potentis* (palimpsest: *rex potens*) *qui* (palimpsest: *quia*) *expugnabunt* (palimpsest: *expugnabit*) *eos et ducent captiuos*. By changing *rex potens* of the palimpsest to the genitive or by regarding it as a mistranslated Hebrew nomen rectum in a construct-phrase, we make sense of the interpolator's version: the Roman soldiers who hit Jerusalem hard in quelling a rebellion in 4 b.c. (Josephus *Ant.* 17.10, 1-11, 1 (250-299) served the "king" Augustus, but Augustus was not present. For "murdering troops," cf. 2 Kings 24.2.
[17]Latin as in n. 16, except for reading *occidentes et rex potens* here. The "powerful king" Antiochus IV had just conquered Egypt; cf. Isa 19.4. The last words of the chapter, *aliquos crucifigit circa coloniam eorum*, probably belong to the interpolator (see Josephus *Ant.* 17.10, 10 (295)). No crucifixions are reported in connection with Antiochus' expedition in 169 or with that of the Mysarch.

The intelligible part of ch. 7 deals with impious gluttonous men of power of a sort not mentioned in the historical sources reflecting the time between the expedition of the Mysarch and the publication of Antiochus IV's decrees against Jewish religious observance. Hence, all of ch. 7 may be post-Herodian interpolation.

If our reconstruction is correct, the words of the seer contain the reactions of a contemporary to the wickedness of the high priests who defiled the temple, to Antiochus IV's capture and sack of Jerusalem and the burning of part of the temple (presumably, a gate),[18] to the expedition of the Mysarch (probably), and to the persecution including the imposition of the idolatrous cult. These are the last important historical events known to the original author, who says nothing of pious armed resistance to Antiochus IV. Hence, our seer wrote early in the persecution, in winter or spring of 167/6 B.C.[19]

II. Attestation of the Text in Josephus

Our seer's prophesy, even when brought up to date in post-Herodian times, proved to be false. Yet his words survived long. Since they were placed in the mouth of Moses, they were probably written in Hebrew. They survived to be translated into Greek and the Greek to be translated into our extant Latin text. Can it be that no other surviving Jewish work took note of the Testament of Moses? The influence of our seer's words may be reflected in 1 Macc 2.29-38 and in 2 Macc 6.11, but there is no way of showing that the author of either book read our seer's work.

Josephus, however, was a proud believer in the veracity of Jewish prophecy, especially that of Daniel.[20] If the Testament of Moses could have been translated into Latin, it also could have reached the eyes of Josephus. There is more than one indication that Josephus knew the Testament of Moses.

Writing of the Zealots at *JW* 4.8, 3 (388), Josephus says,

> There was an ancient saying of inspired men that the city would fall and the sanctuary would be burnt according to the laws of war when civil strife shall befall the city and native hands shall be the first to defile God's sacred precinct. This saying the Zealots did not disbelieve, yet they voluntarily fulfilled it.

Our seer predicts that high priests will defile the temple (5.3-4) and that dissension and injustice will prevail in Jerusalem (5.2-6),

---

[18]See above, n. 14.
[19]See 1 Macc 1.54.
[20]See Josephus *Ant.* 10, 11, 7 (267-81); 12.7, 6 (322).

surely to the point of constituting the civil strife described in detail in 2 Macc 4.1-5.10. The "chief men" of Test Mos 6.3 could well include chief men of the feuding factions. At Test Mos 6.9 there is a prediction that part of the temple will be burnt. No other text is known from which Josephus could have derived his "saying of inspired men." Hence, there is a good chance that he derived it from the Testament of Moses. If so, we learn also that Josephus and the Zealots accepted our seer's work as inspired. Indeed, in its present version, Test Mos 6.8-9 lends itself to being read as a description of the conquest of Jerusalem by Vespasian and Titus.

Another possible allusion to our seer's work stands at Josephus *Ant.* 12.5, 4 (256). There, Josephus appears to be drawing on both 1 and 2 Maccabees, but neither source says, as does Josephus, that crucifixion was the punishment for violation of the ban on circumcision. That fact appears only at Test Mos 8.1.

III. The Sect to Which the Author Belonged

To what groups of Jews did our seer belong? Josephus and the Zealots could be eclectic in dealing with earlier sectarian literature, so that we cannot identify the author's position with that of Josephus; the seer's ideology of martyrdom certainly does not qualify him to be a proto-Zealot. Taxo, however, resembles the pietist martyrs of 1 Macc 2.29-38 and 2 Macc 6.11, who probably called themselves $H^a sidim$.[21]

One passage in our seer's work is very strange and may be important for identifying his sect. At 4.6 the seer alludes to Cyrus' decree allowing the return to the exiles. At 4.7 he goes on to say,

> Then some part of the tribes will go up and return to their appointed place, and they shall build it anew and surround it with walls.[22]

Our author may be drawing on Isa 61.4 (especially in his expression "build anew"), as if he saw the prophecy there partly fulfilled in the events. If so, he saw only partial fulfillment, for he goes on to say in v. 8,

> Only two tribes will remain steadfast in their established (?) faith, grieved and groaning because they will not be able to offer up sacrifices to the Lord of their fathers.[23]

---

[21] See 1 Macc 2.42.
[22] *Tunc ascendent aliquae partes tribuum et uenient in locum constitutum suum et circumuallabunt locum renouantes.*
[23] *Duae autem tribus permanebunt in praeposita fide sua, tristes et gementes, quia non poterint referre immolationes domino patruum suorum.*

The seer probably took "grieved and groaning" from Ezek 9.4, where the words refer to the scrupulous minority, scandalized over the abominations of the majority. However, at this point the seer mentions no abominations. Yet, as we have his words, he says that even after the building of the second temple and after Nehemiah's walling of Jerusalem, scrupulous Jews of the two tribes who returned from exile will still be unable to offer up sacrifices to their God! Unlike the seer of Enoch 89.73, our author says nothing of violations of the laws of purity which might have made the sacrifices invalid. If we take him literally, he here denies the cultic validity of the second temple!

We may be sure that there were Jews who so rejected the second temple and did so on the basis of Deut 12.8-14, Isa 66.1-3, Jer 7.3-15, Ezek 24.21, and Lam 2.7. Though a miracle had attested God's election of Solomon's temple (2 Chr 7.1-3), no miracle had yet attested His election of the second temple.[24] But our author accepted the book of Ezra-Nehemiah and bitterly complained when wicked priests and gentiles violated the second temple. In contrast, the author of Enoch 90.6-18 says nothing about desecrations of the temple, complaining only of the slaughter of Israelites. The absence of the temple from our seer's description of the glorious End is not significant. If he believed that Israel was to be raised to heaven, he must also have believed that the temple would be, too, in accordance with Isa 2.2 and Mic 4.1. Our seer and his audience took Isa 2 and Mic 4 for granted. Therefore he had no need to mention the future of the temple. It was the sectarian author of Enoch 90.28-29 who had to mention it, for he was teaching the relatively new doctrine, that the second temple would be replaced by a new structure brought by God himself. Hence, we may be sure that for our seer the second temple is not to be replaced; it is good enough.

What, then, should we make of our seer's statement which seems to deny the cultic validity of the second temple? Either a word has fallen out, presumably a translation of Hebrew $l^eraṣon$, "acceptably," or else, for our seer "to offer up sacrifices" by itself meant "to offer up sacrifices acceptably" in the sense that God would respond to them with miracles.[25] The rabbis, heirs of the Pharisees, were well aware of how

---

[24]See Ezra 3, 6. The purpose of the legends at 2 Macc 1.19-2.8 is to deny or explain away charges that the second temple was not fully God's chosen place. See my commentary.

[25]See Ezek 20.41-44 and Mal 1.10-13 and 3.4 in the context of its entire chapter; Ps 51.18-21.

the second temple lacked important sacred attributes even while they revered it.[26] Thus, our seer could well have been a proto-Pharisee.

We can be quite certain that our author does not stand in the tradition of the Essenes of Qumran with their sectarian solar calendar and its 364-day year and its 49-year Jubilee.[27] At Jub 50.4 the time of Israel's entry into Canaan and Moses' death is placed in the fiftieth 49-year Jubilee, in the year of creation 2450. Our seer places the death of Moses in the year of creation 2500, in the fiftieth 50-year Jubilee (1.2). On the other hand, the apocalypse of Enoch 85-90 is intimately connected with the tradition of the Essenes of Qumran and their calendar. It stands with the study of that calendar at Enoch 72-82, and the sectarian author of Jub 4.18-20 alludes to the apocalypse. The Enoch apocalypse thus may well represent proto-Essenes who admired Judas Maccabaeus.[28]

IV. The Kings at 2.7 and the Speaker of the Prayer at 4.1-4

We all owe a debt of gratitude to R.H. Charles, whose commentary first opened up many of the secrets of our text. However, one way of showing gratitude is to improve upon his foundation. At 2.6 Charles perceived that our seer was discussing the twenty rulers of the southern kingdom, including Athaliah. We may improve upon Charles' translation as follows:

> Seven shall build walls round about, and I shall beset nine, but <four> shall violate the covenant of God....

Besides mistranslating "beset" as "protect,"[29] Charles divided the rulers of Judah into three groups in arbitrary fashion, of the rise, of the period of power, and of the decline. In fact, the Biblical histories reveal a far more complex pattern of ups and downs. Rather, the seer has accepted the judgments passed on the rulers by the Chronicler. Seven were largely righteous: Abijah, Asa, Jehoshaphat, Uzziah, Jotham, Hezekiah, and Josiah; they built moral and physical walls to strengthen Israel (cf. Ezek 23.30, Ezra 9.9, and Mishnah *Abot* 1.1). Nine sinned enough to be beset by divine chastisement: Rehoboam, Jehoram, Ahaziah, Joash, Amaziah, Jehoahaz, Jehoiakim, Jehoiachin, and

---

[26] See Louis Ginzberg, *Legends of the Jews* (Philadelphia, 1928) 6, 377-78, n. 118, and my commentary to 2 Macc 1.19-2.8.
[27] See Shemaryahu Talmon, "The Calendar Reckoning of the Sect from the Judaean Desert," *Scripta Hierosolymitana* 4 (1958) 162-99.
[28] See my *I Maccabees*, pp. 41-42.
[29] For *circumibo* here as "beset," cf. Ps 59 (58).15 and Ps 88 (87).18 in the Hebrew, the Greek versions, and the Vulgate.

Zedekiah. Four were so wicked as to be outright idolaters: Athaliah, Ahaz, Menasseh, and Amon.

Charles jumps to the conclusion that the speaker of the prayer at 4.1-4 is Daniel. I shall show elsewhere that Dan 9 was written after the Testament of Moses. Nothing suggests any connection between the prayer in Dan 9 and the prayer here in Test Mos 4.1-4. Rather, if the speaker of the prayer is human, he would be Isaiah, who did utter prayers for Israel (25-26; 27.4; 63.7-64.12). Our author readily uses the Hebrew expressions of his own time,[30] but he still draws heavily on Isaiah. The "King on the lofty throne" comes from Isa 6.1. "That this people should be your chosen people" probably reflects Isa 43.20; 45.4. "Round about <shall> be the gate of foreigners and the place where there is vast pride," may well mean that the Israelites will be enclosed by the gates of Babylon ("Bab-El" literally means "Gate of God"), the place of pride, as might be derived from Isa 43.14; 62.10 and 13.19. "Look down and have compassion upon them, heavenly Lord," reflects Isa 63.15. However, the seer probably intended that the speaker of the prayer should be taken as an angel. He calls the speaker "one who is in charge of (or 'concerned with') them," an expression which is never used of a prophet but appears to be taken from Job 33.23, "If there be concerned with him an angel, a mediator, one of a thousand..." (*'im yēš 'ālāw mal'āk mēlīṣ 'eḥad minnī 'alep*), where the request of the angel is said to bring God's salvation upon the sufferer. The expression "who is in charge of" (*ᵃšer 'al*) is also regularly used of royal ministers and hence is appropriate for ministering angels.[31] Angels also defend Israel's cause at Dan 10.13, 21 and at Enoch 89.77.

V. The Meaning and Original Text of 8.4-5

There can be no doubt that all of ch. 8 deals with the persecution and the imposed idolatrous cult. One would expect the climax to come in v. 5 with a reference to the Abomination of Desolation. However, 8.5 appears to be incoherent and unintelligible. The Latin text of 8.4-5 has

> *Nam illi in eis punientur in tormentis et igne et ferro, et cogentur palam baiulare idola eorum, inquinata quomodo sunt pariter continentibus ea. Et a torquentibus illos pariter cogentur intrare in abditum locum eorum et cogentur stimulis blasfemare uerbum contumeliose, nouissime post haec et leges quod haberent supra altarium suum.*

---

[30] See Avi Hurwitz, "Adon Hakkol," *Tarbiz* 34 (1964-65) 224-27 (Hebrew).
[31] 1 Kgs 12.18; 2 Kgs 18.18; Isa 22.15, etc. Alternatively, a royal minister is called *śar–* ("chief of..."), as are the angels at Dan 10.20-21; see, e.g., Gen 21.22; 37.36. For an angel making a request similar to Test Mos 4.1-4, cf. Zech 1.12, G.N.

The words following the last comma are ungrammatical, for a neuter singular relative pronoun has as its apparent antecedent a feminine plural noun, and a verb in the imperfect subjunctive follows a main verb in the future indicative. Perhaps we may ascribe the irregular sequence of tenses to the inelegant Latin translator. The long sequence of verbs listing the dreadful acts which Jews will be compelled to perform suggests that yet another verb should stand where *leges* ("laws") does, perhaps *locare* or *ligare* ("place," "affix"). If so, we may translate the passage,

> For therein they shall be punished with tortures and fire and sword and shall be forced publicly to haul their idols, polluted as they are like those who hold them. By their torturers they shall be compelled to enter their secret place (*sc.* the Holy of Holies), and by whips they shall be compelled to blaspheme the Word with abusive language, and finally, after these atrocities, even to place over their altar that which they were holding.

Antiochus' act of desecration was all the more heinous because he made Jews haul the idolatrous objects and fasten them to the temple altar.[32]

---

[32]See Babylonian Talmud, *Abodah zarah* 42a (statement of Raba) and Mishnah, *Abodah zarah* 3.5, and see also my commentary to 1 Macc 1.54-59.

9

Apocryphal Book of Baruch

Scholars agree that the apocryphal book of Baruch cannot have been written by Jeremiah's secretary Baruch: a contemporary of Nebuchadnezzar could not have committed the blunder of taking Baltasar (= Belshazzar = Bel-shar-uṣur), who was the son of Nabonidus (King of Babylon from 556 to 539) and turning him into the son of Nebuchadnezzar (Bar. 1.11-12).[1] Nevertheless, the book is a puzzle. It appears to be an incoherent compilation consisting first of a prose introduction (A), ascribing the book to Baruch in the fifth year after the burning of Jerusalem by the Chaldaeans (1.1-14). Baruch is said to have read the book aloud to a mass-meeting of Jewish exiles in Babylonia, who thereupon took up a collection to send money to Jerusalem. Surprisingly, we are told (1.7-9) that there was a community of priests and other Jews in Jerusalem, headed by the priest Yoakim son of Hilkiah son of Shallum, and that two months earlier Yoakim[2] had received, surely by an act of Nebuchadnezzar's grace, the silver vessels which Zedekiah had made to replace the golden ones which had been taken to Babylon when King Jechoniah was exiled. The exiles write to Yoakim and his community to employ the money for sacrifices. The Jews in Jerusalem are told also to pray for the life of Nebuchadnezzar and his son Baltasar and to read Baruch's book aloud when making their confession in the temple on festivals and anniversary fast-days. The prose introduction is followed by a prose prayer of confession (B; in 1.15-

---

[1] See Carey A. Moore, *Daniel, Esther, and Jeremiah: The Additions* from *The Anchor Bible* (Garden City, New York, 1977), XLIV, 255-266.
[2] The Greek has only a pronoun, but normal syntax in Greek and Hebrew requires that the antecedent be "Yoakim," and so does the probable propagandistic intention of the author.

3.8).³ Then comes a poem on Torah (C; in 3.9-4.4): Torah is wisdom, a great gift from God; by departing from it Israel suffers grievous captivity; by adhering to it Israel is happy. Nothing is said of vengeance upon the enemy. Finally, in 4.4-5.9 there is a poetic message of consolation to Israel (D): Israel is still being punished for her sins; her grievous sufferings are described, but God will soon take *vengeance* on Israel's persecutors and gloriously restore the nation. Nothing is said of the Torah as wisdom, and the eager expectation of vengeance seems to contrast with the prayers for Nebuchadnezzar and his son mentioned in the introduction.

No less perplexing is the problem of the date of the book or its constituent parts. Definite clues for a date have been hard to find, with Ewald proposing ca. 350 B.C.E. as the date for Bar. 1.1-3.8 and Whitehouse putting at least A, B, and D in the years after the destruction of the temple in 70 C.E.⁴

Clues to the date of Baruch have been overlooked because scholars viewed the prose introduction as a collection of ridiculous errors and anachronisms. Though the text may have minor gaps and corruptions, its outline is clear and it can be made to reflect the situation of the Jews of Judaea under Seleucid rule in 163 B.C.E.⁵

---

³There is no reason to divide 1.15-3.8 into a "Confession for the Palestinian Remnant" (1.15-2.5) and "Prayers for the Exiled Community" (2.6-3.8), though Moore does so (pp. 257-258, 276-294). In 1.17-2.5 the author gives a detailed account of why the people should be ashamed of their sins, and at 2.6 he rightly repeats the formula of shamefaced confession with which he began in 1.15. The disasters mentioned in 2.7 are those listed in 1.20-2.5. Hence, 1.15-2.5 and 2.6-3.8 are tightly linked together. Moreover, according to the writer, the Jews in Jerusalem are being asked to recite the contents of the book, but everything has been written by Baruch, who is the spokesman of the entire nation, of the Jews in Jerusalem as well as of those still in exile. Except for those who were still unborn in 586, the exiles have experienced everything mentioned in 1.15-2.5. Thus, they, too, can recite 1.15-2.5. On the other hand, the Jews in Jerusalem must feel solidarity with their exiled brothers. Thus, the prayers in 2.6-3.8 befit the Jews in Jerusalem, too.

⁴See Robert H. Pfeiffer, *A History of New Testament Times with an Introduction to the Apocrypha* (New York, 1949), pp. 413-423; R.H. Charles, ed., *The Apocrypha and Pseudepigrapha of the Old Testament* (Oxford, 1913), I, 574-576; Otto Eissfeldt, *The Old Testament: An Introduction* (New York and Evanston, 1965), pp. 592-594.

⁵Other scholars on independent grounds have suggested a similar dating. See Charles C. Torrey, *The Apocryphal Literature* (New Haven, 1945), pp. 61-63; Pfeiffer, *op. cit.*, 415-416, 418-419. Bar. 1.15-3.8 certainly echoes the prayer in Dan. 9.4-19, a chapter written after the sabbatical year began in autumn 164 B.C.E.; see below and Jonathan A. Goldstein, *I Maccabees* in *The Anchor Bible* (Garden City, New York, 1976), XLI, 43. One ought also to consider the relationship of Bar. 1.15-3.8 to the fragments from Qumran, 4Q Dib Ham,

Bar. 1.1-2 may be translated, "These are the words of the book which Baruch son of Neriah son of Mahseiah son of Zedekiah son of Hilkiah wrote in the fifth year...on the seventh day of the month, at the anniversary of the time when [*en tôi kairôi hôi*][6] the Chaldaeans took and burned Jerusalem." I have indicated a gap in the text because the designation of the month has been lost from the text, but it is easy to restore.[7] According to II Kings 25.8, the Babylonians occupied Jerusalem in the fifth month on the seventh day of the month. Since the number of the month duplicated the number of the year, it was lost from Bar. 1.2 by one of the most common scribal errors (*en tôi etei tôi pemptôi en tôi mêni tôi pemptôi* became *en tôi etei tôi pemptôi*).[8]

Thus, the book of Baruch pretends to have been written exactly at the beginning of the fifth year after the forces of a king did violence to Jerusalem. There is now peace, and priests have resumed sacrificial worship at the site of the temple. Even some temple vessels have been restored. The book shows interest not only in the king but, strangely, also in his son.[9] Several messages dominate the book. Some are found in more than one of its four sections and thus tie the book together as a

---

published by M. Baillet, "Un recueil liturgique de Qumran, grotte 4: 'Les paroles des luminaires,'" *Revue biblique*, LXVIII (1961), 195-250. Baillet (p. 238) dates the fragments paleographically at around 150 B.C.E.

[6]For the translation, cf. Bar. 1.14 and I Macc. 4.54 and II Macc. 10.5.

[7]Many scholars have done so; see Moore, *op. cit.*, p. 269.

[8]One might have expected the author to have followed instead the text of Jer. 52.12 where the occupation and burning are dated on the tenth of the month. By the second century B.C.E., however, the faithful were familiar with such contradictions in scripture and could harmonize them, e.g., by suggesting that the occupation occurred on the seventh and the burning on the tenth (B.T. Ta'anit 29a).

[9]1.12. But cf. Cyrus' proclamation to the Babylonians, which speaks of prayers to be offered for Cyrus and for Cambyses, his son. The author of Baruch probably knew nothing of Cyrus' proclamation. His model should have been Jer. 27.7, but he departs from that model by not mentioning Nebuchadnezzar's grandson. He is writing against a background where only two royal generations are important. The year-count begins with the year of the fall of Jerusalem and exile of Zedekiah; cf. Ezek. 1.2, where the year-count begins with the exile of Jehoiachin. (See also Ezek. 8.1, 20.1, 24.1, 26.1, 19.1, 31.1, 32.1, 33.21, 40.1, Jer. 52.31.) Jewish year-counts in this period treated any fraction of a year before 1 Nisan as the first year and thereafter numbered a new year every 1 Nisan. See my *I Maccabees*, pp. 22-25, and cf. Hayim Tadmor, "Kronologiah," *Entsiqlopediah miqra'it*, IV (1962), 264-69. The practice of the books of Ezekiel and Jeremiah is to date by regnal years of kings of Judah as long as there was a king of Judah they regarded as legitimate. Thereafter, they dated from the exile either of Jehoiachin or of Zedekiah, from the deposition of a last king of Judah. Baruch is made to follow the same procedure.

unit. The messages can be listed as follows: The Jews for the time being are to obey the foreign conqueror patiently (1.11-12; 4.25); though there has been a partial remission of their punishment (1.7-8; 5.7-8), they must still serve the rest of the sentence imposed for their sin; meanwhile, they should confess their sins, repent, give absolute obedience to the Torah, and pray humbly for complete redemption (1.13-3.8; 4.27-28). Israel's true glory is the Torah, the only true wisdom, given to her by God (3.9-4.4). After completely serving the sentence imposed for her sin, Israel will have the joy of seeing God's vengeance on her enemies and her own vindication (4.5-5.9; 2.34-35). No human agency but God alone will being Israel's triumph (4.17, 27, 34-35; 5.1-4). We shall show that this combination of dramatic background and messages fits the late winter or early spring of 163 B.C.E.

Only once in all Jewish history was a stable community of Jews able to resume sacrificial worship at the site of the temple but four years after Jerusalem was burned. Should we not expect that fourth anniversary to be the real background which evoked the fabrication of the fictitious setting described in Bar. 1.1-9?

Here are the facts. Antiochus IV sent against Jerusalem a punitive expedition under the command of Apollonius the Mysarch which burned the city.[10] According to I Macc. 1.29, the expedition occurred "two years" after the sack of Jerusalem by Antiochus IV. The sack can be dated with strong probability in September or October of 169 B.C.E.[11] The "two years" of I Macc. 1.29 can mean anything from one year plus an appreciable fraction up to two full years.[12] In my commentary on Dan. 7.25 I shall show that the expedition of Apollonius occurred before Nisan (April 1-29), 167.[13] Thus, the expedition could have fallen as early as November 168, or as late as March 167. In sending the expedition, Antiochus began a series of outrages against Jerusalem. In Nisan 167, Antiochus IV published his decrees banning the characteristic rituals and abstinences of Judaism and imposing upon the

---

[10] I Macc. 1.29-31; Jonathan A. Goldstein, *I Maccabees*, pp. 4-5, 211-213; cf. II Macc. 2.24-26.

[11] See Goldstein, *I Maccabees*, p. 207. All Julian dates in this article are approximate and are based on Richard A. Parker and Waldo H. Dubberstein, *Babylonian Chronology* (Providence, Rhode Island, 1956). Brown University Studies, XIX.

[12] See Goldstein, *I Maccabees*, p. 212.

[13] *Ibid.*, pp. 42, 163, and 213, but the discussion there requires a correction. The words of Dan. 7.25 cannot be taken as measuring the 3 and a half years from the expedition of the Mysarch. Rather, the years are measured from the publication of the king's decrees against Jewish observance.

Apocryphal Book of Baruch

Jews a cult which all sources present as pagan.[14] In Kislev (December) of that year the king enforced his decrees by setting up the Abomination of Desolation upon the temple altar.[15]

What had happened by the time of the fourth anniversary of the burning of Jerusalem? I have argued that the Jewish calendar became defective during the persecution and that the Jews under Judas Maccabaeus had celebrated the first Hanukkah and pious Jewish priests were again offering the regular daily sacrifices already in October 164.[16] In any case, they must have been doing so by December, since on a fully intercalated calendar the first day of Hanukkah that year would have fallen on December 14.

Till now, we have been able to date the composition of the book of Baruch and the fourth anniversary of the burning of Jerusalem as early as November 164. If, however, Baruch was indeed composed against that background, its contents and the facts of history preclude so early a date. The Jews repossessed the temple and cleansed it without the king's authorization.[17] Certainly the royal government during the reign of Antiochus IV did nothing to restore temple vessels. Under Antiochus IV the persecuted Jews received only the amnesty recorded at II Macc. 11.27-33: Jews no longer were to be compelled to violate the Torah. They still were denied the power to punish Hellenizing Jews who violated the Torah, and they still were not conceded the right to control the temple and exclude apostates from it. Only Antiochus V, after his father's death, issued a document (preserved at II Macc. 11.23-26) granting those privileges to the Jews.[18] The book of Baruch preaches absolute loyalty both to the Torah and to the king. How could one preach that message at a time when the king still denied the Jews the right to control the temple and to punish apostates?

The news of the death of Antiochus IV reached Babylon on some day in Kislev (November 20-December 18), 164 B.C.E.,[19] and reached Antioch and Judaea somewhat later. Lysias, the chief minister at Antioch, owed to Antiochus IV his office and also his position as

---

[14]Antiochus IV intended it to be a Jewish cult, purged of pernicious accretions. See Goldstein, *ibid.*, pp. 125-160. On the date, see n. 13.
[15]I Macc. 1.54;,59.
[16]Goldstein, *I Maccabees*, pp. 165, 273-281.
[17]See *ibid.*, p. 273, and my *II Maccabees, The Anchor Bible*, Vol. XLIA (Garden City, N.Y., 1983), note on 10.1-8.
[18]See my notes on the documents of II Macc. 11.23-33 in my *II Maccabees*. On the date of the letter at II Macc. 11.23-26, see below, n. 23.
[19]A.J. Sachs and D.J. Wiseman, "A Babylonian King List of the Hellenistic Period," *Iraq*, XVI (1954), 202-204, 208-209.

guardian of the heir to the throne.[20] On his deathbed Antiochus IV appointed his official Philip to be the guardian of his heir. Lysias was at least to be deposed as guardian and to be subordinated to Philip. Probably he was also deposed as chief minister. Lysias refused to accept his deposition. Thus, it was to the interest of Lysias' regime at Antioch to conceal as long as possible the fact that Antiochus IV was dead. The fact could not be concealed very long. Lysias soon made the child heir king, and the helpless Antiochus V appointed Lysias chief minister.[21]

Months earlier, by early spring, 164,[22] the pious Jews had received the amnesty ending the persecution. Their insubordinate seizure and purification of the temple was embarrassing to the government but was probably not an item demanding immediate attention and action in the busy opening days of a regime established contrary to the expressed will of the dying king, a regime opposed by that portion of the royal army which was with Philip. The first full confirmation at Jerusalem of the death of Antiochus IV may well have been the letter of the new king announcing his accession and his new conciliatory policy toward the Jews. In my commentary on Daniel I shall argue that the publication at Jerusalem of the letter preserved at II Macc. 11.23-26 was the "justification of the Holy" mentioned at Dan. 8.14 and that it occurred about February 8, 163.[23] Even if I should be wrong in my interpretation of Dan. 8.14, we have found reason to believe that the act of the Seleucid regime restoring the temple to the Jews cannot have come in December 164, and probably did not come before late January 163. But the imaginary background of the book of Baruch goes a stage farther than the restoration of the site of the temple to the Jews. It speaks of a restoration of temple vessels. Any such restoration in 164 or 163 B.C.E. should have been reflected in our sources, but they, on the contrary, exclude it.[24] As we shall see, we can reconstruct, with considerable probability, a time in the late winter or early spring of 163 when the Seleucid regime may have *offered* to return temple vessels to the Jews. Accordingly, the fourth anniversary of the burning of Jerusalem by Apollonius the Mysarch, if reflected by the book of

---

[20] I Macc. 3.32-33.
[21] I Macc. 6.14-17; 55-56. See also II Macc. 9.19-29; 10.10-11, and my notes thereto in my *II Maccabees*.
[22] II Macc. 11.30; 33 (at least the month in 11.30 and the year in 11.33 are correct); *Megillat Ta'anit*, 28 Adar.
[23] On the true date of the letter at II Macc. 11.23-26, see Goldstein, *II Maccabees*, pp. 414-15. On Dan. 8.14, see for the present Goldstein, *I Maccabees*, p. 43, but for "January 28" read there "February 8."
[24] I Macc. 4.49, cf. II Macc. 10.3.

Apocryphal Book of Baruch   197

Baruch, must have come no earlier than February 163 B.C.E., and the expedition of the Mysarch can have come no earlier than February 167.

We have now to consider how the messages of the book of Baruch fit the time in 163 B.C.E. of the fourth anniversary of the burning of Jerusalem. By then, there had been a considerable restoration of the fortunes of persecuted Israel, and the persecutor was dead. Jews could again punish their fellow-Jews if they violated the Torah. The prophesies of Daniel and others, predicting that God's great redemptive transformation of the world would occur in 164 B.C.E. or with the death of Antiochus IV had not been fulfilled.[25] Nevertheless, many pious Jews believed that the age of Israel's subjection to foreign empires was over, but many others disagreed. The holders of the two views soon faced each other in bitter conflict.

Judas Maccabaeus, believing that the Jews no longer owed obedience to the Seleucid king, revealed in late winter or early spring of 163 his plan to besiege the Akra, the citadel of Jerusalem, which was occupied by Seleucid forces. Though Judas gained enough support to carry out the siege, the many Jews who did not believe that the age of Israel's subjugation was over viewed the siege as an act of rebellion against a legitimate sovereign, as an act forbidden by God. *Jews* were quick to report Judas' act to the king. Such Jews, if they were pious, would certainly preach the messages of the book of Baruch: patiently obey the foreign king, and pray to God to act in His own time to redeem Israel. Judas Maccabaeus and his followers must have been quick to charge that these pious opponents were traitors to the Torah: the dynasty to which they were obedient had only shortly before tried to abolish the Torah, and the besieged citadel contained sinful Hellenizers who had deserted the Torah for "Greek wisdom."[26] Thus, propaganda by the pious opponents of rebellion in 163 B.C.E. would have had to contain material like Bar. 3.9-4.4, to demonstrate that the message was truly Jewish and reflected commitment to the Torah. Like Jeremiah,[27] the pious proponents of obedience in 163 could believe that for the present their peace and prosperity depended on the kings from the conquering dynasty, but God in His own time would take vengeance on the cruel rulers who had exceeded His commands.

If such was the course of the author's argument, he handled the transitions artistically. Bar. 3.9-13 moves gracefully from the theme of

---

[25]See Goldstein, *I Maccabees*, pp. 39-47.
[26]See I Macc. 6.18-27; Goldstein, *I Maccabees*, pp. 315, 319, 323-325. The proposal to besiege the Akra came before the siege itself. On the date of the siege, see Goldstein, *I Maccabees*, pp. 315-318.
[27]See, e.g., Jer. 25.1-14; 27.6-8; and 29.1-14.

sin and confession in 1.15-3.8 to the theme of Torah as wisdom in 3.9-4.4. Bar. 4.5 moves from the near-paradox of 4.4 (that despite being subjugated Israel is happy through possessing the Torah), to the theme that her punishment is temporary and will be followed by glorious vindication.

Changes of style in the Greek have led scholars to deny that the book of Baruch is the product of a single author.[28] However, these changes may well be intentional and probably display the artistry of a single translator who turned the Hebrew, now lost, into Greek. The prose of 1.1-3.8, in content as well as style, closely follows the book of Jeremiah and is obviously translation-Greek based upon a Hebrew original.[29] Sentences in 1.1-3.8 are usually connected by *kai* ("and"), reflecting Hebrew *w-*; and where a sentence explains the previous sentence, it begins with the particle *hoti* ("because"), reflecting Hebrew *kī*. On the other hand, the poetry of 3.4-4.4 and 4.5-5.9, in content and style, closely follow those of Job and the Second Isaiah.[30] In those sections, as in Job and (to a lesser extent) in the Second Isaiah, sentences are usually connected by *de*, reflecting Hebrew *w-*, or by no particle at all; and where a sentence explains the previous sentence, the particle *gar* is used, reflecting Hebrew *kī*. Scholars have found the Greek idiom to be elegant enough to make them suggest that the Greek is the original and not a translation from the Hebrew, though evidence in ancient authors suggests the whole book had a Hebrew original.[31] Even the Greek of 3.9-5.9 contains Hebraisms and clear cases of misreading or mistranslating a Hebrew original.[32] The difference in Greek style, between 1.1-3.8 and 3.9-5.9, may reflect only the change from prose to poetry. The book of Jonah, too, changes from prose to poetry in the psalm of 2.3-10. For Jonah, we have both the Hebrew and the Greek. The Greek of the psalm faithfully reflects the absence of *w-* in the Hebrew poem, though the prose of the Greek of Jonah reflects the Hebrew in monotonously linking sentences by *kai*; and in Jonah 2.10, where the Hebrew was *w-*, the Greek has *de*, just as in the poetic part of Baruch.[33] One might object that the book of Jeremiah, too, contains both prose and poetry, and though the author of Bar. 1.1-3.8 imitates

---

[28] See Pfeiffer, *op. cit.*, pp. 412-413; Moore, *op. cit.*, 303-304, 313-314.
[29] See Henry St. John Thackeray, "The Greek Translators of Jeremiah," *Journal of Theological Studies*, IV (1903), 261-266; Moore, *op. cit.*, pp. 257-258, 268-290.
[30] Moore, *ibid.*, 298-301 *(passim)*, 303, and pp. 309-312 *(passim)*, 313.
[31] See Pfeiffer, *op. cit.*, pp. 417, 419; Moore, *op. cit.*, pp. 259, 261, 313-314.
[32] See Robert R. Harwell, *The Principal Versions of Baruch* (Diss. Yale; privately printed, 1915), pp. 54-56; Pfeiffer, *op. cit.*, pp. 419-421, 422-423; cf. Moore, *op. cit.*, 303, 313-314.
[33] Cf. Harwell, *op. cit.*, p. 60.

the prose of the Greek Jeremiah, the author of 3.9-5.9, with his use of *de* and *gar*, departs widely from the poetry of the Greek Jeremiah. The objection would hold only if one supposed, with Thackeray, that the Greek translator of Bar. 1.1-3.8 was identical with the translator of Jeremiah 29-52.[34] One may rather suppose that the Greek translator of Baruch noticed how the Hebrew author changed style and content and followed scriptural models, Jeremiah for 1.1-3.8 and Job and Isaiah for 3.9-5.9. In rendering the respective sections, the translator of Baruch then would naturally imitate the existing translations of Jeremiah or of Job and Isaiah.

Hence, the book of Baruch is a coherent unit and its message and dramatic setting make sense in 163 B.C.E. Then, as in the imagined time under Nebuchadnezzar, Jews knew of a king who perpetrated ruinous acts in Jerusalem and knew also of his son. Then, as in the imagined time, four years had elapsed since the ruinous acts of the king. Antiochus IV and his successors were kings over Babylon, and Jews believed that biblical prophesies against Babylon and her kings would be fulfilled against the Seleucid empire.[35] After 586 B.C.E. and before the Roman conquest of Judaea in 63 B.C.E.,[36] there was only one foreign ruler who perpetrated ruinous acts at Jerusalem, Antiochus IV. Propaganda calling upon Jews four years after the ruinous acts to obey

---

[34] See n. 29. I do not see how any test can distinguish for us whether the Greek translator of Baruch 1.1-3.8 was identical to the translator of Jeremiah 29-52 or, rather, imitated him. Emanuel Tov (*The Septuagint Translation of Jeremiah and Baruch: A Discussion of an Early Revision of the LXX of Jeremiah 29-52 and Baruch 1.1-3.8* [Missoula, Montana, 1976]), argues that the original Greek version of the entire book of Jeremiah followed the style we now find in Jeremiah 1-28. Tov holds that the peculiarities common to Jer. 29-52 and to Bar. 1.1-3.8 are due to revisions carred out by a later editor upon both. Then the original Greek translation of the entire book of Baruch could indeed have been done, as we have suggested, by one man, who in 1.1-3.8 imitated the Greek Jeremiah and in 3.9-5.9 imitated the Greek Job and Isaiah.

[35] Antiochus' ruinous acts, like Nebuchadnezzar's, left Jerusalem "deserted by her sons" (I Macc. 1.38-40). In scripture, "north" is used both of the Babylonian kingdom (Jer. 6.22; 10.22; 16.15; 31.7; and cf. 25.9) and of the Seleucid empire (Dan. 11.6; 7; 8; 11; 13; 15; 40; perhaps also Joel 2.20). See also Goldstein, *I Maccabees*, p. 488. The text of the prophesy at Isa. 13-14 says it is against the king of Babylon. Jason of Cyrene in II Macc. 9 sees it fulfilled in the dath of Antiochus IV; see George W.E. Nickelsburg, Jr., *Resurrection, Immortalty and Eternal Life in Intertestamental Judaism* (Cambridge, Mass., 1972), Harvard Theological Studies, XXVI, 79-80.

[36] The Roman conquest in 63 B.C.E. cannot be the background of the book of Baruch. Pompey was not a king, his sons were not involved with the Jews, and he did not depopulate Jerusalem. Only a few individuals were deported. See Josephus, *Antiquities*, xiv, 4.4-5.70-79.

such a ruler and his son could have been written only in the reign of Antiochus V.

Can a Jew who knew the book of Jeremiah have written such propaganda? The writer at Jer. 52.29 dates the second exile of Jews from Jerusalem by Nebuchadnezzar (586 B.C.E.) in the king's eighteenth year and goes on in verse 30 to speak of a third exile from Jerusalem in the king's twenty-third year (582/1). Thus, a few months after Baruch's imagined message, Jews at Jerusalem, far from enjoying a partial restoration in security, suffered a fresh disaster which belied the message! One might try to solve the difficulty by suggesting that the author of Baruch read in Jer. 52.29, not "eighteenth," but "nineteenth" (as at Jer. 52.12 and II Kings 25.8). If he did, the third exile for him would have occurred some four years after the second, shortly before the time of Baruch's message. But then it is strange that the author, in Bar. 1.2, took no note of the third exile. Rather, we must conclude that the author knew, not the version of Jeremiah underlying the Masoretic text, but the version underlying the old Greek translation, from which Jer. 52.28-30 are absent.

Up to this point, I have argued that the content of the book of Baruch excludes the possibility that the book was written before the news of the death of Antiochus IV reached Jerusalem. Nevertheless, at Bar. 1.11 the destroyer king and his heir are mentioned together, as if both were alive. To complete my argument, I must explain how an author, working in the reign of Antiochus V, would have been impelled so to couple the king with his heir. The explanation is easy.

If a preacher writing in 163 B.C.E. chose to compose propagandistic fiction set in the reign of Nebuchadnezzar, there was no way in which he could make his composition mirror every detail of the present. Nebuchadnezzar's acts were quite different from those of Antiochus IV. The Babylonian king's destruction of Jerusalem involved no attack on Judaism, unlike the atrocities of Antiochus IV. Jews knew that Nebuchadnezzar was still alive four years after the fall of Jerusalem,[37] whereas Antiochus IV was dead four years after the outrages of 167 B.C.E. The propagandist did nothing to call attention to the differences. He spoke of the four-year interval and mentioned Nebuchadnezzar with his supposed son and heir Belshazzar.

---

[37]We have seen that the author of Baruch did not know Jer. 52.29-30, but he could learn elsewhere that Nebuchadnezzar lived beyond the time of Baruch's message. Daniel 4 tells how Nebuchadnezzar was turned into a beast for seven years and then recovered his reason. If the king's time as a beast had come before the destruction of Jerusalem in 586, surely the fact would have been reflected in Kings, Chronicles, or Jeremiah. Hence, for the author of Baruch, Nebuchadnezzar survived the fall of Jerusalem by at least seven years.

Antiochus V was indeed the son and heir of Antiochus IV. Moreover, the propagandist may have had good reason to mention a counterpart of Antiochus IV even though Antiochus IV was dead. Besides being a monstrous persecutor, that is to say, a tyrant, Antiochus IV was also a usurper.[38] Jewish prophesy and Greek political theory denied legitimacy to tyrants.[39] The legitimacy of Antiochus V as king depended entirely on the legitimacy of Antiochus IV. A preacher of loyalty to Antiochus V could thus have felt the necessity of mentioning the obligation of loyalty to Antiochus IV.

One could object that the king and his son might instead reflect Vespasian and his son Titus. A pious Jew could have counseled obedience to the Roman empire in the fifth year after the Romans destroyed the temple. However, two authors who wrote at the latest in the first century B.C.E. probably drew on the book of Baruch; they are the historian whose work is abridged in II Maccabees[40] and the writer of Psalm of Solomon 11.[41] Evidence inside the book of Baruch also

---

[38] See Otto Mørkholm, *Antiochus IV of Syria* (København, 1966), pp. 38-50.
[39] See Goldstein, *I Maccabees*, pp. 72, 324.
[40] I demonstrate this in my commentary to II Maccabees, p. 301. See also Nickelsburg, *op. cit.*, pp. 106-108.
[41] On the close parallels between Bar. 4.36-5.9 and Psalm of Solomon 11.3-8, see Moore, *op. cit.*, pp. 314-316. Moore there rightly notes the fact that Bar. 5.8 is in the past tense, whereas the rest of the consolations to Jerusalem are in the future or the incipient present. (Moore wrongly treats the verb of Bar. 5.9 as past, too, and says nothing of 5.7.) In the prophetic books of the Bible, the perfect tense is frequently used to speak of future events. However, in Isa. 40-66, which served as the model for Bar. 4.5-5.9, there are almost no instances of such perfects rendered by a past tense in the Greek (see, however, Isa. 49.18). Furthermore, a late writer like the author of Baruch probably meant his Hebrew perfect tense to reflect past time, especially if he changed from imperfect to perfect; see Eduard Y. Kutscher, *The Language and Linguistic Background of the Isaiah Scroll (1 Q Isa^a)* in Studies on the Text of the Desert of Judah, ed. J. van der Ploeg (Leiden, 1974), VI, 351-352, 355-356. There is no such change in Psalm of Solomon 11, which is uniformly in the past tense. Moore infers that therefore Psalm of Solomon 11 cannot have been based on Baruch. Presumably Moore thinks that otherwise Psalm of Solomon 11, too, would have exhibited the change of tense.

But there are good reasons for the change of tense in Bar. 5.8-9 and for the absence of one in Psalm of Solomon 11. The author of Baruch believed that the entire book of Isaiah was written by a single prophet who lived before Jeremiah's secretary Baruch. Baruch therefore could have known Isaiah's prophesies. The book of Baruch asserts (1.7-9) that Isaiah's prophesies of a return of the temple vessels (52.11-12) and of a repopulation of Jerusalem have already been partially fulfilled. The past tense of "commanded" in Bar. 5.7 probably refers to the prediction of Isa. 40.4. The past tense in 5.8 probably indicates the fulfillment of one of Isaiah's prophesies (41.19). The author of the

precludes the time of Vespasian and turns us back to 163 B.C.E. We have deliberately postponed to this point our detailed treatment of the strange mention of the return of temple vessels to the priest Yoakim (Bar. 1.7-9). It is demonstrably a fiction,[42] but a propagandist

---

Hebrew original of Psalm of Solomon 11, on the other hand pretended that Solomon, who lived long before Isaiah, was the writer; consequently, he cast his work entirely in the prophetic perfect tense, which the Greek translator rendered as past. The author of the Psalm of Solomon went on in verse 8 to pray for the complete fulfillment of the prophesy in his own day. Had the Psalm of Solomon lain before the author of Baruch, who also found the prophesy incompletely fulfilled, he, too, would probably have included the prayer. Thus Bar. 4.36-5.9 is surely earlier than the Psalm of Solomon 11 and very likely served as its model. See also Wilhelm Pesch, "Die Abhängigkeit des 11. salomonischen Psalms vom letzten Kapitel des Buches Baruch," *ZAW*, LXVII (1955), 251-263, and Joachim Schüpphaus, *Die Psalmen Salomos* (Leiden, 1977), p. 55, n. 216.

[42]The author of Baruch wrote carefully. He did not want his words to be exposed as fiction. Nothing was known of Baruch's last years. The Jews who fled to Egypt after the murder of Gedaliah included only the survivors of those who had been living at Mizpah under Gedaliah's protection, plus the people led by Johanan the son of Kareah, and the unwilling captives Jeremiah and Baruch (Jer. 41.10-18; 43.4-6). Some of the poor could have remained in Judaea (Jer. 40.7), especially in view of the modest number of the exiles (Jer. 52.28-30). Baruch had the reputation of being even a more eager advocate of submission to the Babylonian king than Jeremiah (Jer. 43.3), so that readers of Bar. 1 could think that Baruch later either induced Jews of Judaea to remain in the homeland or persuaded exiles to return. Among the Jews thus to be found in Judaea in the reign of Nebuchadnezzar there could well have been priests. No high priest Yoakim is known from that period, but the priest Yoakim mentioned in Baruch is called the son of Hilkiah, and thus could have been the great uncle of the last preexilic high priest Jehozadak (I Chron. 6.13-15 [Hebrew 5.39-41]). We learn from Jer. 41.4 that sacrifices could be offered at the ruined site of the temple. A reader of Jer. 27.16-28.17 could well conclude that the gold vessels of the temple taken to Babylon with Jechoniah-Jehoiachin (II Kings 25.12-13) would not quickly return to Jerusalem, but that the vessels taken with Zedekiah might soon be restored. Hence, there was nothing incredible in Bar. 1.1-9. Completely in accord with the doctrines of Jeremiah and Baruch are the instructions to the Jews at Jerusalem in Bar. 1.11-13, to pray for the welfare of the king and his son, to serve them loyally, and to pray for their own forgiveness; see Jer. 29.1-14; 43.3. The author in Bar. 5.8 probably again presents Baruch as having witnessed a partial restoration; see n. 29.

Pfeiffer, *op. cit.*, p. 418, saw an incongruity in the poem on Torah, at Bar. 3.10, "Why, Israel, why is it that you have grown old in a foreign land?" Could this be said to an audience of Jewish exiles in 582 B.C.E.? It could. King Jechoniah was present to hear Baruch's words (Bar. 1.3); by 582 B.C.E., he and many others had been in Babylonia for some 15 years. Moreover, the reference to "growing old" may be figurative and derived from Hos. 7.9.

Nevertheless, if there had been a return of exiles or of temple vessels in the reign of Nebuchadnezzar, surely the fact would have been mentioned in

perpetrates a fiction only if it is useful in his own time. Four years after the destruction of the temple by the Romans there was no priest offering sacrifices on an altar in Jerusalem, and there was no sign that the Romans would restore temple vessels to the Jews. Certainly Jewish sacrifices were being offered in Jerusalem in 163; there is evidence that a priest Yoakim was prominent there; and there are clues allowing us to guess that the Seleucid government in that year offered to restore temple vessels to the Jews. Let us study the evidence and the clues.

On receiving the news that Judas Maccabaeus and his followers were besieging the Akra, the regime of Antiochus V in mid-163 B.C.E. moved to suppress the rebellion. According to II Macc. 13.3-8, the Seleucid government, before attacking the Jewish rebels, first refused to confirm in office the unpopular and corrupt Hellenizing high priest Menelaus and then had Menelaus executed. If Menelaus needed confirmation, he must have lost his authority over the Jews, either de facto or de jure. Judas Maccabaeus never exercised high priestly authority. Who became the leading priests when Menelaus lost control? Shortly after Menelaus' fall, perhaps immediately, Alcimus, whose Hebrew name was "Yakim," a shortened form of "Yoakim," replaced Menelaus as high priest.[43] I have argued elsewhere that Alcimus was a pious Jew.[44] Throughout his tenure as high priest, Alcimus was conspicuous for his loyalty to and dependence on the Seleucid kings.[45] The royal government must have installed him in hopes he was a personality capable of pacifying the turbulent Jews. An unknown could hardly rally support. Alcimus must have been prominent previously among the Jews, as a pious priest, loyal to the dynasty. In the narrative of Baruch, Yoakim is only priest, not high priest. Similarly, at the beginning of Judas' siege of the Akra, Alcimus was only a prominent priest, not high priest.

---

canonical scripture. "Evil-Merodach's" release of Jechoniah-Jehoiachin is recorded at 11 Kings 25.27-30 and Jer. 52.31-34, and Cyrus' release of the temple vessels is recorded at Ezra 1.7-11, and yet nothing is said of Nebuchadnezzar's supposed release of the temple vessels in Jeremiah, Ezekiel, Deutero-Isaiah, Daniel, II Kings, II Chronicles, or Ezra. Therefore the return of the Jews and temple vessels to Jerusalem spoken of in Baruch must be fictitious.

[43]Josephus, *Antiquities*, xii, 9.7.385, xx, 10.3.235; cf. II Macc. 14.3. Although most witnesses to the text of Josephus give the Hebrew name as *Iakeimos* or *Iakimos*, mss. A, M, E, and the Latin give it as *Iôakeimos*, *Iôakimos*, or *Ioachim* at *Antiquities*, xii, 9.7.385; and E and the Latin have the *o* at *Antiquities*, xx, 10.3.235, 237.

[44]Goldstein, *I Maccabees*, pp. 332-336.

[45]I Macc. 7.1-25; 9.1; 23-27; 54-57; II Macc. 14.3-26.

Furthermore, Josephus says that one of the successors of Antiochus IV did return to the Jews of Antioch all the copper votive offerings taken from the temple during the sack of 169 B.C.E.[46] The return of the temple vessels to the Jews of Antioch is strange. One would expect to have them returned to the temple in Jerusalem. The phenomenon looks like a face-saving compromise. Perhaps a Seleucid king offered to return the vessels "to the Jews," surely meaning to the temple in Jerusalem, but a rebellion in Jerusalem then prevented the fulfillment of the offer. The regime of Antiochus V could have made such an offer to Alcimus, in the hope that pious Jews would then be induced to withdraw their support of the siege of the Akra. When the siege nevertheless continued, the regime may have withdrawn the offer, and either Antiochus V or a later Seleucid may have turned over the temple vessels to the loyal Jews of Antioch. Josephus does not specify which later Seleucid made the return. However, the chronology and content of the book of Baruch gave us reason to date the work in 163 even before we considered Alcimus and the temple vessels, and the strange fiction in Baruch of Nebuchadnezzar's return of the temple vessels demands explanation. By supposing that Antiochus V in 163 made an offer to or through Alcimus to return the temple vessels, we find all pieces of the puzzle falling into place. The fit can hardly be coincidental. As a witness contemporary with the events, the book of Baruch fills out the vague hints in Josephus, and we may take it as fact that Antiochus V made the offer through Alcimus,[47] that the offer

---

[46] *War*, vii, 3.3.44.

[47] Professor Saul Lieberman has called my attention to the legend concerning Yaqim (=Yakim) found at Midrash Tanḥuma, ed. Buber, Toledot, section 10, p. 132. The text of the Oxford manuscript, printed by Buber, is somewhat corrupt, though the meaning is clear. Buber himself in his commentary cites the reading of the Parma manuscript, which may be rendered as follows: "[When old Isaac was about to bless the disguised Jacob,] he foresaw that wicked men were destined to be descended from him, and he did not wish to bless him. When Jerusalem was conquered in the time of Yehoyaqim [the Oxford manuscript has *Yaqum* (error for *Yaqim*)], he said, 'the gentiles are afraid to enter the temple.' What did he do? He entered and brought out the candelabrum. When Isaac foresaw him [Yehoyaqim], he did not wish to bless Jacob because of him; [as it says in scripture,] 'He did not recognize him.' But as soon as he foresaw that he [Yehoyaqim] repented, immediately 'he smelled his garments [$b^e g\bar{a}d\bar{a}w$, punningly read as $b\bar{o}g^e d\bar{a}w$, his (repentant) traitors] and blessed him [Gen. 27.23].'" See the comments on this text at Bereshit Rabbah 65.27, p. 741 Theodor-Albeck. One might infer from the tradition in Midrash Tanḥuma that Yaqim felt guilty for delivering temple vessels to Antiochus IV, though he may have done so under duress. One could imagine the repentant priest as eagerly seeking the return of the vessels from Antiochus V. However, it is hazardous to use the story in Midrash Tanḥuma as a historical source. In

Apocryphal Book of Baruch 205

failed to secure its purpose, and that Antiochus V or a later Seleucid turned the vessels over to the Jews of Antioch. We may also be confident that the book of Baruch was written in 163 as propaganda for Alcimus and his followers, pious Jews who were loyal to the Seleucid government in the belief that God's time for the liberation of the Jews had not yet come.

Bar. 1.15-3.8 has so much in common with Dan. 9.5-19 that the resemblances cannot be coincidental.[48] Although most scholars agree

---

other sources the guilty priest is not named "Yaqim" but "Yosi from Shitah," and his death follows close upon his delivery of the candelabrum. (See Bereshit Rabbah 65.27, pp. 741-742 Theodor-Albeck.) I think the tradition in Midrash Tanḥuma is an incomplete and corrupt version of the tradition in Bereshit Rabbah, where two stories are told, one of Yosi from Shitah and the other of Yakim; the authority underlying the tradition in Midrash Tanḥuma forgot the story of Alcimus and wrongly remembered the subject of the other story as Alcimus, not as Yosi from Shitah.

[48]Bar. 1.15-16 parallels Dan. 9.7-8, having in addition (probably from Jer. 32 [Greek 39].32) the mention of priests and prophets. Bar. 1.17-18 parallels Dan. 9.5-6; 10, but lacks the mention of (true) prophets, either because it was awkward to speak of them after mentioning false prophets in Bar. 1.16, or because the writer saved for Bar. 1.21 his allusion to true prophets. Bar. 1.19 parallels Dan. 9.15 but goes beyond Daniel in saying that Israel's disobedience goes back to the remote past and extends down into the present. Bar. 1.20 parallels Dan. 9.11, having in addition "to this day" (cf. Dan. 9.14) and the reference to the time of the curse and the covenant (probably derived from Jer. 11.4-5). The sins and disasters in Bar. 1.19-20 go back to the remote past. To focus on more recent sins, the author of Baruch in 1.21-22 has material beyond that in Dan. 9; nevertheless, 1.21 again parallels Dan. 9.6, 10. Bar. 2.1-5 parallels Dan. 9.12-13a, with amplification based on Deut. 28.13; 37; 53-57, and Lev. 26.29. The reader's mind has been pulled away from the main subject by the amplification in Bar. 2.3-5, so the author resumes the main topics of Bar. 1.15, 19, 21; 2.1-2, by repeating them in Bar. 2.6-9, verses exactly parallel to Dan. 9.7-8, 11-14. Bar 2.10 is parallel to Dan. 9.10. Bar. 2.11-12 is parallel to Dan. 9.15, with amplification in Bar. 2.11 derived from Jer. 32.20-21. Bar. 2.13-17a is parallel to Dan. 9.16-19; however, there is no parallel in Dan. 9 for the prayer in Bar. 2.14 for the favor of Israel's foreign masters (see below). Bar. 2.16-17 expresses concern only for the nation and lacks the prayer for Jerusalem in Dan. 9.18. Bar. 2.17b-18 probably reflects lack of belief in the resurrection and would thus be the one doctrinal point wherein the author disagrees with the author of Daniel, though on the good authority of Isa. 38.18, Ps. 30.10, 115.17-18, etc.

Bar. 2.19 parallels Dan. 9.18; from here on, the author of Baruch, unlike Daniel, sharply distinguishes the sinful ancestors and kings of the past from repentant Israel of the present (see below).

At this point, the author of Baruch hs paralleled everything in Daniel except the reference to God's mercy in Dan. 9.9. Hence, as one might expect, Bar. 2.20-26 has no parallel in Dan. 9, though it can be viewed as identifying what were the teachings given through the prophets (mentioned in Dan. 9.7, 10) and what were the consequences of disobedience to them.

that the prayer in Baruch is based upon that in Daniel, the recent commentary of Carey A. Moore still considers that the prayer in Daniel might be based upon the one in Baruch or that both draw on a common source.[49] I shall treat elsewhere the problem of how and when Daniel 9 was written. The chapter may have more than one stratum, but in its present form it probably dates at the latest from autumn 164.[50] If my views on Daniel and Baruch are correct, the two prayers were written almost contemporaneously, but the prayer in Daniel is the earlier.

The prayer in Baruch contains more than the prayer in Daniel. Careful examination of the additional material[51] shows that the prayer in Daniel served as a model for the one in Baruch. The same examination also confirms our theory that the prayer in Baruch was written against the background of 163 B.C.E. Some of the additional material is mere elaboration of shorter allusions in Daniel. Significant, however, are the following. Except perhaps for one ambiguous passage (9.15), Daniel confesses only sins of the past, sins from before the destruction of the temple. Bar. 1.19 unambiguously states that the sins have continued into the present. Daniel prays only for complete deliverance; Bar. 1.14 prays that the foreign rulers of the Jews will favor them. Daniel does not find it necessary to specify any particular

---

Bar. 2.27-3.2 has no parallel in Dan. 9, but can be viewed as an expansion of the reference to God's mercy in Dan. 9.9. The final petitions in Bar. 3.3-8 are also unparalleled in Dan. 9 and present very sharply the distinction between the sinful ancestors and repentant Israel. God's mercy is only for the repentant.

[49]Moore, *op. cit.*, pp. 291-293; Pfeiffer, *op. cit.*, p. 415. Moore's arguments for leaving the question open are very weak. The first reason for regarding Dan. 9.5-19 as the earlier and as the model is not merely that the prayer in Baruch is longer but rather that the excess maerial in Baruch is demonstrably intrusive. See n. 48; Pfeiffer, *op. cit.*, p. 415, and B.N. Wambacq, "Les prières de Baruch (1, 15-2, 19) et de Daniel," *Biblica*, XL (1959), 464-475. A second reason for believing in the priority of Dan. 9.5-19 is that the reading in Daniel is usually closer to older biblical models than the reading in Baruch. Moore's counter-examples are weak or wrong. He suggests comparing Bar. 1.16 and Dan. 9.8 with Neh. 9.32; but Dan. 9.8 is probably based rather on Jer. 2.26. He suggests comparing Bar. 2.12a and Dan. 9.15c with I Kings 8.47c. It is true that I Kings 8.47c and Bar. 2.12a have three verbs and Dan. 9.15c has only two, but all three verbs have appeared already in Dan. 9.5. Finally, Moore suggests comparing Bar. 2.15b and Dan. 9.18c with Deut. 28.10. But Bar. 2.15b does *not* parallel Dan. 9.18c; rather, Bar. 2.16-17a does. Bar. 2.15 is probably an expansion of "for the Lord's sake" in Dan. 9.17 and Bar. 2.14 (perhaps based upon Ezek. 39.7; see also Ezek. 36.23; 37.28; II Chron. 6.33). Dan. 9.18c, with its concern for the city rather than the nation, is not derived from Deut. 28.10 but from some such verse as II Kings 27.7 or Jer. 25.29.

[50]For the present, see Goldstein, *I Maccabees*, p. 43.

[51]See n. 48.

sin. In contrast, the author of Baruch goes to great trouble to stress, first, the sin of the Jews in not submitting loyally to the king of Babylon and, second, the punishment thereby incurred (2.20-26). The author does so at a point where he has already reflected everything in Dan. 9.5-19 except the allusion to God's mercy in 9.18. That allusion is expanded at Bar. 2.27-3.2. If Bar. 2.20-26 had been omitted, no one would have missed the verses. Clearly, the author is concerned that Israel sins in the present and has still to be ruled by foreign kings and must not risk the dire punishment rebellion against them would incur. These are the issues stressed by the loyalist pious Jews in 163.

I believe that the seer in Daniel, who had predicted God's and Israel's eschatological triumph for the beginning of the sabbatical year in Tishri 164 B.C.E., met the challenge of the failure of his prophesy by moving the time of fulfillment to Tishri 163, the end of the sabbatical year.[52] The writer of Baruch seems to have had his doubts about the resurrection of the dead (2.17-18), but otherwise he agreed with the prophesies of Daniel; he, too, held that God's time was near. But the author of Baruch altered the prayer of Daniel 9 in order to warn Israel that the sin of rebellion could prevent the great redemption.

The author seems to believe that he and his followers can dissociate themselves from the rebellious sinners. Whereas at Dan. 9.18 the lack of merit belongs to "us" (to all Jews), at Bar. 2.19 it belongs to the rebellious ancestors and kings. At Bar. 3.7 "we" (the pious Jews) have purged ourselves of the sin of our rebellious ancestors. Indeed, from 2.19 through 3.8 he sharply distinguishes "us" (repentant Israel) from "our ancestors" or "our kings," the rebels. Judas Maccabaeus and the besiegers of the citadel are the bearers of the false and wicked tradition. As a typical sectarian Jew, then, the author of Baruch viewed himself and his group as the "true Israel."[53]

---

[52] Goldstein, *I Maccabees*, p. 43.
[53] The author was not an earlier member of the sect found at Qumran. Members of the sect designated the months by ordinal numbers, not by Babylonian names, and a Babylonian month-name occurs in Bar. 1.8. The animal apocalypse of Enoch 85-90 seems to belong to the ancestors of the Jews of Qumran, and in Enoch 90.1-9 there is no sign that the pious members of the author's sect broke with Judas Maccabaeus on the issue of besieging the Akra; see Goldstein, *I Maccabees*, pp. 41-42, n. 12. Thus, it is not surprising that no fragments of Baruch have been found at Qumran.

10

Review of Doran's *Temple Propaganda**

As preserved, II Maccabees is strange: it consists, first, of two letters (1.1-10a and 1.10b-2.18) urging the Jews of Egypt to observe the festival of deliverance which Jews now call Hanukkah. Abruptly after the second letter comes a preface (2.19-32) in which the writer claims that he is about to present an abridgment of a longer historical work by one Jason of Cyrene, of which we now possess no other trace. The professed abridger's work, which can be called "the epitome," follows (3.1-15.39), tracing in a highly peculiar and emotional style events which befell the Jews from the reign of Seleucus IV (187-175 B.C.E.) down through the victory of Judas Maccabaeus over Nicanor which probably occurred in 161 B.C.E.[1] The abridger does not tell us what his own name is.

The present thin and somewhat poorly executed[2] study by Robert Doran nevertheless contains some good contributions to understanding the purpose and character of II Maccabees.

Thus, Doran examines (pp. 24-46) some interesting aspects of the grammar and style of the epitome, demonstrating how it consistently

---

*Robert Doran, *Temple Propaganda: The Purpose and Character of 2 Maccabees.* Washington: Catholic Biblical Association of America, 1981 (The Catholic Biblical Quarterly Monograph Series. v. 12). Pp. viii + 124. $4.50.

[1] See Jonathan A. Goldstein, *I Maccabees* ("Anchor Bible," vol. 41; Garden City, N.Y., 1976), pp. 341-42.

[2] Examples of minor errors: on p. 19, lines 1, 2, and 6, for "inviolability" read "sanctity" or "holiness," and in line 5, for "neglects" read "fails to assert the sanctity of" (here Doran has given an inaccurate paraphrase of my own statements); on p. 20, for *ederon* read *epheron*; on p. 43, for "die" read "kill"; on p. 47, for "unseat" read "make trouble for"; on p. 61, for "hubritic" read "hubristic"; on p. 111, for "Macedonians" read "Lacedaemonians."

displays "a nicety of syntax that one associates with classical, literary writers. The author shows himself capable of writing good Greek."

Doran strives to show how the epitome fits into the patterns of ancient tales, Jewish and non-Jewish, of how a god miraculously defended his temple and his chosen territory from enemies (pp. 47-51, 72-74, 98-104). Expanding on a note by Elias Bickerman, he puts an end (pp. 77-78) to the misinterpretations which have made *arithmōn* in II Macc. 2.24 refer to historical statistics; rather, it should be translated "lines of text."

On pp. 79-97 Doran also does well in setting the epitome in the context of ancient historical works and abridgments and in demolishing the notion that a genre of "pathetic" or "rhetorical" history evolved in the Greek literature of the Hellenistic era, and that the epitome is a surviving example of that genre. Rather, the epitome fits patterns prevalent in Greek historiography from the classical period on. Doran's discussion here draws heavily on the works of Thomas W. Africa and F.W. Walbank.

The claim of the writer in II Macc. 2.19-23 that he is abridging a work by Jason of Cyrene has been questioned. In his unpublished German dissertation, Wolfgang Richnow suggested that the writer's claim is a fiction contrived for the purpose of winning greater attention for a work that was really entirely his own. Doran presents a good refutation (pp. 81-83) of Richnow's hypothesis.

Much less satisfactory are other aspects of Doran's book. His treatment of the prefixed letters (pp. 2-12) is superficial. He denies that either one of them contains an implicit polemic against the schismatic Jewish temple at Leontopolis in Egypt. He can do so only because he has failed to perceive the numerous Scriptural allusions in the first letter and their implications, and because he has failed to discern the thread of argument which unites the apparently disparate sections of the second letter.[3] Indeed, he quotes and rejects (p. 10) my description of the second letter as a "reasoned attack upon challenges to the holiness of the second Temple prevalent at the time."

Doran finds (pp. 11-12) no trace of opposition between the partisans of the Jewish temple of Leontopolis and those of the Temple of Jerusalem, noting that a good case can be made that a member of the Jewish community at Leontopolis wrote propaganda favoring the Temple in Jerusalem. He might have cited also the fact that Onias IV, founder of the schismatic temple, himself surely valued the Temple of

---

[3]See Jonathan A. Goldstein, *II Maccabees* ("Anchor Bible," vol. 41A; Garden City, N.Y., 1983), pp. 138-49, 158-63.

Jerusalem.[4] Doran has failed to perceive what was the issue. The first and second letters were written by persons who held the same views as those of the strongest partisans of the Temple of Jerusalem – that it was still (or again) the place which the Lord has chosen (see Deut. 12.13-14) – thus excluding the legitimacy of any other Jewish temple. The partisans of the temple of Leontoplis did not deny all holiness to the Temple at Jerusalem. They did, however, hold that the site had been disowned by God with the destruction of the first Temple, and that it was not (or not yet) the Chosen Place which would exclude any other.[5]

According to Doran, the first letter is "lopsided," with its long introductory prayer and its references to Jason and to the Days of Tabernacles in Kislev, which would be unintelligible today if we did not have the epitome. Moreover, he finds both the first letter and the epitome peculiar among the Hellenistic Jewish works earlier than Paul and Josephus, because they use the Greek root *katallag-* in the sense of "reconcile." For him these facts suggest that the first letter "has been edited [selectively] and prefixed to the epitome," presumably as an introduction to it.

In fact, if the letter has been edited to service as an introduction to the epitome, the editor did an amazingly poor job: as an introduction, II Macc. 1.1-10a should have been intelligible to the reader before he reached chapters 3 through 5 and 10.5-7. Properly understood, the first letter contradicts the epitome.[6] Although the contradiction was subtle enough so that it did not prevent the attachment of the first letter to the epitome, it argues strongly against the theory that the letter has suffered selective editing. It seems cryptic to us only because we are not familiar with the facts which were well known to the senders and receivers of the document. The use of the root *katallag-* in the sense of "reconcile" is a poor argument for connecting the letter with the epitome. The Greek root probably reflects the Hebrew root *slḥ* ("forgive").[7] Words from the root *katallag-* are never used to translate *slḥ* in the extant Greek versions of the Hebrew Bible. The absence of *katallag-* in the sense of "reconcile" from those versions, however, is no proof that Jews writing Greek did not so use the Greek root before the time of Paul and Josephus. Such arguments from "early silence" are hazardous. Indeed, the adjective *eukatallaktos* occurs in III Macc. 5.13; the Greek root *diallag-* in the sense of "reconcile" is fully

---

[4]See *ibid.*, p. 16.
[5]See Jonathan A. Goldstein, "The Tales of the Tobiads," above, p. 140.
[6]See my *II Maccabees*, p. 25.
[7]*Ibid.*, p. 143.

interchangeable with *katallag-*[8] and occurs in Greek translations from the Hebrew Bible and Ben Sira.[9] *Katallag-* is used by Josephus in *AJ* vi 7.4.143-44, *diallag-* in *AJ* vi 7.4.151; in both places the words occur parallel to the Greek root *syngnō-* ("forgive").

Doran recognized (pp. 6-7) that the account of the death of Antiochus IV in the second letter (II Macc. 1.13-16) is irreconcilable with that in the epitome (II Macc. 9). He perceives (p. 10) in the Greek of the second letter (unlike that of the epitome) Hebraisms or Aramaisms. These facts, according to him, demonstrate that the second letter and the epitome are not by the same author. Nevertheless he still finds it possible to say that the second letter and the epitome "are certainly compatible"! He has failed to perceive other contradictions between the two which make them still less compatible than would appear at first.[10]

Doran proceeds (pp. 12-23) to refute the attempts of Schunck, Bunge, Bickerman, Habicht, and myself to discover the sources which lay before Jason of Cyrene or the abridger. In some instances he has done well, especially in refuting suggestions that the writer was sloppy in combining two sources into one narrative. Rather, one should assume that throughout the writer was a literary artist able to digest the material from his sources and use them to write a coherent narrative in his own vocabulary and style. Doran shows correctly that the account of events in II Macc. 12 is so different from that in the parallel narrative in I Macc. 5, that one cannot deduce from the similarities between them that both drew upon a common written source (pp. 14-16).[11] Doran, however, goes beyond these achievements to assert (p. 23) that "source-criticism...has failed to turn up 'sources' in the technical sense."

In fact, although Doran here may mean "sources incorporated verbatim," historians and the scholars he criticizes do not so restrict the word. For them sources in the accepted technical sense are the materials from which a writer has constructed his narrative. The arguments of Schunck and Bunge demonstrating common sources for other sections of I Maccabees and the epitome than I Macc. 5 and II Macc. 12 are mostly sound.[12]

---

[8]Büchsel, "*allassō*," in *Theological Dictionary of the New Testament*, ed. by Gerhard Kittel, I, 253.
[9]I Reigns 29.4; Symmachus' version of Isa. 60.10 and Ps. 29(30).6 and 68(69).14; Sir. 22.22 and 27.21.
[10]See my *II Maccabees*, pp. 25-26, 347-48.
[11]Cf. my *II Maccabees*, pp. 434-37.
[12]See *ibid.*, pp. 32-41.

Doran agrees (p. 112) that Jason of Cyrene wrote more than a generation after Heliodorus' attempt to seize the deposits at the Temple (narrated in II Macc. 3); therefore, Jason must have learned the story from one or more sources. The story of the thwarting of Heliodorus is overfull and has him thwarted in two ways. Each way is an example of a different pattern of miracle tales current in Greece and in the ancient Near East. Although Herodotus has narrated a story conforming to each pattern in telling about how the Persians were prevented from sacking the temple of Apollo at Delphi, he carefully presented the two stories as coming from two different sources.[13] Despite being a literary artist, the writer in II Macc. 3.24-29 has put into his narrative details which contradict each other.[14] Should we not conclude, in opposition to Doran (pp. 19-20), that the writer, unlike Herodotus, has combined details from two sources into one narrative?

There are important defects in Doran's chapter on the structure of II Maccabees (pp. 47-76). He devotes considerable space (pp. 49-51) to showing how the writer has dealt with the problem of how to tell the story of God's thwarting of Heliodorus and still leave Heliodorus alive to kill Seleucus IV. Surely the writer never had to face that problem He nowhere connects Heliodorus with the death of Seleucus IV. Furthermore, the writer was a historian, not a writer of fiction. The fact that Heliodorus failed (for whatever reason) to seize the deposits at the Temple is well attested.[15] The writer could only draw upon his sources.

In the epitome, the story of Heliodorus serves the important function of showing how God, in the absence of Jewish sin, normally protects the Temple in Jerusalem. It is strange, therefore, to find Doran saying (p. 51) that "it hardly deserves the elaborate treatment is receives in 2 Maccabees. It is, after all, an isolated incident which does not influence further historical developments."

When the writer in II Macc. 4.22 tells how Antiochus was received in Jerusalem with the ceremony due a Hellenistic king, he does so with no hint that such a reception was sinful. He wishes rather to show how cordial were the relations between the king and the Jews before he became the rod of God's anger (contrast Doran, p. 52).

---

[13]Herodotus, viii, 36-39.
[14]See my *II Maccabees*, pp. 210-11. Doran, however, is right in pointing out (pp. 20-21) that the pluperfect *erripto* fits its context, being parallel to the pluperfect *epeplērōto*.
[15]See my *II Maccabees*, pp. 196-99.

The cult imposed upon the Jews by Antiochus IV was not "the final step in the attempt to assimilate the Jews to other nations" (p. 53).[16]

Two problems have long troubled commentators: how does II Macc. 8.30-33 fit into the narrative of the epitome? Were there two commanders named Timotheus or only one? If there was only one, he is alive in 8.30, killed in 8.32, mentioned as defeated and perhaps killed in 9.3, alive again in 10.24, killed in 10.37, and alive again in 12.10-25. If so, surely our literary artist has produced an incoherent narrative. Doran briefly states the problems (pp. 58-59) and does nothing whatever to solve them. He dismisses (p. 59, n. 32) my solution as not correct and very subjective. Let others judge whether he is right.[17]

The narrative of II Macc. 9 should leave very little doubt about why the writer has presented the letter of Antiochus IV to the Jews (verses 19-27). Although the writer has misunderstood the letter, for him it substantiated the assertions that he had just made in verses 14-18.[18] Whether the letter is authentic or forged, the flattery in it of the recipients is purely conventional, and even the writer and his first readers must have regarded the flattery as hypocritical. Obviously the Jews had been fighting a bitter war against the king. The writer not only describes that bitter war against a monarchy widely popular in the Greek world;[19] he also condemns accepting Greek-style citizenship and imitating the Greeks as deadly sins (4.9-17). At least the abridger and perhaps Jason of Cyrene, too, used the Greek word "barbarian" to refer to Greeks and Macedonians (2.21). Greeks reading such a work would hardly feel kindly toward Jews. Yet Doran suggests (pp. 60-61) that the letter is included for an apologetic purpose, to demonstrate "that the Jews are good and reliable *citizens*" (sic! italics mine).

Other scholars and I have maintained that II Macc. 10.1-8 has been displaced from its original position after 8.36. By such displacement the chronological sequence of the death of Antiochus IV and the purification of the Temple in the abridged history was made to conform to that in the second letter. Doran argues against that theory (pp. 61-62), but his arguments are unsound.[20]

---

[16]The writer of the epitome does not say so! On the true character of the imposed cult, see my *I Maccabees*, pp. 125-59, and my *II Maccabees*, pp. 84-112.

[17]See my *I Maccabees*, pp. 296-97, and my *II Maccabees*, pp. 338-40, 351-52, 395-96.

[18]See my *II Maccabees*, pp. 355-71.

[19]See Otto Mørkholm, *Antiochus IV of Syria* (København, 1966), pp. 55-63.

[20]See my *II Maccabees*, pp. 345-56.

His treatment of II Macc. 11 and the letters quoted there (pp. 64-67) depends on Habicht and is inadequate. To explain why the writer presented the letters, Doran again has recourse to the notion that the writer had an apologetic purpose. For Doran the letters demonstrate that the Jews are not antisocial and do not hate Gentiles, because they contain the (conventional and perhaps hypocritical) flattery in verse 19, the repeated statements that what the Jews desire is the right to follow their own customs (verses 24 and 31), and the evidence of their readiness to deal with pagan Romans (verses 34-38). Doran's suggestion is no more plausible for the documents in II Macc. 11 than it was for the letter in II Macc. 9.19-27.[21]

The same notion that the writer of the epitome has an apologetic purpose dominates Doran's discussion of II Macc. 14.1-15.36 (pp. 68-70, 76). For him the key text is Alcimus' characterization of the pious Jews as factious and turbulent in 14.6-10, a charge which Doran finds significantly contradicted in 12.2 and 14.18-25; not the Jews but their enemies are disturbers of the peace. Similar charges, similar contrasts, and similar language are found in Greek Esther 3.13 and 8.12 and in III Macc. 3.26 and 6.15. In all three sets of passages Doran finds the same apologetic purpose of defending the Jews against charges of antisocial behavior, presumably before an audience of Greeks. Taken in isolation, the three sets of passages can be so interpreted, but hardly if taken in their contexts.[22]

The patterns of the three sets of passages are to be ascribed rather to the tendency in propaganda, especially Greek, to portray the enemy

---

[21] See my *II Maccabees*, pp. 55-63, 406-38.
[22] On how II Maccabees constitutes a context in which an apologetic purpose is improbable, see my remarks above in connection with the letter in II Macc. 9.19-27. As for Greek Esther, see Elias Bickerman, *Studies in Jewish and Christian History* (Leiden, 1976-), Part I, pp. 267-71. The following factors impede regarding III Maccabees as having an apologetic purpose: the description of Dositheos in 1.3; the portrayal of the bolder loyal Jews in 1.22-23; the remark in the prayer in 2.13, "We have been put under the rule of our *enemies*"; the similar prayer in 6.10-15, which calls the Ptolemaic government "enemies" and its Greek deities "vanities," and beseeches God to make Gentiles cower before His might; the widespread joy of the Gentiles over the plight of the Jews (4.1, 5.24, 41); the approval of the rejection by the majority of Jews of equal citizenship with Alexandrians (2.30-32; cf. 3.21-23), and of the way the majority sought and accomplished the slaughter of three hundred of the minority who had accepted the king's offers (7.10-15). As for the mention of good Greeks in 3.8-10, it probably is intended not to defend Jews before a Greek audience but to preach to Jews that friendly relations with Greeks are possible and desirable in a time like the mid-120s B.C.E., when Ptolemy VIII cruelly punished the Greeks of Alexandria and at least put fear into the hearts of his Jewish subjects (cf. Bickerman, *Studies*, Part 1, p. 272).

as factious and turbulent, a tendency which was all the stronger in Judaea and in the Hellenistic empires during the incessant civil strife of the reigns of the later Ptolemies, Seleucids, and Hasmonaeans.[23] Especially in such a period, if one wanted to persuade the dominant power (the king, the emperor, or the Roman republic) to act against a person or a group, one would have to show that that person or group opposed the interests of the dominant power. The dominant power usually aims at preserving stability in its sphere of influence. The enemy must therefore be shown to oppose stability. To persuade Seleucus IV to act, the pious Onias III intended to use against his Jewish enemy Simon the same charge of promoting instability that impious Alcimus brought against the pious Jews led by Judas Maccabaeus (II Macc. 4.6, 14.6-10). The Christian Paul was still a Jew when his Jewish opponents came before the Roman authorities and brought the same sort of charges against him (Acts 24.2-5). Greeks came before the Roman authorities to use the same method against their Greek enemy Nabis,[24] and Carthaginians did the same against their Carthaginian foe, Hannibal.[25] Clearly, one did not have to be an Antisemite to bring such charges, nor were the Jews unusual in being the target of them.

Individual Jews in any period might be hotheads vulnerable to being portrayed as enemies of stability, but between the time of the Babylonian captivity and the revolt of Judas Maccabaeus the Jews as a group were astonishingly loyal to the pagan sovereigns whom they believed God had placed over them.[26] Even later the Hasmonaeans Jonathan, Simon, and John Hyrcanus I often gave remarkably loyal service to pagan kings.[27] Outside Judaea Jews were even more consistent in their loyalty. In III Macc. 3.3-6, 6.25-26, and 7.6 the author writes of the loyalty of the Jews of Ptolemaic Egypt as a recognized fact; in II Maccabees and even in I Maccabees the authors show how the Jews acted only in self-defense and abstained from aggression. Such presentations are probably not the exaggerations of an apologist but rather the simple truth.

There is another feature characteristic of the charges brought against the Jews in many of these ancient tales. During the centuries when Jews were remarkable for their loyalty, when enemies in history

---

[23]See Bickerman, *ibid.*, pp. 271-74, and the accounts of the reigns of the later Hasmonaeans in the works of Josephus.
[24]Livy, xxxiv, 33.6-8, 48.5-6.
[25]Livy, xxxiii, 45.6-7, 47.3-6.
[26]See my *II Maccabees*, pp. 148-51.
[27]I Macc. 10.15-11.7, 11.26-53, 11.57-12.48, 15.1-26; Josephus, *Antiquities*, xiii, 8.3-4.245-51.

or in fiction wished to argue that the ruling power would be justified in taking action against the Jews, they usually did not point to the Jews' general behavior but rather took advantage of the strangeness of the commandments of the Torah and of the way the Jews obeyed those commandments even when they conflicted with the decrees of their pagan sovereign. These, too, were recognized facts. Haman, the hater of Jews, might say, "Their laws are different from all other people, and they do not keep the laws of the king" (Esther 3.8), but the pagan Hecataeus of Abdera, who had some admiration for the Jews, still described their way of life as "misanthropic" or "antisocial" (*apanthrōpon*) and "xenophobic" and stressed that they adhered to their laws even against the decrees of their pagan rulers.[28] Hence comes what we find in the narratives of Esther, Dan. 3 and 6, and the books of Maccabees. Again, bringing such charges is not peculiar to Antisemites, and the Jews are not peculiar in being their victim. The Achaean Greek Aristaenus in 195 B.C.E. argued in the same manner to urge the Roman Flamininus to act against the Greek Aetolians – "They have only the shape of men; they live under rules and practices more savage than any barbarians, yes, then any wild beasts."[29] The stories in Esther, Daniel, and the books of Maccabees are in no way apologies aimed at a pagan audience to defend the Jews against the charges of Antisemites. The writers glory in the way the Jews with God's help prevailed over pagan enemies. They aim to urge a Jewish audience to observe the Torah and keep the faith.

Doran's hypothesis of the apologetic purpose of the writer of the epitome becomes still less plausible when combined with the date he suggests (p. 112) for the composition of the work, the early reign of John Hyrcanus I, beginning with the aftermath of the death of Antiochus VII in 129 B.C.E. Although in that period John was aggressive against Idumaeans and insubordinate to Seleucid kings, he received the admiration of Greek Athens and Pergamum and enjoyed repeatedly the support of Rome.[30] Even earlier Hasmonaeans had good relations with Sparta and Rome.[31] Eventually some Greek writers did portray Hasmonaean Judaea as aggressive and tyrannical in its expansion, as we find in Strabo.[32] One might suppose that the need to defend

---

[28] Diodorus, xl, 3.4 and Josephus, *Against Apion*, i, 22.190-93.
[29] Livy, xxxiv, 24.3-4.
[30] See the account of John's reign in my chapter, "The Hasmonaean Revolt and the Hasmonaean Dynasty," in *The Cambridge History of Judaism*, ed. by W.D. Davies and Louis Finkelstein (Cambridge, 1987), vol. 2.
[31] I Macc. 8.17-32, 12.1-23, 14.16-24, 15.15-24.
[32] xvi, 2.37, C. 761 (based on Posidonius?).

Hasmonaean Judaea against such charges before an audience of literate Greeks arose later in the reign of John Hyrcanus I, when the Greek cities of Scythopolis and Samaria were conquered,[33] but perhaps even then a Greek audience might not have regarded the two cities as innocent victims. The impression we find in Strabo probably became widespread first among Greeks as a result of Alexander Jannaeus' conquests of the Greek cities within the borders of the land claimed as their ancestral heritage by the Jews, and as a result of his policy of requiring the inhabitants of those cities to become Jews or face expulsion.[34]

Doran's argument (pp. 111-12) for dating the writing of the epitome is particularly weak. According to him, "the epitome contains a threat against adopting foreign ways and a desire to show the Jews as respecters of the rights of Gentile sovereigns and cities," and he believes that the aggressive policies of John Hyrcanus I in his early reign ran counter to those teachings of the writer: John conquered the Idumaeans and forced them to accept Judaism; he maintained foreign mercenaries; he plundered the tomb of David[35] as Menelaus had plundered the vessels of the Temple. Therefore, Doran suggests that the epitome was written early in the reign of John and in opposition to his policies.

Does the evidence allow such inferences? There is sympathy in the epitome for good Tyrians (4.49) and for the good Greeks of Scythopolis (12.29), but even the Scythopolitans receive an admonition from Judas Maccabaeus to remain friendly to the Jews. It is doubtful that the Scythopolitans were still friendly when their city was conquered in the later reign of John. As for the Idumaeans, one might rather infer from II Macc. 10.15-23 that the writer would have approved of John's treatment of them. No ancient source accuses John of adopting foreign ways or even objects to his employment of foreign mercenaries. Though seizing the contents of a tomb might be viewed as a crime,[36] there is no reason to think that an ancient Jew or pagan would equate it with the sin of Temple-robbery. But even if such an equation could have been made, it is poor logic to use the report of Menelaus' conduct to date the writing in the reign of John Hyrcanus I.

---

[33] Josephus, *War*, i, 2.7.64-65; *Antiquities*, xiii, 10.2-3.275-81.
[34] *Ibid.*, 15.4.395-97, and see my discussion of the religious background of John's treatment of the Idumaeans and of Jannaeus' aggressive policies in my chapter in *The Cambridge History of Judaism*.
[35] Doran should have cited the text which proves that John's subjects could have viewed his use of the treasures in the tomb as sinful (Josephus, *Antiquities*, xvi, 7.1-2.179-88).
[36] See above, n. 35.

Doran stresses that the epitome has as its main purpose to tell how, in the absence of sin, God defends the Temple and Judaea. If an element of the narrative serves that purpose, the writer surely included that element for that reason; there is no way to draw here a valid inference that he also intended to cast aspersions on John. In the narrative of 4.32-50 the elements serve the main purpose of the epitome: the Temple robberies perpetrated by Menelaus and Lysimachus are part of the accumulation of sin in Judaea; the robberies lead to the further enormity of the murder of Onias III; they lead also to the riot in Jerusalem in which (surely with the miraculous help of God) an unarmed mob prevails over three thousand armed men and brings retribution upon the Temple robber Lysimachus; the riot in turn leads to the further enormity of Menelaus' securing through bribery his own acquittal and the execution of the three innocent emissaries of the Council of Elders.

If one wishes to date the writing of the work of Jason of Cyrene (and of the epitome after it), one should proceed rather from elements of the narrative which do not serve one of its main purposes but rather, if omitted, would not impair those purposes. Such elements can be found in the traits ascribed to Judas Maccabaeus. It would be enough to describe Judas as the instrument of God in winning victories after the Jews had suffered their punishment and repented and God's wrath had turned to mercy. Let us examine, of the instances where the writer goes beyond what is necessary in portraying Judas,[37] one which can be very useful for dating the work of Jason of Cyrene.

In II Macc. 10.20-23 members of a force under Judas' brother Simon besiege Idumaean enemies but take a bribe from some of the besieged and let them slip out. Maccabaeus himself prosecuted the men for treason, executed the guilty, and pressed the siege to a victorious conclusion. The story has two main purposes. It shows that even after God's wrath turned to mercy, Jewish sin could impede a Jewish victory, and it serves to discredit Simon, the founder of the hereditary line of Hasmonaean princely high priests. The writer needed only to present Judas as the righteous commander who finally brought victory. Yet he goes out of his way to show how Maccabaeus did not assume he had the power to punish the culprits but used due process against them: he prosecuted them before the assembled leaders of the people and executed *those who were guilty of treason*. We are to infer that he executed no others. What is the purpose of this detail? One might

---

[37]Other instances are less useful for dating; e.g., the way Judas the commander abstains from making a command decision on his own authority and rather consults the elders (13.13), surely intended to contrast with the autocratic behavior of later Hasmonaeans.

suggest that it is aimed at the presumption of Judas' brother Jonathan, who took upon himself the powers of a Biblical judge and began to "wipe out the wicked from Israel."[38] But I have demonstrated that the writer has committed the kind of historical errors which would have been impossible in the lifetime of Jonathan or even of Simon.[39] And the story is of the use of due process against those who commit the treason of aiding the enemy in time of war; it tells of the punishment of the guilty alone. Only one known incident of Hasmonaean history conspicuously suggests itself as the target envisaged by our writer in so portraying Judas: the great atrocity of King Alexander Jannaeus. When Jannaeus punished those Jews who had called in against their own king the army of the Seleucid Demetrius III Akairos, he had eight hundred of those Jews crucified on his own royal authority, and while they were still alive, *slaughtered their children and wives* before their eyes.[40] Jason of Cyrene contrived his portrait of Judas to contrast with Alexander Jannaeus. If so, we find one more confirmation of my own date for the writing of the book in the reign of Jannaeus.[41]

---

[38] I Macc. 9.73.
[39] See my *II Maccabees*, pp. 55-63, 71, 274, 391-95.
[40] Josephus, *War*, i, 4.4-5.92-97; *Antiquities*, xiii, 13.5.376-14.2.383.
[41] See my *II Maccabees*, pp. 71-83. Doran also says (p. 113) that "I see no reason to suppose the epitome to have been written outside Jerusalem; ...the fervor for the Jerusalem Temple is a strong argument for it." Rather, the errors in the epitome about the geography of the area (see my *II Maccabees*, pp. 12, 389, 391-95, 439-40, 442) argue strongly against the hypothesis. Furthermore, there is the same sort of fervor in Philo, *Legatio ad Gaium*, 29-32.188-242 and 36-42.290-333. Should we infer that those passages were written in Jerusalem?

11

How the Authors in I and II Maccabees Treated the "Messianic" Promises

I. Introduction

Great were Jacob and Moses and Balaam and the prophets of Israel for their prophecies which were fulfilled in history down to the fifth century B.C.E. In many ways, greater still have been the same prophets and the seers of the books of I Enoch and Daniel for the impact of their prophecies which were still unfulfilled in the second century B.C.E. and even later. Those unfulfilled prophecies each promised one or more of the following: the permanent liberation of the Jews from exile, from foreign rule, and from all mishap; the erection at Jerusalem of a temple more magnificent than Solomon's, which God Himself would choose as His own Place, glorifying it and making it secure from desecration and destruction; the rule over the Jews of a great and just king from the dynasty of David; their exaltation to imperial primacy among the nations; the conversion of the gentiles to follow the ways of the true God; the coming of a permanent era of peace; the resurrection of the righteous dead; and the punishment of all the wicked, past and present. Many of those prophecies omitted any mention of a king, but already Isaiah displayed the tendency to focus the fulfillment of such promises upon the coming of a single royal figure.[1] From Isaiah on, prophets might predict that that king would accomplish some or all of the great things promised by God. On the other hand, some religious spokesmen might hold that God himself or other persons would fulfill

---

[1] Isa. 9.1-6, 11.1-10; in this paper I follow Jewish tradition and treat Daniel not as one of the books of the Prophets but as one of the Writings (Hagiographa).

all or most of the promises before the coming of the royal figure; then, that king would at least henceforth be the good ruler of a great restored Israel.

Beginning with some writings of the first century B.C.E. and perhaps earlier,[2] that royal figure came to be called "the LORD's anointed," "the Messiah" (Hebrew and Aramaic: *mšyḥ*; Greek: *christos*). This eschatological meaning of "Messiah" cannot be found in the Jewish Bible. Scholars have struggled with the problem of explaining how the usage could have evolved.[3]

The prophetic books of the Hebrew Bible all date either from the time of the kings of Israel and Judah or from the exilic and postexilic periods. It is not surprising that most if not all of the aforementioned

---

[2]Writings of the first century B.C.E.: Psalms of Solomon 17-18 (see Nickelsburg, *Literature*, pp. 203-4, 207-9, and J.H. Charlesworth, "From Jewish Messianology to Christian Christology"). For the Qumran texts containing the word *māshīaḥ* in this sense, see *ibid*. As for possible earlier use of the word in this sense, one should take note of the messianic passages in the Testaments of the Twelve Patriarchs. Part or even most of the Testaments of the Twelve Patriarchs may go back to the first quarter of the second century B.C.E.; see Elias Bickerman, *Studies in Jewish and Christian History*, Part II ("Arbeiten zur Geschichte des antiken Judentums und des Urchristentums," Band IX; Leiden: Brill, 1980), pp. 1-15, 19-23, and the third paragraph from the end of George W.E. Nickelsburg's paper in this volume. But the messianic passages of the Testaments may well be Christian interpolations. See Bickerman, *Studies*, Part II, pp. 6-8; de Jonge, "Chriô ktl. C III. Apocrypha and Pseudepigrapha," *TDNT*, IX (1974), 512-13; and Charlesworth, "Jewish Messianology."

The "Parables of Enoch" (I Enoch 37-71) are difficult to date, but I think the mention at I Enoch 56.5 of the Parthians as a menace to Judaea excludes their having been written before the first century B.C.E. (see Nickelsburg, *Literature*, pp. 214-23). Moreover, the "anointed one" of the Parables is a heavenly being (see Nickelsburg, "Salvation"), and nothing is said there about his being born on earth to the dynasty of David. True, the language used to describe him and his actions is taken from Isa. 11 and Ps. 2. Isa. 11 is indissolubly connected with the line of Jesse and David. The anointed king of Ps. 2 is not necessarily descended from David, but he certainly is said to be king on Mount Zion. The figure in the Parables may indeed receive the epithet "anointed" because it was used to refer to the Davidic kings (II Sam. 19.22, 22.51, 23.1, etc.). On the other hand, the heavenly being of the Parables, like the Persian king, Cyrus, is a power from outside Judaea who brings vindication to the suffering righteous, so that his epithet "anointed" may be taken from the description of Cyrus at Isa. 45.1. See also Charlesworth, "Jewish Messianology."

[3]On the use of *mšyḥ* in the Jewish Bible, see Hesse, "Chriô ktl. B III. *Māshiah* in the Old Testament," *TDNT*, IX (1974), 501-5, and Jacob Liver, "*Māshīaḥ*," EM, V (1968, 508-9). As examples of scholarly efforts to explain the evolution of the eschatological term, see Hesse, "Chriô ktl. B IV. The Development of Messianic Ideas in Israel," *TDNT*, IX (1974), 505-9, and Liver, "*Māshīaḥ*," 507-26.

promises of the canonical prophets (like Zech. 1.12-13) essentially have to do with a coming time of God's favor which will put an end to the effects of the wrath of God that was kindled in the time of the kings of Israel and Judah.

The first centuries of the postexilic period could only have been puzzling for faithful believers: the glorious prophecies of restoration uttered by the true prophets were not being fulfilled. Yet a believer could hardly conclude that those inspired utterances were false. Fulfillment would come, but later. There had to be some explanation for the delay; usually, the faithful found it in present or past sin. That solution, too, posed difficulties: Moses, Isaiah, Jeremiah, and Ezekiel predicted that in the Age of Mercy after the end of the exile God would never again let his wrath fall upon Israel; indeed, in that Age the Chosen People would never again come to sin. The evidence we have from the period after the return from the exile shows the peculiar predicament of the Jews. Despite the joyous proclamations of the postexilic prophets, despite the return of many exiles to the Promised Land, despite the completion of the second temple, it was clear to believing Israelites that they were still living in the "Age of [God's] Wrath."[4]

The first temple, in accordance with Deut. 12.5-14, had been God's Chosen Place so as to bar the offering of Jewish sacrifices at any other location. The miraculous fire from heaven which was said to have attested God's election of Moses' tabernacle (Lev. 9.24) and Solomon's temple (II Chron. 7.1-3) never came down upon the altar of the second temple. Also lacking from the second temple were the ark and Moses' tabernacle and its sacred furniture, which were reported to have been placed in Solomon's sanctuary (I Kings 8.4, II Chron. 5.5) and which had never been recovered after its destruction in 586 B.C.E. The absence of those objects, too, might imply that the second temple was not the Chosen Place. For long centuries it remained inferior to Solomon's, and it was as vulnerable as the Jews themselves, though no one desecrated it until Antiochus IV sacked it in 169 B.C.E. Even so, many Jews held the second temple to be God's Chosen Place, equal in this respect to the first temple. However, many other Jews, indeed, entire sects, held the second temple to be incompletely holy or even completely unfit for the

---

[4]Prophecies about the Age of Mercy: Deut. 30.6, 8, 10, Isa. 54.9-10, Jer. 31.30-39, Ezek. 11.17-20, 36.24-29, 37.21-28. The expression "Age of Wrath" is found at CD 1.5-6; cf. Ezra 9.7-9, Neh. 9.30-37. Some of the relevant texts pretend to have been written in the time before the return from the exile: Dan. 9.12-19, 24, I Bar. 2.4-3.8, I Enoch 89.58-90.8. On the date and purpose of I Baruch, see Jonathan A. Goldstein, "The Apocryphal Book of I Baruch," above, pp. 191-208.

offering of sacrifices. If it was not God's Chosen Place, Deut. 12.5-14 would no longer forbid the existence of other Jewish sacrificial shrines. Jews might be free to recognize the legitimacy of other holy places, such as the Samaritan shrine on Mount Gerizim.[5]

More disappointments tested the faith of the Jews in the Age of Wrath. Taught by their tradition to expect that their God would perform miracles for them, they found none in their own time; knowing that God sent His true prophets to reveal His will to their ancestors, they themselves found fewer and fewer true prophets and finally none at all.[6] From lessons preached by Jeremiah, Ezekiel, and the book of Chronicles, they learned that God Himself had set over them their foreign rulers and would punish them severely if they rebelled. Accordingly, Jews for centuries were loyal to their pagan kings.[7] If the signs of the times should indicate that the delay was coming to an end, Jews would infer that the complete fulfillment of the prophecies was imminent, and some of them might rise in revolt while others might expect that God by Himself would accomplish all.

The events of the years from the 170s down to 134 B.C.E., narrated in I and II Maccabees, were epoch-making in the history of the Jews and in the development of Jewish eschatology. In particular, a series of disasters came upon the Jews, contrary to God's promises through the true prophets, that nothing of the kind could happen after the return from the Babylonian exile.[8] In 169 B.C.E. King Antiochus IV sacked the temple and Jerusalem;[9] in 167 his commander Apollonius perpetrated a massacre in the Holy City and took large numbers of Jews captive;[10] later in 167 Antiochus IV imposed upon the Jews an idolatrous cult and made death the penalty for obeying the Torah and for refusing to observe the imposed cult.[11]

The response of most believing Jews to those disasters was to search the scriptures for guidance. Surely they were part of God's plan. Surely the true prophets must have foreseen them and given instructions how to respond. But no prophet had predicted that Israelites in their own land would be forced to worship idols! Nevertheless several prophets had predicted a time of terrible troubles during the Last Days before

---

[5] Goldstein, *II Maccabees*, pp. 14-16.
[6] Goldstein, *I Maccabees*, pp. 12-13.
[7] Goldstein, *II Maccabees*, pp. 150-51; I Bar. 1.1-12, 2.21-24; and cf. Rom. 13.1-7.
[8] E.g., Isa. 51.7-8, 22; 55.4-10; Jer. 30.23-40, 32.37-44.
[9] I Macc. 1.20-28, II Macc. 5.1-23; see also Goldstein, *I Maccabees*, pp. 49-51, 207-9, and *II Maccabees*, pp. 246-61.
[10] I Macc. 1.29-40, II Macc. 5.23-27; see also Goldstein, *II Maccabees*, pp. 261-66.
[11] I Macc. 1.44-64, II Macc. 6.1-11.

the Great Redemption.[12] Pious Jews were quick to assume they were living in that penultimate time of troubles.

In the period between 167 and 161 B.C.E. pious Jews made up for what the true prophets had failed to do: they produced texts in which the disasters of their own time were "predicted" and in which God's spokesmen gave counsel for the present and hope for the future.[13] Two sets of these texts thereafter exerted profound influence on the evolution of messianic figures in the beliefs of Jewish and Christian sects: Dan. 7-12 and I Enoch 85-90.[14] In both sets, the real author's present closely reflects events from the times of Judas Maccabaeus.[15] In both we find the belief expressed that the present sufferings of the Jews are the last climactic stage of seventy periods of punishment imposed by God for heinous sins committed before the destruction of the temple (Dan. 9.24, I Enoch 89.56-67). If the authors by skill or luck had an accurate chronology, the sins occurred ca. 654 B.C.E., in the reign of Manasseh, archsinner among the kings of Judah. If the persecutions were part of a sentence imposed by God, what could the pious do but endure them until God's appointed time for their release? The authors tried to predict the coming of that time.

In Dan. 7.13-14, 22, appears the prediction that imperial power will come to the grievously persecuted righteous Jews ("the Saints of the Most High"). The collectivity of those "Saints" is there symbolized by a figure described as like a "human being" or "Son of Man." A Jew (or Christian) who thought of deliverance as coming through superhuman beings and of power as being exerted by kings could easily take that figure to be a superhuman savior (despite the descriptive epithet, "human being!") or a king. Nowhere in the book of Daniel is there an allusion to David. Dan. 12.2-3 is the earliest Jewish text to predict in absolutely unambiguous fashion a resurrection of the righteous dead for glory; it also predicts a punishment of the wicked. Dan. 7 reached its final form in 167, and one can demonstrate that Dan. 7.25 means that the prediction would be fulfilled with the coming of the sabbatical year in Tishri, 164 B.C.E.[16] Dan. 12.2-3 can be shown to

---

[12]E.g., Isa. 24-27, Ezek. 38-39, Zech. 12-14, Mal. 2.2-4.

[13]On the Testament of Moses, I Enoch 85-90, and Dan. 7-12, see the discussion at Goldstein, *I Maccabees*, pp. 39-46, and *II Maccabees*, pp. 90 (n. 34), 92-94, 106-9.

[14]I speak of "sets" because the sections of Dan. 7-12, though they may well all be by the same author, were written at various intervals between 167 and 163 B.C.E. The same is true of the rewritings which produced the present text of I Enoch 90.6-39 (see n. 18).

[15]See Goldstein, *I Maccabees*, pp. 40-44.

[16]*Ibid.*, p. 42.

have been written before Antiochus IV marched eastward in June, 165, and Dan. 12.11-12 predicted that the great fulfillment would be complete by August 12, 163, 1,335 days after the desecration of the temple altar on 25 Kislev, 167. Throughout Dan. 7-10 the second temple is held to be God's Chosen Place.[17]

I shall demonstrate elsewhere that I Enoch 90.6-39 is the result of a series of rewritings of a text first composed at the end of the third century B.C.E.; the rewritings all occurred in response to events in the career of Judas Maccabaeus, before his death in 160 B.C.E.[18] The writers' sectarian beliefs were different from those of the author of Daniel, and the passage is largely, if not completely, independent of Daniel.[19] The messianic elements of the extant text may (or may not) all go back to the earlier original. In any case, the passage as it stands is a remarkably early example of bringing together around a single royal figure the fulfillment of most if not all of the messianic prophecies. The text does not contain the word "Messiah," and there is some doubt that I Enoch 90.33 refers to a resurrection of the dead rather than to an ingathering of the living exiles.[20] Unlike the book of Daniel, I Enoch 90.6-39 contains a figure demonstrably connected with David.

The commanding figure of I Enoch 90.37-38 is surely royal and rules over Jews and gentiles after the great fulfillment, after all wickedness has been defeated and all pagans converted and humanity restored to the longevity which characterized the patriarchs (symbolized in Enoch's vision by the sheep and other animals turning into bulls).[21] We are thus entitled to speak of him as a Messiah. His person and those of the remiss angelic shepherds of God's flock in I Enoch 89.59-90.25 are derived from Ezek. 34, where "David" will rule over the Chosen People after God delivers them from evil and brings retribution on the bad shepherds. Both in Ezekiel and in I Enoch, the great king comes after

---

[17]*Ibid*, pp. 42-44.

[18]In my book *Chosen Peoples*. See for the present Goldstein, *I Maccabees*, pp. 41-42, esp. n. 12.

[19]*Ibid.*, p. 42; I hope to treat elsewhere the problem of the relationship of I Enoch 85-90 to Dan. 7-12.

[20]One would expect so miraculous and so longed-for an event as the resurrection to receive more elaborate treatment (contrast Dan. 12.2-3) and to be narrated in less ambiguous language. Nevertheless, if I Enoch 103-4 comes from the first half of the second century B.C.E. (see Nickelsburg, *Literature*, p. 150), the expectation of a resurrection there would suggest that the writer meant one in 90.33.

[21]Cf. Jubilees 23.26-31 (by an author who shares the views of the seer of I Enoch 90).

the great miracles and divine judgments have occurred. He has no role in accomplishing them. From the fact that I Enoch 89.59-90.25 is derived from Ezek. 34, we can infer that at least one can call this Messiah "David." Did the writer of that text think it was a mere matter of the king's bearing that name? The writer was at least a spiritual (and perhaps a physical) ancestor of the Qumran sect, who certainly believed in a Messiah descended from David. Accordingly, we may assume that the Messiah of I Enoch 90.37-38 also is descended from David.[22] The writer holds that all offerings at the second temple were unclean (89.73) and predicts that it will be replaced by another which will descend from heaven (90.28-29).

The authors of Israelite prophecy were seldom if ever interested in the remote future, and the audiences who preserved their works were

---

[22] On the connections of I Enoch with the Qumran sect, see for the present the cautious remarks of Nickelsburg, *Literature*, pp. 53-54, 90-94, 149. For the Qumran texts referring to a Messiah descended from David, see van der Woude, *TDNT*, IX (1974), 517-20.

John J. Collins, "Messianism in the Maccabean Period," this volume, has challenged my assertion here, that the person of the commanding figure of I Enoch 90.37-38 and those of the remiss angelic shepherds in I Enoch 89.59-90.25 are derived from Ezek. 34. Collins finds my assertion "far too simple." "The imagery," he writes, "of the *Animal Apocalypse* is not simply derived from Ezekiel 34 or any one source. The white bull, specifically, does not figure in the imagery of Ezekiel at all, and even if it did, we could not automatically assume that it had the same meaning in its new context."

I never asserted that the *imagery* of the "Animal Apocalypse" was derived from Ezek. 34, though in part it surely was. The imagery by which the Israelites' superior ancestors, the patriarchs, are portrayed as bulls and the hostile nations by various wild beasts and birds – that imagery is the original creation of the author of the "Animal Apocalypse." On the other hand, his portrayal of the Israelites, beginning with Jacob's sons, as sheep is a scriptural commonplace.

But where else but from Ezek. 34 did that author derive his idea (I Enoch 89.61-90.17) that *remiss* shepherds would tend the LORD's flock, letting them be scattered among the wild beasts (I Enoch 89.75; Ezek. 34.5-6) and abandoning them to be destroyed and devoured by predators (I Enoch 89.61-90.17; Ezek. 34.5-8), while, moreover, the shepherds themselves kill, destroy, and eat the sheep (I Enoch 89.69-70; Ezek. 34.2-3, 10)? Where else but from Ezek. 34 did he derive his idea that thereafter God would put an end to the shepherds and would Himself take charge of the sheep, gathering together the dispersed (I Enoch 90.20-33; Ezek. 34.9-16) to a good pasturage (I Enoch 90.20; Ezek. 34.13-14), while also punishing any evil members of His flock (I Enoch 90.26-27; Ezek. 34.16-22), and thereupon would place in power over them a shepherd-protector of patriarchal character (a white bull in I Enoch 90.37; "David" in Ezek. 34.23)? If the whole scheme of shepherds plus ruler is taken from Ezek. 34, surely the great white bull is a Davidic Messiah. Parenthetically, we may note that Zech. 11.3-7, too, probably depends on Ezek. 34.

chiefly interested in the present and in a future which included little if any more than their own lifetimes. For Isaiah the "end of days" or "days to come" (*'aḥărīt hayyāmīm*) of his chapter 2 were probably no more remote than that.[23] Certainly the writers of the predictions in I Enoch and Daniel believed they were living in the last days before God's great intervention.

Thus, signs of the times could lead Jews of the second century B.C.E. to expect imminent fulfillment of the glorious prophecies, and Dan. 7-12 and I Enoch 85-90 as well as other texts attest that Jews who lived in the times narrated in I and II Maccabees had such expectations. Nevertheless, the word "Messiah" (whether in transliterated Hebrew or in Greek) does not occur in either book of Maccabees. The writers who produced them certainly knew the predictions of the Torah and the Prophets. One can demonstrate that they knew Dan. 7-12 and perhaps also I Enoch 85-90.[24] The writers believed that important aspects of the Age of Wrath had run their course and were now past. Yet the books contain no hint of the expected coming of a wonderful king descended from David or of a figure called the "Son of Man." This surprising fact demands explanation. The causes can be found in the character of the content of the two books.

I Maccabees is a history written to demonstrate the right of the Hasmonaean dynasty, descended from the zealous priest Mattathias and his son Simon, to be hereditary high priests and princes ruling the Jews.[25] Never does the author write anything that would suggest there was doubt among Jews concerning God's election of the second temple. From clues in the book and from other evidence one can establish that it was written ca. 90 B.C.E., in the reign of the Hasmonaean king, Alexander Jannaeus.[26] We shall refer to the author as the "Hasmonaean propagandist."

II Maccabees is composite. It begins with two letters, each written to induce the Jews of Egypt to observe the festival commemorating the purification in 164 B.C.E. of the temple of Jerusalem. The first letter (II

---

[23]Jeremiah's use of *'aḥărīt hayyāmīm* shows that its meaning is relative to what the speaker had in mind: "at the end of the predicted course of events," which might be relatively brief (as at Jer. 23.20) or (as at Jer. 30.25) a matter of many years (though not of centuries). It may well be that Isaiah himself meant the events of chap. 2 to be taken as following immediately upon the purging of Israel described in 1.24-31.

[24]On Daniel, see Goldstein, *I Maccabees*, pp. 42-52, and *II Maccabees*, pp. 63-69, 305-6. On I Enoch, see Goldstein, *I Maccabees*, pp. 95-96 (through line 2), 374; *II Maccabees*, pp. 495, 499.

[25]Goldstein, *I Maccabees*, pp. 1-21, 62-78.

[26]*Ibid.*, pp. 62-78; Goldstein, *II Maccabees*, pp. 71-83.

Macc. 1.1-10a) contains nothing connected with messianic figures, and we shall not consider it further. Let us call the second letter (II Macc. 1.10b-2.18) "Ep. 2" (for "Epistle 2"). Ep. 2 is an important document for our study. It purports to have been sent by the Jews of Jerusalem and Judaea and by Judas Maccabaeus to Aristobulus, the Jewish philosopher of priestly stock, and to the Jews of Egypt; in fact, it was forged late in 103 B.C.E., long after the death of Judas in 160. The bulk of the letter (1.18-2.18) serves to prove that important aspects of the Age of Wrath have ended forever, especially some which had cast doubt on God's election of the second temple. The letter concludes with a vigorous expression (2.17-18) of confidence in the present situation of the Chosen people and of hope that God will speedily fulfill his promises and put an end to all aspects of the Age of Wrath.[27] Ep. 2 also contains a prayer for the end of the Age of Wrath (1.24-29). Obviously, the author believed that Age had not yet completely ended.

We shall call the remainder of II Maccabees the "Abridged History." Demonstrably it was originally separate from the two letters. It is an anonymous abridgment of a history by one Jason of Cyrene of the wars of Judas Maccabaeus and his brothers. Nothing further is known of the unabridged work or of its author or of the abridger. One purpose of the Abridged History is to oppose the dynastic claims of the Hasmonaeans. Another is to demonstrate that although the second temple is not yet the exclusive location for sacrificial worship demanded by Deut. 12.5-14, there are important senses in which it is now God's Chosen Place. From the content of the abridgment and other evidence, one can infer that the unabridged work was written by 86 and the abridgement by 63 B.C.E.[28]

I Maccabees

The predictions of Daniel and Enoch are never mentioned in I Maccabees, but the attitude of the Hasmonaean propagandist toward them is clear. He knew that the course of history had proved them false: there had been no miraculous manifestations of God and His power after the coming of the sabbatical year in 164 B.C.E. and during the lifetime of Judas Maccabaeus. The Hasmonaean propagandist was intensely hostile to the following fundamental teachings of the book of Daniel: (1) that God Himself decreed the persecution of the Jews by Antiochus IV as the last stage of their punishment for sins committed some 490 years before (Dan. 9.24); (2) that therefore Jews ought to

---

[27]Goldstein, *II Maccabees*, pp. 157-67.
[28]*Ibid.*, pp. 3-24, 71-83.

accept the divine decree and suffer torture and death as martyrs until the appointed time for God's intervention, at most a few years away (Dan. 7.21-27, 9.24, 11.33, 35, 12.10-12); (3) that those pious Jews who perished would be resurrected and rewarded (Dan. 12.2-3); and (4) that the Hasmonaean revolt at best was a "small help," and it was an act of "slippery treachery" (ḥălaqlāqōt) for pious Jews to join forces with the Hasmonaeans (Dan. 11.34).

The Hasmonaean propagandist held, on the contrary, that the recent sins of Hellenizing Jews had provoked God into using Antiochus IV as His punishing instrument; unresisting martyrdom was disgraceful and brought the martyrs no reward but only their own deaths.[29] False, in his view, was the belief in the resurrection, which served to compensate the martyrs for their suffering.[30] He went out of his way to contradict the mistaken predictions in Dan. 7-12 and wrote barbed parodies of their words to point up their falsity.[31]

The Hasmonaean propagandist had less reason to hate the revelations in I Enoch 90, which endorsed the career of Judas Maccabaeus. But he resented their falsity: God did not perform His great intervention while Judas Maccabaeus still lived. He also seems to have resented the effect those revelations must have had on Judas, inspiring him to believe he would not be killed but would live to see that great intervention, so that he went into battle against overwhelming odds and lost his life. The barbed remarks at I Macc. 9.27 may well allude to the falsity of I Enoch 90.[32] Moreover, the seer of I Enoch 90.37-38 reiterated the prediction of a Messiah descended from David. The Hasmonaean propagandist, on the contrary, wrote to prove that God's instrument for bringing permanent victory to the Jews was the Hasmonaean dynasty,[33] and he took care at I Macc. 2.57 to hint that God's election of David's dynasty might not be permanent.[34] At

---

[29]See Goldstein, *I Maccabees*, pp. 4, 12, 226, 227-28, 231-32, 235-36.

[30]*Ibid.*, pp. 12, 227.

[31]*Ibid.*, pp. 45, 47-48. I am puzzled why Collins, "Messianism," should say that my detection in I Maccabees of parodies of the words of Daniel is overly ingenious. Let others decide whether he is right after reading my arguments.

[32]*Ibid.*, p. 48.

[33]*Ibid.*, pp. 4-12, 63-78.

[34]*Ibid.*, pp. 240-41. Collins, in "Messianism," finds insecurely based my assertion that there is a hint at I Macc. 2.57 that God's election of David's dynasty might not be permanent. I here restate the basis. At I Macc. 2.57 David is said to inherit the throne *eis aiônas*, an expression which usually means only "for ages," but on my own showing (*I Maccabees*, p. 240) in some contexts means "forever." Not I alone, but also ancient scribes who believed in the eternal royal rights of the dynasty of David took *eis aiônas* at I Macc. 2.57 to mean only "for ages" and therefore altered the text to make it say "forever"; see

the very least, he quoted the resolution of the Jews, that the Hasmonaeans had the right to be princes and high priests over the Chosen People "Until a true prophet shall arise."[35] Writing in the reign of King Alexander Jannaeus, the author of I Maccabees knew of the strong claims of the king's father, the Hasmonaean prince John Hyrcanus, to be a true prophet.[36]

The Hasmonaean propagandist could not deny the authority of the glorious predictions which constituted so important a part of the words of the accepted "true" prophets. Indeed, as a believing Jew with high hopes for the future, he had no desire to cast doubt on those predictions. One might expect him to make every effort to prove that they were being fulfilled through the Hasmonaeans.

The predictions of how God after the end of the Babylonian exile would bring about a great restored Israel in a perfected world can be divided into two classes: those which could conceivably be fulfilled by Jewish mortals (e.g., conquest of Moab, Ammon, and Philistia; military security for Judaea),[37] and those which could be fulfilled only by a supernatural power (e.g., creation of new heavens and a new earth, resurrection of the dead, streaming of the gentiles of their own free will to Jerusalem to learn the ways of the God of Jacob).[38] The Hasmonaean propagandist does not touch the predictions which could be fulfilled only by a supernatural power,[39] but he exploits some of his opportunities to suggest that Hasmonaeans fulfilled those possible for

---

my *I Maccabees*, p. 241. Further confirmation for my inference that the propaganda of the Hasmonaeans denied the permanence of the royal rights of the house of David can be found in the bitter complaint at Psalms of Solomon 17.4-6 that the Hasmonaean usurpers denied those rights.

[35] I Macc. 14.41; see Goldstein, *I Maccabees*, pp. 507-8.

[36] Josephus *War* i. 2.7.68-69; *Antiquities* xiii. 10.3.282, 7.299-300; *Tosefta Soṭah* 13.5 and parallels.

[37] Isa. 11.14, Mic. 4.5.

[38] Isa. 65.17, Dan. 12.2 (and Isa. 25.8, 26.14, 19), Isa. 2.3-4.

[39] One might regard, as a pale allusion to and partial fulfilment of the predicted resurrection, the temporary suspension of the power of death which may be claimed at I Macc. 5.54; see Goldstein, *I Maccabees*, p. 304. But in telling of it, the Hasmonaean propagandist does not use his opportunity to echo the language of the prophecies. There is only indirect evidence in I Maccabees on voluntary conversion of gentiles (see Goldstein, *I Maccabees*, pp. 347, 349-50). Though Hasmonaeans may have encouraged the process, the Hasmonaean propagandist makes no claim that they did.

mortals, as we shall see, and one could go on to trace the efforts of Hasmonaeans to fulfill them after the times narrated in I Maccabees.[40]

Interesting, however, is the fact that the Hasmonaean propagandist abstains from using many of his opportunities to portray the members of the dynasty as fulfilling prophecies. Let us give a brief survey of what he might have done and what he actually did.

For the Hasmonaeans and their propagandist, the first decisive step in ending the Age of Wrath was Mattathias' act of zeal: he refused to obey the King's edict to observe the imposed cult, slew a Jew who was about to comply and killed the royal official enforcing compliance, and called upon all Jews loyal to the Torah to follow him into rebellion against the king. Thus he broke with the doctrine which Jews had followed during the centuries of the Age of Wrath, that the Chosen People must not rebel against their foreign kings because God had placed those kings in power and would punish rebellion.[41] The next decisive steps were the mighty deeds of Judas Maccabaeus and his men as they battled the armies of Seleucid kings. And next were the similar mighty acts of Judas' brothers, Jonathan and Simon. The Hasmonaean propagandist gives due prominence to all these. The Hasmonaeans' acts of insubordination against the kings brought the Jews, not punishment inflicted through the wrath of God, but liberation. For the Hasmonaeans and their propagandist, these facts proved that the Age of Wrath was at least approaching its full end, though the miserable deaths of Judas, Jonathan, and Simon and the vicissitudes of Simon's heirs strongly suggested that God's wrath still had a few more years to act upon the Jews.

The Jews called the Seleucid empire of Antiochus IV "Greece" ($Y\bar{a}w\bar{a}n$).[42] A prophecy of God's great final intervention predicted that He would "make the sons of Zion mighty against the sons of $Y\bar{a}w\bar{a}n$" (Zech. 9.13), and there can be no doubt that this prophecy was being read in Mattathias' lifetime, because there is an allusion to Zech. 9.8 at Dan. 11.20.[43] The author of I Maccabees repeatedly echoes the wording of the Hebrew Bible as he narrates the exploits of his heroes. Would not one expect him to echo Zech. 9.13 at least once, in telling of Mattathias or Judas or Jonathan or Simon or their followers as "mighty against $Y\bar{a}w\bar{a}n$?" Not once does he do so! Indeed, relatively infrequent

---

[40] See Jonathan A. Goldstein, "The Hasmonaean Revolt and the Hasmonaean Dynasty," in *CHJ*, Vol. II, chap. 8.
[41] I Macc. 2.1-26; see Goldstein, *I Maccabees*, p. 5.
[42] C. C. Torrey, "'Yawan' and 'Hellas' as Designations of the Seleucid Empire," *JAOS* 25 (1904), 302-11.
[43] Goldstein, *II Maccabees*, p. 197.

are the Hasmonaean propagandist's allusions, in telling of his heroes, to the books of the Writing Prophets. His most audacious echoes of those books occur in connection with Judas Maccabaeus. In the "Ode to Judas" with which he introduces the great Maccabaeus' career, he says, "His renown spread to the end of the earth, as he gathered together those who were astray" (I Macc. 3.9). The second half of the verse certainly echoes Isa. 11.12; the first half may well echo Isa. 12.5. God is the subject of the verbs in both verses in Isaiah. Surely the Hasmonaean propagandist is portraying Judas as God's agent in the fulfillment of Isa. 11.12 and probably of Isa. 12.5 as well.[44] Less certain[45] but similarly audacious is the probable allusion to Isa. 52.12 at I Macc. 5.53: Judas is God's agent in fulfilling His promise to be the rear guard gathering up the stragglers.[46] At I Macc. 4.58 we read, "The shame inflicted by the gentiles was removed." "The shame inflicted by the gentiles" probably is an echo of Isa. 25.8 and Ezek. 36.4, so as to suggest that God has fulfilled those verses through the dedication of the new temple altar by Judas and his men.

Many of the sects of pious Jews could agree that Judas Maccabaeus was the LORD's agent.[47] More controversial were his brothers, first Jonathan and finally Simon, real founder of the Hasmonaean dynasty.[48] Would not one expect to have the Hasmonaean propagandist apply the language of biblical prophecy to Simon? In fact, in his "Ode to Simon" (I Macc. 14.4-15), he does use at 14.8 the words of Lev. 26.4, Ezek. 34.27, and Zech. 8.12; at 14.9 he uses the words of Zech. 8.4;[49] and one might think that he uses at 14.12 the words of Mic. 4.4 and Zech. 3.10.[50]

In telling of Simon's climactic achievement, the liberation of Israel from tribute-paying bondage, the Hasmonaean propagandist may have

---

[44]Goldstein, *I Maccabees*, p. 245.
[45]Because the allusion, if present, involves only the single word *episynagôn* (Hebrew *m^{e}assēph*).
[46]*Ibid.*, p. 304.
[47]The numerous sects are attested by the irreconcilable character of the surviving pieces of literature emanating from them: the Testament of Moses, Dan. 7-12, I Enoch 85-90, and I and II Maccabees. See Goldstein, *I Maccabees*, pp. 1-34, 39-52, *II Maccabees*, pp. 12-19. Not the least of Judas' achievements was his ability to unite under himself forces from so many irreconcilable groups (I Macc. 3.9, 13; II Macc. 8.1, I Enoch 90.10; Goldstein, *I Maccabees*, pp. 65, 504, *II Maccabees*, pp. 323-24). See also the beginning of my treatment of Judas Maccabaeus in my study in *CHJ*, Vol. II, chap. 8.
[48]Goldstein, *I Maccabees*, pp. 65-66.
[49]Cf. Goldstein, *I Maccabees*, p. 491.
[50]But see n. 60.

echoed prophecies but more likely he avoided doing so! At I Macc. 13.41 we read that "the yoke of the gentiles was lifted from Israel." In fact, what was lifted was the "yoke" of the Seleucid empire, the latter-day Assyria.[51] No Jewish Bible-reader could fail to think of Isa. 10.27 and 14.25, but there is rather good reason to think that the Hasmonaean propagandist deliberately avoided writing an exact echo of those verses. Explainable is the omission of a word corresponding to the Hebrew *subbŏlō* ("his burden") of Isa. 10.27 and 14.25. The Greek of both verses shows that Jews of the Hellenistic period did not know the meaning of the word. But the word ἤρθη ("was lifted") in the Greek text of I Macc. 13.41 probably indicates that the Hasmonaean propagandist used a Hebrew verb from a root different from the one (*sūr*) employed at Isa. 10.27 and 14.25, for at both places in Isaiah the Greek renders the Hebrew word by ἀφαιρεθήσεται, not by a form of αἴρειν, the verb of which ἤρθη is the first aorist passive.[52]

In most instances, the author of I Maccabees in writing of his heroes, the Hasmonaean brothers, seems deliberately to have departed from or to have avoided the wording of biblical prophecies. Repeatedly he tells of the victories they won in the land of the Philistines, and he also tells of their victories in Ammon, Moab, and Edom, but not once does he echo the prophecies of conquests there.[53]

One can understand the Hasmonaean propagandist's failure to put into his narrative of Jonathan's exploits allusions to prophecies of dynastic glory. The author of First Maccabees was a partisan of Simon's heirs, and Jonathan had descendants who might contest their claims to rule.[54] But the Hasmonaean propagandist takes pains to identify Jonathan as a Judge (I Macc. 9.73). Biblical Judges were not dynastic princes whose sons inherited their power. And even so, the Hasmonaean propagandist does not echo Isa. 1.26 at I Macc. 9.73.

Indeed, though most believing Jews facing the persecution under Antiochus IV probably thought they were living in the prophesied

---

[51] Goldstein, *I Maccabees*, p. 210.
[52] The inference is only probable, not certain, because the Greek verb αἴρειν renders the *hiph'îl* of the Hebrew root *sūr* at Gen. 35.2 and Isa. 5.23 and its *huph'al* at Isa. 17.1.
[53] Prophecies of conquests: Num. 24.17-18, Isa. 11.14, 25.9-12, Jer. 49.1-6, Amos 9.12, Obadiah (esp. 19), Zeph. 2.4-10. The are also prophecies which predict that the LORD will smite Philistia, Moab, Ammon, or Edom but say nothing of Israel as the agent (Isa. 15-16, Jer. 48.1-47, 49.7-22, Zech. 9.5-7); nothing in those texts, however, would prevent a searcher of prophecies from suggesting that the LORD used the Hasmonaeans as his agents in fulfilling them. Hasmonaean victories: I Macc. 3.41 with 4.12-22, 5.1-23, 55-68, 10.67-89, 11.60-62.
[54] Goldstein, *II Maccabees*, p. 31.

time of troubles immediately before the final Great Redemption, the Hasmonaean propagandist regarded that response to the dreadful challenge as disastrously wrong. He displays how such beliefs brought only disappointment and death to those who bravely refused to violate the Torah and waited for God's supposedly imminent fulfillment of the prophecies. He was aware how Judas Maccabaeus' belief that he was living in the time of fulfillment of prophecies misled him to go into hopeless battle and to perish, and he may well have thought similar beliefs led Jonathan to his doom.[55] More than one generation had elapsed by the time he wrote. It was therefore obvious to the Hasmonaean propagandist that the troubles had not been the prophesied prelude to the Last Days.

I do not think that the way he portrays his heroes is entirely due to hindsight. They never ask for the fulfillment of prophecies and never say they are fulfilling them. Yet a Jewish response to the persecution had to be based on scripture. The Hasmonaean response as portrayed in I Maccabees has a consistent character and fits the known conditions of the time. In all probability it is not a mere creation of the author but reflects the actual ideology of Mattathias and his sons.

From the beginning, the Hasmonaean doctrines were so audacious that many pious Jews viewed the party as wicked and opposed it.[56] The Hasmonaeans were ready to engage in acts of war against the royal army, a step which required breaking with the long-held Jewish belief that rebellion would bring disastrous divine punishment. Old Mattathias dared to act on the assumption that a king who commanded Jews to violate the Torah could no longer be ruling Jews by divine right. No prophecy predicted that God's requirement to obey the pagan kings would be repealed before the miraculous end of the Age of Wrath. In Zechariah 9.9-13, before Jews fight Greeks, the Jews have their own king in Jerusalem. Far from having ended at the time Mattathias dared to act, the Age of Wrath was continuing! The old man was a priest, perhaps from a family of some distinction,[57] but he made no claim to have received a new revelation from God either through prophecy or through priestly oracles.

To judge by the account in I Maccabees, Mattathias differed from many of his contemporaries in explaining how the persecution fit into God's plan. According to I Maccabees, the persecutions were not troubles

---

[55]Mistaken beliefs of the pious martyrs: see Goldstein, *I Maccabees*, pp. 227, 235-36, 273-80, 331-32, 371, and cf. Dan. 11.33-35; on Jonathan's death, see Goldstein, *I Maccabees*, pp. 468-69; on Judas', *ibid.*, p. 374, and above.
[56]Goldstein, *I Maccabees*, pp. 64-66.
[57]*Ibid.*, p. 231.

belonging to the Last Days, nor were they the climactic end to the punishment for pre-exilic sin. Rather, in origin they were an ordinary punishment, brought on by the recent sins of Hellenizing Jews, but Antiochus IV, God's punishing instrument, had exceeded his divine mandate as Assyria in days of yore had exceeded hers (Isa. 10.5-34).[58] We may imagine Mattathias as theorizing that a Jew might dare to resist a pagan ruler who had overstepped the mandate of God. If the persecution was merely an excessive act of God's unruly whip, it would do no good to study prophecies of the Last Days. If the present persecution posed unprecedented problems, it would do no good to look in the laws of the Bible for solutions. But the heroes of the biblical narratives had also had to face problems which for those heroes were unprecedented. Mattathias' religious approach as presented by the Hasmonaean propagandist was revolutionary in its time: follow the glorious *examples* of the heroes of the past!

No law, no prophecy justified rebelling against Antiochus. If Mattathias had based his acts upon a scriptural law or prophecy, the careful author of I Maccabees surely would have quoted it. Instead, the author does everything possible to portray Mattathias' act of zeal as equivalent to Phineas' act of zeal in Num. 25. Just as Phineas showed "zeal" and acted on behalf of the "anger" of the LORD (Num. 25.11) and stabbed the sinful couple in their illicit bedroom,[59] the place of their sin (Num. 25.8), so Mattathias was "filled with zeal and anger" and slew the idolater on the altar, the place of his sin (I Macc. 2.24-26).

The Hasmonaean propagandist pushes the principle of following the examples of the heroes of scripture far beyond the point of justifying Mattathias' act of zeal: he has old Mattathias on his deathbed urge his sons (I Macc. 2.51-61) to note the examples of how God rewarded the brave and righteous conduct of Abraham, Joseph, Phineas, Joshua, Caleb, David, Elijah, Hananiah, Azariah, Mishael, and Daniel. The implication is that by emulating the conduct of those heroes, the sons will earn similar rewards: God will regard them, like Abraham, as righteous; they will be raised to high office under kings, like Joseph; they will found a high priestly dynasty, like Phineas; they will hold judgely power, like Joshua; they will receive territory of their own, like Caleb; they will become kings, like David. They may

---

[58]Goldstein, *I Maccabees*, p. 239 (note on 2.49), and compare I Macc. 6.12 with Isa. 10.7. In I Enoch 85-90, too, the angelic shepherds exceed their mandate from God, but there the sin to be punished is Israel's ancient sin, not the recent sin of Hellenizers, and the punishing instruments are superhuman beings.

[59]Here one must render the obscure Hebrew word in Numbers 25.8 according to interpretations current in Mattathias' time. I follow the Septuagint (and the Vulgate).

even aspire to have God perform for them miracles as he did for Elijah, Hananiah, Azariah, Mishael, and Daniel.

Throughout the rest of his book, the Hasmonaean propagandist echoes the language of biblical stories of heroes, from Judges, I-II Samuel, and I-II Kings, in order to base the dynastic claims of the Hasmonaeans on the fact that their accomplishments equaled those which earned such rewards for those heroes.[60] At I Macc. 5.62 the author is at his most audacious in asserting for the Hasmonaeans the prerogatives reserved for David's line in earlier Jewish tradition.

Indeed, he there calls Mattathias and his descendants "that seed of men to whom had been granted the deliverance of Israel through their agency."[61] The expression is strange both in the Greek and in the reconstructed original Hebrew (ăsher lāhem nittᵉnah yᵉšu̔at yiśrā'ēl bᵉyādām). The use of the passive voice is simply an instance of the Hasmonaean propagandist's habitual avoidance of speaking directly of God, but "deliverance of Israel through their agency" is an unnatural way of saying "that they would be the deliverers of Israel." The strange syntax can have come only from II Sam. 3.18, "...The LORD hath spoken of David saying, 'Deliverance of [hōshīa'] My people Israel is through the agency of David My servant....'" The verse in II Samuel refers to David, yet the Hasmonaean propagandist uses its language to refer to the Hasmonaeans![62]

---

[60] Judas Maccabaeus' feats are narrated in words echoing the stories of Joshua, Jephthah, Gideon, Samuel, Saul and his son Jonathan, and especially David; see Goldstein, *I Maccabees*, pp. 244, 246, 247, 248, 251, 260, 261, 263, 264, 265, 266, 270, 284, 296, 298, 300, 304, 305, 320, 342, 374, 375. The Hasmonaean propagandist is careful to have his narrative of Jonathan echo stories only of Joshua and the Judges and Joab, not of royal or princely heroes, because he does not want to imply that Jonathan's descendants deserve a share of royal power; for the passages, see *ibid.*, pp. 377, 381, 384, 393, 395. The narrative on Simon echoes stories of Elijah and especially of Solomon; see *ibid.*, pp. 472, 490, 491-92. I Macc. 14.12 certainly echoes Mic. 4.4 (cf. Zech. 3.10), but the Hasmonaean propagandist probably was most intent on the fact that Simon had equaled the example of Solomon (I Kings 5.5).

[61] "Seed of men" here means "family," but in the Hebrew Bible the expression is used only by Samuel's still childless mother, Hannah, of the child she longs to bear, as she prays to God that she conceive and bear him (I Sam. 1.11). Samuel grew up to become the prophet and judge who brought about the salvation of Israel in his time (I Sam. 7.8-16); see also Goldstein, *I Maccabees*, p. 305, notes on vss. 60-62 and 63.

[62] I give the reading of the Masoretic text of II Sam. 3.18, which has the noun-expression hōshīa' (an infinitive construct), where the Greek of I Macc. 5.62 has a noun, *sōtēria*. There is another example in Samuel of such use of an infinitive construct, at I Sam. 23.20; cf. also Jer. 10.5, and see *Gesenius' Hebrew Grammar*, ed. E. Kautzsch (2d English ed., rev. by A. E. Cowley; Oxford: Clarendon Press,

Thus the echoes in I Maccabees from the biblical histories far outnumber the allusions to the Writing Prophets. By this procedure, the Hasmonaean propagandist avoided two dangers. In the first place, Jews had been disastrously wrong in identifying their own time with the predicted End of Days. If the reigns of the Hasmonaeans should prove to be that very time, well and good, but their claims should not depend upon any particular interpretation of prophecies the meaning of which was a matter of bitter controversy. In the second place, there were predictions about the great postexilic dynasty of kings which could not possibly be dissociated from the line of David, to which the Hasmonaeans did not belong.[63] Hasmonaean claims to have fulfilled any of those predictions would immediately be rejected as illegitimate.

The Hasmonaean propagandist did not wish to give up completely the possibility of leading his readers to believe that Mattathias' sons fulfilled the words of the prophets. Without echoing the words of the prophecies, he could tell of the deeds of his heroes which looked as if they were fulfillments, and he could then leave it to Jewish Bible-readers to infer the point. He seems to have done so repeatedly.[64] Caution thus led the Hasmonaean propagandist to base his case for the rights of the dynasty upon their achievements and how they equaled

---

1910), sec. 114a, p. 347. Most scholars have rejected the Masoretic reading at II Sam. 3.18, following Keil's judgment, "*Hōshīa'* is an evident mistake in writing for '*ōshīa'*, which is found in many mss. and rendered in all the ancient versions" (C. F. Keil and F. Delitzsch, *Biblical Commentary on the Books of Samuel* [Grand Rapids, Michigan: Eerdmans, 1950], p. 303). With the reading '*ōshīa'*, the passage would mean, "Through the agency of David My servant I shall deliver My people Israel." The Hasmonaean propagandist's habitual avoidance of speaking directly of God could easily have turned even the reading '*ōshīa'*, into the strange noun-expression at I Macc. 5.62. Nevertheless, the noun in the allusion at I Macc. 5.62 would seem to attest the infinitive construct of the Masoretic reading at II Sam. 3.18. The author of Psalms of Solomon 17.5-6, who wrote at least 42 years after the Hasmonaean propagandist, had good reason to complain that the Hasmonaeans had usurped the prerogatives of the (hidden or extinct) dynasty of David. Collins, "Messianism," does not say why he is skeptical about my suggestion that I Macc. 5.62 echoes II Sam. 3.18.

[63]II Sam. 7.16 (cf. I Chron. 17.12), Jer. 33.19-26, Zech. 12.8. Pro-Hasmonaean exegesis might twist other passages. E.g., in Isa. 9.6 (cf. 16.5) one might say that only the throne was David's but that members of another worthy Jewish dynasty would sit upon it. Of Ezek. 34 one might say that the king would need only to take for himself the name "David."

[64]Goldstein, *I Maccabees*, pp. 261 (note on I Macc. 3.44-45), 298, 301, 304, 310, 415, 442, 443, 465, 472 (where I should not have spoken of echoes), 473, 474.

those of earlier heroes of scripture; for the most part he avoided making direct claims that they were the fulfillers of the glorious prophecies. His cautious procedure did not suffice to protect Alexander Jannaeus from the dilemmas posed by the words of the prophets for anyone who claimed to be a postexilic king of the Jews. True prophets had promised that the postexilic king would be invincible, winning victories over all neighboring peoples. If Jannaeus did not try to make the predicted conquests, Jews would be quick to regard his rule as illegitimate. In fact, he did attempt to make those conquests. As a result, with every defeat of the king who prophecy predicted should be invincible, Jews regarded him as an impostor with no right to be king and rebelled against him. His long series of wars against foreigners and against his own people shows how he was, in effect, a prisoner of the prophecies.[65]

In another respect the Hasmonaean propagandist was incautious. Although the defeats and deaths of his heroes made it impossible for him to hold that the Age of God's wrath was over, he still believed that the worst part of that Age was past. He has no doubt that Jews now have the right if not the duty to rebel against the pagan kings ruling over them. He holds that in the reign of Simon God had lifted the yoke of subservience to the gentiles which He had imposed upon His sinful chosen people.[66] He asserts that God had chosen the Hasmonaean dynasty to bring permanent victory to Israel.[67] The Hasmonaean propagandist never found an answer to the difficult question, "Precisely what aspects of God's wrath still operate today upon the Jews?" He thus was left without any easy theological explanation for the deaths of his heroes, Judas, Jonathan, and Simon. He tells of the aftermath of Judas' death in language appropriate for narrating an Age of God's Wrath (I Macc. 9.23-27), but he portrays the aftermath of Jonathan's fall only as a time of wicked gentile plotting (I Macc. 12.53). Gentiles can plot against Israel even in an Age of God's Favor. Hardest of all to explain was Simon's death, and the Hasmonaean propagandist tells of it without any theological comment. Jannaeus was trapped by the implications of the title "king." But even if a descendant of Simon refrained from assuming the royal title, the theology of the author of I Maccabees left the member of a dynasty

---

[65]See the discussion of the reign of Alexander Jannaeus in my study in *CHJ*, Vol. II, chap. 8.
[66]I Macc. 13.41.
[67]I Macc. 5.62; the word "permanent" does not occur in that verse, but prophets had promised that God's postexilic Age of Mercy and Vindication for Israel would be permanent (e.g., Isa. 54, Jer. 31.31-40).

supposed to bring permanent victory with no easy way to explain a defeat.

III. The Second Letter at the Head of II Maccabees

To understand the content of Epistle 2 one must know something of its background. Late in 163 or early in 162 B.C.E., the regime of Antiochus V, to which Judaea was subject, passed over Onias IV, rightful heir of the Zadokite-Oniad line of high priests and gave the high priesthood instead to Alcimus, who was not a member of that line. Thereupon, Onias IV left Judaea for Egypt. There, through good service, he earned the favor of King Ptolemy VI and eventually won royal permission to build at Leontopolis in Egypt a Jewish temple where sacrifices were offered to the LORD. Although this schismatic rival to the temple of Jerusalem might seem to be a violation of the prohibitions at Deut. 12.5-14 against offering sacrifices in any place except the one chosen by God, surviving texts show many Jews believed that God in 586 B.C.E. had revoked his election of Jerusalem when he allowed the temple to be destroyed. God had never given the sign which would prove he had chosen the second temple of Jerusalem.[68]

Onias IV and his Oniad family became leaders of the Jews of Egypt and stood loyally by the dynasty of Ptolemy VI and his wife, Cleopatra II. Later, in 107 B.C.E., civil war broke out between Cleopatra III (the daughter of that royal couple) and her own son, Ptolemy IX. In the time of this civil war, the chief Oniads were Chelkias and Ananias, sons of Onias IV. They served Cleopatra III as commanders. In 103 B.C.E., when Ptolemy IX from Cyprus invaded Palestine and attacked Judaea, which was then under the rule of the Hasmonaean king and high priest Alexander Jannaeus, Cleopatra III and her Jewish commanders marched into Asia and beat Ptolemy off. Chelkias died in the course of the fighting, but Oniad Ananias himself endorsed Jannaeus' dynastic claims and convinced Cleopatra not to annex Judaea. Trumped in Judaea, Ptolemy saw that if he could seize control of Egypt, he still might decisively defeat his mother, who was still in Asia with her army. In the second half of 103 he invaded Egypt. The Jews of Egypt, so strongly identified with the cause of Cleopatra III, had much to fear from the hostility of Ptolemy IX. His invasion confronted them with clear and present danger.[69]

---

[68]Goldstein, *II Maccabees*, pp. 14-16.
[69]Hans Volkmann, "Ptolemaios 30," RE, XXIII^2 (1959), 1740-42; Alan E. Samuel, *Ptolemaic Chronology* (München: Beck, 1962), pp. 148-51; Goldstein, *II Maccabees*, p. 162.

The author probably was in Egypt when he forged Ep. 2 in late November or early December, 103 B.C.E. He meant to preach the following messages to the Jews of Egypt in their hour of danger. First, they should observe the festival now called Hanukkah, in honor of the purification of the temple of Jerusalem by Judas Maccabaeus and his followers. That observance would be a symbolic expression of the writer's more fundamental second message: that the temple of Jerusalem was still God's Chosen Place, so that the Jews of Egypt were sinning in accepting or even tolerating the temple of Leontopolis. Third, God's promised salvation for the Jews was being realized in Judaea through the Hasmonaean dynasty of high priests, princes, and kings. Ep. 2 thus endorses the dynastic claims of the Hasmonaeans, but its emphases and arguments are very different from those of I Maccabees.

In the meager narrative in Ep. 2 telling of the supposed events culminating in the death of Antiochus IV in 164 B.C.E. (II Macc. 1.11-17), God is the sole power named as active against the enemies of the Jews; nothing is said of the victories of Judas Maccabaeus and his brothers and their followers. The fact may well reflect the nature of the audience of Egyptian Jews in 103 B.C.E., who, it seems, tended to favor the Oniads and to regard the Hasmonaeans as usurpers. It would have been bad tactics for the author to begin the letter by rousing the hostility of his audience. But all Jews of Ptolemaic Egypt would hear with pleasure of God's victory over the wicked Seleucid king, Antiochus IV.

In the very first verse after the salutation, Ep. 2 implies, in agreement with I Maccabees, that the Jews are now permitted to rebel against their foreign king. The requirement of the full Age of Wrath, that Jews be loyal even to oppressors, has passed away. The bulk of Ep. 2 (II Macc. 1.12-2.15, 18) serves to prove that despite the shortcomings of the second temple of Jerusalem, it is indeed the Chosen Place. God brought gruesome death upon the king who had made war upon the Holy City (II Macc. 1.12-17). God made possible the purification of His temple (1.18, 2.18). The second temple did not need to have the LORD's election of it attested by miraculous fire from heaven, because its fire was in fact the wondrously preserved fire of the first temple (II Macc. 1.19-36). True, the second temple lacked ark, tabernacle, and incense altar, but that fact was God's will; the missing sacred articles would be restored in His own Time of Mercy (II Macc. 2.1-8). The present status of the second temple itself marks an important abatement of God's wrath.

The Days of Purification were a rite celebrating a victory of the Hasmonaeans, however much one might try to minimize the connection between the observance and the dynasty.[70] To ask that those Days be observed was therefore to give some endorsement to Hasmonaeans, at least to Judas Maccabaeus, whose generalship led to the victories which made possible the purification of the temple. At II Macc. 2.17 the author of Ep. 2 went much farther in supporting the Hasmonaeans. If my restoration of the original text is correct, he there presents Judas Maccabaeus and the pious Jews as asserting confidently in 164 B.C.E., "God, Who saved His entire people and restored the heritage to us all will also restore the kingdom and the priesthood and the sanctification."[71]

The writer has just demonstrated that the second temple is God's Chosen Place. Hence, when he employs the word "heritage," he

---

[70]In the Abridged History there is an effort to discredit all Hasmonaeans except Judas Maccabaeus and to minimize the connection.

Collins, "Messianism," calls "unfounded" my theory that the letter in II Macc. 1.10b-2.10 contains implied opposition to the temple at Leontopolis and holds that it is especially incongruent with the setting I propose, "Since the Oniads of Leontopolis supported Alexander Jannaeus." See rather my *II Maccabees*, pp. 25-26, 158-60. The paradoxical position of the Oniads and their temple is a fact of history which no one would have suspected if our sources did not tell us about it. Onias IV surely respected the temple at Jerusalem yet founded a schismatic sanctuary at Leontopolis. The Oniads regarded their own high-priestly line as the legitimate one, yet Ananias of that line refused to exploit an opportunity to depose the Hasmonaean Alexander Jannaeus, for which the price would have been the subjection of independent Judaea to Ptolemaic Egypt. The authorities whose views are preserved in the Mishnah surely believed in the exclusive legitimacy of the temple at Jerusalem but still conceded limited validity to vegetable sacrifices offered at Leontopolis. See my *II Maccabees*, pp. 162-63, and my review of Robert Doran's *Temple Propaganda*, above, pp. 209-20.

[71]For the correct reading at II Macc. 2.17, see Goldstein, *II Maccabees*, p. 187. I emended the text in order to give it good Greek syntax. Without my emendation, the case for regarding II Macc. 2.17 as pro-Hasmonaean propaganda from the reign of Alexander Jannaeus becomes even stronger, for the verse then asserts (supposedly in 164 B.C.E.) that God has already restored to the Jews the kingdom, the priesthood, and the sanctification – at a time when no Jew aspired to be king (least of all, Judas Maccabaeus); when the high priests were appointees of the Seleucid kings, first the impious Menelaus and then the pious Alcimus, who, however, was bitterly opposed by many pious Jews; and when the pagans and apostates, who occupied the citadel of Jerusalem and parts of Judaea, were always able to commit acts of desecration! Jewish claims that the kingdom, priesthood, and sanctification had all been restored were impossible before the accession of the first Hasmonaean king, Judas Aristobulus I. His brief reign (104-103 B.C.E.) was troubled and was too early to have produced some of the allusions in Ep. 2. The combination of allusions and claims thus fits only the reign of Alexander Jannaeus (103-76 B.C.E.).

alludes primarily to its occurrence in Deut. 12.9-14: if Jews possess the heritage, i.e., the Promised Land, they are not permitted to offer sacrifices except at that Chosen Place. One therefore cannot tell whether the author is alluding also to Isa. 57.13, 58.14, Jer. 3.18-19, 12.14-15, 49.8, Zech. 8.12, which predict restoration of the heritage. In any case, he greatly exaggerates the extent of the Jews' recovery of promised territory in 164 B.C.E. Only Jannaeus' vigorous territorial achievements and aspirations could bring anything like literal truth to a claim that the heritage had been restored.

As for "the kingdom and the priesthood and the sanctification," those words are taken from Exod. 19.6 as read in the second century B.C.E., a verse promising those three attributes to the Chosen People.[72] If my reconstruction of the text is right, the writer correctly refrained from having Judas Maccabaeus and his contemporaries claim that in their time God had restored the three attributes promised at Exod. 19.6. Rather, he made them express their confidence, using the future tense, that the attributes would be restored in the near[73] future. For an author writing in 103 B.C.E., only in the reigns of the Hasmonaean kings, Judas Aristobulus I and Alexander Jannaeus, could the Jews have a claim to have recovered the complete triad of kingdom, priesthood, and sanctification, and there is good reason to believe that the Hasmonaeans in the time of Judas Maccabaeus did not yet have such audacious aspirations.[74] Consequently, the author of Ep. 2 here reflects and endorses the achievements and aspirations of Alexander Jannaeus.

We have admitted the possibility that the word "heritage" in I Macc. 2.17 is an allusion to passages in the Writing Prophets, but that is far from being a certainty. The allusion there may be only to Deut. 12.9. If it is, author of Ep. 2, in making assertions about present sanctity of the second temple and about the achievements and aspirations of the Hasmonaeans, has refrained as conspicuously as the Hasmonaean propagandist from echoing the words of books of the Writing Prophets (the author of Ep. 2 at II Macc. 2.7-8 did fabricate unambiguous utterances of Jeremiah to drive home important points).

On the other hand, in contrast to the writer of I Maccabees, the author of Ep. 2 does not hesitate to specify what has not yet been accomplished, i.e., what aspects still continue of the Age of Wrath. He quotes in full the prayer (II Macc. 1.24-29) which, he says, was recited on the Day of the Fire,[75] when the wondrously preserved fire from the

---

[72]Goldstein, *II Maccabees*, p. 188.
[73]Cf. "speedily" (*tacheôs*) in II Macc. 2.18.
[74]Goldstein, *II Maccabees*, pp. 160-61.
[75]See II Macc. 1.18.

first temple was ignited upon the altar of the second. He could have had only one reason to quote the passage: he wanted the Jews of Egypt to use it as part of the observance of the Days of Purification.[76] The prayer asks that God guard Israel and make her holy; that He gather the dispersed exiles and free those who were enslaved among the nations; that He be mindful of the Jews, whom the gentiles despised and abominated; that He take vengeance upon the oppressors; and that He plant His people in His holy Place as Moses said (Exod. 15.17).

This prayer, in alluding to still unfulfilled promises and to continuing aspects of the Age of Wrath, does echo words of the Writing Prophets.[77] Though the great prophetic forecasts for the postexilic era had predicted a prompt ingathering of the exiled Jews[78] and a prompt punishment of their oppressors, the author of Ep. 2 concedes the obvious truth, that those promises were still unfulfilled in 164 and even in 103 B.C.E. Despite the successes and aspirations of Jannaeus, Judaea in 103 B.C.E. obviously still lacked complete sanctification: it still was vulnerable to gentile attack. Nevertheless, the author of Ep. 2 ends with the hope that the last remnants of the Age of Wrath will *speedily* pass away, with the renewed fulfillment of Exod. 15.17, i.e., a new Exodus by which the exiles will return to be planted again in God's holy Place.

As a supporter of the dynastic claims of the Hasmonaeans, the author of Ep. 2 passed over in silence the prophecies which predicted a king descended from David. Like the Hasmonaeans he also passed over in silence the revelations of I Enoch 85-90 and Dan. 7-12 and with them the belief in the resurrection. We may infer that he rejected both the revelations and the belief.[79]

---

[76]Cf. *ibid*.

[77]II Macc. 1.25 contains echoes of Isa. 14.1, 41.8, 44.1-2; II Macc. 1.25 and 27 draw on Ezek. 37.28; II Macc. 1.25 and 28 draw on Jer. 2.3; II Macc. 1.27 looks to Isa. 49.7; II Macc. 1.27-28 draws on Isa. 49.25-26. See also Goldstein, *II Maccabees*, p. 179.

[78]Ingathering: Isa. 27.12-13, 43.3-8, 49.8-12, 22, 60.4, etc. Punishment: Isa. 41.11-12, 49.23, 26, 60.4, 66.14-16, etc.

[79]Collins, "Messianism," questions my inference that the author of the letter in II Mac. 1.10b-2.18 rejected the belief in the permanent royal rights of the dynasty of David. My inference is based not only upon the author's "remarkable reference" (Collins' expression) to the restoration of *the* kingdom (i.e., the promised kingdom, par excellence), but also on the absence of any reference to David's dynasty in the author's prayer for the fulfillment of those divine promises still unfulfilled. The author of the letter makes clear just what those promises are.

IV. The Abridged History

We do not possess the original work of Jason of Cyrene. All we have of it is the anonymous Abridged History. Though I interpret the abridger's preface (II Macc. 2.19-32) as a promise that the abridgment faithfully reflects the original,[80] skeptics may not accept my interpretation or may not choose to believe the abridger kept that promise. I shall use "our writer" in order to have a convenient brief expression, meaning "Jason of Cyrene or the abridger," so as to designate the person responsible for the views expressed in the Abridged History.

Our writer knows that the glorious predictions of the canonical prophets and Daniel were at best incompletely fulfilled, but he keeps his faith that they are true. Furthermore, he knew of the shortcomings of the second temple, but he kept his faith that it was holy. He believed that some aspects of the Age of Wrath had run their course and reached their end. Indeed, unlike the Hasmonaean propagandist, he maintained that truly supernatural miracles had occurred in the Present Age. For our writer, this and other abatements of the Age of Wrath did not mean that all aspects of that Age had passed away. Writing in the first half of the first century B.C.E., he knew (like the Hasmonaean propagandist and unlike the seers of Daniel and I Enoch) that the troubles of 169-164 B.C.E. had not been those of the Last Days. Unlike the Hasmonaean propagandist, our writer defined the conditions of the Present Age as falling far short of the predicted period of Israel's unending bliss. Israel can still sin and, on sinning will bring upon herself and even upon the temple the calamitous wrath of God. Even so, paradoxically, our writer finds it possible to assert that God's promise at Isa. 54.10 is already fulfilled, "God never lets His mercy depart from us. Rather, though He teaches us by calamity, He never deserts His people" (II Macc. 6.16).

On the other hand, our writer is no more successful than the Hasmonaean propagandist in finding a theological explanation for some of the misfortunes of his heroes. Why should pious Onias III have had to face the plotting of wicked Simon and Menelaus, and why should he have been murdered (II Macc. 3.4-6, 4.1-6, 33-34)? Why should Razis have been driven to suicide (II Macc. 14.37-46)? Like the Hasmonaean propagandist, our writer in these instances tells the difficult truth without theological comment.

The Abridged History shows great interest in the sanctity of the second temple. Near the very beginning of the narrative, our writer

---

[80]Goldstein, *II Maccabees*, pp. 190-92.

may well be claiming that prophecies of Isaiah concerning the second temple were fulfilled in the time of the high priest Onias III, for II Macc. 3.2-3 probably draws on Isa. 60.3, 7, 10. Our writer then turns to tell the story of the thwarting of Heliodorus (II Macc. 3.4-39), the first miracle attested for the second temple. It constituted the first important break in the manifestations of the Age of Wrath (II Macc. 3.30 probably draws on Isa. 60.7). God had at last ended his centuries-long abstention from giving supernatural aid to His chosen people.[81] The thwarting of Heliodorus is a fulfillment of Zech. 9.8. II Macc. 3.39 probably contains paraphrase of Zech. 9.8.[82]

Our writer agreed with the Hasmonaean propagandist in holding that the sins of the Hellenizing high priest, Jason the Oniad, and of his followers provoked the wrath of God and caused Him to use Antiochus IV as His punishing instrument.[83] Our writer also agreed that thereupon Antiochus IV in his arrogance exceeded his mandate and went on to persecute the Jews and their religion.[84] In these points, Jason of Cyrene departed from the views of the seers of Daniel and I Enoch, who say nothing of present sin as the cause of God's wrath and regard the persecution as the climactic stage of centuries of punishment for sins committed in the time of the first temple. Our writer, however, need not have felt there was any conflict between his own theological explanation of Antiochus' hostile acts and the views of Daniel and I Enoch, for he surely agreed that the Age of Wrath had begun in the time of the first temple.

Allusions in the Abridged History to I Enoch are faint and questionable,[85] but it is clear that our writer believed in the revelations of Dan. 7-12. He quotes from them and writes his narrative in a manner which shields them from challenge.[86] His strongest allusions to Daniel (II Macc. 7.9, 14) are to the verse predicting the resurrection (Dan. 12.2).[87] After 162 B.C.E. believers in Dan. 7-12 faced difficult problems. The revelations had been correct in predicting that the suffering Jews and their temple would win vindication and that the persecuting king would perish, but many other details in the

---

[81]Goldstein, *I Maccabees*, pp. 12-13, 28, 49.
[82]Goldstein, *II Maccabees*, p. 215. Dan. 11.20 certainly alludes to the same event and draws on Zech. 9.8; see Goldstein, *II Maccabees*, p. 197.
[83]II Macc. 4.10-17.
[84]II Macc. 5.17, 21-22, 7.31, 34, 9.4, 8, 10-18.
[85]Goldstein, *I Maccabees*, pp. 96-97 (through line 2), *II Maccabees*, p. 501.
[86]*Ibid.*, pp. 63-70, 305-6.
[87]*Ibid.*, pp. 305-6. On his allusions to Dan. 8 and 11, see *ibid.*, pp. 306-7, 351, 353, 355.

predictions had proved to be false. The Seleucid empire did not fall in the 160s B.C.E., contrary to Dan. 7.11. Jews did not gain imperial or cosmic power, contrary to Dan. 7.13-14, 27, 12.3. The aftermath of the death of Antiochus IV did not fit Dan. 12.1. The chronology of the events was far from fitting Dan. 7.25, 9.24-27, 12.7. There was no resurrection, contrary to Dan. 12.2.

The procedure of believers ever after was like that of Christian Jerome in his *Commentary on Daniel:* the predictions in Dan. 7-12 which had not yet been fulfilled would be fulfilled at some time in the future. But the wording of Dan. 7-12 made it difficult for anyone who knew the history of the times to dissociate many of those predictions from the years 169-162 B.C.E. Moreover, the time for the future fulfillment of the flagrantly unrealized predictions of the end of pagan empires and of imperial and cosmic power for the Jews was obscure, even where the meaning was otherwise clear. It was best to say as little as possible of the predictions. However, Dan. 12.2, the sole unequivocal prediction of the resurrection in the literature of Jewish revelation, was too precious to give up or pass over in silence. One could read the text in such a way as to believe that the resurrection would indeed come after the death of the impious Antiochus IV, King of the North, but would not necessarily follow that event immediately. Accordingly, our writer loudly echoes Dan. 12.2 to preach belief in the resurrection.

Our writer admired Judas Maccabaeus and strove to discredit all other Hasmonaeans.[88] He knew that the terrible events of the 160s B.C.E. had not been the trials of the Last Days, predicted by the Writing Prophets. But the words of those prophets had done much to determine the actions of the embattled Jews of the 160s, shaping especially their expectations and the form of the supernatural apparitions they perceived. These recognizable effects of the words of the Writing Prophets Jason of Cyrene took over from his sources.[89] Our writer, however, chooses the words of his narrative very carefully. Much as he admires Judas Maccabaeus, in telling of that hero's achievements he abstains from echoes of the Writing Prophets.[90] No Hasmonaean, including Maccabaeus, is to be viewed as fulfilling those words!

Perhaps the most striking scriptural allusion in the Abridged History (II Macc. 8.27) comes from the Book of Samuel (II Sam. 21.10),

---

[88]Goldstein, *II Maccabees*, pp. 17-18.
[89]*Ibid.*, pp. 293, 295-96, 298, 354-55, 386, 392-95, 397-99, 403, 405-6, 442, 495, 501.
[90]In the passages cited in n. 89 from my *II Maccabees*, I was not always careful to distinguish a literal echo of the words of the Writing Prophets from a recognizable effect of those words, taken over by our writer from his sources.

the favorite source for the Hasmonaean propagandist. Characteristically, that allusion in its context refers more to God's appreciation of the merit of the martyrs, than to the achievements of Maccabaeus and his men.[91]

In telling of the atrocious sufferings which came upon Israel, our writer shows deep concern to console his pious readers (II Macc. 6.12-17). He also presents the martyrs as uttering theatrical speeches to encourage themselves and exhort posterity (II Macc. 6.24-28, 7.6, 9, 11, 14, 16-19, 22-23, 27-38). Furthermore, he sought to discredit the Hasmonaean dynasty, which by his time had "usurped" the high priesthood and the kingship.[92] To encourage the pious readers and to discredit the Hasmonaeans, one procedure would seem to have been obviously effective: allude to the glorious messianic promises attached indissolubly to the dynasty of David, as is done in Psalm of Solomon 17. Our writer could have argued as follows:

> Though martyred Israel has to face the tyrant, Antiochus IV, at some time in the future the Chosen People will live secure under the glorious rule of David's heir! Whatever their achievements, the Hasmonaean usurpers have no claim to be fulfilling those glorious prophecies!

The Abridged History, however, contains nothing of the kind. Nowhere does our writer mention David. One would like to know why. Did Jason of Cyrene have evidence that David's line was extinct or had been disqualified by sin? If our writer could predict a resurrection, why could he not predict the coming of a righteous king from the dynasty of David or of David himself? His failure to do so suggests that his sect of Jews, unlike the sect of the seer of I Enoch, no longer even thought of a Davidic king. If that possibility seems strange, let us note how there is no mention of David in the book of Daniel and how the Hasmonaean propagandist could hint that David's line received the kingship only

---

[91] Goldstein, *II Maccabees*, pp. 336-37. On the possible allusion to I Sam. 2.1-10 at II Macc. 6.30, see Goldstein, *II Maccabees*, pp. 287-88, but in writing my comments there I wrongly believed that the great figure at I Enoch 90.37-38 was not a messianic king. Otherwise, I still stand by them.

[92] The abridger in his epilogue might seem to value the Hasmonaean achievement of keeping the Holy City out of the hands of gentiles (II Macc. 15.37), but in the context of the whole Abridged History that achievement is at best small: the same situation prevailed almost throughout the period of the second temple, even under the wicked high priest, Jason. It was interrupted only by the atrocities which began with the sack by Antiochus IV in 169 and ended with the defeat of Nicanor in 162 B.C.E. Thus, in our writer's view, conditions under the Hasmonaean high priests need not have been any better than under wicked Alcimus after the death of Maccabaeus in 160 B.C.E.!

"for ages," not forever.[93] True prophets had promised eternal rule to the line of David and had predicted a glorious Davidic "Messiah." How could many Jewish sects have come to the conclusion that those prophecies were void? We do not know. But the evidence seems to show that important Jewish sects of the second and early first centuries B.C.E. disagreed with the seer of I Enoch 85-90: they did not believe in the coming of a Davidic Messiah.

Abbreviations

CD	Document of the Damascus Covenanters, published in Chaim Rabin, *The Zadokite Documents* (2d ed.; Oxford: Clarendon Press, 1958)
CHJ	*The Cambridge History of Judaism*, ed. W. D. Davies and Louis Finkelstein (Cambridge: University Press, 1984-)
EM	*Entsiqlopediah miqra'it* (Jerusalem: Bialik Institute, 1955-82)
Goldstein, *I Maccabees*	Jonathan A. Goldstein, *I Maccabees* ("Anchor Bible," Vol. 41; Garden City, N.Y.: Doubleday, 1976)
Goldstein, *II Maccabees*	Jonathan A. Goldstein, *II Maccabees* ("Anchor Bible," Vol.

---

[93]At I Macc. 2.57; see above, n. 34. In a paper limited to the writers in I and II Maccabees, I refrain from surveying the opinions on the dynasty of David in the other Jewish sources which survive from the late fourth to the first century B.C.E. I have just shown how peculiar is the silence in II Maccabees on a coming Davidic king. There might be nothing strange, however, about the absence from Daniel of allusions to David. The writers in Daniel might have taken for granted that the imperial power predicted for the Jews would be exercised by a Davidic king. No one can read the mind of those writers, but in my book *Chosen Peoples* and in my commentary on Daniel I shall demonstrate that the traditions which shaped the revelations in Daniel had nothing to do with a Davidic king. Collins, "Messianism," questions my inference that the writer of the abridged history in II Maccabees "no longer even thought of a Davidic king." Again let me point out that my inference is not a mere argument from silence, but an argument from a silence where one would expect an assertion of the rights of the dynasty of David. Throughout our entire volume, *Judaisms and Their Messiahs*, we run the risk of relying upon mere arguments from silence, so incomplete is our evidence. But if there is a silence where demonstrably there should be a statement, the silence becomes eloquent indeed.

	41A: Garden City, N.Y.: Doubleday, 1983)
JAOS	*Journal of the American Oriental Society*
Nickelsburg, *Literature*	George W. E. Nickelsburg, *Jewish Literature between the Bible and the Mishnah* (Philadelphia: Fortress Press, 1981)
PAAJR	*Proceedings of the American Academy for Jewish Research*
RE	*Realencyclopaedie der klassischen Altertumswissenschaft*, ed. Pauly, Wissowa, *et al.*
TDNT	*Theological Dictionary of the New Testament*, ed. Gerhard Kittel (Grand Rapids and London: Eerdmans, 1964-74).

List of Abbreviations Used in Chapters 1, 3, 5-10

Ab	Abot
Ag. Ap.	*Against Apion*
AJ	*Antiquities of the Jews*
Ant.	*Antiquities of the Jews*
AOS	American Oriental Society
Ap.	*Against Apion*
Apol.	*Apology*
AZ	'Abodah zarah
b	Babylonian Talmud
BA	*Biblical Archaeologist*
BB	Baba Batra
B.C.E.	Before the Christian Era
BJ	*Jewish War=Bellum Judaicum*
BJRL	*Bulletin of the John Rylands Library*
BT or B.T.	Babylonian Talmud
CBQ	*Catholic Biblical Quarterly*
CPJ	*Corpus Papyrorum Judaicarum*
EJ	*Encyclopaedia Judaica*
Enc. Jud.	*Encyclopaedia Judaica*
ET	English Translation
F. Gr. Hist.	*Die Fragmente der griechischen Historiker*
GCS	*Die griechischen christliche Schriftsteller der ersten drei Jahrhunderte*
G.N.	Note added by George Nickelsburg
Hag	Hagigah
Hist. Eccl.	*Historia Ecclesiastica*
HTR	*Harvard Theological Review*

HTS	Harvard Theological Studies
IEJ	Israel Exploration Journal
JBL	Journal of Biblical Literature
JCS	Journal of Cuneiform Studies
JJS	Journal of Jewish Studies
JQR	Jewish Quarterly Review
JT	Palestinian (or "Jerusalem") Talmud
Jub.	Jubilees
J.W. or JW	Jewish War
Legat.	Legatio ad Gaium
m	Mishnah
Macc.	Maccabees
Mek.	Mekilta
Mut. nom.	De mutatione nominum
Opif. mund.	De opificio mundi
p	Palestinian Talmud
Praep. evang.	Praeparatio evangelica
RE	Realencyclopaedie der klassischen Altertumswissenschaft, ed. Pauly Wissowa, et al.
REJ	Revue des etudes juives
Sanh	Sanhedrin
SBT	Studies in Biblical Theology
Sib. Or.	Sibylline Oracles
Sir	Book of Ben Sira = Ecclesiasticus
Somn.	De somniis
Sot	Sotah
Spec. leg.	De specialibus legibus
Syr.	Syriake
t.	Tosefta
T.	Testament of
TB	Babylonian Talmud
Test. Mos.	Testament of Moses
ZAW	Zeitschrift für die alttestamentliche Wissenschaft
ZNW	Zeitschrift für die neutestamentliche Wissenschaft

Index

Aaron 58-60

Abdera 5, 13, 15, 22, 164, 165, 171, 217

Acts 6.1 3

Age of Mercy 223, 239

Age of Wrath 223, 224, 228, 229, 232, 235, 241, 243-246

Ahiram 110, 111

Akra 16, 197, 203, 204, 207

Alcimus 203-205, 216, 240, 242, 248

'Alenu 63

Alexander Jannaeus 141, 220, 228, 231, 239, 240, 242-244

Alexander the Great 8, 68, 104, 162, 163

Alexandria 13, 17, 28, 40, 59, 117, 118, 126, 132, 140, 143, 164, 215

Aligarh 5

Amos 7, 172, 234

Antiochus III 18, 116, 121, 124, 127, 131, 163

Antiochus IV 4, 11, 12, 16, 18-22, 24, 32, 119-121, 123, 129-132, 134, 135, 138, 149, 150, 161, 165, 166, 168, 171, 181, 183-185, 194-197, 199-201, 204, 212, 214, 223, 224, 226, 229, 230, 232, 234, 236, 241, 246-248

Antiochus V 12, 19, 195, 196, 200, 201, 203-205, 240

Antiochus VII 144, 145, 217

Apocalypse of Peter 96-98

apocalypse, apocalyptic 13, 96-98, 155, 156, 181, 183, 188, 207, 227

Apollonius the Mysarch 183, 194, 196

archangels 66

Aristeas to Philocrates 6, 27, 133

Aristophanes 15

ark 58, 64-66, 78, 111, 223, 241

Ashurbanipal 104, 105, 108, 109, 111, 159

Atargatis 36

Babylon 17, 65, 106, 156-160, 189, 191, 195, 199, 202, 207

II Baruch 77

Bel 45, 65

Ben Sira 4, 9, 12-14, 18, 30, 132, 140, 145, 164, 171, 172, 212

Bickerman, Elias 8, 13, 18, 27, 29, 44, 62, 67, 122, 127, 139, 142, 168, 210, 212, 215, 216, 222

Cato 9, 10, 17, 31

Christ 20, 84, 86, 90-96, 98, 112, 120

Christian, Christians 13, 29, 33, 38, 44, 48, 53, 57, 61, 63, 64, 66, 67, 69, 70, 76, 80-88, 90-92, 94-101, 112, 182, 124, 215, 216, 222, 225, 247

Cicero 9, 10

Claudius 28

Cleopatra I 116, 117, 120, 123, 125, 128, 146, 149

Cleopatra II 128, 135-140, 142-145, 148, 240

Cleopatra III 128, 136, 138, 139, 142, 144, 145, 240

congraecare 9

Dan. *1-6* 8, 128

Dan. *6:11* 68

Daniel, Dan. 5, 7-12, 16, 20, 24, 26, 68, 94, 102, 103, 116, 118, 126-128, 144, 147, 167, 172, 181-185, 188, 189, 191, 192, 194, 196, 197, 199, 200, 202, 205-208, 217, 221, 223, 225, 226, 228-233, 236, 237, 244-249

David 5, 60, 61, 68, 71, 77, 79, 82, 83, 85-87, 91, 94, 133, 134, 155, 171, 175, 218, 221, 222, 225-228, 230, 236-238, 244, 248, 249

Delos 28

Diaspora 17, 27, 28, 30-32

Dinkler, Erich 87, 91-94, 96-98

Dura 33, 34, 36, 37, 39, 41-45, 47, 48, 50-53, 57-69, 72, 76, 78-89, 92-96, 98-105, 108, 110-112, 114

Edessa 36, 39-41, 43-45, 51-53

Elijah 60, 64, 90-95, 97-99, 236, 237

Enoch *85-90*, I Enoch *85-90* 24, 167, 181-182, 187, 188, 207, 221-223, 225-228, 230, 233, 236, 244-246, 248, 249

I Enoch *37-71* 222

Epistle 2, Ep. 2 *see* II Macc. 1.10b-2.18

Esther 29, 61, 63, 133, 191, 215, 217

Europos *see* Dura

formulary, formularies 33, 44-49

Gaza 71, 82, 83, 85

Gen. *49* 79-81, 112

Gentile, Gentiles 5-8, 11-13, 14, 16, 19-23, 25-28, 30-32, 78, 95, 117, 118, 132, 137, 162-168, 176, 187, 204, 215, 218, 221, 226, 231, 233, 234, 239, 244, 248

Gog and Magog 78, 103, 107

Goodenough, Erwin R. 57-67, 69, 70, 72, 73, 75, 78, 79, 82, 88, 89, 96, 98, 99, 101, 111, 113, 114

grace after meals 62

Graeculus 9, 11

Greek, Greeks 3-24, 26, 27, 29-32, 36, 39, 44-48, 50-52, 54, 59, 64, 66, 67, 82, 85, 91, 92, 96-98, 102-104, 112, 117, 118, 121, 124, 127, 132-134, 136, 138, 143, 148, 156, 162-165, 168, 170-172, 174, 178, 185, 188, 191, 197-201, 205, 210-212, 214-218, 222, 228, 234, 235, 237, 242

gymnasium, gymnasia 6, 10, 17-29, 31, 32

Hasmonaean, Hasmonaeans 12, 25-27, 29, 31, 32, 115, 132, 144, 145, 148, 149, 164, 168, 170-172, 176-178, 182, 216, 217-220, 228-248

Index

Hecataeus of Abdera 5, 13, 15, 16, 22, 164, 165, 171, 217

Hellenism, Hellenistic, Hellenizing 3-21, 24-33, 64-65, 105, 116, 123, 132, 133, 136, 137, 162, 164, 167, 168, 171, 177, 195, 203, 210, 211, 213, 216, 230, 234, 236, 246

Hengel, Martin 4, 12-14, 26, 28

Herod 26, 29, 183

high priest 6, 14, 18, 19, 21-25, 104, 116, 117, 120, 122, 123, 126, 127, 129-132, 134, 137, 140, 141, 145-150, 164, 165, 167, 168, 170-172, 202-204, 240, 246, 248

hokmat yevanit 30

Homer 30

homosexual, homosexuality 5, 6

Hosea 7

Hyrcanus I 161, 171, 172, 216-218

Hyrcanus II 171, 172

Hyrcanus (the Tobiad) 115, 118, 119, 122, 135, 141

idolaters, idolatry 6-8, 15, 17, 20, 23, 25, 27, 31, 101, 189

iconoclasts 84, 87, 100, 101

Isa. *11* 64, 79-81, 83-86, 95, 110, 112, 231, 233, 234

Isa. *12* 95, 233

Isa. *46:1-2* 65

IV Esdras 77

Jacob 31, 47, 63, 70, 73, 77, 80, 83, 101, 111, 113, 114, 165-167, 170, 172-177, 179, 181, 204, 221, 222, 231

Jannaeus *see* Alexander Jannaeus

Jason (high priest) 12, 18-25, 131, 165, 167, 168, 183, 184

Jason of Cyrene 19-21, 30, 115, 121-123, 134, 135, 137, 138, 141, 146-148, 150, 151, 199, 209, 210, 212-214, 219, 220, 229, 245-248

Joel *4.8* 47

John Hyrcanus I 161, 171, 172, 216-219

Jonathan 4, 115, 148, 166, 168, 170, 177, 178, 192, 194, 209-211, 216, 220, 223, 232-235, 237, 239, 249

Joseph (the Tobiad) 115, 117, 119, 124, 131, 146, 147, 164

Jubilees, Jub. 22, 23, 25, 26, 161-179, *passim*, 226

Judaea 7, 15-18, 25-29, 31, 32, 116, 120, 121, 126, 137, 140, 142, 144, 145, 147, 149, 162-164, 170, 175, 177, 192, 195, 199, 202, 216-219, 222, 229, 231, 240-242, 244

Judas Maccabaeus 5, 16, 24, 25, 172-177, 182, 188, 195, 197, 203, 207, 209, 216, 218, 219, 225, 226, 229, 230, 232, 233, 241-243, 247

katallag- 211, 212

Kraeling, Carl 54, 58, 68-75, 79, 81, 88, 96, 104, 111, 113

Leontopolis, temple of 137, 139, 140, 210, 240-242

Lysias 19, 195, 196

I Macc. *1.11* 21, 23

Maccabees, I Maccabees, I Macc., First Maccabees 4, 11, 14, 18, 19, 21, 22, 24, 25, 115, 116, 121, 123, 131, 134, 135, 138-140, 142, 148, 150, 151, 165-168, 170, 172, 174, 177, 178, 181, 188, 192-197, 199, 201, 203, 206, 207, 209, 212, 214, 216, 224-226, 228-239, 241, 243, 246, 249

II Macc. *1.1-10* 25
II Macc. *1.10b-2.18* 229, 239-244
II Maccabees, II Macc., Second Maccabees 4, 5, 12, 16, 18-26, 30, 77, 115-118, 121-123, 130, 131, 135, 137, 138, 140, 141, 143, 145, 147, 148-150, 164, 168, 173, 193-196, 199, 201, 203, 209-216, 218-220, 221, 224, 225, 228, 229, 232-234, 240, 241-250
III Maccabees 147, 215
IV Maccabees 30
Mattathias 25, 228, 232, 235-237
Menelaus 22, 24, 25, 121, 131, 134-137, 167, 168, 183, 184, 203, 218, 219, 242, 245
Merkabah 61-63, 65, 66
Messiah, messianic 60, 61, 63, 64, 77-81, 83-86, 90-95, 98, 99, 101, 112, 113, 171, 221, 222, 225-230, 248, 249
Mishnah 24, 43, 45, 51, 52, 54, 77, 120, 161, 188, 190, 242, 250
Moses 23, 24, 26, 29, 58-60, 63, 64, 72, 76, 87-95, 97-99, 112, 113, 133, 161, 163, 165-167, 171, 172, 181-183, 185, 186, 188, 189, 221, 223, 225, 233, 244
Mount Sinai 87-89, 91-95, 113
mysticism 58-63, 65, 66
Onias II 116, 117, 119, 123, 127, 131, 138, 147, 148
Onias III 18, 119, 121-123, 130-132, 137, 138, 141, 145-148, 164, 165, 216, 219, 245, 246
Onias IV 121, 132, 137-141, 143-151, 210, 240, 242
Orpheus 60, 64, 70, 71, 73, 75, 79-87, 100, 112

P. Dura 11 62, 63
Parthian, Parthians 46, 53, 54, 78, 101-104, 106, 108, 109, 127, 222
Paul 4, 11, 82, 122, 211, 216
pergraecari 9, 11
Persia 68, 78, 102, 103, 105
Pharisees 4, 115, 116, 187
Philo 11, 13, 15, 28, 31, 58-62, 64, 66, 220
philosophers, philosophy 9, 13, 15, 27, 30, 61, 165
Plato 13, 15, 30, 61
present-future prophecy 156, 157
Psalm of Solomon *11* 201
Psalms of Solomon *17-18* 222
Psalter, Utrecht 95
Ptolemy I 125, 126, 164
Ptolemy II 120, 124-126, 139
Ptolemy III 126-128, 144, 146
Ptolemy IV 117, 118, 123-127, 129, 131, 139, 147
Ptolemy V 116, 117, 120, 123-126, 128-132, 146, 148, 149
Ptolemy VI 121, 128, 135-137, 139, 140, 143, 144, 240
Ptolemy VII 135, 139
Ptolemy VIII 128, 135, 136, 138-140, 142-145, 215
Qohelet 13, 14
Qumran 11, 23, 29, 132, 137, 161-163, 170, 188, 192, 207, 222, 227
Rab 63, 66, 103
Rev. *7* 92, 95-97
Romans, Rome 8-10, 14, 31, 44, 63, 77, 78, 85, 103, 182, 201, 203, 215, 217

Index

Rostovtzeff, M. I. 7, 9, 39, 67, 102, 104, 106, 114

royal art, themes of ancient Near Eastern 108-109

Sadducees 141

Salerno ivories 98

Samaria Papyri 33

Samaritan, Samaritans 14, 19, 49, 116, 117, 123, 149, 224

II Sam. *3.18* 237

II Sam. *21.10* 247

I Samuel *6* 65

San Apollinare 87, 89, 91-98, 112

San Vitale 87-89, 93, 94

Sardis 28

Sassanian, Sassanians 46, 63, 68, 78, 101-111

Sefirot 66

Seleucus II 126-128, 148

Seleucus III 119, 127, 128, 148

Seleucus IV 119-123, 129-131, 139, 145-149, 209, 213, 216

Simon I 120, 132, 145, 146

Simon II 119, 120, 123, 129, 131, 132, 134, 138, 140, 145, 146, 164, 171

Smith, Morton 13, 64, 76, 90, 115, 116

Son of Man 225, 228

Stern, Henri 11, 15, 70, 71, 79-83, 85, 86, 124, 126, 127, 133, 134, 137, 141

temple, heavenly 64, 65, 182

temple, second 140, 141, 183, 187, 188, 210, 223, 226-229, 240-243, 245, 246, 248

Testament of Moses 24, 26, 29, 167, 172, 181-190, 225, 233

Testaments of the Twelve Patriarchs 222

Tobiad, Tobiads 22, 115-151 *passim*, 164, 167, 211

Torah 4-8, 11, 13, 15, 17, 18, 20-25, 27, 30, 31, 58, 61, 68, 73, 75, 78, 79, 88, 89, 99, 103, 112, 113, 136, 137, 140, 141, 163-169, 192, 194, 195, 197, 198, 202, 217, 224, 228, 232, 235

Transfiguration 64, 89-97, 99, 112

Tree of Jesse 81

tree-vine 63, 70-76, 78-81, 94, 96, 98, 99, 105, 110-113

Tubias 122, 139

Wisdom 3, 5, 8, 30, 171, 192, 194, 197, 198

yavan, Yawan 11, 232

Zech. *9.8* 232, 246

Zech. *11.3-7* 227

Zenon 16, 121, 122, 125

www.ingramcontent.com/pod-product-compliance
Lightning Source LLC
Chambersburg PA
CBHW032020230426
43671CB00005B/146